Europe On
€387 Million
A Day

Olly Figg

St Edward's Press, England

First published in Great Britain in September 2010

by St Edward's Press Ltd
Court House, Crapstone, Yelverton, Devon PL20 7PS

www.stedwardspress.co.uk

ISBN 978-0-9554188-3-9

Printed by Intype Libra Ltd

Foreword

I defy anyone to read this book and remain an enthusiastic and untroubled Europhile. For it represents as comprehensive and damning account as any of the European Union's tawdry and secretive history, the devious and undemocratic workings of its institutions and the sad parade of shifty election-losers, second-raters, recent communist totalitarians and outright criminals who have come to fill too many of its senior posts.

Olly Figg records in coruscating detail the extent to which the EU now interferes in our daily lives on such issues as fortnightly rubbish collections, the rate of VAT on women's sanitary products, the phasing out of traditional light bulbs, the closure of post offices, and the working hours of our doctors.

While our politicians are happy enough to aid and abet citizens' complaints of "too much red tape", only rarely do they draw attention to those huge and growing areas of life – all of our commerce and industry, social and employment policy, transport, environment, agriculture, fish, and foreign aid – where we have ceded control to the EU and about which we can do absolutely nothing. In all, Brussels is now responsible for about 75 per cent of our laws, leaving us with 170,000 pages of EU diktats to obey – the equivalent of 250 King James Bibles.

Indeed, in some cases, our politicians are happy enough to see Brussels ram through laws which they haven't got the guts to introduce themselves in our own increasingly impotent Parliament.

With the enforcement of the self-amending Lisbon Treaty, economist Ruth Lea has warned, "There will quite simply be no more significant powers left solely with the governments of the member states, and outside the orbit of the EU's formal institutions."

Not only is the EU happy to lift huge sums from us – £16billion gross in cash from the UK alone each year – it then uses these funds to pay many of the constituent parts of the donor nations, such as broadcasters, politicians, think tanks, charities, arts companies, regional development agencies, to join the swelling chorus of praise for the European Union's alleged glories. Ostensibly independent groups such as Oxfam and the National Society for the Prevention of Cruelty to Children are just a few of the thousands who have qualified for EU largesse, so long as they can prove they "pursue an objective which is part of an EU policy" and are thus suckered into the propaganda campaign that says Britain and other once-independent nations are no longer capable of running their own affairs or making their own laws.

"In plain fact, he had now become a millstone to me,
useless as a necklace, and quite afflictive to bear"

From *Bartleby, The Scrivener* (1853) by Herman Melville

"I didn't vote for it myself quite honestly
but now that we're in I'm determined to make it work"

Basil Fawlty, *Fawlty Towers* (1975)

The EU was formed in 1993 but the abbreviation has sometimes been used in this book to refer to the EU's predecessors – the European Economic Community (EEC) and the European Community (EC)

Contents

Frequently, we have been told that some issues – climate change, foreign policy, world trade, international finance – are so big that they can be tackled only at a supranational level. Yet the EU's initiatives on the environment – biofuels, carbon-emission trading, renewable energy – have thus far proved to be expensive, calamitous, self-defeating disasters. Not to mention the Common Fishing and Agriculture policies.

Efforts to reconcile the conflicting interests of 27 EU countries in foreign policy – on Afghanistan, the Arab-Israeli conflict, the Balkans, Georgia, Iraq, Rwanda – have too often ended in embarrassing, laughable impotence. The attempt to lock the currencies of 16 EU states into one Eurozone – with one interest rate – has proved little more successful.

Despite occasional, flashy displays of foreign aid, the EU's policies towards the developing world have too often been ruinous. Between them, the net effect of the Common Agricultural Policy, high import tariffs and the dumping of EU surpluses has meant that for every euro given to Africa in aid, the EU has taken away some seven euros in thwarted trade.

Not content with wrecking fishing in many northern waters – with up to 90 per cent of each fisherman's catch thrown back into the sea to rot as "discards" – the EU has "leased" vast areas further south and EU fishermen have, over the past 30 years, thus helped halve fishing stocks off West Africa.

Yes, there are some heroes. Former chief accountant and now MEP Marta Andreasen, Dorte Schmidt-Brown, Robert McCoy and many other brave Eurocrats have tried to expose the appalling accounting, lax computer security and outright fraud that have become almost endemic within the EU and its attendant agencies. Yet whistleblowers have been routinely ignored, frustrated, persecuted, traduced – and usually fired.

Even those who are no longer on the EU gravy train – and who might have suffered a bout of late-onset wisdom and remorse – can be kept in line. For even the most senior retired Eurocrats have been silenced with crass and coercive reminders that they can be deprived of their pension if they do not continue to display proper respect and "duty of loyalty to the Communities".

So how can the rest of us escape the clutches of this intrusive, coercive, expensive, inefficient, corrupt, wasteful, lawless, undemocratic octopus? A simple one-line Bill in Parliament – repealing the European Communities Act (1972) – would do it. But since, for the moment, none of Britain's three major political parties shows the remotest sign of following that route, we can at least threaten to withhold from them our vote. We can also do more to probe that yawning gap between the propaganda and the reality of the European Union. We can discuss, debate and dispute.

Clearly, it will be a tough, draining struggle for Britain to return to its former position of autonomy, sovereignty and prideful independence. But this book could indeed prove a key weapon in what threatens to be a long, long fight.

For few other documents have done a better job of marshalling all the arguments – political, social, legal, cultural, constitutional, financial and economic – against our continued existence within the European Union in such an accessible and entertaining manner. I wish the book well and congratulate Olly Figg in pulling off such a formidable tour de force. Readers will feel grateful that he has provided clear, definitive and unequivocal answers to questions that so many in public life have tried, traitorously, to obscure and ignore.

Lord Pearson of Rannoch, Westminster

N ot everyone "does" politics. Even fewer people "do" the politics of the European Union. But politics – especially EU politics – "does" them. And it does them at almost every turn.

Compared with the economy and causes such as the environment and poverty in the developing world, the EU is seen as irrelevant or parochial. It's viewed as a marginal irritation, telling us that whatever else happens market traders must advertise their loose fruit and veg in kilos. Some people might know that the EU's accounts are iffy and that its employees rather prefer life high on the hog.

But that's not the whole story. The EU determines more and more areas of our lives, from the micro (whether you pay VAT on certain toiletries or not) to the macro (under what terms we trade with the world's poorest and how we treat the environment). Far from being marginal, the EU tells us how we must answer the big questions as well as the small ones.

Of course, the procedures and mechanics of the EU are often astonishingly dull. But the effects that the EU has on everyone's lives – whether they're British, Latvian or Malawian – are far from dull.

Most legislation passing through the Houses Of Parliament is not homegrown, it's passed down by the EU. In 2009 the French ministry of justice said that "the proportion of EU legislation in French legislation comprises between 60 and 70 per cent of new laws". In Germany in 2004, a figure of 84 per cent was arrived at after examining the pedigree of all legislation passing through the Bundestag over a five-year period. However, the additional laws passed by the 16 federal Länder – or provinces – were ignored so that figure is probably too high. Gordon Brown, when chancellor, said, "Approximately half of all new regulations that impact upon businesses in the UK originate in the EU."

No one really knows the true percentage of UK laws that originate in the kingdom of Belgium and even if they did it would be fruitless to compare one law with another; no two laws have the same impact or cost. It is more worthwhile to estimate in how many areas the EU legislates and how many it leaves to Westminster. This book, for the sake of argument (and there's rather a lot of it from both camps), says that the EU has control over about 75 per cent of policy areas (eg trade and fishing, to name two[1]) in all of the member states. Here are a few things for which it is responsible:

Higher mobile-phone charges
Looking for a popular gesture, the EU reduced the cost of "roaming charges", the inflated rate that one is charged for using one's phone elsewhere in the EU.

---

[1] See the Appendix (p 337) for the full list, which includes even healthcare

Because telecoms operators exist to make money, they chase the profit bubble wherever it is pushed under the wallpaper. So, most of them recouped the loss by raising the price of domestic phone calls – which we make for the 50 weeks of the year that we are not abroad. People who are based abroad, such as all MEPs but Belgium's, may have viewed the decision more gratefully than others. The *Wall Street Journal* saw through the move: "The 56 per cent of European cellphone users who don't travel outside their home countries, according to a Eurobarometer survey, will surely not be thrilled if their bills rise to accommodate those (typically wealthier) users who do travel. If someone told them their domestic phone bills were likely to go up, this EU brainchild would probably not be as popular as the [EU] Commission appears to think it is now. None of these arguments has so far swayed EU officials, whose chief obsession seems to be boosting the union's public image."[2]

In effect, business travellers used to subsidise people making local calls, but now the situation is reversed – some pay-as-you-go minimum call charges went from 10p to 25p. Not quite such a victory for the ordinary consumer.

In 2008, the EU turned its attention to the fee that different networks charge one another for connecting calls, the so-called "termination charges". The networks, particularly Vodafone, immediately warned the EU that if price caps were imposed on these charges then customer offers such as free handsets would have to be withdrawn and also that, as happens in the USA, those receiving calls might have to be charged. However, at the time of writing, Ofcom (acting as the European Commission's proxy) is recommending a reduction of these fees.

The withdrawal of the open-platform "Routemaster" bus
Once ubiquitous in the capital and elsewhere, they are now a rarity[3]. The replacements (bendy or otherwise) were not universally welcomed by wheelchair users, who lost many dedicated buses. Ken Livingstone, just after he was first elected London's mayor, in 2000, said, "Only a ghastly dehumanised moron would want to get rid of the Routemaster bus." He vowed to retain them but the decision wasn't his to make: it was the EU's. But he was right about the morons[4].

The loss of the right to take unused annual holiday as extra pay
This is just one example of how the EU interferes unhelpfully in the relationship

---

2 *The Wall Street Journal*, 22 February 2007
3 They are allowed to serve a few "heritage routes", such as the number 9 in London, which runs between the Royal Albert Hall and Aldwych
4 The iconic Routemaster bus was a victim of (the Bus and Coach) Directive 2001/85, which makes their operation all but impossible; any plans for their replacement will have to heed this edict

between employer and employee[5]. Nor can "workers" carry unused holiday over to the next calendar year.

Another example is that government websites for jobseekers must, if asked to do so, carry adverts from escort agencies or chatlines looking to recruit workers ("involves sexually explicit dialogue… may cause embarrassment to some", applicants should be "willing to pose naked on webcam", may involve appearances alongside "nude adult images" etc). The Department For Work And Pensions (DWP) says, "Jobcentre Plus has a duty to advertise any legal job." That duty is dictated by the EU. The DWP – which manages the Jobcentre Plus network – has been legally obliged to list such adverts after Ann Summers, the chain of sex shops, took it to court in 2003. A High Court judge, observing EU employment law, ruled that Jobcentres must carry adverts for any work within the law in the "sex and personal-services industries"[6].

The 48-hour week (which is social legislation) is covered later in the introduction.

The warnings on cigarette packets
This directive also stubbed out the name Marlboro Lights: "light" is a banned word, as are "low tar" and "mild"[7].

The fortnightly collection of household waste
This was introduced by local councils in an attempt to encourage householders to recycle more so that the councils could meet superficially worthy but often counterproductive EU landfill targets and thus escape mammoth fines from Brussels.

The influx of over a million people to the UK since 2004
Immigration has advantages and disadvantages but debate about it is essentially pointless when the UK must allow no-questions-asked immigration from 26 other EU countries. Those whom we harbour from war and persecution are a minuscule number compared with the number we must admit from the EU. (Those here "illegally" are also a relatively small number.)

---

[5] *Workers can't trade holidays for pay, EU rules* in *The Guardian*, 16 March 2006. See Directive 93/104
[6] At the time of writing, the ConDem government said that it would outlaw job ads of a sexual nature. Unless EU law changes, any ban would be found to be illegal if challenged, as in 2003. But at least the government got a headline or two
[7] Courtesy of Directive 2001/37 ("This Directive concerns the manufacture, presentation and sale of tobacco products in the member states of the EU, in particular the use of warnings on packets, the prohibition of descriptions such as 'mild' or 'light', the maximum tar, nicotine and carbon monoxide yields" etc)

Besides, the EU, by virtue of Regulation 343/2004 and other legislation such as the Reception Directive, dictates how countries treat asylum applications from "third" (ie non-EU) countries – for instance, any asylum seeker whose application has not been processed within a year is allowed to work, even if he or she has already had an application rejected.

People from outside the EU can become EU citizens after five years' residency in any of the 27 EU member states. They are then, courtesy of Directive 2004/38 EC, free to live anywhere in the bloc, as are their spouse, children, parents and parents-in-law.

All EU nationals in the UK may claim UK child benefit and other family allowances, such as child tax credits, regardless of whether their children are actually with them in the UK. Home Office figures released in February 2008 showed that 796,000 workers from the 2004 accession countries had registered to work in the UK. The self-employed and those choosing not to work do not need to register so the total inflow must have been well into seven figures. Because the EU is essentially borderless internally, it is not known how many later returned but it is known that many renewed their registration. All can receive jobseeker's allowance, housing benefit and assistance with council tax. If they lose their jobs and return to their mother country, they continue to be eligible for a £60-a-week handout from the UK government for up to three months.

In March 2008, it was revealed in parliament that the cost in the previous 12 months for child benefit for non-British EU citizens was £28million. Two months later, the Home Office said that 102,029 non-British EU children (wherever they lived) received child benefit, and there were 58,000 claims for tax credits. In 2009, the Treasury said that child benefit was being paid to 50,586 *non-resident* children (ie almost half the May 2008 total). In 2009, the Irish government discovered that 10,000 children living outside the republic were receiving Irish child benefit, costing the country €20million per annum.

Furthermore, Gordon Brown was always wrong to talk about "British jobs for British workers": all EU citizens have the same rights to UK jobs as the natives enjoy. He promised this – in direct contravention of EU law – as long ago as September 2006[8] until well into his premiership the next year, including at the party conference. (The promise came back to bite him when the oil firm Total ignored local workers for a contract at its Lindsey refinery in 2009.) In 2010's second quarter, 186,000 people started work in the UK for the first time. Of those, 145,000 were born abroad – and more than half of them (77,000) were

---

[8] *News Of The World* interview, 10 September 2006

from EU states. Overall, according to the Office for National Statistics, one in seven of the UK workforce is foreign.

Nor could Mr Brown call for Premiership football clubs to field more British players[9] at the expense of EU nationals: that, too, would have been illegal (and has been since the famous Bosman ruling of 1995, which every football fan knows)[10].

The inability to deport many foreign murderers and rapists

Also by virtue of Directive 2004/38 EC, we cannot deport an EU citizen after he has served his sentence, however appalling the crime, be it rape or murder[11]. Gordon Brown said, early in his premiership, "If you commit a crime you will be deported from our country. You play by the rules or you face the consequences. I am not prepared to tolerate a situation where we have people breaking the rules in our country when we cannot act. That will be toughened up."[12]

If a Mancunian serves a prison sentence in HMP Wandsworth he is not afterwards "sent back" to Manchester from London; the principle is no different throughout the EU member states. That's why the Italian-born killer of headmaster Philip Lawrence could not be deported from the UK on release.

Of course, the opposite applies during a criminal investigation: just as a suspect can be "extradited" from Manchester to London for questioning, so can a suspect be shuttled from any EU province to any another, courtesy of the European Arrest Warrant (EAW). The EAW allows for extradition, sometimes for petty offences and often without even prima facie evidence, to another member state, where habeas corpus, trial by jury and other British niceties are not always offered.

---

[9] *Brown's mission: British players for British clubs* in *The Guardian*, 14 November 2007

[10] Not to be confused with the Uefa and Premier League rule that every squad must have eight "homegrown" players. As the EU explained: "'Homegrown' players are defined as players who, regardless of their nationality or age, have been trained by their club or by another club in the national association for at least three years between the ages of 15 and 21. The Uefa rule does not contain any nationality conditions" (EU Commission press release, 28 May 2008).
Fifa's "6+5" proposal, whereby a team must start with at least six players eligible for the *national* team in the country that the club is based, is contrary to EU law. Brown's plan was similar to Fifa's not Uefa's

[11] This is one of the Four Freedoms guaranteed by the original Treaty Of Rome (see Chapter 1: "Background"). It was amplified by Directive 2004/38: "expulsion orders may not be issued by the host member state as a penalty or legal consequence of a custodial penalty"

[12] *The Times*, 25 July 2007

The EU states are becoming a single jurisdiction. However, it is a single jurisdiction subdivided into areas with often very different laws. British judges are now powerless to stop people (be they British or not) being deported from the UK for a crime that is not even on the UK statute book – and even if the alleged crime were committed in the UK rather than the member state issuing the extradition request (Greece, for example, has successfully issued an EAW against a Briton whose supposed crime was committed in London)[13].

Home Information Packs (Hips)
The useless, expensive and unpopular packs were opposed by estate-agent trade bodies, the Council of Mortgage Lenders and buyers themselves. The Law Society described Hips as "the worst piece of consumer legislation in 50 years". So why did the Labour government, in the face of universal opposition, persist with them, lying that they would "speed up the house-buying process"? Because one of the packs' components, an "energy performance certificate" (EPC), is required by all homes sold or rented throughout the EU. The Labour government had to comply with EU law and so used Hips, an idea that had been kicking around for a while, as the vehicle for these certificates[14]. However, Labour "gold plated" the EU order in two ways: by making the EPCs (and the rest of the Hips) mandatory from when properties were put on the market, not just when finally sold or rented; and by surrounding the EPCs with local-authority searches that no buyer's solicitor would trust.

The ConDem Coalition could not totally get rid of Hips because of the mandatory EPCs, which at £60 were always the most expensive component. The Tories, when in opposition, said EPCs were "useful" and did not let on that they could not get rid of them anyway. Homeowners face a fixed penalty fine of £200 if they do not provide a EPC, which has to be at least commissioned (if not available), when a property is marketed for sale or rental (the certificates are valid for 10 years, whatever changes are made to the property – that's "useful"?). The EU, then, is not responsible for HIPs – that was Brown – but it can be blamed for EPCs.

The complicated system of measuring letters and parcels
The Post Office's "Pricing In Proportion" system, whereby letters and parcels must be measured as well as weighed, was introduced to comply with Directive

---

13 The EAW's companion piece, the European Investigation Order, is covered in the Appendix

14 The EU Directive, 2002/91 (Energy Performance Of Buildings), can be read at tinyurl.com/2ho4wf – the EPCs are in Article 7: "Member states shall ensure that, when buildings are constructed, sold or rented out, an energy performance certificate is made available to the owner or by the owner to the prospective buyer or tenant"

97/67, the EU Postal Services Directive, which states that "prices must be geared to costs". Postcomm was explicit about the reasons for the change back in 2004: "Royal Mail believes that SBP [size-based pricing] meets the need for more cost-reflective pricing that is identified within the European directive" but you would now be hard pushed to find the origin of this nuisance.

The closure of Post Office branches
In addition, and in order to comply with the supplementary Directive 2002/39, the EU forced the Royal Mail to open up to competition, with the result that lucrative bulk-mail contracts and the like, which used to subsidise the network, have been cherry-picked by newcomers (eg DHL/Deutsche Post).

Perhaps even more seriously, EU rules on state aid have meant that government subsidy, currently £180million per annum, must be capped (and sustainable) so that, in real terms, less and less money is available to prop up the network. That is why 2,500 branches were given a death sentence in 2007. So, just as it becomes, care of the EU, more complicated to send things through the post and therefore more necessary to visit a post office, post offices are closing.

In this country, about 4.2million people receive social-security benefits via the Post Office Card Account. Because of EU rules on competition, this scheme, too, has had to be put out to tender, just as TV and driving licences had been (the loss of which cost the Post Office £168million per annum). Fortunately but unexpectedly, the contract, which had cost the Post Office £1billion to set up, was retained and not lost to PayPoint, which would have resulted in another 3,000 branch closures.

The sell-off of a large stake in the Royal Mail, almost certainly to a foreign company, is also a provision of this directive[15]. In 2009, over 100 Labour MPs rebelled over plans for the part-privatisation of the Royal Mail, even though a sale is mandated by Brussels and it cannot remain in public hands. Part-privatisation was never abandoned by Labour, merely delayed when a decent price could not be found; the sale was put in what used to be known as the second post. As with the railways (see below), at least some of Royal Mail will parcelled up and sold – to operators from another member state or to American venture capitalists or whomever (employees might have a small stake). The Tories could not stop this happening even if they had wanted to, which they did

---

[15] The Hooper Report, properly called *Modernise or decline: Policies to maintain the universal postal service in the United Kingdom (an independent review of the UK postal services sector)*, published by DBERR on 16 December 2008, makes several references to EU involvement in the postal service. For instance, box 12 on page 81 mentions that "European directives require that all European postal markets must be fully open to competition by 2012"

not. In opposition, Ken Clarke was in agreement on this with his opposite number, Lord Mandelson, a fellow supporter of the EU. In office, the ConDem coalition said "we will seek to ensure an injection of private capital into Royal Mail", without admitting why.

Fridge mountains and car mountains
These twin epidemics of fly tipping were a direct consequence of EU legislation. See "Neighbourhood" for more.

Children's booster seats in cars
The compulsory wearing of booster seats for every child under 12 and under 4'5" was introduced to comply with Directive 2003/20, which is covered later. The EU is also responsible for all other areas of road safety, including the newly legal random breathalyser tests coming soon to your high street, as well as alcohol limits themselves – and the forthcoming requirement for cars to keep their headlights on at all times[16], regardless of the waste of energy and the fact that motorcyclists will no longer be as noticeable.

The privatisation of the railways
Being in office at the time, the Tories were blamed for this but were not wholly responsible.

Directive 91/440 "requires member states to make railway undertakings independent by giving them a budget and system of accounts which are separate from those of the State" and "to have separate accounting for railway infrastructure (track and related equipment) and the operation of transport services as such. The aim here is greater transparency in the use of public funds, but also the ability to measure the actual performance of these two branches better. It is with this requirement in mind that a number of member states have in recent years set up bodies which manage the railway infrastructure but are separate from the railway companies, which continue to manage the carriage of passengers and freight". The directive was implemented here as part of The Railways Act (1993).

The separation of track from stock has often been the cause of huge nuisance and has probably been the cause of at least one fatal disaster. Anyone calling for

---

[16] As per *Hansard (Commons)*, 4 February 2008, column 7AWW: "Jim Fitzpatrick [transport minister]: The UK has been successful in arguing against the introduction of mandatory use of dipped headlamps during daylight hours by drivers of existing vehicles. This outcome has been welcomed by motorcycle user groups. However, from early 2011 all new types of passenger car and light van will have to be fitted with dedicated daytime running lamps in accordance with the relevant European directive. By summer 2012 all new vehicle types will have to be so fitted." He admitted that this would increase fuel consumption by 5 per cent

the re-nationalisation of the railways, or merely the re-fusion of the infrastructure companies with the actual carriers, will have to argue with the EU. (You won't win – see "European Court Of Justice" on p102.) Eventually, the Royal Mail will go the same way as British Rail.

Genetically modified food

The decision on whether or not to allow the growth or sale of genetically modified food in the UK is not our government's to make. See "Neighbourhood" for more.

The banning of hundreds of health supplements

Under Directive 2002/46 hundreds of apparently safe vitamins and health supplements have been outlawed. Since August 2005, only those on the EU's "approved list" of 112 products can be sold, in a reversal of our "whatever is not illegal is legal" way of doing things.

Health and Safety Executive

Yes, much of that, too (how to climb a ladder, the permitted decibel levels of bagpipers and orchestras, etc), stems from a 1974 act of parliament that implemented one of our obligations to the EEC, which we had joined the previous year. The Health And Safety Executive is the "UK Focal Point" for the European Agency For Safety And Health At Work. The UK's Food Standards Agency (see later in the introduction) has a similar relationship with the EU's Food Safety Authority: it's a proxy. We always had our own (necessary) health-and-safety standards. The Health And Safety Executive aggregated those – and added a very great number we never needed nor asked for.

The levying of VAT on toiletries such as condoms and tampons

In this country, both of these items attract VAT at 5 per cent. So for every £10 spent almost 50p goes to the VAT man. A Treasury press release on the Budget of 2000 (dated 21 March) explains why: "European law allows sanitary products to be taxed at a reduced rate. The UK has agreed with its European partners not to extend its zero rates beyond those in place on 31 December 1975. Therefore, it is not possible to reduce the rate of VAT on sanitary products to zero." [17] It doesn't matter who's "in power" here: we have no control over the VAT rate on prophylactics, women's sanitary products and many, many more items. See "VAT" in "Cash" for more on this.

---

[17] See also another UK Treasury press release, from June 2006, produced when the rate on condoms also went from the standard UK rate of 17.5 per cent to 5 per cent: "Under EU law, the UK is permitted to reduce the rate of VAT on a prescribed list of goods and services, but is not permitted to introduce new zero rates"

That list – some of which is looked at in more depth later – soon adds up to interference and might give the correct impression that we are no longer in control of many areas of life. But it is by no means the extent of Brussels lawmaking, it's merely a selection from the 170,000 (that's not a typo: one-hundred and seventy thousand) pages of EU law we must abide by. Supporters of the EU say that it does not interfere and that the British tabloid newspapers invent myths (occasionally they do but the list given here is, unfortunately, far from mythical; bent bananas appear later). If the EU didn't interfere, what would be the point of it – and what is it doing with its time and our money?

How many Westminster MPs does it take to change a light-bulb policy? None. That decision, too, is made over their heads by Brussels, and is why ordinary incandescent light bulbs are being phased out[18].

Many rules and regulations might look like domestic regulation but they are dictated by the EU. Just as the Ten Commandments might look like Moses's word as he came back down the mountain, they were from the Almighty. For those who prefer their metaphors secular, Brussels is our executive's overriding earpiece.

The EU is useful for unpopular lawmaking. Domestic politicians can say with a clear conscience, when challenged about a counterproductive law, "Not us, guv – it was Brussels. Blame the Eurocrats." And so MPs can get on with the "sexier"

---

[18] They will be banned for use in the home by 2012 and replaced throughout the EU with "energy-saving" "compact fluorescent" (CFL) bulbs that, while often lasting longer and consuming less electricity, depend on five times the amount of CO_2 in production and contain levels of mercury far higher than barometers, whose supporting industry the EU saw fit to abolish. Many people complain that the bulbs do not last even a month, others say that the things lose as much as a third of their brightness after a few weeks. The CFLs have even been known to change a television's channels.
And, for CFLs to work at optimum levels, they must be left on permanently. Also, they cannot be fitted to about half of the UK's existing fixtures, including dimmer systems. They can induce migraines and their dull light has been linked to eczema and skin cancers.
Here's Defra's advice, from 2008, if one of the CFLs breaks: "Vacate the room and ventilate it for at least 15 minutes. Do not use a vacuum cleaner, but clean up using rubber gloves and aim to avoid creating and inhaling airborne dust. Sweep up all particles and glass fragments and place in a plastic bag. Wipe the area with a damp cloth, then add that to the bag and seal it. Mercury is hazardous waste and the bag should not be disposed of in the bin. All local councils have an obligation to make arrangements for the disposal of hazardous household waste." Can all that really be ecologically sound?

side of governance[19]. However, most MPs never quite spell out, if they even know, the true extent of their impotence by, say, reminding us that they are responsible for only a small proportion of UK legislation – for then we would rightly wonder what purpose they serve and whether they deserve their salaries and allowances. It sticks in the craw when MPs can even think of asking for larger salaries just as they cede, via voting for the Lisbon Treaty, more of their power to others. But at least one Tory knows that a lot of legislation passing through the House is not homegrown.

When he was an MP, Boris Johnson wrote: "The other day, a transport minister announced in a nannying New Labourish way that we should all start taking more care of our offspring in the back of the car... This was presented to the public as a thoughtful government recommendation... In so far as that was the intended impression, it was grossly misleading. The minister was really trying to prepare the public for the time when these ludicrous plastic cushions or seatettes will become a legal requirement, and they will be imposed on us not by parliament but by Brussels... This directive, 2003/20/EC, has been dreamt up by some well-meaning but insatiably interfering official, no doubt in close co-operation with representatives of the European Association of Plastic Seatettes and Child Restraint Appliance Manufacturers... As for the notion that the directive can be somehow modified or attenuated by British MPs, in the process of enactment into British law – well, that is a complete joke. I sit on European standing committee B, watching EU legislation come in like a tide, and there is nothing we can do to interrupt or object. We are far less use than the Russian Duma under Lenin. It is a farce, and it is no way to govern a country."[20]

The problem with this system is that domestic politicians find that they have increasingly less dominion, for the EU knows only accrual; MPs soon discover that important areas are no longer in their fief. A good example of this came during the 2005 general election campaign when the then Tory leader Michael Howard promised to limit immigration if elected, but was told by the president of the EU Commission, José Manuel Barroso, that he could not promise to do any such thing – immigration and asylum were by no means the exclusive business of national governments but were now the EU's "competence"[21].

Two year later the Labour government nationalised Northern Rock, a move that attracted the attention of our supreme government in Belgium. The European Commission requested information from the authorities about the bailout,

---

[19] If you were an MP, would you rather spend parliamentary time trying to save your local hospital, or discussing the matters covered by Regulation 1462/2006? See page 2 of tinyurl.com/ycfruwl
[20] *The Daily Telegraph*, 22 April 2004
[21] The EU's command of immigration is covered in the Appendix

concerned that it might violate EU state-aid laws if such support led to distortion of the banking market. A spokesman for Neelie Kroes, the [EU] competition commissioner, said the ban on government subsidies to banks could be waived in exceptional circumstances of "systemic risk", but not on a long-term basis: "We're monitoring the situation," he said. (The financial crisis is covered in "The euro".) As mentioned, Gordon Brown's "British jobs for British workers" is another example of making a promise he could not deliver, because EU nationals – whether Poles, Portuguese or Hungarians – have the same employment rights as native Britons; it would be illegal under EU law to ringfence jobs in the manner that Brown had promised. Even in 2008, years after the railways were privatised in order to comply with an EU directive, very senior Tories tried to justify the sale as if it were a policy of the Major government rather than an order from Belgium.

Next time a national politician of whatever stripe – whether in government or aspiring to be – makes a promise, see if he or she even has or would have jurisdiction in that area. The chances are slim. (The coalition agreement of 2010 is groaning with measures that are contrary to EU law. The Tories were told that some of these – such as giving small businesses a quarter of all government contracts – were illegal under EU law as long ago as 2006. Other measures are mentioned later.) Politicians may not even be aware that the power had long ago been given away. But that nice Mr Barroso can often be relied on to put them right. It is as if the Houses Of Parliament were a local council – a county or borough one, say, not merely a district one and the European Union is central government. And, by voting for the Lisbon Treaty and its provisions, our MPs slashed their already short job specs. Soon they will have nothing more to do than rubber stamp EU law (which they can, if so minded, debate – but never amend) and justify their remuneration.

Here's how one writer describes the set-up: "The EU's power is easy to miss. Like an 'invisible hand', it operates through the shell of traditional political structures. The British House of Commons, British law courts, and British civil servants are still here, but they have all become agents of the European Union implementing EU law. This is no accident. By creating common standards that are implemented through national institutions, the EU can take over countries without necessarily becoming a target for hostility... The EU's obsession with legal frameworks means that it transforms the countries it comes into contact with, instead of just skimming the surface."[22] They are not the words of a eurosceptic. The quotation is from a paper published by a *pro*-EU think tank.

---

[22] Centre For European Reform, February/March 2005 (Issue 40)

Here is a genuine eurosceptic, the columnist and author Christopher Booker: "[The EU] has never attempted to replace the existing structures of Europe's national governments, but has gradually taken over their powers from behind the scenes. The familiar landscape of national governments, parliaments, monarchies, judicial systems has all been left in place. But they have been subtly hollowed out from within, so that as their powers have gradually been transferred to the new system of government above them, most people have remained blissfully unaware of what has happened."[23]

You may have seen some Britons use a dark-coloured passport sleeve that fits over the burgundy EU passport. Crucially, the sleeve omits the words "European Union" in order to mimic the navy UK ones that disappeared in the 1990s. This inexpensive and faintly amusing self-deception is also a metaphor for lawmaking in this country: the EU "fits inside" the UK, whence it goes about its business. The replica passport sleeve acts like "the shell of traditional political structures": outwardly, it looks like a UK construct, but it hides the active EU element.

The EU likes to boast how few people work for it, even if it does underestimate how many people are on its payroll. However, it can be argued that if our own Department For Environment, Food And Rural Affairs (Defra), for instance, is dancing to the EU's tunes ("they have all become agents of the European Union implementing EU law", according to an EU sympathiser) and not Westminster's then it, too, is working for the EU.

The UK's Food Standards Agency (FSA) is another body that can only permit or ban what the EU – via the European Food Safety Authority (EFSA) – dictates, and is quite open about it. In the summer of 2007 there was a tabloid clamour for several food additives that had been linked to cases of hyperactivity to be banned from drinks and meals often marketed to children. When asked by parents' groups (and newspapers) to outlaw these ingredients, the FSA admitted that it could act only on orders from above (Brussels). A referee might look supreme on a football pitch but he is implementing only what the Football Association says. There's no point asking the ref to change the offside rule – you have to go higher than that, to the real rule makers. And that's what campaigners discovered.

In March 2008 the issue was raised again when a £750,000 Southampton University research report recommended the banning of six food additives or "E" numbers (yup, the "E" means "Europe" as in EU, further stressing primacy in yet another area) which had caused impulsive and inattentive behaviour in

---

[23] Speech to Bruges Group conference, *Integration Marching On*, October 2005

children. The list comprised sunset yellow (E110), quinoline yellow (E104), carmoisine (E122), allura red (E129), tartrazine (E102) and ponceau 4R (E124)[24]. But any Europe-wide, or even UK-wide, ban on the artificial additives – very commonly found in sweets, drinks and medicines etc – was ruled out by the EFSA.

According to the *Times*, food campaigners reacted furiously to the decision and demanded that Britain took unilateral action to remove the additives from food. But even if all UK confectioners poured away their garish palettes of additives, the problematic E numbers could still not be barred from imports – and so foreign suppliers (in the EU and elsewhere) would merely fill the gap.

The EFSA said that the research was too limited to apply to the general population. The university report had found that children given drinks containing a cocktail of controversial E numbers and the preservative sodium benzoate (E211) became boisterous and inattentive[25].

As a result, the FSA proposed that its board members consider phasing out all six colourings by the end of the year because of "an accumulating body of evidence" linking them to hyperactivity in susceptible children. Dame Deirdre Hutton, the FSA chair, had no problem with saying that her hands were tied: "The evidence we have suggests it would be sensible for these [additives] to be taken out of food. We would like to see the use of colours phased out over a period. That does require mandatory action by the EU."[26] In the meantime, any ban, the FSA said, would have to be voluntary. And, as mentioned, such a ban (which the major UK supermarkets later observed) left the market open to imports and less scrupulous domestic operators.

The "acquis communautaire" is the rulebook of the EU – the sum of its laws (eg the sale of loose fruit and veg etc *must be* by the kilo, but our retailers and traders may display, in writing no bigger, the equivalent pounds and ounces if they want to; if they sell exclusively in pounds they risk a risk a fine or six-month prison sentence and the confiscation of their equipment), policies (eg whether to allow the commercial planting of GM crops) and practices (eg buying the fishing rights of developing countries).

"Communautaire" means "community" in its adjectival sense, or "federal". At Tony Blair's behest, Valéry Giscard d'Estaing amended the EU Constitution that he had drafted, in order to remove certain words that would have frightened British voters. He said, "I rewrote my text with the word 'federal' replaced by

---

24 These came to be known as the "Southampton Six"
25 *The Times*, 17 March 2008
26 BBC news online, 10 April 2008

'communautaire', which means exactly the same thing"[27]. No more unexpectedly, the noun "acquis", from the past participle of "acquérir", is cognate with our "acquirement" (via their Latin forebear "acquirere") and identical in meaning. The *Oxford English Dictionary* notes: "Acquire often suggests a continued, sustained, or cumulative acquisition (eg to acquire poise as one matures), but it can also hint at deviousness (eg to acquire the keys to the safe)." Both senses – "sustained" and "devious" – are apt. As is the sense of "acquisitive".

This cumulative body of legislation must be adhered to by all states, be they current or candidate members. Countries have – voluntarily, it is true, but not always openly – given their lawmaking power in all these many areas to the EU. A Czech prime minister, Václav Klaus (now president), observed: "Every time I try to remove some piece of Soviet-era regulation, I am told that whatever it is I am trying to scrap is a requirement of the European Commission." Those in favour of this set-up say that the countries are "pooling" or "sharing" sovereignty. Sharing sovereignty is like sharing a secret or sharing virginity: the act destroys it.

When Bulgaria and Romania were preparing to join the EU, their parliaments had to absorb all 170,000 pages of the acquis[28], the equivalent of 250 King James Bibles. There is a "like it or lump it" approach to the acquis and derogations or exemptions are extremely rare. In the UK, road signs in miles and the sale of beer by the pint are dog-eared and isolated examples, trumpeted by pro-EU campaigners as "evidence" that we are not ruled by Brussels. Those who don't think we are ruled by the EU should try selling loose fruit or veg *without* metric measurements. Yes, imperial measures are tolerated – but the absence of metric is not. Imperial measurements such as pounds and ounces, thanks to our derogation from Directive 80/181[29], are allowed to co-exist with metric (so long as they are not in bigger type or writing) but they are not allowed to exist by themselves. Ironically, although the pint has been "saved", a pint glass can no longer carry the crown symbol but must instead have a "CE" marking, as if to say, "Enjoy your 568ml measure of beer but never forget who's really in charge here."

Once an area of "competence" – either a lazy or disingenuous translation of the French "compétence" that's more readily understandable as "jurisdiction" – has been "communitised" (ie ceded or surrendered) it cannot be reclaimed by a

---

[27] *Wall Street Journal*, 7 July 2003. A federation, such as the United States Of America, allows its constituent parts far more latitude than does the EU, which is closer to being a state in and of itself than a federation
[28] *How big is the acquis communautaire?*, www.openeurope.org.uk
[29] It can be viewed at tinyurl.com/yhdudm

country. This characteristic of the acquis attracts various metaphors: a ratchet (the most popular), a salami slicer, a dog's choke collar, a one-way street, a diode, etc. The acquis serves primarily to season the disparate (Finland and Cyprus, for example) into the homogeneous: if two or more countries share a rulebook they will become indistinguishable – that is also the main purpose of the euro – and therefore help to achieve the EU's famous goal of "ever closer union". Closer and closer – it's like a game of grandmother's footsteps.

There is also a domino effect: if you lay down a law allowing the free movement of people throughout the Union (which is why we can't deport murderers and rapists born in other EU nations), then a law allowing extradition between the subdivisions of this unit, even if the alleged offence is not a crime in the country of expulsion, is a logical consequence. You may or may not like this consequence but it is difficult – though not impossible – to argue that it doesn't follow. This is "competence creep" and is just one method by which the EU encroaches on more and more areas of our lives.

The single market is a great driver of integration – that is its main purpose. As with the European Arrest Warrant or the euro, the EU first creates a zone – a single market in goods and services, a 16-province currency bloc, an extradition agreement, whatever. Then the EU spots local discrepancies within the zone. These doomed displays of diversity can be judicial (different criminal statutes), fiscal (a government overspending by more than 3 per cent of GDP) or mercantile (weights and measures). Once spotted, these idiosyncrasies are then used as an excuse to promote integration because they would otherwise provide local advantage or cause confusion and compatibility problems in the other provinces: the differences are harmonised.

How many "competences" are really necessary for the smooth running of the single market (rather than for creating a single polity) is anyone's guess. Nafta, the free-trade area formed by the USA, Canada and Mexico, has very little of the EU's bureaucratic baggage and no loss of national sovereignty. Similarly, the World Trade Organisation, which regulates international trade deals, doesn't tell countries that they mustn't deport one another's criminals. The British MEP Daniel Hannan[30] wrote: "Although it is reasonable to accept a degree of harmonisation of cross-border questions, Brussels is currently administering a number of policy areas of essentially domestic concern: farming, fishing, employment law, industrial relations, the status of local government, the interpretation of human rights, transport policy, immigration, defence, energy policy."

---

[30] Thanks to YouTube, he later made the most viewed European parliament speech ever: a three-minute demolition of Gordon Brown in March 2009, when the PM visited Strasbourg

He has also explained the genesis of Brussels lawmaking, from the point of view of successive British governments patronising the public: "Stage One is mock incredulity: 'No one is proposing any such thing. It just shows what loons these sceptics are that they could even imagine it.' Stage Two is bravado: 'Well, all right, it's being proposed, but don't worry: we have a veto and we'll use it.' Stage Three is denial: 'Look, we may have signed this, but it doesn't really mean what the critics are claiming.' Stage Four is resignation: 'No point complaining now, old man: it's all been agreed.'"[31]

The *Times* had a similar take on the process: "It is at first denied that any radical new plan exists; it is then conceded that it exists but ministers swear blind that it is not even on the political agenda; it is then noted that it might well be on the agenda but is not a serious proposition; it is later conceded that it is a serious proposition, but that it will never be implemented; after that it is acknowledged that it will be implemented but in such a diluted form that it will make no difference to the lives of ordinary people; and at some point it is finally recognised that it has made such a difference, but it was always known that it would and voters were told so from the outset."[32]

It should not be underestimated how often this method of governance suits domestic politicians, who might not otherwise be able to sell a certain measure to either the public or parliament. If "the gentleman in Whitehall really does know better what is good for people than the people know themselves", but is concerned that no one will believe him, he can smuggle in his medicine via the unarguable diktats of the EU, "gold plating" them if he needs. Democracy loses out: laws arrive that are untempered by opposition argument and debate. In return, the EU gets "more Europe" spread around, bringing a single polity into sharper and sharper focus. Everyone is happy (except the voter).

Another problem with this system of government is that our own parliament cannot legislate in certain areas even if it wants to – it simply does not have the ultimate say in many areas of everyday life. This is the opposite of unnecessary legislation, which the EU is best known for. A good if unfortunate example came in 2006 when MPs from both main parties proposed to make reflective strips on HGVs mandatory so that lorries in particular could be seen clearly at night and so about 70 lives a year might be saved. At the same time, a requirement for all left-hand-drive lorries using British roads to have better passenger-side mirrors fitted was proposed (these lorries are eight times likelier, according to HMG, to be involved in serious or even fatal accidents in the UK). The then transport minister, Stephen Ladyman – who knew of what he spoke because he had been caught speeding three times, once had nine points on his licence and had

---

[31] *The Daily Telegraph*, 26 January 2005
[32] *The Times*, 28 August 2002

admitted to owning a GPS-based road-camera detector – advised that in each case parliament could take no such action unilaterally because it would be against EU law: road safety is, as already mentioned, the EU's ultimate responsibility, what's called an "occupied field". In other words, a no-go area for domestic parliaments[33]. So, we have to wait for the EU to catch up. And, until it does, people will die needlessly[34].

When we joined the "Common Market" in 1973, we were not joining a free-trade area. Some of those who voted 'yes' to remaining in the EEC in the 1975 referendum complain now that the EU is not what they voted for, in the manner of a wife complaining that her husband is not the man she married. While the wife may have a point – her charming fiancé may have turned into a slobbish husband – the disgruntled voter who wanted only free trade does not. The truth was always there ("ever closer union"), in the large print of the Treaty Of Rome (see "The background"), although it was not pointed out in 1975.

The EU never was a free-trade area. It was and is a customs union. The two have something in common – members of both enjoy tariff-free imports and exports *among themselves*. This fact tends to blind people to the crucial difference between the two set-ups. A free-trade area lets its members negotiate their own bilateral terms for trading with outside (or "third") countries. In a customs union, however, there is a common external tariff, set centrally, when any member trades with a "third" country. A free-trade area is to a customs union as a holiday camp is to a prison, perhaps an open prison but a prison nevertheless – it's easy to confuse the single market with a closed shop. To revisit the spousal analogy, a free-trade area is an open relationship in which each partner has their own terms for seeing others, whereas a customs union is a marriage with definite and equal parameters about the manner in which one can see others, which is why we had to forsake the Commonwealth (sorry), among many others, for membership of the EEC. But you don't have to marry your neighbours to sell them things. The EU itself can have free-trade agreements with other countries (eg Mexico and South Africa) and there is no reason why the UK could not have

---

[33] "Were we to try to change the legislation in the way suggested, our partners in the European Union would certainly object and take infraction proceedings against us... the amendment and the clause are redundant and perhaps illegal," Stephen Ladyman MP, quoted in *A fatal confusion*, eureferendum.blogspot.com, 29 March 2006. The site added that Italy had passed similar legislation – and *then* sought permission from its true government, the one in Brussels. Our government felt it could not follow the Italians' cavalier lead, and so opted instead to wait for the EU to legislate.
See also *Utterly powerless*, eureferendum.blogspot.com, 18 December 2008
[34] See *The EU and Road Safety*, written by one of the MPs after he had come up against the EU when trying to save lives, in *The European Journal*, October 2006 (not to be confused with the EU's *Official Journal*). Available from www.europeanfoundation.org/journals.html

the same free-trade only relationship from outside the European Union.

Many laws underpinning the single market are ruinous. The European Working Time Directive [EWTD], for instance, greatly reduces the UK's competitiveness and even prevents many hospitals' A&E depts from operating, because of a ban on doctors working more than 48 hours a week. In the *Observer* on 17 September 2006, Ian Gilmore, president of the Royal College of Physicians, said: "The pressure on medical staff due to reducing junior doctors' hours to comply with the EWTD has made it increasingly difficult to maintain full emergency services running 24 hours a day in many hospitals." Also, 48-hour weeks mean more staff handovers, and a doctor's working week might have to finish while she's in the middle of an operation. Gilmore's successor, Sir Richard Thompson, said the EWTD had been a "complete disaster" for both patient care and training: "We are not providing the service or the training that we require. I cannot over-emphasise the damage to service provision and to training."

The British Medical Association (BMA) wrote in a May 2004 briefing paper: "Following the application of the 48-hour limit, the hours of junior-doctor cover that will be lost each week as a result of the implementation of the [EWTD] will be between 208,296 and 476,638 – equivalent to between 4,300 and 9,900 junior doctors working an EWTD-compliant 48-hour week. This is the main factor that makes the EWTD for junior doctors such a huge issue." The doctors also lost the right to free accommodation, worth about £5,000 per annum, because they were no longer deemed "on call" but "working". A 2008 BMA survey found that 64 per cent of junior doctors believed that compliance with the EU's 48-hour working week would have a "negative overall effect" on their training. When asked what they were worried about most, a third feared an impact on the quality of their training while a further 32 per cent were concerned about the impact on their ability to learn the skills needed to practise safely[35].

At the end of 2008, the BMA warned that the NHS would face serious problems when the hours of junior doctors were limited. Hospitals could find themselves short-staffed, the BMA said, which would threaten the quality of care patients receive[36]. Infringements of the EU law would result in hospital trusts being fined up to £5,000 each time. In February 2010, a BMA survey of 1,500 junior doctors found that 40 per cent were "working on understaffed rotas as UK hospitals struggle to cope with the introduction of the EWTD".

Two months after the EWTD was introduced, the Royal College of Surgeons said in a report that "lives were being lost because patients had to be switched

[35] Press Association, 10 April 2008
[36] *The Guardian*, 30 December 2008

between up to four doctors every 24 hours, instead of being cared for by the same team round the clock. Junior doctors used to work 80-hour weeks, staying on call at all times and sleeping in the hospital. Surgeons said that this had guaranteed continuity of treatment."[37]

In April 2009, John Black, president of the Royal College of Surgeons, warned that "Patient safety is going to be reduced. People are going to die because of this... The vast majority of doctors think EWTD is dangerous." The *Guardian* reported that Dr Don MacKechnie, vice-president of the College of Emergency Medicine, which represents the 2,500 doctors who work in casualty departments, said A&E units might have to close temporarily as a result of the EWTD. "Hospitals are already struggling to recruit enough of the more senior junior doctors to work in their A&E units," MacKechnie said[38].

The following month Black told the *Mail On Sunday* that "it is not an exaggeration... that operations will be cancelled and wards closed down... Unless the government comes to its senses, the result will be catastrophic for the NHS, with patient safety on a knife edge, surgeons not being properly trained, waiting lists going up again and even hospitals closing. We have already reached the point where patients' health has been endangered. There is a serious risk of units in hospitals having to close to emergencies, with resulting chaos, not to mention the danger and inconvenience brought about by patients going long distances to a hospital that has enough staff to stay open. This is truly a nightmare, and I despair that the government will not take action."[39] Just before the 2010 election, he warned that there was "overwhelming evidence that safe and effective hospital cover, especially at night, cannot be sustained" because of the EWTD.

After the election he warned the ConDems that "without action we are going to see a generation of specialists with less experience than any that have gone before". He said: "To say the European Working Time Regulations have failed spectacularly would be a massive understatement. Despite previous denials by the Department of Health that there was a problem, surgeons at all levels are telling us that not only is patient safety worse than it was before the directive, but their work and home lives are poorer for it." In response, the Department of Health said: "We will not go back to the past with tired doctors working excessive hours, but the way the directive now applies is clearly unsatisfactory and is causing great problems for health services across Europe." Black would later find that waiting times for elective surgery had doubled compared with 18 months earlier, and said: "If you have the same number of patients, no more

---

[37] *The Sunday Times*, 11 October 2009
[38] *The Guardian*, 11 April 2009
[39] *The Mail On Sunday*, 31 May 2009

doctors and ask them to work less then it is inevitable that the time available for elective procedures will reduce and waiting lists grow."

Marjan Jahangiri, professor of cardiac surgery at St George's Hospital in London, said: "We have created a generation of surgeons who lack technical skills and operate within a 'clocking off' culture where they do not feel personal responsibility for their patient." By the time she became a consultant, she said, she had performed 900 operations whereas today's senior doctors are qualifying after fewer than 300. Across the country, 980 consultant and trainee surgeons were surveyed. Four fifths of the consultants and two thirds of the trainees said that care had suffered since the 48-hour week had been introduced. One surgeon said: "The most insidious problem is that [the EWTD] fosters the concept that you are responsible for a patient only for a shift. A consultant surgeon has a particular and continuing responsibility – [but] we are training clock watchers whose work-life balance is more important than anything else."

According to the BBC: "NHS Grampian revealed it had employed 60 additional staff in order to comply with the EWTD... [it] said employing the 60 extra staff was part of the reason it was facing a £900,000 financial deficit this year." The item concluded: "Unions have warned that the 48-hour weekly limit could harm the quality of training for junior doctors."[40] In a 2010 *Nursing Times* survey, 70 per cent of respondents said the 48-hour week had led to gaps in cover for patients.

A study in the Royal College of Physicians' journal, *Clinical Medicine*, found that the length and frequency of sick leave among medical trainees doubled in the 12 months after the introduction of the 48-hour week, by reducing the number of staff on duty and thus putting extra pressure on others. Dr Hugh McIntyre, the report's lead author, said, "The directive may have failed in its primary purpose: that of promoting the welfare of employees."[41]

In a letter to a newspaper, Ken Darby, the treasurer of an Abbeyfield residential home wrote, "From time immemorial the [residential-home] housekeeper has been given a flat and required to sleep in five days a week. Now under EU working-time regulations 'sleeping in' is classified as being 'on call', and that counts as 'work'. The housekeeper having worked during the day is no longer allowed to 'work' overnight, and thus it is deemed that she need not be supplied with a flat. However, in the best interests of the residents we would still like her to 'sleep in', and so we must declare her flat as a benefit in kind to the Inland Revenue. The cost to us is £3,000 per annum. The employer is then charged

---

[40] BBC news online, 4 August 2009
[41] *Reduction in hours fails to cut sick days of junior doctors, study says* in *The Times*, 1 April 2010

21

12.8 per cent in National Insurance contributions. The tax burden on the employee has to be compensated for by raising her salary... this sort of complication, added to the plethora of bureaucratic nonsenses emanating from Brussels and Whitehall, is killing the voluntary sector"[42].

Carers who accompany the disabled (for instance) on holiday are classified as being "on call" the entire time, even when asleep; as soon as one carer has been away for 48 hours, he or she has to return to the UK and then another carer takes over; the extra travel and other costs mean fewer holidays.

In 2009 a temporary reprieve of the EWTD was announced and doctors at 38 NHS trusts were granted a derogation: they could work 52 hours (averaged over six months) until 2011, in certain specialties such as obstetrics and paediatrics.

There are problems also for firemen. They, too, are classed as working when only on call. Most are part-time and already have a main job so are prevented from working as firemen for more than a few hours a week because their salaried work has taken up most of their 48 hours.

There are problems in other sectors as well. In January 2009, the British Constructional Steelwork Association organised a petition to try to preserve the opt-out from the 48-hour week. Simon Boyd, contracts director at Reid Steel, who led the campaign, said: "If this is introduced, it will have a devastating effect on the industry. It will mean that projects take longer to complete and employees will lose out financially. Imagine the amount of stress put on managers and employees having to do more in less time. This could see an increase in accidents... The impact could be severe, and end in many companies going out of business. The industry needs to be flexible through peaks and troughs. If our ability to expand and contract the workforce [through overtime at busy periods] is lost, that will kill our competitive edge."[43]

A government spokesman said: "Losing the opt-out would cost the UK billions in costs to industry and lost earnings. We are determined to defend it and welcome all support from businesses and workers." In April 2009 the opt-out from this requirement (for the private sector only) was debated long into the night by MEPs – with no apparent sense of contravening the spirit of the law... A stalemate meant that the opt-out, as used by the UK and other countries, was safe in the private sector. Some of the first people to notice the effect of the new laws were cabinet ministers: their chauffeurs could no longer work for them all week. Ministers had to make do with relief drivers, some of whom had to be told the way.

---

[42] Letters, *The Daily Telegraph*, 4 May 2007
[43] *Contract Journal*, 27 January 2009

If Americans, for example, wish to supplement their wages by putting in 80 hours' overtime at Christmas they can do so. In his study of the English language, *Mother Tongue*, Bill Bryson wrote: "When companies from four European countries – France, Italy, Germany, and Switzerland – formed a joint truck-making venture called Iveco in 1977, they chose English as their working language because, as one of the founders wryly observed, 'It puts us all at an equal disadvantage.'"[44] That's the thinking behind much EU legislation: to reduce relaxed and versatile economies, such as ours, to the sclerotic European model; to put us all at an equal disadvantage (ostensibly so as not to skew the single market). Large companies tend to favour EU legislation because it damages their smaller rivals, which are less well equipped to absorb it, more than it does them.

The laws essential for the single market aside, it would take a spectacular level of churlishness to disagree with all other EU legislation; some laws are welcome (don't try to change them when they become outdated or counterproductive). However, if a law is sensible and desirable – one to end slavery, or to clean up the air, or to grant universal suffrage, or to prohibit sending little boys up chimneys – we can pass it ourselves. We in Britain have a very proud record of doing so. If other countries wish to emulate us by passing the same laws, all well and good. In terms of lawmaking, what does the EU confer on us that is otherwise unavailable? Conversely, is it wise to give up our right to legislate in certain areas, especially when we often need to change tack quickly?

Most international co-operation needs no treaties or regulations. If an American tourist sends a postcard from Beijing to Chicago, it will arrive within a week and without hassle. Its journey is no more than a combination of aeroplanes and reciprocal arrangements between the postal services of the USA and China. It's not formalised; it just is. It's a good example of unfettered international give and take, and its convenience does not come bundled with legions of unwarranted laws that are, furthermore, of no relevance to the favour granted. Looking at the Pricing In Proportion shambles at our Post Offices, we should be thankful that airmail and its ease of use predate the EU.

The publication of the new edition of *Halsbury's Laws of England*, the encyclopedia of all the laws of England, was covered by the *Daily Telegraph* which noted that the doorstop-sized volume had been produced just five times in the past 100 years[45]. The fifth edition, said the paper, has 102 volumes – nearly twice as many as the fourth edition in 1987. The publisher, Simon Hetherington, said he had to make room for 900 new acts of parliament and 30,000 extra pieces of legislation in the new edition.

---

[44] *Mother Tongue* by Bill Bryson (Penguin, 1991)
[45] *The Daily Telegraph*, 29 April 2008

"It is unarguable that there is more written law than ever before, and the growth of it has been accelerated over the last three decades," Mr Hetherington said. "A great deal emanates from Europe – either with direct effect or because the UK is obliged to give effect to European enactments in UK legislation."

Law governing employment had grown from half a volume to two volumes. Road traffic law doubled to two volumes. Domestic governments are certainly not afraid of drafting unnecessary legislation, usually the Something Must Be Seen To Be Done Even If Legislation Already Exists (Favourable Tabloid Headline) Bill, but the EU – with, let's not forget, competence in the areas of employment and road traffic law – is no slouch either. Mr Hetherington said he thought ministers should sometimes stop legislating and pause while waiting for existing measures to bed in. Unfortunately, three quarters of our laws come from Belgium and ministers can do nothing to stop them. Ministers might be better off pausing and doing nothing else.

Legislation from Belgium can be in the form of "regulations", which pass into law immediately; legislatively, they "don't even touch the sides". "Directives" are given to national parliaments to implement within a certain time limit – they are sometimes "gold plated" – ie given unnecessary and resented flourishes by domestic legislators keen to a) keep themselves and their enforcement colleagues in work and b) smuggle in other provisions. The final tablet to be handed down is a "decision", which is intended for a specific individual or company etc[46]. None of the three is negotiable once "done at Brussels", as the legal wording has it. You'll find the year of the legislation before the oblique in the case of directives, after it in the case of regulations.

Famously, no parliament can bind its successor; each intake can if it chooses unpick the work of any of its predecessors. Such an arrangement is now largely meaningless because EU-derived law, which is the lion's share of new legislation, lasts in perpetuity (or until the EU changes its mind) and it cannot be undone by national parliaments.

Reviewing a *eurofacts* paper by Vaughne Miller, Dr Helen Szamuely[47], head of research at think tank the Bruges Group, wrote on the EU Referendum blog:

---

[46] Article 288 of The Treaty of the Functioning of the European Union: "A regulation shall have general application. It shall be binding in its entirety and directly applicable in all member states. A directive shall be binding, as to the result to be achieved, upon each member state to which it is addressed, but shall leave to the national authorities the choice of form and methods. A decision shall be binding in its entirety. A decision which specifies those to whom it is addressed shall be binding only on them. Recommendations and opinions shall have no binding force"
[47] She blogs at yourfreedomandours.blogspot.com

"In 2006, the EU Commission produced 76 directives, 1,795 regulations and 781 decisions; the Council [of Ministers] obliged with 101 directives (inc 38 with the European parliament), 238 regulations (inc 43 with EP) and 264 decisions (inc 21 with EP). That gives us a total of 177 directives, 2,033 regulations and 1,045 decisions or, in other words, 3,255 pieces of legislation…"[48]

In that year, the UK parliament passed 55 Acts (including one to welcome Bulgaria and Romania into the EU) and 3,599 Statutory Instruments (SIs), which are pieces of "secondary legislation" that piggyback existing Acts. Parliament has little power to amend or change SIs and a debate on any of them is almost unheard of. The EU-inspired SIs hitch a ride on the European Communities Act 1972: SI number 113 in 2006, for instance, was The Feeding Stuffs And The Feeding Stuffs (Sampling and Analysis) (Amendment) (England) Regulations 2006, which tells us that "the secretary of state makes these Regulations in exercise of her powers as a minister designated for the purposes of section 2(2) of the European Communities Act 1972 in relation to the common agricultural policy of the European Community and measures in the veterinary and phytosanitary fields for the protection of public health"[49]. This is dull stuff, which is one reason why national politicians are so keen to outsource their chores to Belgium.

Many other SIs rely on the same 1972 Act. But even if one counted how many do so (while remembering to include those SIs that, although they do not depend on or cite the 1972 Act, are nevertheless doing EU business in other ways, such as amending EU-derived Acts), it's still difficult to arrive at a meaningful figure because laws differ hugely: the Dangerous Dogs Act (not EU-derived), for example, cannot be usefully viewed alongside the Finance Act, which makes the UK Budget law. There's no real point in trying to ascertain, by quantitative analysis, the proportion of homegrown legislation compared to EU legislation. (That said, it's well over half.) Also, if the EU did not exist, some of its legislation would need to be issued anyway. Those laws laws cannot reasonably be blamed on the behemoth – although their imperfect and untailored drafting can be, which is why it would make more sense to legislate with the needs of each country and its people in mind. And that can be done only at the national level.

Which leaves trying to estimate the number of policy areas that are bossed by Brussels (eg fishing, trade) and the remainder (eg sending our armed forces into southern Iraq). This book says it's about three quarters. Some bodies, including the think tank Open Europe and the British Chambers Of Commerce, have estimated the cost of EU business laws as a proportion of the cost of all business laws. Their figure is around 72 per cent. Using UK government impact

---

[48] *Some data on legislation*, eureferendum.blogspot.com, 26 April 2008
[49] All Acts and SIs can be found at www.opsi.gov.uk/acts

assessments, Open Europe also calculated that in 2009 the EU proportion of the regulatory cost of all legislation was 99 per cent for the Food Standards Agency, 91 for the Health and Safety Executive, 86 per cent for the Department of Transport, 75 per cent for Defra and 74 per cent for the Department of Communities and Local Government.

Every year the Adam Smith Institute announces "Tax Freedom Day" (ie "How long do we have to spend working for the government, rather than ourselves?"). In 2010, it was 30 May. In the same way, we should also celebrate "EU Freedom Day", the notional day after which all laws *originate* in Westminster and are aimed at the specific needs of the domestic electorate. As it stands, EU Freedom Day is around 1 October. Or, if you prefer it the other way round, the UK parliament legislates for its electors until March 31 every year (pro rata) and then from 1 April until 31 December it's the EU's turn. Although most of those days feel like April the first.

In one respect it is a good thing that EU law cannot be debated – and hence cannot be amended – in national parliaments. If it were debated, EU Freedom Day would be even later and there would be even less time to introduce "homegrown" laws. Boris Johnson is not the only Tory to point out the increasing redundancy of parliament. Peter Lilley proposed a Ten Minute Bill on 3 June 2008:

"When I was a minister it was a frequent occurrence that officials would say, 'No, minister, you can't do that' because it was within the exclusive competence of the European Union... Few voters, or even members of this House, fully realise how many powers have been, or are about to be, transferred elsewhere. There are three reasons for this. The first is that governments of all persuasions deny that any significant powers are being transferred. The second is that, once powers have been transferred, ministers engage in a charade of pretence that they still retain those powers. Even when introducing measures that they are obliged to bring in as a result of an EU directive, they behave as though the initiative were their own.

"Indeed, ministers often end up nobly accepting responsibility for laws that they actually opposed when they were being negotiated in Brussels... At first sight, it is odd that Ministers – who, in this government, are not normally slow to blame others – should nobly defend and accept responsibility for Brussels' legislative progeny, in whose conception they have often played little part. They prefer to claim paternity rather than admit impotence – the fate of the cuckold across the ages.

"The third reason is that... those who support the transfer of power from here to supranational institutions should logically accept that our pay should reflect the diminution of our responsibilities. But, strangely, all the Euro-enthusiasts whom I asked to sponsor the Bill declined to do so without explaining why. Too many members are happy to avert their eyes from what is happening, so long as they retain the prestige and emoluments that were appropriate to a fully sovereign parliament."[50]

Mr Lilley did not want less pay; he wanted power restored to Westminster instead.

Any new law is three times likelier to have originated abroad than at home. If our legislators are having their legislating done for them, what do we pay them so much for? Why do we pay for their conservatories, bath plugs and moats? And when those MPs vote to give away more of their own powers (which had only ever been lent by us), how can they then argue for a pay rise?

Leaving the EU is not as simple as getting up from the dinner table. Its laws permeate our statute book. To leave would be like trying to remove sugar from a cup of tea. But that's not to say that leaving is undesirable. The first chapter argues that Britain has only herself to blame for the EU.

---

[50] *Hansard (Commons)*, 3 June 2008, column 644

CHAPTER 1: THE BACKGROUND

Before its May 2004 expansion (Poland, Cyprus, Slovenia et al), the EU15 countries fairly closely described the area occupied by the Holy Roman or Habsburg Empires. After the Holy Roman Empire a short man with something of a Napoleon complex – Napoleon – came along. He forged an empire along similar lines to Charlemagne's but, as the noted historians ABBA remind us, "at Waterloo Napoleon did surrender".

Now, the European Union has "united" the continent as never before. José Manuel Barroso, the president of the European Commission, calls the present EU the "world's first non-imperial empire". Looking ahead in 2006 to the accession of Romania and Bulgaria, he called the expansion a "reunification of our European family". If that unification – whenever he may have been referring to (have Poland and Ireland really been yoked together before?) – is deemed a success worth repeating, why did it ever come unstuck? Will it not come unstuck again? We shall find out. In the meantime, how did it come about this time round?

The EU has had more British input than most people realise or acknowledge. Those who seek greater integration seethe that "la perfide albion" had anything to do with their beloved "projet", while British eurosceptics kick themselves. Thinkers and doers as diverse as Dante, Victor Hugo and Leon Trotsky have proposed a "united states of Europe". One man who went as far as calling for a "kind of united states of Europe... to begin now", in a speech at Zurich University in 1946, was Winston Churchill. However, he added the caveat that such a scheme was suited, like siestas and suppositories, to continental Europe but not to Britain, which should be "associated but not absorbed"[51]. He had mooted the idea well before the war when in opposition and was to repeat the call when in postwar opposition, even marching from parliament to Downing Street (Clement Attlee was interrupting his tenure) to call for a Council Of Europe. He then set up the Council, with one of his sons-in-law, Duncan Sandys, in 1949, having previously set up the integrationist Anglo-French United European Movement with him in 1947.

In June 1940 Churchill had even seriously entertained and then rejected the idea, put to him by a French civil servant and former cognac salesman called Jean Monnet, that there should be Franco-British Union. It was thought by then

---

[51] "We have our own dream and our own task. We are with Europe, but not of it. We are linked, but not comprised. We are interested and associated, but not absorbed"

that the Entente Cordiale of 1904 between France and Britain was quite enough foreplay and that full union should follow[52].

Jean Monnet was a former head of the League Of Nations, where in the 1920s he had met Arthur Salter, a British civil servant who later became a Tory MP and then peer[53]. Their friendship and discussions led to the Briton's book, *United States Of Europe*[54], which became Monnet's – and the EU's – lodestar. Its key chapter, "The United States of Europe Idea", ends with: "And if it is true that a large measure of economic rapprochement can only come as counterpart of political rapprochement, that is no reason for waiting before making a beginning. Each can obviously help the other, and an advance on either line would mean advance on both."

When it began to look likely that the Great War of 1914-18, "the war to end all wars", would not in fact end all wars but may even have sown the seeds of another, Monnet became ever more determined that his organisation, what we know now as the EU, would be supranational (that is, it would exist over and above national governments, which would be subservient to it) not intergovernmental, as were the League and its successor, the United Nations.

In 1944, just after the Allied liberation of France, Monnet bought a house in Versailles from a Swedish politician. He insisted on negotiating the price in US dollars but on the day of the deal demanded to pay in francs. The Swede accepted. The very next day the franc was devalued, meaning Monnet effectively got the house for a hundredth of the agreed price. By extraordinary coincidence, Monnet was at the time a member of the French Committee for National Liberation, which oversaw the devaluation[55].

After World War II, Monnet was in charge of French economic recovery and in this role saw an opportunity to advance his ambitions for Europe. In 1950, he chose Robert Schuman, the French foreign minister and a former PM, to announce his scheme to meld much of Europe and her resources into the European Coal and Steel Community (ECSC). This was known as the "Schuman Plan", though it was Monnet's work. Because coal and steel were the prerequisites of war it was hoped that surrendering them to a collective authority would take the cudgels out of everyone's hands – but particularly West

---

[52] See *Franco-British Union: a personal view*, an essay in *Cross-Channel Currents: 100 Years Of The Entente Cordiale*, edited by Richard Mayne et al (Routledge, 2004)
[53] For the best account of the genesis of the European Union, see *The Great Deception* by Christopher Booker and Richard North (Continuum, 2005)
[54] *The United States Of Europe* by Sir Arthur Salter (George Allen & Unwin, 1933)
[55] *Brussels Sprout* column, *Private Eye*, 14-27 November 2008

Germany's, who was too contrite to argue. Schuman said that he wanted France and Germany (then led by Konrad Adenauer) "to embrace so closely that neither could draw back far enough to hit the other". In the words of Sir Humphrey Appleby, "[the Germans entered the EEC] to cleanse themselves of genocide and apply for readmission to the human race"[56].

What of Britain? Having just nationalised the coal and steel industries, the prime minister, Attlee, did not feel like handing them over. When the decision had to be made, in 1950, he was abroad. Monnet, not wanting British involvement, which he thought would tend away from the supranational to the intergovernmental, sought a quick decision from the nation that had spurned his offer of union exactly 10 years earlier. He sent a mandarin to seek out Herbert Morrison, who was deputising for Attlee. Morrison was in The Ivy, the fashionable Covent Garden restaurant. After some thought, Morrison said to the go-between, "It's no good. We can't do it. The Durham miners will never wear it [the Schuman Plan]." His grandson, Peter Mandelson, might well have given a different answer – but possibly from the same restaurant. However, the joke at the time in the Labour Party was that "Monnet is the root of all evil"[57].

Meanwhile, across the Atlantic, US president Harry Truman realised that there must be a friendly bulwark against Stalin's Russia. In return for the generous sips of Marshall Aid – some $12.5billion of it[58] – that Truman gave to an economically bedridden Europe was the promise to promote trade by means of reduced trade barriers. Uncle Sam backed a united Europe because he knew that it might well keep Uncle Joe behind the Caucasus. This helped to morph the Coal and Steel Community into the customs union of the European Economic Community (EEC), with the same six players[59], in 1958. Britain did not consider joining this either. It would have necessitated sharing her nuclear resources ("the Six" were pre-nuclear) and forgoing the lively and multilaterally beneficial trade she enjoyed with her empire, which, by a process of reverse alchemy, was by then turning into the Commonwealth.

But by the early 1960s Britain, still smarting from humiliation in Suez, was an economic basket case. Dean Acheson, the US secretary of state who had helped

---

56 *Yes Minister*, series 2, episode 5
57 *The Time Of My Life* by Denis Healey (Michael Joseph, 1989)
58 "A Marshall Plan announced today would be worth closer to $740billion": *Dollar Diplomacy*, a review by Niall Ferguson of Greg Behrman's *The Most Noble Adventure: The Marshall Plan and the Time When America Helped Save Europe* (Free Press, 2007) in *The New Yorker*, 27 August 2007. The review says that Behrman believes "the Marshall Plan [was] instrumental to the process of European economic integration, presaging today's European Union"
59 The Benelux (Belgium, Holland and Luxembourg), Italy, France and West Germany

to set up Nato and who was most responsible for administering Marshall Aid, famously said that "Britain has lost an Empire and has not yet found a role". Such criticism spurred the prime minister, Harold Macmillan (and, later, Harold Wilson) to fold Britain's hand into the EEC. But French president Charles De Gaulle twice rejected Britain's application, and is said to have explained in private his refusals with the words, "One cock on the dungheap is quite enough". When De Gaulle was replaced by Georges Pompidou and Wilson gave way to Heath in 1970, Britain was finally allowed to "negotiate". This involved Heath – and another of Churchill's sons-in-law, Christopher Soames, who was Our Man In Paris – agreeing to disastrous terms that Heath then lied about to the Commons and the nation. The price included full access to our fishing stocks, for the Six had hastily concocted the Common Fisheries Policy and rightly scared off Norway, which backed out of the talks sharpish.

We acceded in 1973 and, two years and a change of PM later, Wilson hosted the UK's only national referendum, on continued membership of the "Common Market". His government – bar Tony Benn and some others – campaigned for a yes along with the woman who had just been elected leader of the Tories and who would later be famous for repeatedly saying "No" to the EEC (one of the few leaders brave enough to oppose "the project" while still in office). The two-to-one verdict in favour of the status quo was a victory for misinformation and cemented the country into the EEC for the foreseeable future.

In 1984, during her second term in power, Margaret Thatcher secured the UK's famous but shrinking rebate – "le chèque britannique". Encouraged by that success and keen to see a transparent internal market, she pushed for what became the Single European Act (SEA), even guillotining debate on it in the Commons. The SEA had been the brainchild of Altiero Spinelli, an Italian communist and fervent federalist after whom a building of the EU parliament in Brussels is named. (He specifically cited British federalists of the interwar years – such as William Beveridge and the Federal Union – as his political and intellectual models.)

Although Jacques Delors was the Commission president at its creation, the precise details of the single market were mostly worked out by a British Commissioner nominated by Thatcher: Lord (Arthur) Cockfield. Unknown to her, the SEA was the first half of an audacious power grab and it opened up many more policy areas to EC control. (After learning this, she did not reappoint Cockfield to Brussels.) The SEA was a perfect demonstration of Salter's observation that "an advance on either line [economic or political] would mean advance on both"; the economic integration of the single market was also a political integration. The European Union, as it was to become, courtesy of the SEA and Maastricht, its successor treaty, was the one union that Thatcher conspicuously failed to tame. In his resignation speech in 1990, Geoffrey Howe said her obstinacy over "Europe" was a reason for his going – and that precipitated her going.

The Maastricht Treaty completed the sentence that the SEA had started, and transformed the EC into the European Union. The EU might well have risen up without Salter, Churchill, his two sons-in-law, and Lord Cockfield but they were among its prime movers. Another Briton, Richard Mayne, was personal assistant to Monnet during the Coal And Steel Community years, then he was PA to Walter Hallstein, the first president of the Commission, and was then PA again to Monnet for several years in the Sixties. Mayne, who headed the European Commission's office in London at the time of the UK referendum, wrote an essay for the centenary of the Entente Cordiale, entitled *The Franco-British Father Of Europe: Jean Monnet*, and translated his biography into English.

It's hard to argue that the European Union is a totally foreign construct. It has had British input, both intellectual and then financial. To oppose the EU is to oppose something that might never have existed in its current form without Britain.

In the next section, there's a look at what Monnet and Salter – with help later from some other Brits – created. First, here are the main dates:

Timeline of treaties and expansion

1950 The Schuman Declaration (9 May)
Five years and 24 hours after VE Day, a plan for European peace was initiated. It's this day, 9 May, that's celebrated as "Europe Day" (the practice has not extended to Britain).

1951 The Treaty Of Paris
The treaty establishing the European Coal and Steel Community, the forerunner of the EEC, is agreed.

1955 Monnet's Action Committee for the United States Of Europe convenes the Messina Conference, which paves the way for the Treaty Of Rome.

1957 The Treaty Of Rome (25 March)
Consciously aping the first Roman Emperor, Augustus, by their choice of venue, the Six sign the Treaty Of Rome, which established the European Economic Community (EEC).
The European Atomic Energy Community (Euratom) is created the same day. The Treaty stated as one of its goals "ever closer union between the peoples of

Europe" and was enacted 1 January 1958, in time to beat De Gaulle's Fifth Republic to the statute book. The lawyers were in such a rush to win this race that the Italian state printers were not ready and so the "treaty" being signed in the famous photograph is in fact a pile of blank pages. Exactly 50 years later, the Lisbon Treaty was a constitutional blank cheque.

The Treaty established the "four freedoms": that of the movement of capital, goods, services and people throughout the member states.

1958 In July, the Common Agricultural Policy is set up by the Stresa Conference. It came into force in 1962 and Germany found herself subsidising the land (France) she had tried to steal a generation earlier.

1960 European Free Trade Association (Efta)

Britain fancies some free-trade action but not the shackles of the EEC and so forms a rival club with Austria, Denmark, Norway, Portugal, Sweden and Switzerland making "the Seven" of Efta. For a time, therefore, Europe was at Sixes and Sevens. Many claim it still is.

1963 Treaty Of The Elysée

France and Germany promise to consult each other over foreign policy in future. Had they done this in 1940 we might have been spared the EU.

"England is an island, maritime, and linked through its trade, markets and food supplies to very diverse and often distant countries. In short, the nature and structure and economic context of England differ profoundly from those of the other states of Europe," announced De Gaulle when vetoing Britain's first of three applications to join the EEC. He would veto us again four years later.

1967 In July, the European Community (EC) is formed by merging the EEC with Euratom and the ECSC.

1973 Accession of the UK, Ireland and Denmark to the EEC

The UK (as a result of the European Communities Act 1972), Ireland and Denmark join "the Six" (the Channel Islands and the Isle Of Man do not follow the example of Guadeloupe and other French islands – as well as French Guiana – in joining). In a referendum the previous year, Norway, in the spirit of Groucho Marx, decided not to join a club that would have it as a member. It also saw no good reason to surrender its fish stocks.

1975 Referendum in the UK

Harold Wilson holds the only national referendum in the UK's history – whether we should remain in the "Common Market". Cross-party support (yes, even Thatcher, the new Tory leader, urged voters to remain in the EEC) and massive funds – the yes side outspent the no by 10 to one – preserved the status quo by 68.3 per cent to 32.8. By chance, only if you were alive when the Treaty Of Rome was signed 18 years earlier were you old enough to vote.

Which pro-EEC newspaper, warning of the aftermath of a no vote, do you think carried the headline "A day in the life of Siege Britain: NO COFFEE, WINE, BEANS OR BANANAS TILL FURTHER NOTICE"? Well, *The Independent* was 11 years away from its first edition, and it wasn't *The Financial Times*. It was… *The Daily Mail*. Such was the hegemony of the pro side. On the no side were a few Labour rebels (including Tony Benn and Barbara Castle) and Enoch Powell.

1979 In March the Exchange Rate Mechanism (ERM) is formed: the Dutch guilder, German mark, French and Belgian francs, Danish crown, Irish punt and Italian lira are harnessed within narrow bands. Twenty years later they – bar Denmark – go on, with others, to form the euro.

1981 Greece joins the EEC.

1984 Draft Treaty Establishing The European Union
Much too ambitious for most people to accept, Altiero Spinelli's text nevertheless pointed towards the next two treaties.

1985 Greenland leaves the EEC
Having been largely autonomous since 1979, Greenland, as a result of a 1982 referendum, divorces from the EEC, the only country ever to do so. Under the terms of the settlement, she grants her former partner limited access to her fish in return for a large annual cash sum.

1986 Single European Act
A timetable for the completion of the single market and an announcement of economic and political union, it also spread Qualified Majority Voting (QMV, see p87) over 37 more areas (the Treaty of Rome had 38 already). The legal equivalent of a marriage proposal even if most treated it with rather less seriousness at the time.

Spain and Portugal join EC.

1987 Morocco's application to join the EC is rejected after someone points out that it's in Africa not Europe.

1990 Britain joins the Exchange Rate Mechanism.

1992 The Maastricht Treaty

In 1991, the year that the Union of Soviet Socialist Republics was formally dissolved and the year that Yugoslavia bloodily reminded everyone how the fragile Balkans gave us the word "Balkanise", the EC decided to unify, to become the European Union, to move in the opposite direction. (It was the EC's recognition of Slovenia and Croatia as sovereign states that accelerated the Yugoslav break-up; the former was, in 2007, the first 2004 EU entrant to use the euro and the latter, close to membership, is top of the EU's dance card.)

The Maastricht[60] Treaty abolished 41 vetoes and included the commitment to economic and monetary union (EMU). We, Denmark and Sweden had an opt-out from the third and final phase of EMU and so avoided the euro. Formally, Maastricht was the first "TEU" (Treaty of The European Union) treaty and the Treaty of Rome is TEC (Treaty of The European Community).

In a national referendum, the French narrowly voted (a shade under 51 per cent) to accept the Treaty but the Danes rejected it. In a referendum the following year, the Danish voted the other way, while continuing to opt out of the single currency and some other trappings. In EU politics, no rarely means no for long.

Switzerland is accepted into the EC but "does a Norway" and declines membership.

16 September: "Black Wednesday" sees the UK and Italy thrown off the bucking bronco of the Exchange Rate Mechanism. The UK learns its lesson. Italy does not and enters the euro six and a half years later.

1994 Norway again remembers Groucho Marx's maxim, at the eleventh hour, and forgoes EU membership.

1995 Austria, Finland and Sweden join the EU.

1997 Labour and the Tories both commit in their general election manifestos to a referendum before euro membership.

Treaty Of Amsterdam

A leap forward in QMV (19 vetoes were lost), the treaty also recognised the Schengen Convention, and beefed up the Common Foreign and Security Policy first declared by Maastricht. This involved creating a "High Representative for Foreign Affairs". Among the loss of competences were the areas of asylum and immigration (from outside the EU).

---

[60] Maastricht is a Dutch town near the Belgian and German borders whose name literally means "bridge of Maas" (the river Meuse)

2001 Treaty Of Nice

This paved the way for the Constitution and included a clause that gave the president of the Commission the power to sack a commissioner. Imagine a company that waited 45 years to give its chief executive the power to sack a high-ranking executive.

Elsewhere, the veto was surrendered in 43 more areas. The Charter of Fundamental Rights first appears here, as a non-legally binding annexe.

This is the treaty that the Irish, who are promised a referendum if anything changes their constitution, got "wrong" the first time of asking. They got it "right" at the second time of asking, in 2002.

2003 Convention On The Future Of Europe (the Constitution)

It was in this document that the permanent president of the EU idea was first mooted, as was the foreign minister. It would have bestowed many more competences on the EU, as well as vaporising more vetoes. The Charter of Fundamental Human Rights would also have had a legal basis. Compared to the Lisbon Treaty, however, even the Constitution lacked ambition. It was signed, in what now looks like hubris, on 29 October 2004 (see Appendix).

A Swedish referendum opposes joining the euro (56 per cent to 42; with 2 per cent undecided). (The Danes had come to the same conclusion three years earlier with a 53-47 split.)

2004 Cyprus, the Czech Republic, Estonia, Hungary, Latvia, Lithuania, Malta, Poland, Slovakia and Slovenia join the EU on 1 May.

Blair performs a U-turn and grants a referendum on the Constitution, a promise repeated in the Labour general election manifesto a year later. This bounces Jacques Chirac into granting a plebiscite in France.

2005 The Spanish vote in favour of the Constitution. It had been explicitly stated by Barroso's spokesman that it would be best to start having referendums in countries most likely to vote yes. (Spain had received about €85billion in EU funds since accession.) However, the French (55-45) and Dutch (61-39) vote non/nee to the Constitution and so let Blair off the referendum hook soon after his third election win. Luxembourg, pointlessly (the document was dead) and somewhat predictably, later votes yes.

2007 Bulgaria and Romania join the EU on 1 January.

Lisbon Treaty signed – not ratified – on 13 December.

2008 Cyprus and Malta join the eurozone on 1 January.

12 June: referendum on Lisbon Treaty in the Republic Of Ireland, which was constitutionally bound to offer one. The noes win it by 53.3 to 46.7 per cent.

2009 Slovakia joins the eurozone on 1 January.

2 October: Ireland votes again on Lisbon. Just as in the UK's 1975 vote, the populace is lied to and the pro-treaty side is allowed to spend 10 times as much on advertising as the no side. Not surprisingly, the yes vote wins by a margin similar to 1975's: 67.1 to 32.9 per cent.

1 December: Lisbon Treaty enters into force in the 27 provinces. The Lisbon Treaty amended TEC (the Treaty of the European Community, which had started life in 1957 as the Treaty of Rome) and TEU (the Treaty of the European Union, which had started life in 1992 as the Treaty of Maastricht), occasionally shuffling articles between the two.

Also, Lisbon renamed TEC as the Treaty on the Functioning of The European Union (TFEU). The two treaties continue to be known as "the Treaties". Where quoted, "the Treaties" (TEU and TFEU) are as amended by Lisbon.

The consolidated version of TEU (ie Maastricht amended), produced by the EU in May 2008 and still available on its website in 2010, ended "Done at Maastricht on the seventh day of February in the year *one thousand and ninety-two*"[61], which dates it from about the time of the First Crusades. And that is roughly where democracy in the European Union returns to. See the Appendix (p320) for more on Lisbon.

2010 Herman Van Rompuy becomes EU president on 1 January.

---

[61] http://eur-lex.europa.eu/LexUriServ/LexUriServ.do?uri=OJ:C:2008:115:0013:0045:EN:PDF

CHAPTER 2: THE APPARATUS AND APPARATCHIKS

What the EU isn't

There are some things with which the EU is confused, including some things with which it would dearly love to be or have been confused, eg the Eurovision Song Contest (really it would), the 1992 Olympics in Barcelona, and football – all of which it has tried or is trying to co-opt[62]. Let's start with things it has nothing to do with.

The Eurovision Song Contest

Although Eurovision voting has little in common with democracy, it has nothing to do with the EU, and is also a year older than the Treaty of Rome. Norway has had an up-and-down relationship with both irritations.

Eurostar

It's popular, it usually works and is, therefore, entirely unrelated. It's also a great example of international co-operation succeeding without the interference of an expensive supranational bureaucracy[63].

Council Of Europe (COE)

This is the outfit that Winston set up, in Strasbourg in 1949, and is not part of the EU although the EU parliament, on its monthly shuttle, borrows a COE building named after him. Preferring the consensual to the coercive, the Council of Europe was eclipsed in influence as if it were just another wishy-washy League Of Nations by the European Coal and Steel Community soon after the latter was formed.

Nevertheless, the COE now has 47 members – the EU plus Russia and ex-Comecon states, Efta countries outside the EU (Norway, Liechtenstein, Iceland, Switzerland) and others. You have to be a COE member before you knock on the EU's door – Turkey is a member. Turkey aside, the COE is known as a halfway house for countries trying to go straight after experimenting with communism or other types of authoritarianism.

Its most famous institution is the European Court of Human Rights (ECHR). Mentions of taking one's case "to Europe" usually means the ECHR, especially if one's "rights" are involved (a jailed rapist's right to consume pornography etc).

---

[62] See "Propaganda" on p172 for examples of the EU trying to grab glory from unrelated ventures

[63] However, the EU did give us some of our own money back to pay for a tiny fraction of the St Pancras Eurostar development

Although not legally binding, its decisions are rarely ignored[64]. The ECHR is often confused with the EU's European Court Of Justice (ECJ, p102), which is in Luxembourg.

The ECHR gave us the Convention for the Protection of Human Rights and Fundamental Freedoms, usually known as the European Convention on Human Rights. The Human Rights Act (1998), enacted in 2000, made it part of UK law although UK citizens had always had access to its remedies. Parts of the Convention were borrowed by the EU's Maastricht and Amsterdam Treaties. The enactment of the Lisbon Treaty meant that the EU itself, not just its member states, acceded to the ECHR and it now formally recognises ECHR judgments. (The Lisbon Treaty's Charter of Fundamental Rights, covered on p347, cherry-picks both COE rights and UN rights, as well as ECHR and ECJ case law.)

Some people think that the Treaty Of Rome (1957) outlawed capital punishment throughout the EEC. Those who do not think this include the relations of Hamida Djandoubi, a Tunisian executed by guillotine on 10 September 1977 in Marseilles. Nowadays, however, a renunciation of capital punishment, which is proscribed by the European Convention on Human Rights, is, along with COE membership, a prerequisite of joining the EU.

The EU's flag was adopted from the Council Of Europe in the mid 1980s, around the time of the Single European Act. The 12 gold stars on a blue background were not a reference to the then 12 member states: the COE designed the flag in 1955 and chose 12 stars because they "symbolise perfection and completeness and bring to mind the months of the year, the labours of Hercules, and the Apostles". Nowadays, the EU strongly brings to mind a specific labour of Hercules – the cleaning of the Augean stables – as well as those apostles who collected tax.

At the same time, the EU also swiped the COE's anthem, which it had chosen in the early 1970s: "Ode To Joy", the fourth and final movement of Beethoven's Ninth Symphony (which so roused Alex in *A Clockwork Orange*).

UEFA European Cup
Although it changed its name at the same time as the EC changed its name to the EU and is now called the UEFA Champions League, it is popular and, therefore, entirely unrelated. Because of this continuing popularity, the EU is trying to muscle in on the sport's governance.

---

[64] In the UK, not all police forces have deleted the DNA and fingerprints of the innocent from the national database, despite a 2008 ECHR ruling. And "stop and search" police powers continued for a long time after a separate ECHR judgment

Euromillions Lottery
Pots of money? Apportioned randomly? What could Euromillions have to do with the glorious project?

Eurobonds
Again, no

What the EU is

Those who agree with Otto Von Bismarck's saw — "People who enjoy eating sausage and obeying the law should not watch either being made"[65] — will be delighted: it is near impossible to see how all of those EU directives and regulations are made, such is the secrecy of the Commission and the Council Of Ministers. (Apologists say that we do not see the minutes of cabinet meetings in Number 10, either. That is true but we can remove a cabinet in general elections.)

The EU is rather allergic to transparency and democracy. When electorates are given a say in EU matters they tend to vote against further integration, as the French, Dutch and Irish famously did. They then find that they are ignored or are asked to vote again. A character in Somerset Maugham's play *The Circle* says that "Sincerity in society is like an iron girder in a house of cards." Truly democratic habits in the EU would be the iron girder in its house of cards. In a 2007 interview with the *Financial Times*, then foreign secretary David Miliband argued that making the EU more democratic should not be a focus for the government: "I've been convinced for years that the greatest challenge facing the European Union is about delivery rather than about internal democracy; that the root to respect in European hearts is through delivery, that it's the delivery deficit rather than the democratic deficit that should be the focus of our attention."[66] (Without any sense of embarrassment, the EU's budget for 2009 included "Budget Line 190401: Promoting democracy around the world: £91.7million".)

In addition to Miliband, even Eurocrats acknowledge the democratic deficit but nothing is ever done about the missing democracy because its absence is "a feature not a bug". It *is* the point, not an unwelcome by-product, and has been

---

[65] The Iron Chancellor also said, "I have always found the word 'Europe' on the lips of those who wanted something from other powers which they dared not demand in their own name." Quoted in *Europe: A Concise Encyclopedia Of The European Union* (Fourth edition, Profile Books, 2004; the third edition is at www.euro-know.org/dictionary) by Lord (Rodney) Leach
[66] *The Financial Times*, 10 July 2007

ever since Monnet saw that the democratic and intergovernmental League Of Nations did not halt the irresistible rise of European fascism in the 1930s. The thinking was: "Hitler was elected. Therefore, elections are bad. We cannot trust the people again."

The two principal causes of the deficit are the fact that only the unelected Commission can propose laws, and the fact that a country's representative (who is at least elected but not with an EU job in mind) is often outvoted by other countries' representatives. John Stuart Mill explained why there would have to be a democratic deficit in the EU a century earlier when he wrote that: "Free institutions are next to impossible in a country made up of different nationalities. Among a people without fellow-feeling, especially if they read and speak different languages, the united public opinion, necessary to the working of representative government, cannot exist."[67]

Many people when leaving a job snaffle something as they go, such as a dependable stapler. Monnet, the architect of the EU, stole the League Of Nations' entire structure, which is why the EU includes, as did the League, a Secretariat (the Commission), a Council of Ministers, a parliament and a Court of Justice[68]. Crucially, however, he made the EEC supranational (ie governments who sign up to it are subservient to it) rather than intergovernmental (as the League was and the United Nations is).

It's a shame he didn't steal the democratic element, but there we are. Here is what he did steal, the machinery that produces most of this and 26 other countries' laws. Its six main elements are known as "the (EU) institutions".

The European Commission
Every member state provides a commissioner, whose oath of allegiance is to the EU, not to his or her home country: as the Treaties say, "The members of the Commission shall be chosen on the ground of their general competence and *European commitment*" [emphasis added][69]. The men and women give an

---

[67] *Considerations On Representative Government* (1861)
[68] This similarity was first pointed out in *The Great Deception* by Booker and North
[69] From TEU 17(3). See also TFEU 245: "The members of the Commission shall refrain from any action incompatible with their duties. Member states shall respect their independence and shall not seek to influence them in the performance of their tasks. The members of the Commission may not, during their term of office, engage in any other occupation, whether gainful or not. When entering upon their duties they shall give a solemn undertaking that, both during and after their term of office, they will respect the obligations arising therefrom and in particular their duty to behave with integrity and discretion as regards the acceptance, after they have ceased to hold office, of certain appointments or benefits. In the event of any breach of these obligations, the Court of Justice may,

undertaking before the European Court of Justice: "to be completely independent in the performance of my duties, in the general interest of the Communities [ie the EU]; in the performance of these duties, *neither to seek nor to take instructions from any government* or from any other body" [emphasis added]. EU judges also swear this oath. MEPs do not: that tells you everything you need to know about their importance – they are not bound.

It shouldn't really matter, then, which countries have commissioners, because commissioners are not allowed to act in their countries' interests, only in the Union's. This isn't always how the oath is interpreted: exceptions follow.

From the next term onwards (November 2014), according to TEU 17(5), the Commission must "[correspond] to two thirds of the number of member states, unless the European Council, acting unanimously, decides to alter this number". Under the Nice Treaty, there had to be fewer commissioners than member states. It didn't matter how many fewer, just fewer. Therefore, any country would, if the Commission were limited to 26, have been without a commissioner for five years in 135 (there are 27 members, each would take it in turns to lose a commissioner for a five-year period). That's perfectly bearable, especially as the commissioner cannot act in his or her country's interest anyway. Under the Lisbon Treaty, however, the number of commissioners must be no more than two thirds of the number of members (ie 18 of 27). So, every member state must go without a commissioner for five years every 15 years. The promise that every country would keep its commissioner, made as part of an unsavoury package to reverse the Irish referendum of 2008, had no legal basis: the Treaty states that there must be no more than 18. Eventually, the ECJ will enforce this provision. Ireland was better off under Nice, but that's not what she was told before her second referendum.

Only the Commission can initiate laws and because EU law has primacy over national law, the Commission, or "college", is our true cabinet: Brussels is head office, while the Houses Of Parliament and the Bundestag etc are just regional franchises, subservient to the commissars in the Berlaymont, the Commission's Brussels home. Its unelected commissars work to five-year terms, issue diktats, employ security men with a nice line in sunglasses and armoury, and enjoy outsize vehicles with darkened windows.

As Tony Benn, no fan of the EU, has said, "In the course of my life I have developed five little democratic questions. If one meets a powerful person –

---

on application by the Council acting by a simple majority or the Commission, rule that the member concerned be, according to the circumstances, either compulsorily retired or deprived of his right to a pension or other benefits in its stead"

Adolf Hitler, Joe Stalin or Bill Gates – ask them five questions: 'What power have you got? Where did you get it from? In whose interests do you exercise it? To whom are you accountable? And how can we get rid of you?' If you cannot get rid of the people who govern you, you do not live in a democratic system." One cannot look at the Commission, the EU's executive and enforcement body, without recalling these questions. (Benn is pretty much the ace of trumps when anyone tries to play the "opposition to the EU is for right-wing xenophobes" card.)

Romano Prodi, a former EU Commission president, knew what type of ship he was steering: "But what is the Commission? We are here to take binding decisions as an executive power. If you don't like the term 'government' for this, what other term do you suggest? I speak of a European government because we take government decisions."[70] For the hard of thinking, he repeated himself a month later: "Here in Brussels, a true European government has been born. I have governmental powers, I have executive powers for which there is no other name in the world, whether you like it or not, than government."[71] We all say things when we're drunk on power, but in vino veritas.

Many people don't care if the laws by which they must live are made in La Paz or Bratislava – one bunch of self-serving, self-publicising, self-important and self-promoting men and women is pretty much the same as any other on the planet, they maintain. That much is true. However, those in Westminster and local government have to watch their backs every four years or so in case you tip them out of a cushy job and they are forced to visit an executive headhunter. The threat of unemployment focuses the mind – that is why it is important that those who control our lives should be elected and must thereafter look to us for re-election; we should be looking over their shoulders and breathing down their necks, because anything else is not democracy. Sadly, the EU elite feels no such threat.

"The distinguishing quality of parliamentary government is, that in each stage of a public transaction there is a discussion; that the public assist at this discussion; that it can, through parliament, turn out an administration which is not doing as it likes, and can put in an administration which will do as it likes," wrote Walter Bagehot[72]. The Commission is your "administration". There is no point trying to "turn it out". Karl Popper once said, "I personally call the type of government which can be removed without violence 'democracy', and the other 'tyranny'."

---

[70] *The Times*, 27 October 1999
[71] Speech to the European parliament, November 1999
[72] *The English Constitution*, introduction to the second edition (1872)

But perhaps the real power lies with the éminences grises, the senior Eurocrats or civil servants[73]. As a former commissar, Günter Verheugen, said, "The whole development in the last 10 years has brought the civil servants such power that in the meantime the most important political task of the [then] 25 commissioners is controlling this apparatus. There is a permanent power struggle between commissioners and high-ranking bureaucrats. Some of them think: the commissioner is gone after five years and so is just a housekeeper, but I'm sticking around… too much is decided by civil servants."[74] He also put the eurosceptic case well when he said: "[The Commission is] a bureaucratic monster whose tentacles leave no village untouched and with nothing better to do than chop off every difference and blend it into the European sauce." In other words, to season the disparate into the homogeneous.

The UK has had one president of the Commission: Roy Jenkins[75] (1977-1981), who had come third to Jim Callaghan and Michael Foot in the Labour leadership election the previous year. Not only is the EU Commission unelected, its members have very often *lost* an election to get there (eg Lords Kinnock and Patten, who both lost in 1992 despite being on different sides).

The Berlaymont, the Commission's home, was built in 1967. The EU then leased it from the Belgian government and staff worked there until 1991, when asbestos was discovered and the building was emptied. (The Commission occupied the nearby Breydel building from 1991 to 2004.) A press release of 5 December 2000 admitted that asbestos removal did not begin until 1995 and lasted until 1999, over a year behind schedule. All the while, the rent was being paid at £8.7million a year. Since 2002, the EU has owned the building. It told the parliament on 17 December 2002 that "the Commission's total payment will be €553million and its share of the renovation costs is set at €503million".

Berlaymont Babylon

The all-powerful Commission comprises José Manuel Barroso, its Portuguese president, and his 26 commissioners (or commissars), many of whom add greatly to the gaiety of nations.

Despite being the only institution that can legislate, and do so over and above

---

[73] See Bruno Waterfield's essay in *No Means No!*, 8 December 2008, available from www.manifestoclub.com
[74] *Sued Deutsche*, 4 October 2006
[75] In 1971 he had led, in defiance of a three-line whip, 69 fellow rebel Labour MPs into the aye lobby to vote for Ted Heath's European Communities Bill, more than cancelling out the 33 Conservative refuseniks, and thereby ushering in Britain's membership of the EEC. How could Brussels not reward him?

national parliaments that cannot argue with it, it is unelected: commissioners are nominated by their mother country, their posts decided by the Commission president. Between them they have 42 "directorates-general" (DG) or ministries, each headed by a director-general (salary between €15,000 and €18,000 per month – about £160,000 per annum).

Because so many of the 2004-2009 Commission are quoted in this book and half are also in the 2009-2014 Commission, it's useful to have a look at the previous "college" as well.

The November 2004 to 31 October 2009 crew could say that of its commissioners:

One, who had an embezzlement conviction in France that could not be reported, was in charge of justice
One, who had been tried on a charge of fraud, was in charge of stamping out fraud
One had links to the underworld in her home country
One warned that the alternative to further EU integration was the gas chamber
One, who thought the benefits of the EU were heavily outweighed by its costs, was in charge of enterprise
One, from the country with possibly the EU's worst per capita pollution record, was in charge of the environment
One came from an area not fully signed up to the Common Fisheries Policy and was, of course, fisheries commissioner
One whose husband did handsomely from the Common Agricultural Policy was in charge of – you can guess the rest
Until October 2008 one of them was Peter Mandelson

And at least seven were – to borrow the argot of alcoholics – "recovering" communists.

Mr Barroso replaced Romano Prodi, a former PM of Italy, in November 2004. However, on 27 October 2004 he had to withdraw his original list of 24 commissioners an hour before parliament was due to vote on it. Several selections had caused some MEPs offence. Although the MEPs could not block individual commissioners they could block the entire Commission and Barroso saw a beating coming his way.

Rocco Buttiglione, Italy's first choice and her then European affairs minister, was problematic. Investigated in 2002 but never charged by the Monagesque authorities over money laundering[76], he was a Catholic philosopher-politician who was rather more "Rome" than "Treaty Of Rome".

It was wrongly reported that he had described homosexuality as a sin at his "hearing", a three-hour interview in front of the committee of the European parliament whose brief most closely matches that of the commissioner-designate. In fact, it was a left-wing MEP who mentioned "sin", asking Buttiglione how he could reconcile Catholic teaching on homosexuality with a role as anti-discrimination commissar. Buttiglione replied that that there is a world of difference between morality and legality, and that his private religious opinions certainly would not prevent his championing the rights of minorities. However, he did say, "The family [unit] exists in order to allow women to have children and to have the protection of a male who takes care of them." And he attributed Europe's low birth rate to the fact that women "concentrated too much on their careers" and not enough on babies. The committee feared he would not be able to disentangle the "sin" of homosexuality from the "sinner" and so voted that he should not have the brief, which included the area of discrimination. Those who knew him argued that he disapproved of discrimination. Josep Borrell, then president of the European parliament, described Buttiglione's comments as shocking, and said that perhaps if he, the Italian, were in charge of beetroots it would not be so serious. Alas, the committee further voted that he should have no other portfolio, be it vegetable or social. Though not binding, the committee's votes were a warning to Barroso. (Singing from exactly the same hymn book as Buttiglione, Ruth Kelly would be later appointed minister for women and equality in this country.)

Another 2004 nominee was dropped: Ingrida Udre, a former basketball player from Latvia who had been nominated for Taxation and the Customs Union. The deep ironies in the 2004 Commission and the appointments meted out to its officers started with her: one of her bodyguards was charged in Latvia with bribing a customs officer. Her problems really started at her hearing when she said she supported tax competition. She was also – deep breath – fairly eurosceptic. Have a guess why the ticket inspector chucked her off the gravy train: was it her euroscepticism or her support for tax competition? Either would have done. She was replaced by a lifelong communist from Hungary. There were mutterings that László Kovács, Hungary's man, knew too little about energy, so Latvia's second choice got that brief. And Kovács got Udre's tax brief. If only Udre had instead been able to sport a criminal record, or had bolstered a soviet.

---

[76] *The Daily Telegraph*, 20 October 2004. "Separately, [Buttiglione's] senior aide is facing trial for fraud in Italy, and is the subject of a string of criminal inquiries including a case involving the alleged disappearance of £4million of Italian and EU money"

The second attempt at forming a Commission was put to the European parliament a month later. Again, it wasn't without incident. On 18 November the Ukip's then leader Nigel Farage broke a perpetual embargo – in the French media at any rate – and revealed to the Strasbourg parliament that France's nominated commissioner had a criminal record (he was a true "conviction" politician). This is Farage's speech:

"Mr President [Borrell], Mr Barroso said: 'I think my team is of high quality.' Well, let us conduct a human audit. I am mindful that audits are not very popular in the European Commission and that auditors – if they do their job properly – get fired, but nonetheless here goes:

From France we have Mr Barrot, who will take on transport[77]. In 2000 he received an eight-month suspended jail sentence for his involvement in an embezzlement case and was banned from holding public office for two years.
From Hungary we have Mr Kovács, who will take on taxation. For many years he was a communist apparatchik, a friend of Mr Kádár, the dictator in Hungary, and an outspoken opponent of the values that we hold dear in the West.
His new empire will produce taxation policy and he will look after the customs union from Cork to Vilnius.
From Estonia we have Mr Kallas, who for 20 years was a Soviet Party apparatchik until his newly acquired taste for capitalism got him into trouble. However, to be fair, he was acquitted of abuse and fraud but convicted of providing false information[78]. He is going to be in charge of the anti-fraud drive! You could not make this up!
From the UK we have Mr Mandelson, who will take on the trade portfolio. He, of course, was removed twice from the British government, but to be fair, he is one of the more competent ones!
From the Netherlands we have Mrs Kroes, who will take on competition. She is accused of lying to the European parliament. These may be only allegations, but they are made by Mr Van Buitenen and should be listened to.
Ask yourself a question: would you buy a used car from this Commission? The answer simply must be 'no'! Even if they were competent and even if this were a high-quality Commission – sorry, Mr Barroso, but I do not think it is – we would still vote 'no' on the political principle that the Commission is the guardian of the Treaties; the Commission is the motor for integration; the Commission initiates the legislation that is damaging our businesses across Europe so badly; the Commission is the embodiment of all that is worst

---

[77] He moved to Justice in 2008
[78] This wasn't quite true: when finance minister of Estonia, Kallas was convicted and then cleared on appeal of a $10million abuse and fraud allegedly carried out four years earlier when he was head of the national bank. He was also acquitted, after the case had been referred to a lower court, of the charge of providing false information. The prosecutor in the last case decided to appeal that decision.
However, Estonia's chief prosecutor overruled him, took over the case and decided to end the appeal. Kallas had been represented by Indrek Teder, who happened to be the law partner of the justice minister. All were members of the Reform Party – which Kallas led and had founded

in this European Union; the Commission is the government of Europe and is not directly accountable to anybody…" [79]

Despite this and other objections, the Barroso Commission was approved by 449 votes to 149 (with 82 abstentions). It was finally sworn in, three weeks late, on Monday 22 November 2004. The Bulgarian and Romanian commissars joined on 1 January 2007.

The first Barroso Commission was acting without remit after its term expired on 31 October 2009: there's no legal basis in the Treaties for a "caretaker" Commission. Hearings for the new "college" ran from 11 to 19 January 2010. There had been rumours that the Socialist grouping in the parliament would object to the whole "college" on account of the centre-right Bulgarian nominee, Rumiana Jeleva, whose answers about her financial interests had not satisfied every MEP.

Jeleva, Bulgaria's foreign minister and deputy of the EPP group of centre-right MEPs in the European parliament, came under scrutiny even before her hearing. In December 2009 the Bulgarian and German media discussed her husband, Krassimir Jelev, who was branch manager of the Central Co-operative Bank in the port of Burgas. The bank was thought to be part of the secretive TIM business group, which had often been linked to Russian funds of less than transparent provenance[80].

At her hearing, for the job of Humanitarian aid, Jeleva was mightily unconvincing about her role in a company called Global Consult. She said that her involvement with it ended in 2007, when she became an MEP. A Bulgarian MEP from an opposition party claimed that Jeleva owned the firm until April 2009 – in violation of Bulgarian law. She hadn't listed Global Consult in the register of MEPs' interests in Brussels (some of her declarations were, unusually, unsigned) but apparently did declare the company in a national register back home. Michael Cashman MEP (ex-*EastEnders*) asked Jeleva if there were anything that she may have left out of her register of interests "that she may now wish to tell the committee [of MEPs] and are there any current business interests not currently declared?"

Later, another opposition Bulgarian MEP accused her of having been CEO of a firm, ETKO Schneiders, set up in Liechtenstein by the country's communist secret service[81]. It also looked as if the price for which she claimed to have sold

---

[79] The YouTube clip of this speech is at tinyurl.com/2xsr9c
[80] *EurActiv*, 16 December 2009
[81] *Jeleva chaired firm set up by communist secret services, says MEP* in *EurActiv*, 19 January 2010

Global Consult – €2,500 – represented only a quarter of the cash in its bank account.

She had been shaky on geography (despite a focus on Yemen in the media, she did not know where the Gulf of Aden was) and had said that the situation in the DR Congo, about which it was obvious she knew nothing, was a consideration for a director-general not her. She had been rather better when dancing the rumba for charity on Bulgarian TV the year before. Hours after her hearing, Haiti was devastated by an earthquake. Humanitarian aid would be her brief.

During the following week, Mr Barroso gave her lukewarm backing, reminding MEPs that she had twice been elected to their parliament – but he did not refer to her dismal hearing. The next day she resigned and was replaced by the Bulgarian PM with Kristalina Georgieva, a World Bank official, who would have been a smarter first choice. Jeleva also resigned as Bulgarian foreign minister.

When Jeleva's job had first been threatened by the centre-left group of MEPs, the EPP then whispered that it would decapitate a leftist commissar-designate. This would be Maroš Šefčovič, a Slovak, who had five years earlier supposedly accused ethnic Roma of exploiting his country's welfare system. Even before his hearing, an EPP spokesperson said, "I don't think that the future vice-president of the European Commission, responsible for such sensitive issues as recruitment, as equal opportunities, as gender, can have such discriminatory views on this." In the end, there was no retaliation by the EPP.

The vote of consent for the current "college" was on 9 February 2010 (two weeks late). The Commission was approved by 488 votes to 137 (with 72 abstentions) and sworn in the next day to run until 31 October 2014. This was over three months after Barroso's first gang had run out of road.

So, here are the men and women, "Barroso II", who dream up most of our legislation. The Commission press release that announced them to the world made no mention of any of their mother countries.

President
José Manuel Barroso (Portugal)
Salary: €293,073 (€24,422.80 per month)

Mr Barroso is possibly the only person in the world who has claimed to be influenced by both Chairman Mao and Margaret Thatcher. He first came to attention outside Portugal in 2003, just before the invasion of Iraq, when he hosted the summit between the Spanish PM, Blair and George W Bush on the island of Terceira in the Azores.

In 2009, he was re-elected unopposed for another five years. Although soundly communautaire and deeply pro-integrationist, he was nevertheless a compromise candidate and a joke to many EU heads of government. Conservative MEPs, who are popularly supposed to be eurosceptic, mostly voted for him. Labour MEPs mostly did not (a member of the EPP, he's not a socialist).

His officials admitted in 2006 that 11,000 sq ft of illegal Indonesian rainforest wood had been used on the thirteenth floor of the Berlaymont, where the president's suite is located.

There are seven vice-presidents of the Commission and each receives a salary of €265,465 (€22,122.10 per month); they're marked below by an asterisk. The other 19 commissars bump along on €238,919 per year. A British cabinet minister gets about €160,000 per year.

If Mr Barroso is unavailable, the order of deputies is: Viviane Reding, Joaquín Almunia, Siim Kallas, Neelie Kroes, Antonio Tajani, Maroš Šefčovič (Ashton does not deputise).

Agriculture and rural policy
Dacian Ciolos (Romania)

Ciolos is a former agriculture minister and it was on his watch, in 2008, that EU agri-funds to Romania were frozen because of fraud. He is now in charge of farm subsidies, which are the largest part of the EU budget, for the whole 27-nation bloc.

Schooled in France, which he regards as his "adopted country", and married to a French woman, Ciolos has worked for the Commission before and his appointment delighted France's President Sarkozy who rightly thought that the Common Agricultural Policy (CAP – see p237) would be safe in the Francophile's hands. The press in France and Romania dubbed him "France's second commissioner" and he's a friend of the first, Michel Barnier (see later), the fiercely pro-CAP commissioner, who said that Ciolos would be "independent, but I will give him my opinion". At his hearing Ciolos said that "reform [of the CAP] does not mean decreasing the budget" and "If it were just up to me, I can assure you we would have a lot more money [for subsidies]". The EU, he claimed, had made enough concessions for the World Trade Organisation's Doha round of talks. The developing world has been warned…

From 2004 to 2009 this post was held by Mariann Fischer Boel (Denmark). One should be in favour of people in government having experience of the real world, particularly if such experience is relevant to the job in hand. Marianne had been an agriculture minister in her home country. But her experience didn't end there: her husband earned €136,914 from the CAP in 2006. But it was her husband Hans – not she – who owned the farm. No conflict of interest at all. Besides, she said, she had received CAP payments when she was Denmark's agriculture minister[82] and therefore part of the EU's Agriculture Council (see Council Of Ministers). One thing that wasn't fine was her forgetting to tell her national parliament that she had banking and sugar shares. Fortunately, these were disposed of before she assumed her exciting EU role.

In July 2006 she said that in her upcoming review of the CAP (a predictably damp squib in 2008), the Commission should check whether funds were being handed out efficiently and, if not, it may be necessary to "impose top and bottom limits to what farmers can receive". That was part of her husband's income she was talking about. Three months later she ruled out cutting the CAP's budget in the 2008 review of EU financing. She explained, "These are busy days in the kitchen – lots of pots are boiling at the same time. Rather than keeping the door to the kitchen sealed I have decided at an early stage to give an impression of what is boiling under our lids."

The Treaties state that "the members of the Commission may not, during their term of office, engage in any other occupation, whether gainful or not" and that only commissioners whose "independence is beyond doubt" should be chosen for a post.

Budget and financial programming
Janusz Lewandowski (Poland)

At his hearing the economist and former MEP wasn't give too hard a time – he used to lead the parliamentary committee that "grilled" him, and he started by flattering some of its current and former members. He said that he favoured an EU tax in principle but "Europe is probably not ready yet for [it]. It could prove detrimental for our links with the citizens." A tax on financial transactions was a possible new way to fund the EU budget, he agreed, ignoring the fact that such taxes end up being paid by the consumer (or a firm's employees or a pension fund's portfolio etc: there's no such thing as a victimless tax). He was, however, against a tax on text messages, a proposal from the head of the committee.

---

[82] Her successor, Henrik Høegh, the Danish minister for agriculture (at the time of writing), also of course sits on the Agriculture Council. He received €604,787 in CAP payments between 2000 and 2008 (his children also did well). As part of the Council, he is involved in discussions about the future of the CAP – as Mariann had been, first as part of the Council then as a commissar.
In 2005 the Dutch minister for agriculture, Cees Veerman, who had farms in Holland and France that he described as "his pension", threatened to resign when his PM backed reform of the CAP.
In 2010 the campaigners Centre For Open Politics wrote to Defra's permanent secretary about the new cabinet minister, Caroline Spelman: "[She] is in charge of negotiating subsidies, quotas and tariff barriers at the EU Agriculture Council, giving rise to a clear conflict of interest between this official role and her close links to a company [founded by her and her husband] which has in the past lobbied or may be intending to lobby over such matters"

Now that the EU can sign treaties as an entity in its own right, it lacks only two things available to real countries: the ability to declare war; and the means to raise direct taxation. It is dependent on levies from cash-strapped national governments and would much rather get money straight from the citizen. Although the "carbon" revenue would supposedly stay with national treasuries, it's not hard to see at least some of it ending up in the Commission's coffers, as with VAT. Eventually, it would all go directly to the Commission after the EU has argued that it sets the rate and therefore should scoop it all up as well.

Lewandowski came round to the idea of EU taxation in August 2010: "If the EU had more of its own revenues, then transfers from national budgets could be reduced. I hear from several capitals, including important ones like Berlin, that they would like to reduce their contribution." And who'd make up the shortfall? The citizen, who is anyway financing "national budgets" through taxes. Disingenuous is the politest word. If there were a tax on financial transactions, the UK (because of the City) would be hardest hit of anywhere in the EU – perhaps ten times harder than even Germany and France. An aviation tax would also unfairly single out the UK, home to Europe's busiest airport. Taxation without representation gave George III problems in America…

In much the same way that "social funds" bypass national governments to go to the "regions" (see p107), the EU wants to bypass national governments when it *collects* money. It wants "own resources" (in EU jargon) to come directly from the serfs. There have been several ideas – an EU tax on text messages etc – but none has yet joined the 1 per cent of VAT receipts which the Commission already gets (sent in via national treasuries). Giscard d'Estaing told Gisela Stuart MP, when she was helping him draft his Constitution: "British people will have to realise that the Union cannot survive without an independent stream of income."

From 2004 to 2009 this post was held by Dalia Grybauskaité (Lithuania). A martial arts black belt and former finance minister back home, she was keen to grab more of the UK's rebate for the 2007-2013 budget period: that was her job. Blair gave it to her. She maintained she was never a communist party member but took a PhD at Moscow University in 1988 and worked at Leningrad University during the 1980s. It would have been unlikely, but not quite impossible, that someone not politically "reliable" would have been allowed to do so. She said some sensible things about the Common Agricultural Policy, which are repeated in that section and in "Cost". She became her country's first female president in July 2009.

Climate Action
Connie Hedegaard (Denmark)

She held the same position in the Danish government, earning the nickname Ms Climate. When the Danish capital held the COP-15 UN Conference in

December 2009 she was chairwoman but resigned when the shindig ran into difficulties in its second week and the EU was outmanoeuvred in Copenhagen by the big boys.

Once her country's youngest ever MP, she left politics to pursue journalism, becoming a TV presenter. Now back in politics, she was dubbed one of *Time* magazine's 100 most influential people for 2009 – then along came the Copenhagen debacle. At her hearing she said: "In my universe, nuclear is not a renewable source." She has since shown strong support for an EU carbon tax.

The *Guardian* reported that she had not told the truth about when, as Danish climate minister, she had first known about VAT fraud on Danish carbon permits:

"The EU's climate chief is facing pressure to explain her failure to crack down on a loophole that allowed alleged fraudsters – a large number of them based in Britain – to make millions of euros through Europe's emissions trading scheme. Confidential documents show that Connie Hedegaard had been informed about fraudsters targeting the Danish carbon registry to enable them to trade in credits last summer [2009]... Previously, Hedegaard had denied knowing about the suspected fraud until a Danish newspaper reported it in December 2009. 'I was never informed about this until last autumn,' she had told the *Guardian*. But a confidential [Danish] climate ministry report appears to have been signed with Hedegaard's initials, indicating she was made aware of the problem in August... When invited to clarify her position... she admitted seeing the confidential document, but denied she should have acted last summer because 'it was just a normal criminal thing – somebody making fraud on VAT'."[83]

Competition
* Joaquín Almunia (Spain)

A veteran Spanish socialist, he was in charge of Economic and monetary affairs in the previous Barroso Commission. At his hearing for the job of handing out billion-euro fines to companies such as Microsoft and Intel, he said he also was in favour of a "Tobin" tax, although "I know it's a very difficult tax to implement".

He was formerly the keeper of the discredited Stability and Growth Pact (SGP – see "The euro" on p152), whereby any country that overspends by 3 per cent of GDP is, theoretically at least, fined. He let off Italy for breaking the SGP in summer 2005, while France, Greece, Holland and Germany looked at their shoes. He even shook his fist at Germany early in 2006 but nothing changed; the pact is permanently broken by the bigger states, especially since the recession.

---

[83] *Europe's climate chief under pressure over 'missing' emissions traders* in *The Guardian*, 24 May 2010

Who knows what might have happened if countries, particularly those in the eurozone, had been held to the terms of the pact?

In 1998, Almunia, despite being leader of the Socialists (PSOE) in Spain, was defeated by Josep Borrell in an open vote of PSOE members to be candidate for PM. When Borrell later stood down following a financial scandal (and was then made president of the European parliament), Almunia took the PSOE to its worst electoral defeat since the 1970s and resigned. During his tenure as minister for employment and social security in Spain, unemployment had soared to an unprecedented 22 per cent.

As parliamentary spokesman for PSOE, he defended former home secretary José Barrionuevo, who was convicted of organising and funding illegal armed actions, principally involving the anti-Eta group GAL. In 2001 Almunia said: "Only to those who have hate as their motto could it appear normal that a person such as Barrionuevo should be in prison for doing what he did as minister of the interior, which was to put great courage into the struggle against Eta."

In May 2006 Almunia predicted that all 25 EU countries – including the UK – would be in the eurozone within 10 years. But he has admitted that the euro has not increased trade within the EU: "The share of intra-EU trade over Gross Domestic Product has stabilised since 2000."[84]

In September 2006 *FT Deutschland* criticised the lobbying undertaken by him and a fellow commissar, Frenchman Jacques Barrot (see below), for securing increases in subsidies for their countries' banana farmers. The paper cited the rise in funds from €242 to €257m, and argued: "Needless to say, 96 per cent of that flows to the overseas territories of Spain and France... sometimes events in the EU are a bit like events in a banana republic."

In July 2009 Almunia told a Spanish newspaper that it is "not very democratic" to hold referendums on new EU treaties. He and his wife own four properties.

From 2004 to 2009 this post was held by Neelie Kroes – see Digital agenda (below).

Development
Andris Piebalgs (Latvia)

Piebalgs was energy commissar in the last "college". A former teacher and communist, he was finance minister in post-USSR Latvia but resigned after just one year when the Baltija Bank, the country's biggest, collapsed in May 1995, a victim of mismanagement and fraud.

---

[84] *The Wall Street Journal*, 15 March 2007

Rolf Linkohr, a German ex-MEP and power-company lobbyist who sat on the boards of two energy companies, was an adviser to Piebalgs when he was energy commissar. The German had to resign in February 2007 when it was pointed out that his conflicts of interest were obvious. Piebalgs said he did not to know of Linkohr's other jobs[85]. In his new job Piebalgs reports to Cathy Ashton.

From 2004 to 2009 this post was held by Louis Michel (Belgium), who was development and humanitarian aid commissar. In 2003, when he was Belgium's foreign minister, Michel called Blair a "belligerent grandstander" and is said to have leaked the story that Peter Mandelson wanted an £80,000 Maserati as his official EU car.

His uneasy relationship with democracy was evident from the time of the Nice Treaty when he said: "I personally think it is very dangerous to organise referendums when you're not sure to win them. If you organise a referendum and you lose the referendum, that's a big problem for Europe." (His first act when appointed Belgium's deputy PM and foreign minister was to appoint his 24-year-old son as regional director of Wallonia.)

When he was appointed, a British newspaper said that "allocating humanitarian aid, an EU activity notorious for financial irregularities, to the former Belgian foreign minister Louis Michel" was an unwelcome move. Why so?

In 2001, he was accused, in a Belgian civil court, of covering up a corruption scandal involving the mass sale of EU entry visas by the Belgian embassy in Sofia to organised-crime groups. A lawsuit served by a diplomat, Myrianne Coen, who had been first secretary in the embassy, alleged that her ambassador, Koenraad Rouvroy, was tied to the Russian mafia and had created fictitious companies to request EU visas for the criminal underworld. Michel had succeeded earlier in preventing a parliamentary inquiry into this by pleading with Belgian MPs to hold off for the sake of the country's reputation during Belgium's six-month EU presidency[86].

He later angered the US when trying to use the Belgian universal jurisdiction law of 1993, making war-crimes complaints against several US officials. The law allowed Belgian courts to rule on crimes against humanity regardless of the nationality of the perpetrator or where the crimes took place. Despite criticism from the US, Michel said there was "no reason to fear this law". General Colin Powell was among those targeted, along with former president George Bush Snr, over alleged war crimes during the 1991 Gulf War. The law was scrapped in November 2003 after Michel came under intense US pressure. Michel had himself fallen foul of the same law when he was accused by an opposition party of authorising illegal arms sales to Nepal in June 2003.

---

[85] Peers also fund lobbyists as advisers (eg *The Independent*, 27 June 2008). Just because it happens elsewhere does not make it OK in Brussels. Peers also accept money to try to amend legislation (eg *The Sunday Times*, 1 February 2009). So long as the law is not based on an unchangeable EU directive, they might have a chance, otherwise they are merely breaking a different law – and ripping off their clients

[86] *The Daily Telegraph*, 6 September 2001

At his 2004 hearing, Michel was questioned about his relationship with Belgian-Kiwi businessman George Forrest, who owned mines in DR Congo. Bart Staes MEP criticised Michel for failing to keep his distance from Forrest when Belgian foreign minister. Staes pointed out that Forrest had been cited in a report by a United Nations panel in October 2002 on the looting of DR Congo's natural resources.

In March 2007, the Corporate Europe Observatory believed that there was a potential case of conflict of interest involving Etienne Davignon, an adviser to Michel on the role of the private sector in the economic development of sub-Saharan Africa. Mr Davignon was a board member of – and held 11,111 shares in – Suez, the French energy company, which was promoting the privatisation of public electricity and water supply services in Africa.

Michel stood down in June 2009 to become an MEP. After he'd been in his new job just a few hours, *The Parliament* reported that he had criticised the European parliament's "many procedures, rules and regulations". Michel said, "I admit that it is only my first day but the impression I get is that this a very bureaucratic institution, perhaps even more so than the Commission."

Digital Agenda
* Neelie Kroes (The Netherlands)

She was competition commissar in the previous "college", becoming famous for fining Microsoft and Intel hundreds of millions of euros. A high-profile Dutch woman, she met Steve Jobs of Apple and Mick Jagger when considering how music should be sold online in the 27 provinces. Her 2010 hearing was lacklustre – her well-wishers blamed this on her having to chase miscreant multinationals instead of revising for the new brief. She had to return for another hour's questioning, in camera, a week later. She promised to extend the (double-edged) ban on high roaming charges when it expires in 2011.

"Nickel Neelie", supposedly Holland's answer to the Iron Lady, submitted a 14-page document on her past business interests when going for her first EU job in 2004 (by 2010 she was admitting to €1million in shares). That hearing was much livelier. Understandably, MEPs expressed concern over Kroes' possible conflicts of interest with her previous business career. Paul Van Buitenen, the whistleblower turned MEP, accused her of misleading the Dutch parliament while a director of the firm Ballast Nedam and took her to task for her role in providing subsidies to a Rotterdam tanker company. He also said that she had accepted money and put it into a slush fund, but could not provide proof. She denied allegations by other MEPs that she facilitated bribes or wrongly helped friends arrange business in Indonesia, describing the claims as "unfounded and nonsensical".

She had been on the boards of many big European companies, including Lucent Technologies, Thales, Dutch Railways, (Dutch) McDonald's, PwC, ProLogis Intl, KLM Assurances, Royal P&O, Nedlloyd NV, and Volvo AB, but severed all her business ties and placed her share portfolio in a blind trust.

Kroes had been a non-executive director of MMO$_2$ plc, the British mobile-phone company, when the previous competition commissioner, Mario Monti, alleged that they unfairly charged foreign companies to use its network. On 2 August 2004, the *Wall Street Journal* reported that she would be questioned by the European parliament on whether she should judge a pending case against MMO$_2$. Within a week of her 2004 appointment she had to absent herself from five anti-competitive hearings because they involved companies with which she had past or present ties at board level. However, on 21 October 2004 the front page of the *Wall Street Journal* reported that Kroes had failed to declare work she did for Lockheed Martin.

In May 2006 *Le Monde* reported that Kroes had been accused of maintaining contact with a property developer believed to be involved with Dutch organised crime. The businessman, Jan-Dirk Paarlberg, had been on trial since 2004. According to the Dutch Public Prosecutor's office, he was a member of Willem Holleeder's criminal organisation, which had a record of extortion, forgery and money laundering. Kroes and Paarlberg are certainly involved: in 2001 he was guarantor on a home loan for her, but she denied that there was any continuing link between them. *Volkskrant* reported that Kroes not only did business with Paarlberg, but also acted as his lobbyist by introducing him to the municipality of Rotterdam, with which he hoped to secure an important contract. Kroes admitted in an interview with the paper that she introduced Paarlberg also to "banks, pension funds and investors", but said she participated in meetings only "very occasionally". She denied offering Paarlberg free offices and insisted that she broke all links with him in June 2004, a few months before becoming commissioner. In 2010, the Dutch authorities seized Paarlberg's property, car, Picassos and Renoirs although he had not been convicted of any crime.

Economic and Monetary Affairs
Olli Rehn (Finland)

At his 2010 hearing, he did not rule out fining Greece for running a supersize budget deficit. How this would reduce Greece's deficit is not clear. MEPs doubted that he had the backbone to haul countries into line.

He was enlargement commissar in Barroso's first Commission. The last time Finland's borders were redrawn, in 1944, its neighbour, Russia, did particularly well, so the Finns know a bit about enlargement even if it is at their expense. His job was to pretend to Turkey that it could join the EU (France and Germany will see that it never does), and to warn the country continually that its behaviour – such as not opening its ports to Cyprus – meant that it had a "one-month window" to save its accession status. Despite not opening its ports, Turkey is still in talks. Mr Rehn also welcomed Bulgaria and Romania into the club, at least one of them before she was ready.

An ex-footballer and ex-MEP, Rehn ran the office of Finland's last commissioner, Erkki Liikanen. Mr Liikanen fell along with the rest of the Commission in 1999 but was reappointed despite having denied his wife had signed business contracts with the Commission (until a journalist presented those contracts), and despite being ultimately responsible for the unjustified suspension of whistleblower Paul Van Buitenen, whose mental stability he had questioned.

From 2004 to 2009 this post was held by Mr Almunia – see Competition (above).

Education, Culture, Multilingualism and Youth
Androulla Vassiliou (Cyprus)

Formerly health commissar, Vassilou, a former First Lady of Cyprus, now has a duff portfolio. However, it should allow her to keep an eye on her other rather juicier portfolio – the almost €3million of shares that she declared in the register of interests in 2010, up from €600,000 declared in 2008. She also has €768,870 in bonds and €300,000 in savings at the Central Bank Of Cyprus, as well as a €3million property portfolio.

Some might take issue with her appointment, saying that she hadn't had the grace to lose an election before joining the Commission: she has been elected several times, including to the presidency of several UN bodies and twice to the Cypriot House Of Representatives (HOR), from where she was an alternate on the Convention for the Future of Europe (ie the EU Constitution-drafting process). A 2008 Commission press release boasted that "as a member of the European affairs committee [in the HOR] she participated very actively in the harmonization process of Cyprus with the Aquis [sic] Communautaire". How her country must thank her.

When swine flu was discovered in Mexico and elsewhere in 2009, Vassiliou said that people "should avoid travelling to Mexico or the United States unless it is very urgent for them". This statement would have mattered – jobs in the travel and leisure industries might have been lost – if anyone trusted the EU. But it was irresponsible and ignored the fact that is up to national governments to issue travel advice.

"The societal role of sport is a very important aspect of sport policy and I really intend to work on that," she said at her 2010 hearing.

From 2004 to 2009 this post was held by Ján Figel' (Slovakia), who was commissar for education, training and culture. Figel' declared when given the portfolio that it was not his "primary choice".

Before January 2007 Figel' had the multilingualism portfolio, but he ceded it to Leonard Orban (Romania). Orban's first proposal was that regional Spanish tongues, such as Catalan, Basque and Galician, be recognised as EU languages. He was then slow in getting the draft Lisbon Treaty translated from French into languages spoken rather more widely than those three Iberian languages (eg English). A former European integration minister in Romania, he looked after a condescendingly minor portfolio ("would suit first jobber" in employment-advert speak, if such terminology is still allowed by EU law). The original Romanian nominee, Varujan Vosganian, withdrew his candidacy over allegedly unsuitable ties to big business.

Employment, Social Affairs and Inclusion
László Andor (Hungary)

Andor is an economist, leftist intellectual and former board member of the European Bank for Reconstruction and Development, which is not an EU body, funded as it is by around 60 countries, including the USA, Mexico and New Zealand, as well as the EU's European Investment Bank. Discussing overtime, Andor said at his hearing that "since we have economic and monetary union, I think that opt-outs are, in general terms, never the best solution." This lack of backing for opt-outs means that not only the NHS but also the whole of the private sector might one day be told how and when it can work, courtesy of the Working Time Directive, which he thought there was a "compelling case to revisit". He likes to be thought of as a "post-Keynesian" and once received an apology from the *Financial Times* for suggesting he was ever a communist.

From 2004 to 2009 this post was held by Vladimir Špidla (Czech Republic), who was commissar for employment, social affairs and equal opportunities.

A Czech former PM, whose CV also showed time spent as a sawmill worker, scene shifter, dairy-industry worker and construction worker, Špidla got the Brussels job after a heavy electoral defeat back home, his party earning just nine per cent of the vote in the 2004 European elections.

He was pro-equal opportunities – except for smokers. It was he who confirmed to a Scots MEP in August 2006 that companies in the EU could advertise for "non-smokers". (The views of Ken Clarke, the pro-EU erstwhile tobacco salesman, are not known.)

At the fag end of his time in Brussels, he issued the following press release: "the Commission has sent a reasoned opinion to the United Kingdom for incorrectly implementing EU rules [Directive 2000/78] prohibiting discrimination based on religion or belief, disability, age or sexual orientation in employment and occupation. In the reasoned opinion sent to the United Kingdom, the Commission pointed out that exceptions to the principle of non-discrimination on the basis of sexual orientation for religious employers are broader than that permitted by the directive." This "reasoned opinion" was telling the government that the Muslim Council Of Great Britain, for instance, cannot discriminate, on grounds of sexuality, against Graham Norton if he ever seeks employment with them. It affected Catholic adoption agencies and others too.

The press release also said: "We call on the UK government to make the necessary changes to its anti-discrimination legislation as soon as possible so as to fully comply with the EU rules. In this context, we welcome the proposed Equality Bill and hope that it will come into force quickly." This became Harriet Harman's 2010 Equality Act. Some people wondered why the ConDems did not repeal it – they couldn't (even if they'd wanted to) because it was implementing unarguable EU directives.

Energy
Günther Oettinger (Germany)

He was apparently Merkel's third choice, although they're from the same party back home, where he had been president of Baden-Wuerttemberg since 2005. His hearing was dull, despite his admission that "If the Copenhagen summit [of 2009] showed us one thing, it is that the EU isn't big enough for world authority when it comes to countries like China." He was widely criticised for a eulogy he gave in 2007 for Hans Filbinger, a former president of his Land, whom he very inaccurately described as an "opponent of the Nazi regime". In 2000 Oettinger sang the (strictly verboten) first stanza of the national anthem, best but wrongly known by its opening line "Deutschland über alles". He declared €500,000 worth of stocks and shares but was twice forced to change his entry on the register of interests – the only commissar who had to do so. He had apparently omitted several trusteeships and connections, including to energy firm EnBW, which sponsored a German basketball team he was involved with. He denied a conflict of interest[87].

From 2004 to 2009 this post was held by Mr Piebalgs – see Development (above).

Enlargement and Neighbourhood Policy
Stefan Füle (Czech Republic)

Füle and Mr Šefčovič (from Slovakia, see below) were both communist party members – but only because they wanted to be diplomats, their spin doctors said. Both were also students at the prestigious Moscow State Institute of International Relations, the diplomatic school of the Russian foreign ministry. In Soviet times, admission to the MGIMO was largely reserved for children of

---

[87] *EurActiv*, 17 August 2010

party members and "approved cadre"[88]. Füle backed full EU membership for Turkey at his hearing and swatted aside questions about his commie past.

From 2004 to 2009 this post was held by Mr Rehn – see Economic and monetary affairs (above).

Environment
Janez Potočnik (Slovenia)

At his 2010 hearing Potočnik, the son of a farmer, told MEPs that his own son had recently crashed the family's hybrid car.

He was science and research commissar in the last Commission and was saddled with several anti-US white elephants (eg Galileo, and the European Institute of Technology, the EU's version of MIT). In 2007 he launched a new agency to fund a "champions league" of scientists, hoping it would solve problems such as climate change and epidemics. The European Joint Research Council was given a budget of €7.5billion for 2007-2013. It pronounced in 2008 that the EU's own biofuels policy (see p228) was best abandoned. He's in favour of a carbon tax. See "Neighbourhood" (chapter 4) for more on this brief.

From 2004 to 2009, this post was held by Stavros Dimas (Greece). A former Wall Street lawyer and Greek finance minister, Dimas represented the country with perhaps the worst environmental record in the EU: Greece has been hauled before the ECJ so many times that its trips to Luxembourg must have greatly increased its carbon footprint. Dimas unwittingly exposed the EU's priorities when, in February 2007, he traded in his Mercedes-Benz for a less thirsty and less flatulent Japanese marque (he already owned a Honda). Overlooking his commitment to "reducing emissions", his Commission colleagues criticised him for not buying an EU car. He admitted to owning four properties in the register of interests.

Health and Consumer Policy
John Dalli (Malta)

Back home in Malta, Dalli failed to win his party's leadership in 2004. A few months later he resigned as foreign minister amid allegations of nepotism, at least one of which was fabricated and led to a prison sentence for its forger. Dalli was later "absolved" (in the Maltese PM's words) of the other allegation – buying airline tickets for his ministry through a travel firm in which his daughter and ex-chauffeur had an interest – despite the fact that the Maltese auditor general had never made public his report into the affair. John Dalli, an innocent man, had, therefore, resigned for no good reason.

---

[88] *EU Observer*, 26 November 2009

For his current job, Dalli resigned several hefty directorships and business interests, as well as his position as social-policy minister in Valletta, but he has properties in Malta and Tripoli. At his hearing, he promised to be a consumer's champion, and to produce a "cloning directive" to regulate the sale of products made from cloned meat. One of his first actions was to authorise, after a 13-year tussle, the planting of genetically modified potatoes throughout the 27-member bloc, against the wishes of Italy, France, Austria and others.

It's often thought that the EU has nothing to do with healthcare. The 48-hour week shows that it does. Other equally important examples (the Emissions Trading Scheme and the Health Services Directive) are covered later. The NHS has had an outpost in Brussels since September 2007. The NHS Confederation said at the time: "EU policy and legislation are having an increasing impact on the NHS as a provider of services, as a business and as a major employer in the EU. Recent ECJ decisions have clarified how EU internal-market rules apply to health services, which will have wide-reaching implications for the NHS. In addition, with forthcoming EU legislation on cross-border healthcare, it is extremely important that the NHS is positioned at the heart of EU developments."

The form E111, which provided reciprocal healthcare in EEA countries in the event of illness or accident, has been replaced by the EHIC card, which also covers Switzerland. It is a good idea to get one: you pay dearly for EU membership, take what you can. Just because you're in prison doesn't mean you should reject the food. See ehic.org.uk

From 2008 to 2009, this post was held by Androula Vassilou – see Education (above).

From 2004 to 2008, this post was held by Markos Kyprianou, who was formerly Cyprus's finance minister. Not keen on smoking, he said at his interview that he wanted it outlawed in public places throughout the EU by 2009. Several countries, including the UK, may well have enacted exactly this type of legislation at domestic level because they realised that the EU would make them do so sooner or later anyway. As a bonus, this sort of pre-emptive lawmaking lets EU provinces act as if they are autonomous.

He was never famous outside Brussels or Cyprus despite proposing a ban on "Made in Britain" stickers on food products and wanting cigarette packet-style warnings on booze, such as "Drinkers die earlier" and "With each draught you can inflict brain damage to your embryo". The highlight of his tenure was an "EU-Canada agreement to simplify import rules for bovine semen and other achievements under the EU-Canada veterinary agreement" (2005). He made his excuses and left the Commission in the spring of 2008, returning home to become foreign minister in the new communist government.

From 2007 to 2009, the Consumer Protection post was held by Meglena Kuneva (Bulgaria). She did not trouble the radar but in summer 2008 proposed making "fire-safe" cigarettes mandatory across the EU, in the hope that the cigarettes – which stop burning after a few seconds if not smoked – would reduce the number of deaths from fires. (The multimillion-euro EU subsidies to tobacco farmers would be untouched.) She also wanted to limit to five hours a week the time spent by people listening to mp3 players at high volume, then decided she wanted to limit the volume. On leaving the Commission, she was appointed head of its Bureau of European Policy Advisers and is a "political counsellor" to Mr Kallas. She's also on the board of French bank BNP Paribas.

Home Affairs
Cecilia Malmström (Sweden)

Formerly an MEP, she resigned to become her country's EU minister and has now returned to Brussels. When last in the city she had campaigned to keep the EU parliament from travelling to France once a month. The other reason that one might look kindly on her is that she has said that the salaries and perks given to commissioners are unreasonably high. On top of a "transition payment" of €41,000 when she took office, she gets a salary of €20,000 per month, an additional €3,100 a month for living abroad, €574 in family allowances, €681 in child allowances and €486 in school allowances, according to *Sveriges Radio*.

She's apparently in favour of scrapping the Common Agricultural Policy. However, she is in favour of more EU integration in justice and home affairs. See pp342-6 and pp348-51 for the more chilling aspects of her remit.

Industry and Entrepreneurship
* Antonio Tajani (Italy)

Tajani is one of the founders of Berlusconi's Forza Italia (he has shares in Berlusconi's company Mediaset as well as a similar stake in a rival broadcaster) and was transport commissar at the tail end of the previous Commission.

Before the second Irish vote on the Lisbon Treaty, Tajani campaigned for a yes on a whistle-stop tour of Ireland with Ryanair's Michael O'Leary. Irish MEP Joe Higgins called on Tajani to resign, saying: "Ryanair is one of the biggest airlines in Europe. It has already and may come into further conflict with the European Commission [over O'Leary's plans to buy up more of Aer Lingus – the Commission had vetoed one takeover bid, on competition grounds]. It puts the commissioner in an utterly compromised position to have travelled around Ireland in a Ryanair plane, campaigning alongside Mr O'Leary."

One of Tajani's first initiatives concerned tourism: "Taking holidays is a right. As the person responsible for Europe's policies in this economic sector, it is my firm belief that the way in which we spend our holidays is an excellent indicator of our quality of life... attention must be paid to young persons and families at a disadvantage who – for various reasons – also face difficulties in exercising their full right to tourism. As commissioner for transport I successfully defended passengers' rights. The next step is to safeguard their right to be tourists."

So, "tourism is a right" and certain groups should get EU-subsidised intra-EU holidays. Which business sector might benefit from such a policy? Low-cost carriers? Might Ryanair benefit in any way from the scheme?

From 2008 to 2009, this post was held by Günter Verheugen (Germany), who was enterprise and industry commissar. He was often on the money. He described the Galileo project (see p274) as "in some ways a dumb project"[89], talked a great game about cutting bureaucracy and was right to point out that the single market costs €600billion (but provides only €160million in benefits). He promised in September 2005 to roll back the acquis to a mere 50,000 pages, having described the EU as a "bureaucratic monster" and saying, "Much of industry feels under pressure from too much legislation. So this is our number one priority, it is going to be my hobby horse for the next few years." Unfortunately, he was forced to dismount.

Although married, he was pictured in German newspapers in October 2006 hand in hand on holiday in Lithuania with his chef de cabinet, Ms Petra Erler. Two months later, pictures of the former enlargement commissar and his paramour, both naked on a Lithuanian beach, surfaced. Imagine for a moment that you are Mr Barroso, the head of a supranational government, and that one of your ministers had been photographed almost totally naked on holiday. Bearing in mind that Prof Verheugen wears only a baseball cap in the later photos, would you have said, as Barroso did in Verheugen's defence, that "people's private spheres" should be respected? Verheugen himself said, "I consider that the question of where and with whom I choose to spend my August holidays is a purely private matter which does not concern anyone other than my wife, who was informed about it."

Some cynics believe that his comments about Eurocrats having too much power – and thus stymieing his efforts to reduce bureaucracy – prompted the publication of the pictures, which were weeks old. Another group of cynics believes that he knew he was about to be exposed by Eurocrats seeking to undermine him – and so he then put up a populist smokescreen about overbearing bureaucracy. You paid his money, take your choice.

In June 2007 he was pictured leaving Ms Erler's house with her early in the morning, and a friend of his wife later said that he'd confessed to the affair in January 2006 – three months before the East German was promoted from adviser to chef de cabinet (€9,045 to €11,579 a month, or €138,948 a year), a role that cannot under Commission rules be carried out by a lover. "There was no relationship beyond friendship at the time of the promotion," Verheugen said in October 2006. "And that remains the situation today."[90]

---

[89] *Handelsblatt*, 24 May 2007
[90] *The Times*, 11 June 2007

Angela Merkel had to intervene to prevent his sacking. Prof Verheugen maintained that he and Ms Erler were not and had never been lovers, as did Ms Erler. He remains married, as does she.

What of his bonfire of regulation? In 2007, a 30-year-old directive concerning the knots in wood was repealed, as was one concerning the size of loaves of bread. In 2009, the rules on some misshapen fruit and veg were relaxed. Having spent almost two decades denying that there were any such rules on the curvature of bananas and cucumbers, the EU decided to relax those same rules. "It's just tabloid hysteria," Commission spokesmen would often say: however, for straight bananas, see Regulation 2257/1994; for straight cucumbers, see p124.

After leaving the Commission, Verheugen took a job as vice-chairman of "global banking and markets in Europe, the Middle East and Africa" with the nationalised Royal Bank of Scotland, without first notifying his old employers. The rules state that Mr Barroso's outfit must be told about any employment accepted within a year of leaving. Although Verheugen did not oversee the Commission's rules on allowing (temporary) state aid to RBS and other banks, all Commission decisions are collective.

According to the *Economist*, he was often spotted doing sudoku puzzles in Commission meetings.

Institutional Affairs and Administration
* Maroš Šefčovič (Slovakia)

A former ambassador to Israel and Slovakia's permanent representative to the EU from 2004 to 2009, Šefčovič went to the same communist finishing school as the Czech commissar Mr Füle (see above). He now uses the diplomatic skill he learned from commies to help Baroness (Cathy) Ashton, a former CND treasurer, to set up the External Action Service which represents us all abroad in "third countries". At his hearing he claimed he "honestly" could not remember disparaging the Roma in 2005. His declaration of interests includes "a car garage in Bratislava".

Internal Market and Services
Michel Barnier (France)

France secured this job as part of the deal that saw Ashton become EU foreign minister. Despite once saying that Barnier had the "charisma of an oyster", Sarkozy told *Le Monde*: "The English are the big losers in this business."

At his hearing Barnier said that "I'm almost as phlegmatic as the Brits. Let there be no fears in your mind – I am not going to be taking orders from Paris or London or anywhere else. I can give you that cast-iron guarantee. I have a British director-general whose name I put forward myself – but he is not there as a Briton but as a Community official. These are people who are committed to defend the general European interest." He even quoted Adam Smith. The British bureaucrat he trumpeted was Jonathan Faull, formerly head of the Commission's justice department; he is Barnier's director-general of internal market affairs. Faull has been in the Commission since the 1970s and even headed its propaganda department between 1999 and 2003.

Barnier also said at his hearing that he believed in a "strong City [of London]" but backed plans to regulate hedge funds: "Those who manage hedge funds shouldn't be afraid of [the Alternative Investment Fund Managers Directive]. It's in their interests." (Few of them realise this, and even fewer were to blame for the recession.) Barnier, like Almunia and other commissars, was in favour of a financial-transaction tax. However, he then changed his mind and backed an upfront levy on banks, which critics said would further encourage "moral hazard" (recklessness caused by the knowledge that someone would pick up the pieces). These national pots would be called "resolution funds" and the Commission planned to absorb them into one pan-European fund by 2014.

Barnier was commissioner for regional policy from 1999 until 2004 in the Prodi "college". He was then French foreign minister when the country voted no to the Constitution. Two years later he became Sarko's agriculture minister. According to the *Financial Times*, Barnier "took an interest in environmental protection in the 1980s, before it became fashionable, on one occasion forcing builders of an alpine motorway to construct a tunnel for passing toads". However, for his opinion of the environmentally disastrous Common Agricultural Policy, see p246.

From 2004 to 2009, this post was held by Charlie McCreevy (Ireland). Known as "Champagne Charlie" back home, he first had a run-in with EU institutions in 2000, when he had been forced to back down after wrongly trying to appoint an underqualified and disgraced former judge, Hugh O'Flaherty, who had just resigned, to the vice-presidency of the European Investment Bank (salary then £147,000).

In December 2005 McCreevy foisted new regulations (Mifid) on the City which would account for 70 per cent of all new red tape the following year, a threefold increase in interference.

In March 2008 he quite rightly preferred to attend the Cheltenham National Hunt Festival rather than a plenary session of the European parliament (the economic affairs committee) and was later sarcastically awarded a toy horse, with a harness and saddle in shocking baby pink, on his return from Gloucestershire to Belgium[91]. Ironically, in 2006, he had threatened legal action against Germany, Finland, Sweden, Italy, Holland and

---

[91] *Brussels Sprouts* column, *Private Eye*, 18 April-1 May 2008

Hungary for restricting the operation, advertising and promotion of bookmakers while they allowed national lotteries within their borders.

During the first referendum campaign in Ireland, in 2008, he said that "no sane and sensible person" would have read the Lisbon Treaty (echoing Ken Clarke and other europhiles at the time of the Maastricht Treaty). "I don't expect ordinary decent Irish people, or anywhere in the globe, to be sitting down and spending hours and hours reading sections about subsections referring to articles about sub-articles." In 2009 he said that most countries' electorates would also have voted against the treaty if given the chance.

In a speech made back home at the end of 2009, when he was presumably demob happy, McCreevy said:

"What President Sarkozy's statement [about the "English" being the "big losers"] tells us is that he does not see the Commission as a commission for the advancement of European interests. He sees it as a Commission for the advancement of French interests… The French are at home in a Brussels bureaucracy that's almost a copy of how the administration in Paris works. This has, over the years, given the French a huge advantage in knowing how to pull the levers of power. And if you look around the Commission you will see that the French have been masters in getting their key people into some of the most powerful posts… As my successor as commissioner for the internal market, Mr Barnier will have responsibility for all European financial services, accounting, auditing, company law, corporate governance, services of general interest, patents, intellectual property rights, public procurement and the transatlantic financial dialogue. But the tactical positioning and influence of the French in all of these areas and other tangential areas stretches far beyond the European Commission."

In the areas of finance, services, monetary policy and leadership of the euro's European Central Bank (Mr Trichet), the French, said McCreevy, "have scooped the pool, lock, stock and barrel. So I salute President Sarkozy and his colleagues in the French foreign service and the finance ministry for their extraordinary deftness and diplomatic and tactical coups." (A Frenchman, Dominique Strauss-Kahn, is head of the International Monetary Fund.)

At the end of his time as a commissar, the *Irish Independent* revealed that in 2006 he had been given a €1.6million mortgage, with "minimum paperwork involved", for a luxury home on a golf course that had hosted the Ryder Cup. However, the property was worth €100,000 less than the loan and at the time the Nationwide building society's guidelines prohibited 100 per cent loans[92].

He became a non-executive director of Ryanair soon after leaving the Commission. At the time, the airline had notched up seven state-aid enquiries from his old bosses.

---

[92] *The Independent (Ireland)*, 23 December 2009. The property halved in value between 2006 and 2009

International Co-operation, Humanitarian Aid and Crisis Response
Kristalina Georgieva (Bulgaria)

A former vice-president of the World Bank who reports to Ashton, she replaced the feeble and compromised Rumiana Jeleva. At her hearing she told MEPs that it was the birthday of her 89-year-old mother, who wanted her daughter to show European commitment.

When floods devastated Pakistan in summer 2010, she said at a press conference: "Raising the visibility of Europe and making sure that our flag shines when we are abroad helping people in need is something that I find incredibly important." As *EurActiv* reported: "Georgieva said she was telling humanitarian organisations that they should do more to help the EU to help them by flying the EU flag... The commissioner added that the visibility issue was one of the important topics of her political proposal to reinforce the EU's capacity to respond to crises."

Justice, Fundamental Rights and Citizenship
* Viviane Reding (Luxembourg)

She was education and culture commissioner in the Prodi Commission and then Information society and media commissar in the first Barroso Commission.

At Reding's 2010 hearing, for a job that had been lobbied for by the committee interviewing her, she said that her priorities would be to allow member states to adopt common legislation on divorce and to set up a European Public Prosecutor (a measure already in the Lisbon Treaty). She also said she might present an annual report to the European parliament, assessing the implementation of the Charter of Fundamental Rights in EU countries. "You can be sure that fundamental rights, including data protection, will be top of my list," she said. There would be "zero tolerance" of infractions, she promised. She said she was against mandatory body scanners at airports and that they should be used voluntarily by member states.

At her hearing Cecilia Malmström, who has the other half of what used to be one portfolio, denied that she was the "good cop" and Reding the "bad cop". From a civil-liberties point of view, there will be two bad cops.

In September 2003, Reding was de facto head of the European Publications Office in Luxembourg when its officials were investigated by Olaf (Office Européen de Lutte Anti-Fraude), the EU's fraud squad, for suspected irregularities similar to those discovered in Eurostat (see "Fraud and whistleblowers"). It was alleged that Eurostat officials had put forward false contract-cost estimates and then pocketed the leftover money.

Her highly publicised and shamelessly populist measure to reduce phone companies' roaming charges, the premium one pays to use one's phone abroad, is her big achievement. And it led to higher prices for the other 50 weeks when one is not abroad (unless one is, er, a commissar, MEP or Eurocrat, in which case one spends most of the year abroad). She supported "three strikes and you're out" termination of internet access without trial (amendment 138 of the Telecoms Package) – while also campaigning in 2009 to become an MEP on a platform of "high-quality internet access" (she has been elected an MEP four times but is not taking her seat in the 2009-14 parliament).

From 2008 to 2009, Jacques Barrot (France) was justice, freedom and security commissar. He had been regional policy commissioner in Prodi's Commission and then at transport in Barroso's Commission I until Italy's Mr Frattini left justice in 2008 and Barrot took his place.

As Mr Farage revealed, Jacques Barrot received an eight-month suspended jail sentence in Paris in 2000 for embezzlement – legally, "abuse of confidence" – a fact he had not revealed to Barroso. The case concerned £2.5million that went missing around 1990 from the campaign war chest of the Social Democrat Centre, the forerunner of Chirac and Sarkozy's UMP. Barrot, the prosecutor alleged, had been laundering illegal party donations through Swiss bank accounts. Mr Barrot said that he had not been in charge of donations and had been hanged on account of collective responsibility, also saying that Farage's claims about being barred from public office for two years were wrong. In an excellent piece of spin, his supporters claimed that the 1995 amnesty – and generous embargo – that incoming President Chirac granted him were bad news because he might otherwise have been able to appeal and thus be properly exonerated. For not even a split second in 2000, then, was he guilty – the amnesty granted five years earlier immediately overrode the court and its suspended sentence.

The Commission had therefore appointed a man who had received a suspended jail sentence to hold the crime portfolio, whose remit specifically mentions "the detection and punishment of all acts of corruption, confiscation of illicit proceeds and reduction of the opportunities for corrupt practices through the establishment of transparent and accountable public administration standards".

When transport commissar he had an enviable train set in his office that featured many of Europe's fastest systems[93].

In 2006, while honorary president of a French plastics trade association, he successfully lobbied Mandelson to slap a higher tariff on imported (ie non-EU) plastic bags, despite the code of conduct saying that commissioners may hold "honorary positions" in public interest organisations but that "posts held on these terms shall under no circumstances involve any risk of a conflict of interest". His spokesman at first said he had terminated his 30-year presidency of the manufacturers' body the previous month, then the story

---

[93] See *Car crash viewing* in *The Guardian*, 30 October 2006, for a commissioner way out of his depth

changed to the previous year. Barrot refused to release the resignation letter he said he'd written[94].

From 2004 to 2008, the post was held by Franco Frattini (Italy), a Freemason, ex-slalom skier and former foreign secretary. Italy's second choice (after Mr Buttiglione), one of his first efforts was to try to ban the phrase "Islamic terrorist". The EU published a counter-terrorism proposal which called for a "non-emotive lexicon" to describe terrorists. He also proposed sending football hooligans on re-education holidays. In March 2007 he was forced to cancel the contract of an adviser after it was revealed that the adviser was under investigation for fraud by the Italian police. Walter Cretella-Lombardo was investigated over his role in a "recycling scandal" in Calabria involving the embezzlement of €200million of public funds. Cretella-Lombardo ran the Italian finance police's training school and had advised Frattini on cross-border co-operation between judicial and customs authorities. In 2008 Frattini returned to Italian politics as foreign minister.

Maritime Affairs and Fisheries
Maria Damanaki (Greece)

Damanaki comes from a country in an area that is not even fully subject to the EU's Common Fisheries Policy, by which we lose most of our fish to other countries' trawlers. She was a member of the Communist Youth while a student in the 1970s and took part in the Athens Polytechnic uprising against the military junta. She was arrested and tortured by the regime[95]. From 1977 to 1993 she was an MP first for the Communist Party and then with Synaspismos, a non-Stalinist far-left party.

From 2004 to 2009, this post was held by Malta's Joe Borg. Malta also has an exemption from EU fishing laws – their exclusion zone is 25km (ours is 6 miles or slightly less than 10km). Not quite the man to replenish the North Sea.

Regional policy
Johannes Hahn (Austria)

Formerly Austria's science minister, he studied law (which he dropped) and philosophy, although the state broadcaster would later wonder if he could have provided more citations for works he had relied on in his PhD thesis. He was CEO of the gambling group Novomatic, and he felt the need to bring documents to his hearing to try to prove that it had never been involved in money laundering: "I am not trying to duck the question [from MEPs about the firm]. It is an important issue and I want it to be clear that there are no criminal

---

94 *The Sunday Times*, 9 July 2006
95 *EU Observer*, 26 November 2009

investigations against me or anyone else. It is a groundless personal attack against me."[96]

From 2004 to 2009, this post was held by Danuta Hübner (Poland), who's now an MEP (she sat in on Hahn's hearing). Early in her career, she joined the Polish United Workers Party (Communist Party), not leaving until 1987, six years after martial law was imposed in Poland to prevent the communist regime from being overthrown by Solidarity. No stickler for democratic or legal niceties, she said at her 2004 hearing that she believed the Commission should pre-empt the ratification of the EU Constitution by starting to implement parts of it, such as the European External Action Service. (Of course, this was already happening.) "Where innovations brought by the Constitution require implementing measures based on a proposal of the Commission, it should not await the entry into force of the Constitution to start the necessary preparatory work." By February 2007 she sounded as if she might after all prefer democracy: she told a press conference that the enlarged Commission had led to a "presidential system", with Mr Barroso personally steering the most important policies.

She was replaced in July 2009 by Pawel Samecki from Poland, who received, according to Open Europe, a golden parachute of €391,898 (on top of his salary and other perks) when he left in 2010, not even 12 months into the job.

Research, Innovation and Science
Maire Geoghegan-Quinn (Ireland)

Geoghegan-Quinn entered politics by taking over her father's Galway West seat. She is a former justice, Europe, and tourism minister in Dublin.

As justice minister in 1993 and 1994, she inherited a system that allowed her to alter court sentences that were brought to her attention by TDs (MPs). She would mitigate 2,283 – well over half put on her desk. As the *Irish Times* recalled: "In one of the most extraordinary episodes in Irish judicial history, district justice Patrick Brennan felt impelled to take Geoghegan-Quinn to court because she had set aside or changed so many of the sentences he had handed down. He cited, merely as samples, four cases – two driving offences, two fishing offences – in which she responded to representations from Fianna Fáil TDs Seamus Hughes and Tom Moffatt. In one, the civil servant who handled the TD's representations noted: 'Serious offences, moderate fines imposed… I consider intervention inappropriate.' Judge Brennan maintained that these examples [four of 2,283 cases] showed that Geoghegan-Quinn was 'wrongfully interfering with his judicial decisions and has been herself purporting to administer justice by a kind of parallel system which for all practical purposes provides an alternative to an appeal to the Circuit Court… the Constitution never envisaged two systems of justice, one a system of private justice and the other a system of

---

[96] *EU Observer*, 15 January 2010

public justice…' Essentially, she used a power that 'must be exercised… sparingly and for special reasons with proper maintenance of records' as a private service for TDs wanting to do favours for their constituents."[97]

Soon after that judgment, she went on to be a two-term member of the EU's Court Of Auditors. Outside politics, she worked for some of Declan Ganley's companies. He would become famous for opposing the Lisbon Treaty (but not the EU). When nominated for the Commission, she said, "The ratification of the Lisbon Treaty allows reform of internal decision making procedures so that new laws can be brought forward in a more structured, efficient and co-ordinated way." So, despite a brief brush with the principled (if confused) Mr Ganley and nine years of picking through the entrails of corruption at the Court Of Auditors, she still thought Lisbon was a good idea. She has houses in Luxembourg, Spain, America and Galway that were probably not bought with the royalties of her mildly frisky 1996 novel, *The Green Diamond*.

In April 2010, after outrage back home, she gave up her annual €108,000 pension from her time as an Irish parliamentarian and minister, which she was being paid on top of her handsome commissar's wage. Separately, she will soon be able to claim an €81,000 pension from her time in the Court of Auditors. And when she leaves the Commission, there would be no reason not to accept once again the pension from the Irish parliament – as well as a commissar's pension.

From 2004 to 2009 this post (Science and Research) was held by Janez Potočnik – see Environment (above).

Taxation and Customs Union, Audit and Anti-Fraud
Algirdas Šemeta (Lithuania)

When she departed as budget commissar, Dalia Grybauskaité (see above), told French newspaper *Les Echos* that her compatriot's "candidacy does not seem the best but he seems reasonable". MEPs at the ex-finance minister's hearing were concerned that he did not know how to reform Olaf. The EPP group said, "The future commissioner for taxation, customs union and fight against fraud left several questions open and proved he is still insecure in his field." The Socialist grouping agreed. Šemeta and his wife, a journalist, own two apartments in Vilnius as well as two summer homes. He wants a "minimum rate of tax on carbon [dioxide]".

From 2004 to 2009 László Kovács (Hungary) was taxation and customs union commissar. When businesses speak of "The VAT Man" it is this post that they ultimately

---

[97] *Should misuse of power debar EU hopeful?* by Fintan O'Toole in *The Irish Times*, 25 November 2009

have in mind. Kovács once wanted to force several countries to levy VAT on nappies but was dissuaded by several other commissars, who told him that it wouldn't help low EU birth rates.

He led the Socialist Party to defeat in the European parliament elections in June 2004: it won just nine of Hungary's 24 seats; a berth for him in Brussels was a logical career step. Kovács was moved from his original post of energy commissioner due to allegations of incompetence. The European parliament's energy committee said, "Most members of the committee were not convinced by his professional competence in the energy field nor his aptitude to assume the high office he has been proposed for." Despite telling MEPs in private that he had little more knowledge of tax than of energy, he got the tax brief, for there was no other left.

A speechwriter for and friend of the dictator, Janos Kadar, Kovács spent the 1980s attacking Nato and was deputy head of the Department of International Relations on the Central Committee of the Communist Party.

Before Ireland voted on the Lisbon Treaty in 2008 it was denied that a common corporate tax base was on the EU's agenda. This was not true.

In both October 2005 and April 2006 Kovács launched a plan for harmonisation of company tax bases "by 2008".

In October 2006 he told the *Financial Times* that plans for a pan-European corporate tax system would go ahead, despite the objections of seven member states. The following month he announced the plan yet again.

In December 2006 he suggested creating a common corporate tax base alongside co-ordination of exit taxes and inheritance taxes: "If [such co-operation] does not work then we would try with some legally binding solution," he said.

In May 2007 the *Financial Times* reported that he would unveil an updated report on his plans for a common European corporate tax system and would argue that a common corporate tax base would make it easier for companies to trade across borders and would boost jobs and competitiveness.

On 8 June 2007 he told *EU Observer* that national governments "have often prejudiced feelings that any kind of harmonisation and tax-policy co-ordination infringe on their sovereignty in the area, which is not true." He claimed that proposed harmonisation of direct taxation would boost Europe's competitiveness and rounded on a fellow commissar, Irishman Charlie McCreevy (see above), who was a strong critic of tax harmonisation. Kovács told *EU Observer*: "Mr McCreevy is no longer the minister of finance of Ireland. He used to be but now he is the member of European Commission who should represent the community interests."

Towards the end of 2008, as the recession picked off its victims, Kovács announced that he would be holding off from producing any more plans for a co-ordinated tax base until

2010 (by which time it was hoped that Ireland would have been bullied and lied to enough to vote yes to Lisbon).

Another of his contentious projects was an outfit called Eurofisc. Kovács urged member states to agree to give one other access to tax data as part of a plan to combat VAT fraud. Eurofisc officials would be able to view your salary, spending habits and level of savings without your knowledge.

See also Siim Kallas, who was "triple A" commissar last time round, under transport.

Trade
Karel De Gucht (Belgium)

He was i/c development and humanitarian aid at the tail end of the last Barroso Commission. At his hearing in September 2009, the Tory MEP Nirj Deva asked him: "A referendum [on Lisbon] would really bring 'Europe closer to its citizens' but the governments of Europe reneged on the promise when they thought they would lose. You are reported as saying to *Flanders Info* in a 2007 interview: 'The aim of the Constitutional Treaty was to be more readable; the aim of [the Lisbon] treaty is to be unreadable... The Constitution aimed to be clear, whereas this treaty had to be unclear. It is a success.' How do you square that 'success' with your desiring of a 'Europe closer to its citizens'?"

De Gucht naively replied: "While the original Constitutional Treaty was technical, and correct, people didn't read the Lisbon Treaty, they didn't understand the first word about it. No real debate about the Lisbon Treaty could happen. This was a deliberate decision of the European Council."

A former deputy PM of Belgium, De Gucht was person non grata in 2010 in one of its former colonies, the DR Congo, after he described the country as "a land where almost everything must be done again, starting with the re-establishment of the state".

From 2008 to 2009 this post was held by Catherine Ashton – see under Foreign affairs (below).

From 2004 to 2008, the post was held by Peter Mandelson. His appointment was anticipated in a post by Dr Helen Szamuely on the EU Referendum blog that also highlighted the illegitimacy and remoteness of the EU project: "... Much as one rejoices to see Peter Mandelson's career revived and the man himself ensconced in a place where his talents will be appreciated (Brussels), one rather wonders why he should be given the power to negotiate trade deals on behalf of 25 countries... What does he know about Greece, Ireland, Finland or Estonia, to name four random countries on whose behalf he will be negotiating? What do they know of him? Did they elect him or want him? No, of course not. Besides, what will he be negotiating?"[98]

It was Mandelson's grandfather, Herbert Morrison, who, when asked what he thought about the Schuman Plan for the European Coal and Steel Community, said, "The Durham miners won't wear it." Mandy, of course, is rather keen on it and does wear it. Like many who are pro-EU and unlike many of those who are not, he is a monoglot.

Another former communist, he resigned from Blair's cabinet in 1998 and 2001 and did not figure again in the UK public's mind until the "bra wars" in 2006 over tariffs on Chinese imports. (Because the EU is a customs union, individual countries cannot do their own bilateral trade deals. You think we should reduce tariffs on African goods? Well, there's no point writing to your MP or even HM Government – you need to lobby this commissar.)

His time in Brussels was not free of complications or embarrassment. One of his top officials was recorded by the *Sunday Times* offering to divulge highly sensitive EU trade information in return for cash. In a six-month investigation, the newspaper recorded Fritz-Harald Wenig passing secrets to undercover reporters posing as lobbyists for a Chinese businessman seeking insider information. Wenig discussed the possibility of payment or taking a lucrative job with the businessman. He leaked the names of two Chinese companies likely to get special status if the EU imposed a protective tariff barrier against Chinese candlemakers[99]. The information was potentially worth millions to those trading with these companies[100]. The Commission quickly announced a ~~whitewash~~ "comprehensive and thorough" enquiry.

In July 2008, Mandy provoked a dispute at the Doha trade talks in Geneva when he pretended to offer a big cut in European farm tariffs. The proposal to reduce these by 60 per cent (up from 54 per cent) was dismissed by Brazil as "mere propaganda", with her foreign minister Celso Amorim describing the offer as "meaningless... purely statistical gimmickry". Even Mandelson's fellow commissioner Mariann Fischer-Boel said that the offer was "nothing new". And the French trade minister, Anne-Marie Idrac, admitted that the offer had not really changed, saying that the difference between the 60 per cent and 54 per cent was down to whether tropical products were included in the calculations or not. "Was there new progress, new percentages? The answer is no. Peter Mandelson this morning had clarified... what technical discussions have come up with – nothing more, nothing less," Idrac said. Mandy himself subsequently described the 60 per cent proposal as a "reiteration" of the EU's position: "The more we clarify, the clearer it becomes exactly what we are offering," he told journalists.

For his bullying of African, Caribbean and Pacific countries, see p263.

He returned to the cabinet, via the House of Lords, in October 2008. The day before he donned his ermine for the first time, the *Sunday Times* reported that he was close to

---

[98] *They will soon wring their hands*, eureferendum.blogspot.com, 14 August 2004
[99] The economist Frédéric Bastiat was 150 years ahead with *The Candlemakers' Petition*
[100] *The Sunday Times*, 7 September 2008

Russia's richest man, Oleg Deripaska[101]. Deripaska, who was for a time barred entry to the USA, owned Rusal, the world's largest aluminium company. Mandy had been to a drinks party on the Russian's yacht, he said, but denied staying the night. What was more interesting was whether Lord M, when EU trade commissar, had been staying the EU's import tariff on raw aluminium for the benefit of his friend.

Knowing so many billionaires, Mandy may have muddled them up. As the *Guardian* put it: "Commission officials who worked for Lord Mandelson issued a misleading statement about the history of his relationship with Deripaska… Mandelson's officials in Brussels said the two men met 'at a few social gatherings in 2006 and 2007', but had never discussed aluminium. However, Mandelson and Deripaska were seen together at a Moscow restaurant in October 2004, after he had been appointed trade commissioner, but before he formally took up the post… The statement is understood to be based on information provided by Mandelson himself. It is unclear why the business secretary has not corrected it to reflect the earlier meetings… Mandelson's staff confirmed yesterday that he had told them that he met Deripaska in 2006, and they said they knew nothing of previous encounters. In addition to the lunchtime meeting between the two men at Moscow's Pushkin Cafe, Mandelson and Deripaska met for dinner at another Moscow restaurant, the Cantinetta Antinori, in January 2005."[102]

Reporting in 2010, the investigative journalist Richard Pendlebury wrote: "[Mandelson] officially entered office as trade commissioner on 22 November 2004. And EU records show that on 23 November his department began a review of the anti-dumping tariff imposed by the EU on Russian rolled-aluminium imports – the type produced at Rusal's plants… In December 2005, the tariff on cheap Russian rolled-aluminium imports was cancelled. In May 2007, the EU trade commission under Mandelson lowered the duty on imports of unwrought aluminium from 7.5 per cent to 6 per cent, which benefitted Rusal. Then, in January 2009, the EU quietly gave Russia a 3.5 per cent discount on the import duty for rolled aluminium products. Mandelson had returned to Westminster three months before, but the tariff reduction can be traced back to his time in power in Brussels."[103] In 2009, Channel 4's *Dispatches* programme showed that Mandy himself had personally signed off the first such decision, dated 20 December 2005, which exempted Rusal from anti-dumping tariffs.

In a letter published in the *Times* the day after the *Guardian* had questioned his memory, Mandelson corrected the statement from his office that said that he'd first met Deripaska in 2006: "This was not the case: to the best of my recollection we first met in 2004 and I met him several times subsequently."

The following month, Commission spokesman Peter Power confirmed that "the subject of timber duties came up in conversation" between Deripaska and Mandy. Deripaska owned a wood-processing and lumber company, though it was worth far less to him than his metal interests. Power said that Mandelson's claims that he never discussed EU policy

---

[101] *The Sunday Times*, 12 October 2008
[102] *The Guardian*, 24 October 2008
[103] *Mandelson, an oligarch and a £500m deal over dinner that cost 300 British jobs* by Richard Pendlebury in *The Daily Mail*, 22 May 2010

with the Russian businessman referred only to the meeting in Corfu.

There were yet more yacht owners whose businesses benefited from EU trade decisions. Deripaska had enjoyed low import tariffs, which meant he could ship in more of his metal from Russia. Conversely, the famous "shoe wars" – in which Chinese footwear was mostly repelled by high import tariffs – greatly helped EU shoesmiths. While the Deripaska storm was still blowing, the *Mail On Sunday* reported that Mandelson had personal links with Italian tycoon Diego Della Valle, who ran the high-end shoe-and-handbag company Tod's. Della Valle had benefited from EU tariffs imposed by Mandy on Asian shoes. Mandy had first stayed with Mr Della Valle four months after a temporary 20 per cent tariff (proposed by him) had been imposed on millions of cheap Chinese shoes. Mandelson met Della Valle on the Italian island of Capri a number of times, including a cruise on Della Valle's yacht[104]. He was criticised in 2005 for having spent the new year on a yacht off Jamaica as a guest of Peter Brown, whose PR firm Brown Lloyd James had been engaged by a company fighting a case brought by the Commission.

Transport
* Siim Kallas (Estonia)

Kallas was administrative affairs, audit and anti-fraud commissar in the previous Commission and as such was party to the hounding of an investigative journalist (see p191). An ex-PM, he was Barroso's "Triple A" commissar in 2004-2009, which was – in a strong field – probably that Commission's best joke, as Farage noted. In his first term, Kallas set up a useless register of lobbyists.

His gaffes include: "If you lose your wallet and you get it back with the money inside, the problem is over... This perception of widespread error and fraud [in the EU and its institutions] is highly unfair. The spending of money in the EU is under tight control." At his 2010 hearing he said that he was apprehensive about so-called "gigaliners" (80-foot lorries): "I feel uncomfortable on the roads if I see a big truck coming. This is fear. But some people are very enthusiastic about it, so let's talk."[105]

He was a member of the Soviet Communist Party from 1972 until 1990 and edited the official Estonian Communist party newspaper *Rahva Hää l.*

In the previous Commission, this was post was held Antonio Tajani – see under "Industry" – as well as Jacques Barrot and Franco Frattini, who are profiled under "Justice".

---

[104] *The Mail On Sunday*, 19 October 2008
[105] *EurActiv*, 15 January 2010

High Representative of the Union for Foreign affairs and Security
* Baroness (Cathy) Ashton (UK)

In 2008, when searching for someone to replace Peter Mandelson as trade commissar in Brussels, then PM Gordon Brown was asked if he could nominate a woman in order to help to equalise the gender ratio of the Commission. He chose Ashton, the Leader of the House Of Lords, who had steered the Lisbon Treaty through the Upper House. However, her appointment was against the EU's own rules, which state that "[commissioners] must not hold [any other] public office of any kind". As a life peer, Lady Ashton was – and is – a member of the UK legislature. But Brussels was more than willing to waive its own rules for the woman who had helped to wave the Lisbon Treaty through the UK parliament.

In her year as trade commissar she backed a (revived) proposal for textiles, clothing, shoes, leather and furniture imported into the EU fortress from "third countries" to carry a "Made In" label. The costs of this nakedly protectionist EU wheeze would be borne by the importer and retailer in each member state.

It looked as if that was all she was going to be able to put on her CV for 2009. Then, at 5pm on 19 November, she discovered she was being nominated for the foreign affairs post created by the Lisbon Treaty, and was appointed just two hours later, by a text message from Barroso. Brown had wanted to send Mandelson or Geoff Hoon (a europhile former whip who had wanted the job and perhaps in revenge would stage a damp squib of a coup against Brown two months later, having also tried to unseat Blair for Brown in 2006) but they were not female. Once the presidency had gone to a centre-right politician from a tiddly nation (Belgium's Mr Van Rompuy), the foreign minister gig had to go the opposite way. Spain and the UK fitted the bill (they were big and had centre-left governments) but the Spanish – knowing how bad their unemployment and property market were – wanted to keep an economic portfolio. So Great Britain's Cathy Ashton, "a lifelong science-fiction fan who has a life-size Dalek in her living room"[106], it was.

Sarkozy explained at a press conference: "Listen, really, this is important, she [Ashton] played an essential role in getting the Lisbon Treaty through the House of Lords, which wasn't nothing, you will agree. She is one of the British political figures – though it's in no way up to me to judge – who most strongly promoted the Lisbon Treaty issue. I've also had occasion to express my gratitude to Gordon Brown for the responsibilities he shouldered, but right the way through the Lisbon process – and you know how fiercely it was discussed in the United

---

[106] *The Sunday Times*, 22 November 2009

Kingdom – she was constantly in favour of it, she supported him courageously. And, after all, we were very happy to find British political women and men to get it through when a section of the British political class was asking for a referendum, as you know as well as I do... She's someone with great experience and who had the advantage of being Labour, British and a woman."

Ashton has never been elected to any role by the public, serving previously as vice-president of the National Council For One Parent Families, head of a local health authority and vice-chair and treasurer of CND, which she represented at Communist Party meetings (although she maintained that she had no contacts with the Soviet Union and had never accepted money from Moscow).

She had been made a life peer in 1999. As Daniel Hannan put it: "[she's] a lifelong quangocrat who has never once been elected to anything... She steered the Lisbon Treaty through the House of Lords, cancelling the referendum on it that all three parties had promised. She was then appointed to the European Commission [as trade commissar] because Gordon Brown wanted to avoid a by-election. Now, she gets the top job as a kind of compensation to Labour over the rejection of Tony Blair [as EU president]. Every chapter in the story is a denial of the democratic principle." Ironically, she is married to a psephologist, a man who makes a living from asking voters what they think.

After her preliminary 2009 hearing, veteran centre-right German MEP Elmar Brok said, "She clearly still has a lot of learning to do. There are many gaping holes that will have to be filled very quickly." She agreed: "Less than two years ago I took the Treaty of Lisbon through the House of Lords. If I had known what was going to happen to me, I might have paid more attention to my speeches on the (role of) high representative. I have a lot to learn."

At her January 2010 hearing she was careful enough to sidestep most of the banana skins. She said nothing much at all, having learnt to keep quiet since her first hearing (when she had criticised Israel's occupation of the West Bank). What about, MEPs asked her, Russia squeezing energy supplies? The EU should "put pressure on Russia to make sure they see these issues in an economic way not a political one." She wrongly thought that there were EU troops (rather than police) in Afghanistan. Geoffrey Van Orden, a Tory, asked her, "Given that you are now responsible for running EU defence policy, have you ever visited a military unit, apart from Greenham Common?" An Austrian Green MEP spoke more for "Europe" than Cathy, a monoglot, ever will when she told the Brit that she had revealed "nothing specific in your visions".

TEU's Article 34(2) incorporates the contentious bit of the Lisbon Treaty about the United Nations: "When the EU has defined a position on a subject which is on the UN Security Council agenda, those member states which sit on the Security Council [France and the UK do so permanently] shall request that the high rep be invited to present the Union's position." Asked about this at her hearing she said, "You've caught me out – well done – on an issue I don't know about." She now attends the UN assembly as the delegate of the EU, which has its own seat like any other state.

At her 2009 hearing she had said, "This [job] is brand new. I do not have an office, I do not have a cabinet, I do not have a team. I inherited a blank piece of paper and at the moment I have written one or two small things on it."

Her job "a blank piece of paper"? She must have a short memory. When she "took" Lisbon through the Lords in 2008, she said: "The proposal is that we have a high representative who becomes the vice-president of the Commission with *very specific functions* [emphasis added]. That is a defined role within the treaty which is vested in one person... the powers and duties of the [president and] high representative are clearly answered in the [Lisbon] treaty... The Lisbon Treaty does not change the mandate for the high representative, including the provision that he be supported by the European external action service [foreign office and embassies]... Noble Lords have rightly indicated that the high representative brings together the current high representative introduced in [the Amsterdam Treaty; a job carried out by Javier Solana] and the Commission For External Relations [see Benita Ferrero-Rocher, below]... The new title makes it absolutely clear that the high representative will represent the agreed views of member states. He will not in any sense be a foreign minister."[107]

This last statement was directly contradicted by Barroso when he announced Ashton to the world as the EU's "foreign minister". She didn't correct his mistake, perhaps because she was still dumbfounded by the Rubik's cube – with her and Herman's faces on – that Barroso had given to the Swedish PM (his country had the six-month presidency of the EU).

Her job spec is spread around TEU, much of it in Article 18 (pronouns feminised): "The high representative shall conduct the Union's common foreign and security policy. She shall contribute by her proposals to the development of that policy, which she shall carry out as mandated by the Council... She shall ensure the consistency of the Union's external action. She shall be responsible within the Commission for responsibilities incumbent on it in external relations and for co-ordinating other aspects of the Union's external action..."

---

[107] *Hansard* (Lords), cols 1446-1449, 22 April 2008

As well as Article 27: "[the high rep] shall contribute through her proposals towards the preparation of the common foreign and security policy and shall ensure implementation of the decisions adopted by the European Council and the Council... shall represent the Union for matters relating to the common foreign and security policy. She shall conduct political dialogue with third parties on the Union's behalf and shall express the Union's position in international organisations and at international conferences..."

Cathy can also suggest invasions! TEU 42(4) states: "Decisions relating to the common security and defence policy, including those initiating a mission as referred to in this Article ['peace-keeping, conflict prevention and strengthening international security' in (1)], shall be adopted by the Council acting unanimously on a proposal from the high rep or an initiative from a member state. The high rep may propose the use of both national resources and Union instruments, together with the Commission where appropriate." Does the last sentence mean that she can propose the "use of" "the Commission" members themselves in combat (together with "national resources and Union instruments")?

The tasks of "peace-keeping, conflict prevention and strengthening international security", for which the EU "may use civilian and military means" (TEU 43 (1)), "shall include joint disarmament operations, humanitarian and rescue tasks, military advice and assistance tasks, conflict prevention and peace-keeping tasks, tasks of combat forces in crisis management, including peace-making and post-conflict stabilisation". What exactly is "crisis management"? Quelling riots about the effects of the euro on unemployment?

In May 2010 she told the LSE that when she took the Lisbon Treaty through the Lords "had I known what was going to happen to me, I must admit, I might have tweaked it here and there". She still didn't seem to know that domestic legislatures cannot change any part of EU treaties or legislation. Amazing.

She has a £45billion budget (between 2010 and 2013) and 7,000 personnel, designed to comprise, in Javier Solana's words, "the biggest diplomatic staff in the world" – at least 60 per cent of whom must be Eurocrats and not seconded from national foreign ministries, so as to ensure loyalty is to "the Union". The EU has many embassies – it's currently upgrading its 136 "Commission delegations" to be EU delegations that speak for the EU, toeing a line determined by majority vote. Ashton will also have control of military-command structures. Officially, the foreign minister of the country holding the rotating six-month EU presidency is her deputy, as are three of her fellow commissars. The EU ambassador to the USA will be on around €188,000, those to countries such as China on €147,000. All receive a 16 per cent bonus for working abroad.

William Hague, in one of his first acts as foreign secretary, urged Tory MEPs to vote for the EEAS in the EU parliament. Shortly afterwards, only a dozen MPs – out of 650 – opposed the service in a House of Commons vote.

In common with other commissars Ashton receives an annual entertainment allowance of €11,000 and an annual accommodation allowance of €32,500. Added to a salary of £270,000, her total remuneration makes her comfortably the world's best-paid female politician and she grosses more than our PM, Barack Obama and Mr Sarkozy.

Because she "knew where the coffee was", she said she would keep her office in the ultra-integrationist Commission, which represents the EU itself, instead of making a clean break to somewhere more amenable to pretending to represent 27 countries' foreign interests. (Ashton comes from a country that favours Turkish accession to the EU. Mr Van Rompuy, the devoutly Catholic president, does not favour the accession of a Muslim state. There can't be an EU foreign policy.)

Her first test as EU foreign-policy chief – the earthquake in Haiti in 2010 – elicited a sparsely attended press conference, her condolences and a promise of €3million in aid. The Americans, meanwhile, admittedly with the advantage of geography (Port-Au-Prince is a few hundred miles from the US naval base at Guantánamo Bay), sent 19 helicopters, several ships, 3,500 troops, hundreds of medical staff and secretary of state Hillary Clinton (Ashton's equivalent). In addition, Obama promised $100million in aid. Later, the EU promised "140 to 150 gendarmes" for the island and another €27million (of its member states' cash). Ashton did not visit until two months later, but did manage to cross the Atlantic a week after the earthquake to see Clinton in Washington DC.

Instead of attending her first meeting of EU defence ministers, she went to the inauguration of Ukraine's president, despite being head of the European Defence Agency. Around the same time, Barroso's appointment of his former chief of staff, a journalist by training, as EU ambassador to the US was made without consulting Ashton, whose job it is meant to be to appoint EU diplomats. Soon afterwards President Obama backed out of a scheduled EU-US summit, unsure who was in charge.

She has infuriated the EU apparatus by commuting to and from England most weekends, and by not answering her phone after 8pm – a handicap for those calling from places not on the same line of longitude as St Albans or Brussels. Denying these charges, she said, "I'm neither a doctor nor a fireman."[108]

---

[108] *Britain's high representative is letting Europe down badly* in *The Times*, 28 January 2010

Peculiarly, this was the same response that a paparazzo gave who had witnessed Princess Diana's crash and not helped.

Not even six months into his job, her German spokesman, Lutz Güllner, resigned and took a job in the EU's trade directorate. "I had to consider my professional future and decided that it was elsewhere... Cathy is in a very difficult position, mainly because of all the fighting between all the different EU institutions," he said[109]. In May 2010, Mandelson's spokesman had to deny that his master had spread claims that she was going to resign (perhaps in favour of David Miliband), saying, "He thinks she is doing quite a reasonable job." That was quite a plausible denial.

These posts were abandoned for the 2009-2014 "college":

Institutional Relations and Communication Strategy

From 2004 to 2009, this post was held by Margot Wallström (Sweden).

In 2004, after five years as Prodi's commissar for the environment, Wallström wrote a book called *People's Europe: Why Is It So Difficult To Love The EU?* It was her job, as chief publicist or "Mrs PR" as she called herself, to make us love the EU.

Her lowest point was on VE Day 2005, during a trip to Terezin in the Czech Republic where there's a memorial to the time when the place was Theresienstadt, a Nazi concentration camp. She gave a speech in which she said that politicians who resisted pooling national sovereignty – via the upcoming Constitution – risked a return to the horrors of Nazism. Her fellow commissars simultaneously issued a joint declaration stating that EU citizens should pay tribute to the dead of World War II by voting yes to the Constitution. (She and the commissioners also gave the EU sole credit for ending the Cold War.) She denied saying the most distasteful sentence in her speech – "Yet there are those today who want to scrap the supranational idea. They want the European Union to go back to the old purely intergovernmental way of doing things. I say those people should come to Terezin and see where that old road leads" – even though it was in the version of her speech on her website. When a newspaper reproduced the words, the sentence disappeared from her site. It was nations with unpooled sovereignty – Britain, America and many others – that stood up to Hitler and defeated fascism, which was an international movement. She had got the argument entirely the wrong way round.

Two months after invoking Nazism to try to help the EU's cause, she unwittingly revived memories of communism in many of the recent accession states by trying to requisition the Eurovision Song Contest. She said she wanted to "show the EU can dance" and wanted to highlight "the benefits that European integration has brought to its citizens".

---

[109] *Resignation of key aide upstages Ashton's foreign policy plans* in *The Independent*, 26 March 2010

Many of the previous year's intake were reminded of such times of compulsory enjoyment when they were communist – back then it was called "sing or swing". A Czech government source told the *Sunday Telegraph*, "For most of the new members, this plan brought back memories of communist times. There were all kinds of events celebrating everything, and there was one called the Spartakiada, which consisted of singing and dancing for the masses."

On her register of interests she listed two properties and her personal Volvo. She is probably best known for a mind-numbing blog that would credit the sunrise to the EU if she thought she could get away with it. See "Propaganda" for more about her work.

In August 2009, Open Europe reported that she had "earned almost €1.9million in her 10 years as a commissioner, and if she lives to be 85, she will receive another €1.9million in retirement payments. In addition she will receive €450,000 after taxes in a one-off payment [when she stands down] before cashing in €8,000 a month after taxes as a pension for the rest of her life."

Although her job was abolished, the propaganda directorate certainly survives.

External Relations and European Neighbourhood Policy
Benita Ferrero-Waldner (Austria)

Another domestic-election loser, Ferrero-Waldner lost her bid for the Austrian presidency in 2004, having been foreign minister. Some people think she remarried her husband in December 2003 only to assist that campaign. She had been backed by Jorg Haider, the late nationalist politician, who appeared on platforms with her several times during the campaign and presented her with a pig for good luck.

She said at her Commission hearing that foreign-policy integration would, in the long term, "logically lead to the EU being represented at the UN Security Council". Her continual sunniness earned her the name Ferrero-Küsschen ("Ferrero Kiss"), a reference to the name given to Ferrero Rocher chocolates in German-speaking countries. Her job is now part of Ashton's and she joined insurance firm Munich Re.

In October 2008, the Commission revealed some of its freebies. The 27 had admitted receipt of 216 gifts since 2004. There was no requirement to list gifts worth less than €150, nor hospitality, meals or trips – and the donor did not need to be named. As the *Times* reported:

"Transparency in Brussels amounts to a quaint list of curios, such as the 12-volume history of Sicily received by the Italian former commissioner Franco Frattini in December 2004, his only entry on the register. He saw no need to list the skiing weekend with the Bulgarian interior minister, which caused a furore because Frattini had taken a close interest in a report on Bulgaria's progress in joining the EU – a report that was criticised for giving Bulgaria an easy ride. Barroso has declared the highest number of gifts, 80, ranging from a gold fob watch from a head of state to a silver dagger presented by a diplomat. However, he does not list any free cruises, such as the one he took with his friend Spiro Latsis which led to criticism because it followed a decision by the previous Commission to allow state aid to a shipyard owned by Latsis. In 2005 the anti-fraud commissioner, Siim Kallas, said that he wanted the code of conduct to be 'more precise and more exhaustive'… During his tenure as trade commissioner, Lord Mandelson… declared five gifts: a [Montegrappa] pen from a head of state, a glass lamp from a 'private association', a rug and a gold-decorated glass plate from national governments, and a model sailing vessel from 'companies'…"[110]

Early in his tenure Mandelson had been criticised for enjoying time on "Octopus", the 414-ft yacht of Paul Allen, the co-founder of Microsoft. At the time, the software company was fighting the EU in the ECJ. It is not known if the "sailing vessel" declared is a model of that yacht or of the one he more famously graced, Mr Deripaska's. (Or even Mr Della Valle's.)

Nickel Neelie, meanwhile, received a "silver fig leaf and a five-volume German-Slovenian dictionary". The leader in the paper noted: "Rules for declaring interests are structured so that any meaningful act of hospitality goes undeclared. Under the code of conduct, the public cannot know who entertains commissioners or whether they mix business and pleasure in what they choose to call their private time, unless the commissioners themselves choose to say so. Usually, and unsurprisingly, they do not. The code of conduct was drafted in haste by Neil Kinnock in 1999 after the resignation of Jacques Santer's entire cabinet… Commissioners were to preserve the dignity of their office 'in their official and private lives', not least by 'ruling out all risks of a conflict of interests'. All paid activity unrelated to the EU was proscribed. Even royalties from work-related publications were to be given to charity, and political campaigning was to be cleared with the Commission president in advance. This was a document that purported to require full disclosure. In practice it leaves commissioners free to disclose nothing at all about whatever they deem to have been private."

---

[110] *The Times*, 29 October 2008

The Council of Ministers

This is where the Commission's legislative fiat lands first – on a table around which are convened representatives of the member states' governments in a long oval room with little natural light in the Justus Lipsius building in Brussels, opposite the Berlaymont[111] – except in April, June and October when the Council meets in Luxembourg.

The Council comprises the minister relevant to the subject under discussion from each country's parliament – a collective of counterparts – chaired by the minister from the country that has the presidency of the EU (a system that continues to exist even though the EU now has a semipermanent president). For instance, Ecofin (economics and finance) is our chancellor of the exchequer and his 26 equivalents (although Ecofin has been marginalised by Eurogroup, which comprises only the 16 finance ministers of the eurozone and meets before Ecofin). There are eight other Councils. Ecofin and both the Foreign and Agriculture Councils meet monthly, others less frequently.

A general election in the UK, though producing much heat, sound and light domestically, is merely a by election at this level of government, which is where real power lies; if the UK government changes, there's only one change around the table of the Council Of Ministers (and at the European Council), where the really grown-up decisions are made, the type that override domestic legislators and domestic legislation.

As Anthony Coughlan, senior lecturer emeritus in social policy at Trinity College Dublin, has written, "At a national level when a minister wants to get something done, he or she must have the backing of the prime minister, must have the agreement of the minister for finance if it means spending money, and above all must have majority support in the national parliament, and implicitly among voters in the country. Shift the policy area in question to the supranational level of Brussels, however, where laws are made primarily by the 27-member Council Of Ministers, and the minister in question becomes a member of an oligarchy, a committee of lawmakers, the most powerful in history, making laws for 500million Europeans, and irremovable as a group regardless of what it does... Individual ministers obtain an intoxicating increase in personal power, as they are transformed from members of the executive arm of government at national level, subordinate to a national legislature, into EU-wide legislators at the supranational."[112]

---

[111] In 2013, the circus will move next door to a new €315million building called the Résidence Palace

[112] *EU Observer*, 14 May 2007. Coughlan is responsible for the fact that any treaty that alters Ireland's constitution must be put to a referendum, a judgment secured after his legal challenge to the republic's ratification of the Single European Act

It is in the Council of Ministers that countries can sometimes veto laws. Talk of "losing the veto" in certain areas means that such matters become subject to qualified majority voting (QMV), which often makes for scenes that would dignify the Eurovision Song Contest's horse trading. Under QMV, the voting weights of countries correspond roughly to their population, though the smaller countries are massively overrepresented and Germany in particular is shortchanged. The Lisbon Treaty grabbed many areas from veto and took them into QMV. After a general election in the UK, therefore, there is merely – at this level of government – a different British face to outvote in "the Council", be it in the Agriculture And Fisheries Council, Ecofin or the Transport Council.

Of 345 votes in the Council, we have 29 (as do Germany, France and Italy), or 8.4 per cent. Votes must – currently – be backed by a simple majority of member states (14+) and be supported by 74 per cent of the 345 votes cast (255 votes), with countries supporting the proposal representing at least 62 per cent of the total EU population. You need 91 votes to block something. Countries not so keen on galloping integration or "ever closer union" include Poland (27), Sweden (10), Denmark (7) and the Czech Republic (12). It's a long way to a blocking 91 votes – and very often the UK minister will be in favour of the measure anyway, knowing that it would be a tough sell in parliament back home.

From 2014, under the terms of the Lisbon Treaty, proposals from the Commission must be backed, in the Council, by 55 per cent of member states (15+; or two thirds for proposals not from the Commission), with countries in support representing at least 65 per cent of the total EU population. To oppose a measure, you need four countries (up from three in the Nice Treaty), representing at least 35 per cent of the EU population (down from 38 per cent under Nice). Therefore, the UK needs its own 12.4 per cent of the EU population plus 22.5 more from at least three countries to block something. It soon becomes obvious that not a lot gets passed or blocked without the say-so of Germany (16.5) and France (12.9). Proponents of the Lisbon Treaty said that it would "streamline decision making", and they were right if they meant that blocking legislation would become harder.

And you can be outvoted even when you're not. In an October 2006 trade council, when the EU had 25 members, 12 countries voted against imposing extra duties on Chinese shoes for the next two years[113]. Nine countries voted in

---

[113] Which so helped, among others, Mandelson's associate Mr Della Valle of Tod's. When this temporary tariff, which Mandy had put in place, was extended after he had left the Commission, he said, "[this] damages trade, harms the reputation of Europe and forces consumers to pay higher prices at a time when they can least afford it" and he called on the EU to "turn its back on protectionism"!

favour. However, as is the norm, the four abstentions were counted as votes in favour, thereby leading to higher prices for EU consumers.

Defenders of this system of government say that the Council of Ministers, or at least its constituents, is elected by the people and that it is therefore democratic. Have you ever elected anyone whose vote helped to overrule the UK in the Council? It's a good bet that none of your neighbours did, either. The House of Commons EU scrutiny committee put it this way: "We do not believe that democratic legitimacy is secured by the system of voting which allows member states to be outvoted and obliged to introduce changes in their criminal law and procedure with which they do not agree" (3 July 2003). Unlike Westminster, you cannot see how ministers, who are given "the power to commit" by their domestic parliament, have voted. Perhaps our minister wasn't overruled as she said she was. One just never knows. Often there isn't even a vote because delegates fear looking like "bad Europeans" and so oppose nothing and measures go through nem con[114]. No minutes are produced, either.

There is a persistent canard about the EU's power: that it is diluted by EU expansion. At least some of the canard's longevity is down to its being propagated by those committed to surreptitious integration. Anyway, a quick look at the erosion of the veto tells the true story. When countries join the EU, a cry goes up: "Now that we have 27 members [or however many], we can no longer allow vetoes in the area of pebbledashing on semi-detached houses, there are now too many potential veto-wielders: pebbledashing must be made subject to Qualified Majority Voting." And so a new treaty – or Constitution – is drafted that eradicates yet more national vetoes. The great leaps forward in EU integration (such as the Single European Act, the Maastricht Treaty), whether they be via loss of veto in certain areas or even wholly new "competences" (which pave the way for directives in new areas), correlate with enlargements. The Lisbon Treaty – hiding behind the last 12 accessions – is just the most recent example and it ignores the fact that legislation has been passed *more quickly* after the huge expansion of 2004 than before: there was no legislative logjam that required a new treaty. But the desire for "ever closer union" remains undiminished, and it hides behind the closest thing to hand. The Charlemagne column saw this just after the EU's 50th birthday:

"Overall, the EU has been adopting new rules and regulations some 25 per cent faster since enlargement, says a study published by Sciences Po in Paris. Its authors have tracked thousands of proposals, large and small. 'Contrary to much received wisdom,' they conclude, 'the data gathered shows that enlargement has not... brought Europe's machinery to a halt.' Looking for blockages, they find

---

[114] In 2008 the Council chose to release the results of 147 votes (out of a total of 536): 128 of them had been unanimous

that 'old' members have opposed proposals twice as often as new ones... As for talk of new voting rules, these conjure up images of late night cliffhangers, in which new laws scrape through. But that is not how the EU works. In both the Commission and in the Council of Ministers, votes are generally shunned in favour of consensus. Abolishing vetoes still matters, but for a different reason. When laws can be approved by majority vote, governments enter negotiations in a state of fear, knowing that doubters can easily end up isolated; a knowledge that pushes everybody towards compromise, gives the Commission more power and promotes 'more Europe'. If countries have a veto, they can sit out the argument and simply say no. When Eurocrats call for more streamlined decision making, what they mean is making life more frightening for laggards."[115]

The Sciences Po study, *Enlargement: How Europe is adapting*, showed that the Council Of Ministers actually takes votes only a fifth of the time and that, since the 2004 enlargement, the number of legislative acts passed after the first reading went from 34 per cent to 64 per cent. In evidence to the House of Lords, Leon Brittan, who resigned from the Commission in 1999, said that Lisbon's new voting system would be an improvement because it "frankly gives more power to the larger countries and less to the smaller ones", making it more difficult for the latter to be "troublemakers". Charming. But if anyone post-2004 was blocking laws, it was the EU15. The ex-commie states were not "troublemakers".

On 22 June 2007, Renaud Dehousse, the professor who wrote the Sciences Po study, was interviewed by *Libération*. Asked if the proposed Lisbon Treaty was "indispensable", he replied, "Before enlargement in May 2004, it took on average 18 months between the deposit of a Commission proposal and its adoption by the Council and the parliament. Since the entry of the 10 new member states, this has gone down to less than 12 months. In addition, there are no fewer votes, but even a little more than before. The fears of a blockage, including my own, were therefore unfounded."

In December 2007, another academic would echo this study. According to Helen Wallace, a professor at the London School of Economics, the main institutions – the Council Of Ministers, European Commission, European parliament and the European Court of Justice – were functioning as well as ever and the much-predicted gridlock had not happened. "Established working methods and practices have survived the arrival of new member states," she said. "The evidence of practice since May 2004 suggests that the EU's institutional processes and practice have stood up rather robustly to the impact of enlargement." A press release said, "The key finding to emerge from experience so far is that the day-to-day business of the EU institutions continues to be

---

[115] "Charlemagne" column, *The Economist*, 12 April 2007

carried out much as before enlargement, with similar levels of activity and output in and from the main EU institutions. Moreover, there is no evidence so far of a recurrent or polarised cleavage between old and new member states in the development of EU policies... Helen Wallace said: 'Of course these are still early days for assessing the impact of enlargement on the EU institutions, but so far at least there is no evidence of the gridlock that many feared.'"

On 30 April 2008 the *Financial Times* again said that the EU had not ground to a halt since enlargement, but instead had managed to streamline its decision making and shorten meetings. A former German representative to the EU, Wilhelm Schonfelder, told the paper, "Many things work better than before. Discussions are not as long as they used to be." It also noted that the EU adopted more legislative decisions in 2006 than it did on average between 1999 and 2003.

The opinion is also held by John Bruton, an Irish former PM and former EU ambassador to the US. He said after the Irish voted no in 2008: "Many suspected that when the European Union went from 15 members to 27 that everything would stop. In fact the contrary has been the case. I think you can say that the European Union has been *more* active in producing new legislation and new measures."[116]

Once the Council Of Ministers has pronounced, the actual implementation and legislation revert to the Commission, the only legislator. The green light from the Council is called the Commission's "right of initiative". None of this is meant to suggest that the Commission is any way answerable to the Council Of Ministers thereafter, for it is not.

After a June 2006 European Council (popularly known as "summits"), EU leaders agreed to allow television cameras into Council meetings. The UK was the only delegation opposed to the move. Margaret Beckett – then foreign secretary – had opposed televisation, arguing that it would drive deals into the corridors because ministers would not want to be seen by their electorates giving in on issues of national importance. The provision still allowed Councils to hold meetings in private, and did not cover foreign policy, defence and criminal justice meetings. Council meetings are anyway a formality (as mentioned, 80 per cent of the time there's no vote), in which ministers nod through decisions already agreed by civil servants in the Council Working Groups and a body called Coreper.

---

[116] BBC *Newsnight*, 19 June 2008

During downtime between Councils, Coreper (from the French for "committee of permanent representatives" of the member states' civil services) tries to find common ground and creates most of the legal thicket we so love, in conditions of secrecy. It comprises mostly anonymous national bureaucrats, ambassadors to the machine, who work way below ground and concoct 90 per cent of the announcements (and detailed agreements) that are made. The Council is watched over by a powerful French civil servant called Pierre de Boissieu (nicknamed "Cardinal Richelieu" by Eurocrats), the secretary general.

The Council Of Ministers is usually called "the Council" and, formally but confusingly, "the Council of the European Union", but not "the Council of Europe" (Winston's baby), nor "European Council". The head of government of the country that has the rotating presidency is the president of the Council Of The European Union.

The European Parliament

This is the only directly elected body in the EU and it comprises 754 MEPs, 72 of whom represent the UK. Some people do not know that they actually have several MEPs in their "region" (see "Committee Of The Regions"). These people are the lucky ones, for they have less sense of the waste involved.

The elections are held every five years and the next is in June 2014. In June 2009, 736 MEPs took their seats, down from 785 in 2004. Although the Lisbon Treaty allows for a total of 754 MEPs (but only 751 from 2014, when Germany loses three), it hadn't been ratified in all provinces before the 2009 vote. However, the EU ignored its own rules in anticipation of ratification and so an extra 18 MEPs (among 12 countries) were elected. But they couldn't take their seats until after: a) Lisbon was enacted; and b) the three Germans had stood down, which they did not want to do before 2014. So the parliament gave the 18 "observer" status until each member state had re-ratified Lisbon to allow for them. (The change to the Lisbon Treaty had been made in a 15-minute session of Coreper.) In the meantime, the 18 received normal MEPs' salaries and perks, despite not being able to take up office. If it takes the 27 provinces a long time to legislate and the 18 do not sit before 2014, they will have cost €30million (including wages, business-class travel, assistants and office allowances, as well as tax-free per diems) for doing nothing. If they do sit any time before 2014, they will still cost that amount – and for what?

Churchill, after whom one of the parliament buildings in Strasbourg is named, famously preferred to "jaw jaw" rather than to "war war". He'd be keen on this multilingual talking shop: it is almost all mouth, and is part of a body formed to prevent war. But the parliament is slightly more than an extravagantly remunerated sheep dip for diktats – it can, with a two-thirds majority, force the resignation of the Commission. This it achieved spectacularly in 1999 (see "Fraud and whistleblowers") when Jacques Santer's "college", with the toy parliament's gun at its head, eventually fell on its sword.

The MEPs, who have been elected since only 1979 – before then some national MPs would do double duty, sitting domestically and in Brussels, so they could see the city where power had gone – but with an ever decreasing mandate, sit in their hemicycle jabbing away on their touch-pads as they vote on hundreds of measures per hour, as if the producers of *Who Wants To Be A Millionaire?* had peopled the audience with contestants from the multinational quiz *Going For Gold*. And, as with *Millionaire*, there is often no way of knowing how individuals voted.

Every month, there is an obscene oscillation as this parliament – which has no legislative power and can block or amend very few pieces of legislation, let alone repeal laws (the very thought!) – moves between Strasbourg (its formal seat, where it spends one week for plenary sessions, nodding through what was decided in Belgium) and Brussels.

This arrangement allows both Belgium and France to cash in on the indulgent per diems of the attendees and means that neither loses face by not hosting the notional seat of government. However, it involves the ferrying of thousands of MEPs, translators, staff, flunkeys and 4,000 trunks twice every 30 days, at a cost of €200million per annum, burning 13 per cent of its budget. As the *Guardian* remarked: "Strasbourg, whose position on the River Rhine symbolises Franco-German reconciliation after three wars in 100 years, is hard to reach. The ordinary train from Brussels takes five hours, and the airport has so few direct flights that around 300 MEPs fly instead to Frankfurt, 136 miles away. A fleet of 15 lorries making the 220-mile journey south along the two-lane motorway from Brussels to Strasbourg on Friday nights once a month signals to motorists that their taxes are being blown on the world's most costly commute."[117] In addition, the 27 commissars and hangers-on meet in Strasbourg on the Tuesday.

In summer 2008, an upmarket 186mph train service was launched to connect the Belgian and French sites. The existing Belgian train took two hours longer (though it was half the price) and lacked a buffet car – some gravy train! But this was the real deal, a shiny red TGV. Despite the inclusion of a buffet car, the gravy was still a problem for some – because the service left Brussels on Monday mornings at 9.57am, an internal parliamentary memo warned that the arrival of the train at 1.36pm in Strasbourg would "deprive colleagues of their midday break and the possibility of a proper lunch"[118]. The €220 return fare is reimbursed but its 377 seats are reserved for MEPs, Eurocrats and journalists – not "civilians", though it is the Belgian state which funded the service. It was hoped that the service would replace six charter flights, perhaps putting a "green" spin on the unnecessary trips – an April 2007 study commissioned by the European parliament's Green group of MEPs had showed that the monthly commute produced 20,000 tons of carbon dioxide a year, equivalent to the greenhouse gases produced by 13,000 return flights from London to New York.

A million-signature petition from EU citizens calling for an end to the travelling circus was ignored because the "power" share between the two sites is included in the Treaties (since Amsterdam), and their clauses can be repealed only unanimously, a move that France at least would scupper. In January 2009, a petition among MEPs could raise only 268 names, well short of the 393 majority needed for the elite to take notice.

---

[117] *The end of the road for roving parliament?* by Nicholas Watt in *The Guardian*, 1 November 2006
[118] *The Sunday Times*, 1 June 2008

In May 2007, in response to a journalist's question, Sarkozy said that the Strasbourg seat of the European parliament was not up for discussion – it was part of the EU's "founding balance and I do not see how Strasbourg could be negotiable and not the other seats of the European institutions". That November, he also made clear he had no intention of ending the Strasbourg plenary sessions, saying there was "zero flexibility" in the treaties for such a change. A year earlier, it was reported that national and local authorities in France had offered €362million in subsidies to the city of Strasbourg for the 2006-2008 period to support its bid to keep the seat of parliament[119]. This was almost twice the amount pledged for the period 2003-2005.

On top of the subsidy, the Alsatian venue had been bilking the EU on the rent for many years. Annual grift of €2.7million soon starts to add up to real money: in 2006 an investigation by MEPs revealed that the city of Strasbourg had, since 1980, inflated the rent of the European parliament's three buildings, costing taxpayers about £54million. The city caused further resentment by refusing to co-operate with an investigation. The buildings had been owned by SCI Erasme, a Dutch pension fund, that let them to the city, which in turn sublet them to the parliament. The parliament paid rent to the city authorities, who raked off a share before handing the balance to SCI Erasme. In September that year, the European parliament paid €143million for the premises it had been renting. No account was made in the price for rent already handed over – nor for the long-running rip-off.

In the same month, the Court of Auditors accused the European parliament of wasting up to €6million a year on renting empty buildings in Belgium. The parliament had paid €6million per year for an empty building between 1998, when it moved out of the Belliard complex in Brussels, and 2004, when the Committee of the Regions (see later) moved in. Like the Commission, it had wasted millions on property.

It cannot have helped that in January 2006 the EU had to suspend the head of its buildings directorate unit in Brussels, Pierre Parthoens. He had not informed the authorities that he was under investigation for bribing officials in his previous job – perhaps he thought it was a requirement. He did not deny the charges but said he was acting on orders and was afraid to say no. According to German magazine *Stern*, Olaf had twice shelved its own investigations into the Belgian, having linked him to possible exaggerated payments to companies involved in the building of a new home for the European parliament in Brussels. Parthoens had also come under the spotlight in March 2002 when financial controllers questioned a payment to him of €30,000. He claimed a right to the additional

---

[119] *Les Echos*, 15 November 2006

pay because of having to move to Luxembourg, though he had done no more than 15 days' work there during the year. *Stern* quoted an internal memo of the Olaf supervisory committee, which said Olaf had initiated a "fake investigation" into the matter[120].

In August 2008, when the parliament was in recess (which is not to say that it had stopped passing legislation – it never does), ten tonnes of the Strasbourg hemicycle's ceiling fell in. The building was not even 10 years old but, as metaphors go, the collapse of its ceiling was as nourishing for eurosceptics as the spate of disintegrating euro notes in 2006 had been. The next few plenary sessions were held in Brussels, saving €4million in travel and other expenses (although €6million had to be spent repairing the roof). In 2002 there had been an outbreak of Legionnaire's Disease in the water supply because the building was too rarely used, and in July 2009 it was discovered that the metallic beams supporting the parliament's dome were only partially fireproofed and would have lasted just 20 minutes in a fire. At the end of 2009, three concrete ceiling slabs in an office block adjacent to the main building fell to the floor after heavy rain. The problem had been missed even though an inspection had been carried out after the 2008 calamity[121].

The presidency of the parliament is a carve-up between the two main groupings, the Progressive Alliance of Socialists and Democrats (S&D), which is home to New Labour, and the centre-right European People's Party (EPP), formerly home to the Tories (who are now in the European Conservatives and Reformists group). The Lib Dems are part of the Alliance of Liberals and Democrats for Europe (ALDE) while Ukip make up most of the Europe Of Freedom And Democracy group.

In December 2007, the then president of the European parliament was criticised for having a 46-strong entourage. The office of Hans-Gert Pöttering included three drivers, 13 advisers and seven press officers. A conservative estimate of the total running costs of the German MEP's staff alone was €3.5million per annum. After he stood down, *Der Spiegel* reported that he had retained a limousine with driver on call. He should have lost the privilege but his former assistant, the EP's secretary general, Klaus Welle, asked the praesidium of the EP to change the rules.

Apologists for the lack of proper legislative power talk of the "ordinary legislative procedure" (formerly "co-decision"), a process whereby about 60 laws out of an annual total of 3,000 have some amendatory input from the parliament. Increasingly, however, the parliament is being given powers, though not of

---

[120] *EU Observer*, 10 January 2006
[121] *EU Observer*, 14 December 2009

course the power to legislate. As it stands, MEPs can make "written declarations", which are similar to Early Day Motions in Westminster: between one and five MEPs draft a text for signing. It is "adopted" if it garners a simple majority (378) and is then sent to the EP's president who announces it in the hemicycle as the place's "official position". The Commission must then take note and examine the "position" but is not obliged to produce any related legislation.

MEPs can also vote not to "discharge" or approve the accounts. However, they never do, despite the fact that every year the auditors fail to pass the accounts. MEPs might one day also be able to force the resignation of an individual commissar rather than the whole "college".

A British Ukip MEP, Jeffrey Titford, once described a hard day's democracy:

"So we go through this charade, this parody of democratic process [whereby MEPs can speak for only 90 seconds and consensus is the norm], and now come the votes. Now and only now does the chamber fill up, often to near capacity. MEP after MEP takes his or her numbered seat, placing their smart cards in their electronic voting machine terminals. Such devotion to duty is admirable, except that, should the members not be there, their daily allowance will be docked 50 per cent. Should they not meet their other attendance target then their secretarial allowance will be halved also. In little more than an hour in that hemicycle, we may be required to cast 200 votes or more – one vote approximately every 20 seconds – each having a direct effect on the lives of hundreds, sometimes millions of people, led by a bored so-called president who sits at the front, for all the world like a weary teller in some huge bingo hall.

The larger groups [of political parties] sometimes have their version of tic-tac men, who engage in baroque theatricals, holding their arms aloft, thumbs up or down, to tell their members how to vote. At irregular intervals, there are roll call votes. These are cast electronically and the results displayed on a giant screen with an animated picture of a hand putting a slip into a ballot box. Seconds later, after the president has declared the vote closed, the result will flash up on the screen and it is on to the next vote. As soon as the voting is done the chamber empties faster than a cinema on fire. Remember: in this parliament there are no private members' bills. Not a single measure originates in the parliament. Every directive and regulation is written by the Commission, passes through this charade and becomes European law.

That it should become law is preordained. Even if the assembly, struck by some aberration, decide to vote against, it would make no difference. The measure would then go through an additional procedure called 'conciliation' where the vote can be overturned and the original reinstated.

A defining moment for me was having to vote on the 3rd reading of the EU's Late Payment Directive. The 1st and 2nd readings had taken place before June 1999, when we were elected. It was a different parliament voting on the directive, but that made no difference. Unlike in the British parliament, EU measures do not fall with the dissolution of the EU parliament[122]. The machine grinds on regardless of its members, spewing out directives and regulations. This perhaps, above all, brought home to me the nature of my role in the parliament. Individual MEPs are not an essential, or even an important, part of the project. We are interchangeable bit-part actors, spear carriers, participating in a mockery of parliamentary process. Oratory plays no part. Reason plays no part. Conviction plays no part.

Our votes cannot check a directive. We are there merely to furnish the illusion of democracy, providing a veneer to conceal what is a fundamentally undemocratic process. The cast may change, but the show always goes on, with the actors collecting their wages from the stage door and dashing off for a self-congratulatory drink after the show."[123]

In summer 2009, Germany's constitutional court in Karlsruhe had to check that the Lisbon Treaty was compatible with the German constitution. The pro-EU *Financial Times* summarised the court's view: "[Karlsruhe] does not recognise the European parliament as a genuine legislature, representing the will of a single European people, but as a representative body of member states. A particular criticism made by the court is that [the EP] does not behave like a true parliament. There is no formal opposition. There is no grouping that supports a government. While the Lisbon Treaty increases the powers of [the EP], it does not, in the court's view, fix its ultimate shortcoming: that the parliament does not constitute an effective control of EU executive power."[124]

There is some independence of mind in the place. A smoking ban introduced in the European parliament on 1 January 2007 ended after just 43 days. A 12-member committee of MEPs decided the ban was unenforceable after MEPs and staff revolted and smoked in more areas than before the ban.

The UK's 72 seats are awarded by proportional representation and each of our 12 "regions" has between three and 10 MEPs. The London "region", for instance, has eight. In the 2009 Euro elections the Tories and Labour won 27.1 per cent and 21.3 per cent of the vote in London respectively. The Tories were given three MEPs and Labour two, which they awarded from the top of their party lists – those lower down missed out. The remaining three tickets for the gravy train were awarded to a Lib Dem, a Green and a Ukip member, those parties polling between 10.8 and 13.7 per cent each.

You cannot, therefore, vote for a specific candidate (unless he or she is the only

---

[122] In 2009, the parliament began moves to change this arrangement, asking the Commission to withdraw and revise 10 proposals left over from the previous term. Don't watch this space...
[123] Speech to The Bruges Group, 4 November 2000
[124] Wolfgang Munchau in *The Financial Times*, 12 July 2009

candidate for that party in that "region"). Besides, to adapt the old joke, it doesn't matter whom you vote for, the EU will get in. The Tories keep all their incumbent MEPs, most of whom prefer deeper integration, at the top of their lists. You cannot hold an individual MEP to account, which is anyway a job often better performed by the tabloid press.

Since 1979, voter turnout across the EU has fallen from 63 per cent to 56.7 per cent in 1994, to 49.5 per cent (1999) to 45.6 per cent (2004) to 43 per cent in 2009, despite the fact that countries such as Belgium and Greece make voting compulsory.

The EU now includes 27 countries, 500million people (about two thirds more than the USA) and 23 official languages[125]. There are many busy linguists in Brussels – translating from Gaelic into Slovenian is not nearly as straightforward as it sounds, and is just one of 506 permutations. The parliament needs 60 translators on €1,500 a day before it can function. Although it is not a government, the United Nations has a larger reach – and gets by with six languages.

To add to the confusion, the official headquarters of the European parliament are in Luxembourg.

For details of the remuneration packages available to MEPs, see "Perquisites and emoluments".

---

[125] The four that use another member's language are Belgium, Luxembourg, Cyprus and Austria; Ireland's official language is Irish

The Court Of Auditors

Corruption in the EU is commonplace. It's commonplace elsewhere, too, but that doesn't make it OK. Even the most famous quotation about corruption – Lord Acton's "Power tends to corrupt and absolute power corrupts absolutely" – has been corrupted to "Power corrupts".

The Court of Auditors (COA) is the EU's spotlight on financial irregularities but has no powers of recovery and can merely pass its findings to Olaf[126].

When you hear of fraud in the EU institutions, you might happily remember the maxim "Just thank God you don't get all the government you pay for". But there is a limit: at some point the sense of relief fades and you start to ask where your money is going.

The COA is based in Luxembourg and was established by the minor Treaty of Luxembourg (1975). It describes itself as the "financial conscience" of the EU: "[It] examines the accounts of the Union's revenue and expenditure and checks whether the financial management has been sound." Its annual reports are an as-long-as-your-arm charge sheet of eye-popping waste and fraud, and are published in November, making an early Christmas present for eurosceptics.

To celebrate 2007's accounts, Open Europe published *100 Examples Of EU Fraud And Waste*[127], which included the dentist who bought a Ferrari; a Spanish former mayor using funds to open a roadside brothel; a €1,280,000 school for TV glamour models in Naples; grants to Romanian witches; head massages in Newcastle; €100,000 for a ski slope on a flat, sunny Danish island, used for only a day and a half in two years (the recipient had applied as a joke after he and his girlfriend became angry that they could not get to the Alps); claims for non-existent silkworms; etc. A typical year might include 90,000 tonnes of fictitious olives raking in subsidies, and a herd of sheep in Greece that were first devoured by wolves and *then* hit by disease. The 2006 COA report found that half of all cattle declared by farmers in Slovenia did not exist, while a quarter of sheep and goats had similarly disappeared. In Spain, Greece and Italy, payments worth over €2billion to olive-oil producers were either inflated or wrong.

One year, the president of the COA – obviously a stranger to irony – held a

---

126 Olaf has a freephone number (0800 963 595) if you know of anything untoward. But please see the Tillack case in "Fraud and whistleblowers" before ringing
127 www.openeurope.org.uk/research/top100waste.pdf
In 2009, another round-up included €2,500 for the chairman of Porsche's Bavarian hunting retreat; €80,000 for the Swedish city of Malmo to replicate itself in the online game *Second Life*; and €198,500 for a puppet-theatre network in the Baltics. www.openeurope.org.uk/research/top50waste.pdf

champagne-and-caviar reception to present to journalists the COA's report on fraud and waste. (After having told the EU parliament that he would serve the hacks only lemonade.)

Ever since 1995 – the year after the champers-and-caviar debacle – the COA has been unable to sign off the EU's accounts (and, needless to say, it itself has been subject to fraud). In its April 2007 report on the financial affairs of the EU, our own National Audit Office said: "For the twelfth successive year the Court of Auditors decided not to provide a positive Statement of Assurance on the legality and regularity of European Community expenditure [for the year 2005]."[128] Not a hard decision to make, in fairness: the accounts weren't signed off because, in the words of the COA, "the vast majority of the payment budget was again materially affected by errors of legality and regularity".

In November 2007, the EU's accounts achieved their "baker's dozen": 13 years without sign-off by the auditors, this time because "errors of legality and regularity still persist in the majority of EU expenditure due to weaknesses in internal control systems both at the [European] Commission and in member states". The think tank Open Europe calculated that the areas of expenditure on which the COA gave an adverse opinion accounted for 57 per cent of the overall 2006 budget, or £43.4billion. This means that of the £10.5billion given by UK taxpayers to the EU each year, nearly £6billion is open to fraud.

When it doles out the euros, the EU Commission also likes to pass the buck with them. Every year it latches on to the fact that member states too are blamed by the COA. But in its 2007 report the COA pre-empted this defence: "Regardless of the method of implementation applied, the Commission bears the ultimate responsibility for the legality and regularity of the transactions underlying the accounts of the European Communities (Article 274 of the Treaty[129])... in significant parts of the EU budget, the Directors-General [of the Commission] give a more positive account of the legality and regularity of EU spending than is consistent with the Court's audit."

As the EU's former chief accountant said, "I will not sign a payment until I know who Gonzalez or Fernandez is. Yet in many cases the money was paid in advance so the EU never sought proof that it was used for the intended purpose. Why did I have to open a bank account for someone in Honduras and make payment in pesos? Can someone tell me who he is? That's the type of thing I got no answer to. I stopped the payment and said I want the documents – the documents never came. It's true the frauds are committed in the member

---

[128] *Financial Management In The European Union*, April 2007, is available from www.nao.org.uk, as are later reports
[129] After the Lisbon Treaty, this is now TFEU 317

countries but I can tell you it's very difficult to commit them without the intervention of the European Commission itself."[130]

In November 2008 some weasel words and a worrying politicisation had infected the COA's report (on 2007). While there were "weaknesses in the accounting systems", the COA said that the Commission had made improvements in its own internal bookkeeping, which meant that the Commission should have been all the more aware of the vulnerabilities in the external spending. However, the same amount of taxpayers' money was subject to fraud as in previous years. There was no escaping the fact that 92 per cent of the 2007 budget was unclean. In other words, £93billion contained "too high levels of illegality and irregularity". Of the biopsies conducted by the auditors, 54 per cent of the Structural Funds projects (regional policy) and 31 per cent of agricultural transfers were infected with "material errors".

In 2009 the auditors "issued an 'unqualified' (clean) opinion on the reliability of the 2008 accounts". This is like having a clear photograph, except it's of John Prescott. As an accompanying FAQ put it, "The Court gives a clean opinion on the accounts – the problems are in the underlying payments." Spain, Italy and Portugal were responsible for 80 per cent of the errors detected in the spending of "Structural Funds" or (see p129). "Cohesion, which is the second largest policy group [after agriculture], representing almost a third of the budget, remains problematic and is the area most affected by errors... The Court gives adverse opinions on the legality and regularity aspects for the policy groups 'Cohesion', 'Research, energy and transport', as well as 'External aid, development and enlargement'. Payments in these policy groups are materially affected by errors, although at different levels."

The original point about the curate's egg ("parts of it are excellent") is that it was, overall, a bad egg; the curate was trying not to embarrass his host. Overall, the EU accounts are squalid and, literally, a criminal waste of money. The buck, as the Treaties make plain, stops with people that we cannot elect or eject. In 2009, the COA again reminded people that "the Commission retains the overall responsibility for the implementation of the budget".

---

[130] Marta Andreasen, about whom much more in "Fraud and whistleblowers", speaking to the Alliance & Leicester in Birmingham, November 2006

The European Court Of Justice (ECJ)

The ECJ is also in Luxembourg and acts as the EU's supreme court, upholding EU laws, assisted by a lower court, the General Court (called the Court Of First Instance until 2009), which was established by the Single European Act. As with the Commission, member states send one person to serve (though for six years).

In addition, eight advocates-general, the court's highest advisers, deliver legal opinion. Five are usually from Germany, France, Spain, Italy and the UK, with the remaining three posts passed around the 22 smaller countries. (Never let it be said that the EU is a stitch-up that favours the bigger kids in the playground.) As with the judges themselves, the advocates-general tend not to be eurosceptics: the UK's is Eleanor Sharpston QC. It was she who, before her appointment, had prosecuted the Metric Martyrs in the UK. Who sits with her?

According to the writer Mary Ellen Synon, "Vassilios Skouris, the Greek president of the ECJ... is typical of what can pass for a 'judge' in Europe. He is an academic who never worked as a judge until he was appointed to the ECJ in 1999. After just four years' experience on the euro-bench, he was made president of the court. A Finn, Allan Rosas, was never a judge until appointed to the ECJ. The same goes with the Belgian Koen Lenaerts and the Pole Jerzy Makarczyk, who was an academic, an author, a government minister and then head of the Polish delegation at the UN before he was appointed to the ECJ, his first job as a judge. The Hungarian Endre Juhasz was a bureaucrat and diplomat until he was appointed to the ECJ in 2004."[131]

At the ECJ cases are heard by a "full court" of 13 judges, or by three or five judges It rules on cases concerning individuals or companies (eg fining Microsoft), countries (eg if one refuses to buy the other's beef, say – "infringement proceedings"), and other EU institutions (usually the Commission). Its decisions are binding, there is never leave to appeal, and the Courts of Appeal in England and Wales are subordinate to it. In this country, "the highest court in the land" is in fact in Luxembourg City. The ridiculous new Supreme Court in London is subordinate to it.

The ECJ sees its role as interpreting the spirit of the treaties as well as their letter, and defined its purpose in 1960 by saying that it sought to enable "the Community interests enshrined in the Treaty of Rome *to prevail over the inertia and resistance of member states*" [emphasis added]. It's this institution that will decide, among many other things, if Britain's "opt-outs" from the Lisbon Treaty are worthless or not. If you're running a sweepstake on how long it is until we're dragged into line, keep buying a ticket until you draw "Very soon indeed". In

---

[131] *The Daily Mail*, 21 January 2009

2008, Roman Herzog, a former president of Germany, warned that the ECJ "systematically ignores fundamental principles of the Western interpretation of law" and "invents legal principles that serve as grounds for later judgments". He described the reasons given by the ECJ for a judgment on age discrimination as a "fabrication", arguing "to put it bluntly, with this construction, which the ECJ more or less pulled out of a hat, they were acting not as part of the judicial power but as the legislature".

In 2008 a £500million refit doubled the space of the ECJ, gave it a pair of 100m towers and a golden-gauze indoor canopy, which resembles a mosquito net or a jellyfish and shrouds the main court[132].

The ECJ is often confused with the European Court of Human Rights (see "Council Of Europe" in "What the EU isn't") and the UN's International Court Of Justice in The Hague ("the World Court" or ICJ) as well as the newer International Criminal Court (ICC), which is also based in The Hague but, like the European parliament, seems to sit anywhere.

---

[132] *Let there be light* in *The Guardian*, 2 December 2008

The European Council

Often wrongly called "EU summits", European Council meetings comprise the 27 leaders of government (PMs or presidents) of the member states – it's not correct to say "heads of state" because HM Queen, for one, does not attend – plus the president of the EU Commission, in a giant photo op. (Loosely, the European Council is like a Council Of (Prime) Ministers – although exceptions include the fact that it's the French president who attends not the French PM.)

"The European Council shall meet twice every six months, convened by its president," says TEU 15(3). "When the agenda so requires, the members of the European Council may decide each to be assisted by a minister." Before Lisbon, they would be "assisted" by their foreign minister. As the Swedish foreign minister pointed out, after Lisbon was enacted on 1 December 2009, relations between the member states were no longer foreign policy but domestic policy. "As it happens I am persuaded it's a very good idea," he said. "But I can't say all the other foreign ministers share that opinion, to put it politely."

Before the Lisbon Treaty, the leader of the country that had the six-month EU presidency (which, confusingly, continues as before – the country with the biannual presidency manages the day-to-day running of the bloc in all areas except foreign policy) became, in the words of Labour MP Austin Mitchell, "a six-month Moses". Since 1 January 2010, there has been a semipermanent president of the European Council who serves a two-and-a-half year term (renewable once). The first of these is Herman Van Rompuy of Belgium, a 30-month Moses, a semi-permanent figurehead, who can sign international treaties on behalf of 500m people without being answerable to them or anyone else[133].

European Councils have met several times a year, usually including once at the end of each country's six-month term, since the Seventies, when the body was devised by Jean Monnet. The Nice Treaty formalised them and said that they should "provide the Union with the necessary impetus for its development" and "define the general political guidelines thereof". In other words, the European Councils should be Moses's "road map" to the Promised Land of "ever closer union".

Like the EU itself, the accounts of the European Council have been problematic. Although it does not have to reveal details of its budget to the parliament, it has been accused by MEPs of having "black accounts" in its €594million budget, half of which pays its 3,200 staff. The European Council's attitude is that its expenditure is its own business and in 2009 it failed to attend a plenary hearing

---

[133] According to Mandelson's memoirs, Gordon Brown considered quitting as PM to become the first EU president. "If I stood, they would have me," he supposedly said

to discuss its 2007 accounts. It had earlier promised transparency. No EU body with any authority produces minutes or attendance records. At European Councils, however, unofficial notes are taken by the "Antici" (named after an Italian bureaucrat) of national delegations, but are never released.

The Lisbon Treaty made the European Council a formal EU institution, which means that it and its members – such as our prime minister – have to hold the "aims and objectives" of the EU above those of their own countries, as well as "advance the Union's objectives" and "refrain from any measure which could jeopardise the attainment of the Union's objectives" (similar to the oath made by EU judges and commissars, quoted earlier). It's as if you – as a shareholder – were expected at a company's AGM to promote not your own interests but those of the board. Your and their interests might well overlap often but they are not the same thing. Now, a British PM can never again argue for the UK's interests – be they a rebate on our subscription, vetoes in sensitive areas such as taxation and health, or independence of mind in matters of defence and foreign policy. He or she is beholden not to the electorate or Westminster but to the aims of the EU – national interest has been liquidated.

Herman Van Rompuy is a Belgian who's famous for not being famous, but he has the power to call extra European Councils, draw up the agenda of the meetings, decide whether to hold a vote, and whether European Councils should be attended by third countries.

If Van Rompuy is known for anything at all, it's his hobby of haiku writing, eg his "A fly zooms, buzzes; Spins and is lost in the room; He does no one harm" (not quite autobiographical, as will be seen in a moment). He has a caravan. During a recent Belgian election his sister Christine, who belongs to a rival political party, produced a poster of him as a clown. "We have not spoken since," she said. He has called for an EU tax, either in the form of green taxes or levies on financial transactions. His attitude to a Muslim member state can be gauged from his opinion that "The universal values which are in force in Europe, and which are fundamental values of Christianity, will lose vigour with the entry of a large Islamic country such as Turkey."

When he was speaker of the Belgian parliament he once changed the locks on the door of a room so that a vote could not be held on a bill that he had instigated when in opposition a few years earlier in order to cause trouble for the then government. As the Belgian journalist Paul Belien recounts in a devastating profile, "On another occasion, he did not show up in his office for a whole week to avoid opening a letter demanding him to table the [same] matter. His tactics worked."[134] The profile, written in sorrow and anger by a one-time acquaintance, ends: "Now, Herman has moved on to lead Europe. Like Belgium, the European Union is an undemocratic institution, which needs shrewd leaders who are capable of renouncing everything they once believed in and who know how to impose decisions on the people against the will of the people. Never mind democracy, morality or the rule of law, our betters know what is good for us more than we do. And Herman is now one of our betters. He has come a long way since the days when he was disgusted with Belgian-style politics. Herman is like Saruman, the wise wizard in Tolkien's *Lord of the Rings*, who went over to the other side. He used to care about the things we cared about. But no longer. He has built himself a high tower from where he rules over all of us."

Van Rompuy is paid around €320,000 a year, more than any other leader in the West and double what he was on as caretaker PM of Belgium (Obama earns $400,000 or €280,000 a year). He's taxed at just 25 per cent and has a staff of 22 press officers, assistants and administrators, in addition to 10 security agents. The cost of his salary, staff and expenses is €6million per annum.

On his first official tour, of European capitals, he told journalists in Berlin, one of whom had wondered if his appointment had been a disappointment for EU citizens: "No one need feel excited. It's possible that there will be more enthusiasm about me after two years." Or not.

---

[134] *Meet the President of Europe* by Paul Belien in *The Brussels Journal*, 20 November 2009

Sub institutions

The Committee Of The Regions (COR)

The COR comprises 220-plus local-government reps, from all of the "regions" of the 27 EU countries, who go on a jolly every other month. The UK has 12 "regions": eight in England (plus London) and one each for Wales, Scotland and Northern Ireland.

Devolution for the Celtic countries, whatever its merits or disadvantages, was knowingly doing Brussels' work for it, as was the creation of the Greater London Authority (and mayor) in 2000. Although the process was started by the Tories, who enacted the Maastricht Treaty wherein this order to fragment first appeared, the mastermind of the scheme in this country was John Prescott, in his job as Secretary Of State for the Environment, Transport and The Regions. (His time as an MEP in the 1970s, before that assembly was directly elected, may have made him loyal to the EU "project".)

The COR is the Brussels end of the direct line between its pots of cash and the "regions". National parliaments are deliberately bypassed – they're seen by the EU as nothing more than underemployed receptionists who get in the way of "ever closer union". The real sweet talk is between the COR and the artificial "region" in the member state, which is bribed with its own money. (See "Structural funds" in "Cash".)

From the wrong angle, devolution in the UK presents a paradox: how can making Scotland and Wales semi-autonomous, and thus quasi independent, help the EU reach its goal of "ever closer union"? Because the EU prefers to do anything that dilutes the nation state and causes the break-up of countries such as the UK. The EU can then deal with digestible, bite-size and dependent "regions".

When Peter Hain was minister for Europe he advised those calling for a referendum on the Constitution, which he had called a "tidying-up exercise", to put away their placards. He had previously been far less dismissive of eurosceptic concerns. In opposition he wrote, "Federalism also becomes a logical structure given the importance in the modern EU conception of the regions, as evidenced in the Committee Of The Regions established under Maastricht. The whole thrust of EU evolution focuses on both the centre [Brussels] and the region, with the national level receding in influence. Links between Brussels and, for example, Catalonia or Wales can override links with Madrid or London. The

EU's structural funds are geared towards re-distribution or compensation at the regional level."[135]

Larry Siedentop made the same point: "The lure of Brussels for resurgent regionalisms is that it provides a centre which can be played off against the traditional 'oppressors' – ie existing nation states. Thus, Scottish, Corsican and Catalonian nationalists see an unrivalled opportunity to weaken the states to which they are currently subordinated, by using Brussels as a fulcrum against London, Paris or Madrid... This pattern might be called the revenge of the regions."[136]

In its proposal "A modern regional policy for the United Kingdom" in 2003, the UK government argued that member states with GDP per capita above 90 per cent of the EU average should no longer receive structural funds. It was argued that instead of transferring money to Brussels and then transferring it back again (and incurring heavy administrative costs into the bargain), the more developed member states should simply spend the money themselves[137].

In an article in the *Times* in 2003 Gordon Brown, then chancellor, argued: "When the economic and social, as well as democratic, arguments on structural funds now and for the future so clearly favour subsidiarity [returning policy decisions back down to member states where practical, like America's 10th Amendment except that it's never observed] in action, there is no better place to start than by bringing regional policy back to Britain."[138] The structural funds are also hamstrung by restrictive rules about what they can be spent on. The same day, Brown told the BBC that "there are many things that we want to do to encourage local skills and research and development, and local businesses, but we're not able to do because of the existing rules".

A local referendum to try to legitimise the North East England Regional Assembly was rejected by 78 per cent of voters (despite – because of? – the support of Gazza and Sting), and assemblies were eventually put down in summer 2007 by the then new PM, Gordon Brown (although London's

---

[135] From *Ayes To The Left* (Lawrence & Wishart, 1995). The most quoted passage from the book is: "The policy, legally enshrined in the Maastricht Treaty, of a European [Central] Bank independent of democratic control and dedicated almost exclusively to price stability must be reversed. It is economically disastrous and politically dangerous."
However, on the BBC's *Newsnight* on 17 May 2002, he said he wanted to be remembered as "the man who took Britain into the euro because it was in the national interest". Not to join, he said, would be a "betrayal"
[136] *Democracy In Europe* (Penguin, 2001) by Larry Siedentop
[137] *Briefing note: European Communities (Finance) Bill*, www.openeurope.org.uk
[138] *The Times*, 6 March 2003

survived). However, the EU and EU-derived projects don't know the word "no" and so the compartmentalisation, designed to fragment member states and so promote solidarity with Brussels – to divide and rule – lived on via the "regional development agencies" (RDAs, which are even less accountable than the assemblies) and "government offices", which are on the domestic end of the cash line.

"Regions" *must* have offices in Brussels to receive cash, although, tellingly, none bothers to have one in the UK capital. In 2005, the North East "region" had, aside from its compulsory Belgian outpost, eight offices in Asia and the USA alone. Between 2001 and 2008, the nine English RDAs had spent £23.8million on their overseas offices, averaging £3.4million each. Advantage West Midlands had the highest overseas outlay of the nine agencies, having spent £4.2m on offices in the USA, Australia, India, Japan, the Benelux, France, Germany, Sweden and Singapore[139]. A business select committee of MPs described the network of overseas RDA offices as "bizarre" – there were, for example, five different UK regions competing in China – and said that the outposts were "diluting the UK brand". What the MPs failed to understand is that "diluting the UK brand" is the *entire point* of the "regions".

The RDAs have the power to recommend or reject planning applications, something that used to be the preserve of elected councils. "What are the running costs of the unelected senior executives in charge of England's nine Regional Development Agencies?" asked a Radio 4 programme[140]. It went on to tell listeners that one chairman, James Braithwaite of the South East England Development Agency (Seeda), spent more – £51,433.80 – on taxis in a year than all of Britain's MPs put together. And he's only part-time. A year later, it emerged that he had spent £148,000 on taxis in three years, despite working only three days a week. The same freedom of information request revealed that another Seeda official had been on a £7,972 round-the-world trip promoting Seeda by visiting Mumbai, Los Angeles and Singapore[141].

In 2006, Yorkshire Forward, the RDA for the white-rose county, spent £20,000 sending staff to a film festival in Dubai. Most notoriously, Steven Broomhead, chief executive of the North West Development Agency (NWDA), was reprimanded but not sacked for sending a racist joke by text. He enjoyed

---

139 *The Financial Times*, 12 August 2008
140 From information in the public domain but collected in *File On 4* on BBC Radio 4, first broadcast 4 March 2008, and presented by Allan Urry. As will be seen later, the BBC does not like to criticise the EU: not once in the 40-minute programme was the EU mentioned, although it is the only begetter of these atrociously wasteful agencies
141 *The Sunday Times*, 7 June 2009

chauffeur-driven trips to and from rugby cup finals, be they in Cardiff or Twickenham – not forgetting to drop off his friend as well – while his company car stood idle in his driveway. The cost to taxpayers each time was £395. It looks as if they were taken for a ride as well. It is quite proper that Mr Broomhead has a chauffeur: it would clearly be wrong to text jokes about members of the Commonwealth if one's hands were meant to be on the wheel of one's (company) car.

A complaint by a member of the public about Broomhead's excesses was referred, by Margaret Hodge, when she was minister for the regions, back to the NWDA, where it was filed at floor level. That's the beauty of being unaccountable. Not only are you unaccountable, you don't have to represent value for money – or even to represent smelly electors, for you are not elected.

The capital is effectively England's ninth (or first, if you prefer) "region". In other words, Ken Livingstone and Boris Johnson would never have had the opportunity to be mayor were it not for the Maastricht Treaty[142]. Although not ceremonial like the Lord Mayor Of London, the mayor has limited powers compared with, say, the New York Mayor. But Johnson, in his £137,000-a-year job, can pull the rug from under the Metropolitan Police commissioner, and veto major planning applications. He also appoints the head of Transport For London. He can ban booze on public transport, and amend or repeal the congestion charge.

The London Development Agency (LDA), the capital's RDA, is one of the Mayor's instruments. Mayor Johnson found that the LDA, though not found to be corrupt, had spent unaccounted tens of millions of taxpayers' money under his predecessor's reign.

The Taxpayers' Alliance (TPA) reported in 2008 that, since the RDAs' inception in 1999, the quangos had cost every family £600, despite overseeing a drop in growth. The seven English "regions" outside London and the South East (Yorkshire Forward and the rest) enjoyed an average of 40.6 per cent growth between 1992 and 1999. The post-RDA average growth, between 1999 and 2006, was just 36.5 per cent. Between 1995 and 2000 the number of jobs in the seven artificial segments grew by 9.5 per cent. Between 2000 and 2005 the figure was just 3 per cent. The TPA report also revealed that the top 39 earners

---

[142] Johnson, who grew up in Brussels while his father Stanley worked for the Commission and then served as an MEP, has identified the EU with the Roman Empire, noting that the current institution suffers in comparison to its antecedent because it lacks a figurehead, a homogeneous demos and a cohesive sporting spectacle such as the circus – hence, perhaps, the EU's attempts to hijack football and the Olympics

employed by RDAs all had six-figure salaries. The agencies had by then already cost the taxpayer £15.3billion since 1999. In 2006-07, according to the TPA report, the RDAs received £2.3billion from Westminster, £62million from the EU – which mandated them and insists on their continued existence, if a "region" wants to get this money – and they spent £2.6billion[143]. Two years later, the cash was still rolling in: in 2010 Seeda, for example, had a budget of £107million and 270 staff, while the East of England Develoment Agency bumped along on £103million with 228 staff.

The RDAs are funded by business taxes, which they have been known to pay to firms such as JP Morgan (which has received £500,000), while letting much of the rest go to other quangos, which might or might not have some cash left over to give to the vast majority of businesses that employ fewer than 50 people and need the most assistance.

For a long time the Tories pretended that they would liquidate RDAs if in office. When he was local-government spokesman, Eric Pickles, said, "RDAs are unaccountable and unelected and they will be abolished – there is no doubt about that."[144]

Knowing that RDAs were a requirement of the club that he thinks benefits Britain, Cameron in opposition was canny enough never to call for their abolition. But nor did he "slap down" Pickles. In February 2009, a Tory document hinted that the Tories might scrap them[145]. Publicising this document on 15 February 2009, in an interview with the BBC's John Sopel, Cameron said: "You'll see... huge proposals for decentralisation, sweeping away that regional layer, giving more power to local government, to drive it out to the lowest level, so they can help build those strong economies of the future." The same day he told the BBC's Paul Siegert: "We could save some money and give it back to people in tax reductions if we got rid of the regional assemblies and so much of the regional bureaucracy there is." Few people knew the difference between regional *assemblies* and regional *development agencies* so the promise sounded much less hollow than it was. Even fewer people knew that Brown had announced

143 *The case for abolishing regional development agencies* by the Taxpayers' Alliance, 8 August 2008, available from www.taxpayersalliance.com
144 *Public Servant*, April 2008
145 *Control shift: returning power to local communities*: "So we will also give elected local authorities the power to come together to establish new enterprise partnerships that truly reflect natural economic divisions, and to take over from their RDAs the responsibility for economic development within those areas" (p29) and "the Secretary of State will be required to satisfy himself that the areas covered by the new enterprise partnerships reflect natural economic patterns and have strong business leadership before he transfers to them the money currently spent by the RDAs" (p30)

seven months earlier that regional assemblies would be scrapped in 2010 anyway. But Cameron should have known.

A fortnight after Cameron had confirmed that he would not give the people a say on the Lisbon Treaty, the Tories unveiled their RDA policy (which was of course also an EU matter although it was thought impolite to alert people to this fact). By then, Pickles had swapped jobs with Caroline Spelman. She said, "RDAs will... evolve into Local Enterprise Partnerships – leaner, more focused and adding real value to their community clients." A change of name, no more and no less. The Tories could not admit that while the UK was in the EU they were powerless to kill the most expensive quangos of all. In office, the ConDems rebranded the RDAs as LEPs.

The COR must be consulted by the EU Commission and EU parliament, which are then at liberty to ignore it. Its budget for 2009 was £92.5million.

The European Economic and Social Committee (Ecosoc)
The other consultative body of the EU. This 344-strong ragbag of "civil society" comprises heads of consumer groups, union leaders and big-business suits etc.

Ecosoc must be consulted by the EU Commission and EU parliament, which are then at liberty to ignore it. Its budget for 2009 was £59million. It shares the Jacques Delors building in Brussels with the COR.

Lobbyists
Although not an EU institution in the literal sense, lobbyists are certainly an institution in Brussels. If an MEP feels peckish, he can just hail a passing lobbyist. Because the EU is vast and has awesome power, it attracts legions of lobbyists.

In the summer of 2007, Peter Mandelson was given an official rebuke after refusing to reveal details of meetings with industry lobbyists. The EU's watchdog issued the formal censure after a two-year investigation. The European Ombudsman[146], Nikiforos Diamandouros, a Greek who cannot bear grift, ruled that Mandelson's office had been "wrongly blanking out the names of industry lobbyists" in documents released to the public. It said that "disclosure of names

---

[146] TFEU 228: "A European Ombudsman, elected by the European parliament, shall be empowered to receive complaints from any citizen of the Union or any natural or legal person residing or having its registered office in a member state concerning instances of maladministration in the activities of the Union institutions, bodies, offices or agencies, with the exception of the Court of Justice of the European Union acting in its judicial role. He or she shall examine such complaints and report on them" (this promise is repeated in the Charter of Fundamental Rights, Article 43). He and his wise counsel are usually ignored by the EU elites

of individual lobbyists is essential". The failure to reveal this information "would constitute an instance of maladministration by the Commission", said the Greek official's report[147].

However, the Commission estimates that only 2,000 out of about 15,000 have signed up to any code of conduct or register of interests, and it has made any such code of practice voluntary. As the commissioner responsible for it, Siim Kallas, said: "Even with a mandatory registration, there is always the danger that somebody acts in the shadows. Look at the USA – the system is different, but even despite their very strong legislation, their scandals are not small ones."[148] Why have a law against murder? There are still murders in America.

In 2009, it was discovered that the Irish Cheerleading Federation had mistakenly signed up and an Italian businessman had been bombarding the registry with seemingly fake organisations. The Commission admitted that it didn't have the staff to investigate the veracity of every registrant's information[149].

On 16 July 2007 Kallas had launched the scheme, the European Transparency Initiative (ETI), in a speech to the committee on constitutional affairs in the Brussels parliament. He started off by saying that "You all know that much-quoted estimate that some 80 per cent of national laws originate at EU level [indeed we do]... if the estimate is even half right, the interests affected are quite substantial. Think for instance of environment legislation; the port and services directives; quotas in fisheries; tariffs in trade policies, the distribution of EU subsidies... All these files obviously mobilise interest representatives, or 'lobbyists'. Let me be very clear: it is good that we do not take decisions blindly. Indeed, the Commission explicitly recognises that lobbying is both necessary and legitimate."

He went on to reveal that "The NGOs [non-governmental organisations, often charities] have told us they will join the register as suggested... [So] the public will also be able to see what they receive and make up its own mind whether it is possible to receive public money without losing independence. Oxfam, for instance, have received €48million from the Commission over two years to carry out development and humanitarian projects throughout the world, while simultaneously expressing strong critical views on EU trade policy. Last year, Friends Of The Earth Europe received 50 per cent of their funding from the EU and EU national governments – a high proportion for a 'non-governmental

147 *The Sunday Times*, 29 July 2007
148 *An Insider in Brussels: Lobbyists Reshape the European Union*, first published in *VI* (www.vi-tidningen.se) and reprinted by www.corpwatch.org on 18 September 2006
149 *EU Observer*, 27 October 2009

organisation'[150]. Despite receiving €635,000 from the Commission, they were initially very highly critical of our car CO_2 emission proposals."

Without too much cynicism one can see that these lobbying charities are funded by the EU so that it can say that its legislation was demanded by "the people" – via NGOs – and that there is, therefore, a popular mandate for more such lawmaking, particularly in environmental areas, where it hopes to make the most political capital. You see, the whole set-up is democratic after all. It looks a lot like "he who pays the advisory piper calls the legislative tune" but in fact it's usually a case of the Commission finding a piper already playing a tune it wants to hear and then paying that piper to keep hammering the tune out.

To switch metaphors, the ventriloquist should not be surprised by what his puppet says to him. Some EU-funded PR firms even set up dummy "grassroots" action groups, a practice known as "astro-turfing". A familiar Brussels mantra is: "The European institutions pay lobbyists with the goal of being lobbied back by them."

The *Economist* noticed the problem: "Look at the websites of EU-funded NGOs and it becomes clear that one of their favoured activities is to lobby for even more EU money. Thus the European Network against Racism (80-90 per cent Commission-funded) complains truculently that 'the present budget line for anti-racist activities is… insufficient. The network… needs to put pressure on the European institutions with a view to increase this amount.' The spectacle of organisations that receive EU money using their money to campaign for more EU money is only one example of this looking-glass world. It is a world in which so-called NGOs are actually dependent on government for cash; and one in which the European Commission, itself directly financed by Europe's national governments, finances 'autonomous' organisations that campaign for more power and money to be handed to the Commission itself."[151]

Even the BBC eventually noticed. On 6 December 2007, its website reported: "Siim Kallas, [who's] in charge of the EU's anti-fraud operations, said he had been assured this funding [of environmental groups] was not taking place. He said: 'The European Commission is not financing anybody to lobby ourselves – nobody is supported just for being there.' But the EC Environment Directorate has said it does give money to environmental groups to lobby. It says this is an attempt to put such groups on an equal footing with corporate lobbyists in Brussels, although it has admitted this is 'a bit schizophrenic'."

---

[150] Since at least April 2007, Friends Of The Earth Europe's website has stated "Friends of the Earth Europe gratefully acknowledges funding from: EU DG Environment, EU DG Employment & Social Affairs, EU DG Development"
[151] *A rigged dialogue with society* in The Economist, 22 October 2004

Conversely, big business can emasculate legislation at will, using the services of erstwhile Eurocrats, many of whom merely lift the phone and speak to former colleagues who signed their leaving cards with a kiss just a few months earlier. That this happens in other places – although not in the USA – does not excuse it in Brussels.

Günter Verheugen, who could sometimes be mistaken for a eurosceptic in europhile clothing, said when he was a commissar: "What really shocked me was that during the [lawmaking] process I have found many cases [in which] European legislation is triggered by interest groups. It's simply the result of pressure from one interest group that is presented as something that is important for the public but it is not. In reality, it is in the interest of one particular group or even one particular company... I think we should also do more to create transparency at the beginning of the process... I would like to know – if there is a new proposal on the table coming from my colleagues – who has asked for it. Start your document with a paragraph saying who has asked for that piece of legislation."[152]

Prof Verheugen would later get into trouble, as we know, for leaving an EU institution and walking into a corporate job without telling Mr Barroso. However, there is no suggestion that the German has ever acted improperly (except forgetting to tell Barroso about the addition to his CV) or even contacted any EU institution after he left. Nor is there any suggestion that his former colleagues Benita Ferrero-Rocher, Meglena Kuneva or Charlie McCreevy, who all also took jobs in the private sector, have broken Commission or other rules.

Those four have done nothing wrong but others have taken advantage of revolving-door recruitment – employing people from EU institutions to lobby former colleagues. There's a chance that some commissars while in office take care not to endanger the activities of the firm that has lined them up. Such appointments are overseen by the Commission's ethics committee. *EU Observer* profiled it: "The committee is headed by Michel Petite, who performs the job part-time while working for law firm Clifford Chance. He was criticised in 2008 by lobby watchdogs when he moved to the firm to work on anti-trust issues after leaving his job as head of the Commission's Legal Service, where he was responsible for investigating anti-trust charges against Microsoft. Its second member comes from the ECJ, while its third member is Terry Wynn, a British Labour MEP. While an MEP, he chaired the Forum for the Future of Nuclear Energy and was a board member of the European Energy Forum, two cross-party groups that have been criticised as fronts for industry lobbying."[153]

---

[152] Press conference at European Institute of Public Administration. Reported by openeurope.blogspot.com on 15 September 2008
[153] *EU Observer*, 5 May 2010

Kallas's register was eventually produced in June 2008. The rule that lobbyists should expose their books to public scrutiny looks hypocritical given that MEPs, who are paid by the public rather than mega-corporations, voted not to put their receipts in the public domain. (You would also be hard pressed to get minutes of European Council, Council Of Ministers or Commission meetings. Not all parliamentary votes are electronic, either.) At its launch, most criticised the registration system as worse than useless. "Having the choice of registering or not is actually an advantage for lobbyists," said Erik Wesselius of Corporate Europe Observatory, a watchdog. "A company can hire a lobbying firm that is signed up to the register when they are doing 'clean' lobbying that no one would worry about, and hire an unregistered lobbying firm when engaged in more sensitive, 'dirty' lobbying." [154]

Kallas said, "A voluntary solution suits all expectations in the best way. Before we had nothing. This is much more than a self-regulating system." When he launched the ETI in 2005, he had said, "People [should be] allowed to know who [lobbyists] are, what they do and what they stand for," and he had publicly criticised voluntary registries. Those who do opt in to the register are required to list their areas of interest and their clients, but not whom they employ, the actual hucksters. Money spent on campaigns must be disclosed, to the nearest €50,000.

The EU's true relationship with lobbyists was revealed by a leaked 15-page handbook, circulated internally in January 2009 and designed to help staff in the Trade directorate stymie Freedom Of Information requests. *EU Observer* reported on it on 9 April 2009: "[The handbook] reminds DG trade employees that all documents, including emails, are 'in principle subject to disclosure'... 'Each official must be aware that all his/her documents, including meeting reports and emails can potentially be disclosed. You should keep this in mind when writing such documents. This is particularly the case for meeting reports and emails with third parties (eg industry), which are favourite 'targets' of requests for access to documents,' reads the handbook. It asks officials to draft documents 'with the utmost care' while telling them to avoid making references to informal contacts, such as meals or drinks, with lobbyists. 'Don't refer to the great lunch you have had with an industry representative privately or add a PS asking if he/she would like to meet for a drink.' The document also tips off officials on how to narrow down the interpretation of a request for information. It points to a past example where a request referred to DG trade meetings with individual companies, meaning the department could avoid making public its contacts with business lobbyists. As a way of avoiding officials having to blank out parts of documents they release, the guide suggests writing two accounts of meetings, a 'factual' or neutral one that can be released to the public and a more 'personal/subjective'

---

[154] *EU Observer*, 23 June 2008

one with assessments and recommendations for follow-up that need not be disclosed... For its part, the Commission defended the memo. A spokesperson told *EU Observer*: 'Actually we think these are good instructions. It makes clear that no category of documents is excluded [from the FoI regulation].'"

Remember the FSA's problems with banning certain additives? On 21 May 2008, a Swedish newspaper reported that the Commission had paid €13.2million to a lobby group to review the EU's official guidelines on food and nutrition. The group was Eurreca, an extension of the International Life Sciences Institute (ILSI), which is run and funded by the likes of Coca-Cola, McDonald's, Heinz, Kraft, and Procter & Gamble. The article noted that "the ILSI is a controversial organisation... in 2002 it questioned the recommendation to limit the consumption of sugar to less than 10 per cent. The group argued that it wasn't proven that the measure, which was a threat to the soft-drink industry, would help fight obesity."[155] The Brussels Sprouts column in *Private Eye* was also wary: "Many of these companies manage to participate twice in the project through another front organisation, the European Food Information Council, the membership of which largely reproduces ILSI's. Why deep-pocketed food multinationals should be paid from the public purse to develop nutrition recommendations is unclear, but one thing is for sure: ILSI has form. The BBC's *Panorama* investigated it in 2004 for secretly funding a UN study on the role of sugar and carbohydrates in nutrition. We await Eurreca's no-doubt scientifically rigorous and entirely unbiased conclusions in due course."

In short:

European Council: the leaders of the 27 countries meet for a photo op and act as a steering group for:
The European Commission: a law unto itself, it is the executive that makes the laws. It draws its power from:
The Council Of Ministers: "the Council" gives powers to the Commission and comprises the ministerial counterparts of the 27 governments relevant to the matter being discussed (eg fisheries, finance)
The European Parliament: a fig leaf for a one-party state; very little ability to block or amend laws, still less to initiate or repeal them; not unlike the audience in *Who Wants To Be A Millionaire?*
European Court Of Justice: this and 26 other countries' supreme court which upholds and adds to EU law (the "acquis"); it finds for the EU with admirable constancy
Court Of Auditors: independent-minded number crunchers whose valid criticisms are ignored

---

155 *Svenska Dagbladet*, 21 May 2008

The Lisbon Treaty also made the European Central Bank an EU institution.

Lord (Malcolm) Pearson describes it thus: "The unelected Commission enjoys the monopoly to propose all EU law in secret. Their proposals are then negotiated, again in secret, by bureaucrats from nation states, in the Committee of Permanent Representatives [Coreper]. When the horse-trading is complete, the proposed laws go to the Council of Ministers for decision, still in secret, where the UK has 8 per cent of the vote. The EU parliament cannot propose legislation, but can amend and even block some of it. It doesn't do so, of course, because it is loath to delay or derail the gravy train. British governments have promised for many years that they won't agree to any new law in the Council which is still being 'scrutinised' (that's all we can do) in the select committee of either House of Parliament. But they have broken that promise 435 times in the last six years. Our parliament is powerless to change any of the laws, which are then enforced by the Commission and the Luxembourg Court, against which there is no appeal. And they call this 'the democratic deficit'."[156]

---

[156] Letter, *The Daily Telegraph*, 19 September 2009

CHAPTER 3: THE CASH

Our annual subscription

The UK hands over about £192million per week (net after rebate) for EU membership, which is £20,000 a minute. Put another way, that's enough to reduce income tax by 3p or raise the income-tax threshold by £2,000 or halve the council tax on every UK property[157]. Or simply reduce the fiscal deficit. But, don't forget, for that money we get about 60 laws a week, some "oven ready" but some needing additional drafting, delivered from the Kingdom of Belgium.

The annual figures for the current seven-year "budget round" are[158]:

Gross payment, £billion		Rebate	Net payment
2007	14.2	3.9	**10.3**
2008	14.6	4.6-4.7	**9.9-10**
2009	13.7	4.8-4.9	**8.8-8.9**
2010	14.4	3.8-3.9	**10.5-10.6**
2011	14.1-14.5	3.5-4.1	**10-11**
2012	14.1-14.5	3.5-4.1	**10-11**
2013	14.1-14.5	3.5-4.1	**10-11**

These UK Treasury figures were released when the pound bought €1.40 and since its depreciation our contributions have risen (although so have our rebates). The actual sum for the year is decided by the preceding December's exchange rate. In January 2009, when the pound and euro were flirting with parity, our contributions rose greatly to reflect sterling's drop from €1.40 to €1 (or the euro's rise from 71p to £1). So, at a time when the country was at its sickest, it had to find more cash for Brussels. What cost us 71p in times of plenty costs us £1 in times of dearth.

The total EU budget for 2010 is €141,453,000,000 (€141.453billion or about £126,297,321,000). In the words of the travel guide, that's "Europe on €387million a day". The spending amounts to €122.937billion (up six per cent on 2009). Of this, €58billion is spent on agriculture and the environment and €36billion on "social funds" (the "regions"). The difference between the total

---

[157] *Briefing note: European Communities (Finance) Bill*, www.openeurope.org.uk
[158] *Hansard* (Lords), 4 June 2007, column WA154. Generally, member states must pay 1 per cent of VAT revenue, 75 per cent of customs receipts, and some part of their GDP.
Funding is explained in more detail in *How Much Does The European Union Cost Britain? (2008)* by Gerard Batten MEP, available from www.brugesgroup.com

"commitments" of €141billion and the "payments" of €122billion is €18,156,000,000 or about £17billion, some of which is accounted for in "Perquisites". The remainder oils the machine: in 2011, the administrative costs for all EU institutions will climb 4.4 per cent, to €8.3billion.

The UK's rebate was won by Margaret Thatcher at a European Council in Fontainebleu in 1984 with the words "We want our money back". She got some of it, too, until December 2005 when Tony Blair capitulated at a European Council in London of all places and our rebate for the budget round of 2007-2013 was greatly reduced. Figures calculated by House Of Commons researchers suggest that the surrender cost the UK £9.3billion between 2007 and 2013 alone, which is equivalent to £344 per family, whether they are the politicians' favourite "hard-working" variety or those from the layabout community.

Despite this, the UK's net contribution since joining in 1973, *unadjusted for inflation*, is over £180billion. The net contribution since 1973 in real terms is a matter of debate. But you wouldn't be far wrong if you multiplied last year's contribution by the length of membership, ie about £360billion. Then add in the lost fish. The compliance costs. Et cetera, et cetera.

The fact that we then receive some of this back via, for instance, Single Farm Payments (see "CAP" in "Neighbourhood") and occasional municipal projects does not make our outlay any smaller. But it suits EU apologists to pretend it does. Do those apologists think that their income tax bills are smaller just because the UK government "gives back" their money in the form of "five-a-day co-ordinators" and "smoking-cessation officers"? If one pays £10,000 a year in income tax, that figure does not get any smaller when one sees a piece of abstract art worth £35,000 in a hospital foyer.

During the 2007-13 period, Britain will receive €770 per person from the EU (the lowest of any of the 27 members), less than half as much as France (€1,480) and less than a quarter of Ireland's €3,090. France is the largest recipient of EU funds of any member state in absolute terms because it has so much farmland. She will receive €89billion over the period, compared to €46billion for the UK, although we pay 20 per cent more into the coffers[159].

In 2007 alone, the UK received £3.7billion back in CAP and CFP payments (ie out of the £10.3billion net that we handed over) compared with £6.1billion given to Germany, £6.1billion to Spain and £5.2billion to Italy. The biggest winner was France, which received £9.1billion. As for the "structural and

---

[159] *Briefing note: European Communities (Finance) Bill*, www.openeurope.org.uk

cohesion" funds, for boosting "regional competitiveness", Britain's £2.1billion handout was way behind Spain's (£4.75billion), Italy's (£3.96billion) and even rich Germany's (£3.8billion)[160].

Commissioner Verheugen said in 2006 that EU legislation costs European businesses €600billion a year[161], on the basis of a new evaluation methodology of the administrative costs of red tape (compliance costs are a job for another few rainy days). The Commission's estimate of the *benefit* of the single market is around €160billion (a 2002 figure that may since have gone up with inflation but may also have been pegged back by the recession).

The Taxpayers' Alliance noted: "Eurostat figures show that GDP for the 25 EU countries in 2006 is just over €11trillion, so the cost of EU regulation is around 5.5 per cent of EU GDP. Eurostat figures also show that there are 367million people aged 18 or over in the 25 EU countries. This means that the cost of EU regulation is €1,634 per adult in the EU."

Every year the British Chambers of Commerce (BCC) produces a "Burdens Barometer". In May 2008 it concluded that the cumulative cost to business of new regulation in the previous 10 years was £66billion, an increase of more than £10billion since 2007. The BCC estimated that over 70 per cent (at least £46.2billion) of this had been dreamt up in Belgium. By 2010, the total cost of all regulations introduced since 1998 would be £88.3billion.

In 2005 we exported £166billion worth of goods and services to the EU, about 13 per cent of our total GDP (this proportion is shrinking fairly quickly as our exports go more and more to Asia and elsewhere outside the EU). Unfortunately, EU rules and regulations apply to 100 per cent of our GDP, whether it stays at home, goes to Brazil or wherever, not just that 13 per cent. In the same year, we imported £204billion of goods and services from the EU, making a deficit of £38billion. In 2007, the deficit had crept up to £40billion, almost half of which was with Germany. Does the EU need us or do we need it? Whose jobs depend on our membership if we're running a trade deficit? Ours or AN Other's?

Why are Norway and Switzerland so rich despite not being EU members? They pay only a small fee to trade with the EU, comparable to a tariff[162]. It's also true that they have to abide by a small fraction of the acquis communautaire. But McDonald's, as viewers of *Pulp Fiction* are reminded in the "Royale With Cheese" scene, forgoes imperial nomenclature such as "quarter-pounder" in

---

[160] *The Sunday Telegraph*, 13 September 2009
[161] *Financial Times*, 10 October 2006
[162] See page 298 for more on their deal with the EU

most of the "non-imperial empire" (© Jose Manuel Barroso 2007). But America and her companies are not hampered by Work At Height Directives (how to climb a ladder) or other irrelevant nonsense – they just drop the name "quarter-pounder" in the EU but keep it at home. All countries have to make allowances when trading, as British car manufacturers understand when exporting to places that drive on the other side of the road.

Because the EU is a customs union, imports from third countries cost us far more than they would otherwise. The knock-on effect for the consumer is immense. Estimates and criteria vary. In 1998, the CAP cost British consumers £6.7billion and taxpayers spent a further £3.4billion to fund the scheme, the total being equivalent to £250 per year for every man, woman and child, according to Elliott Morley, speaking in 1999, when he was Labour's agriculture minister. Open Europe has suggested that the EU's combination of farm subsidies and trade taxes costs the average family of four £1,500 a year[163].

Even the Treasury thinks the CAP is a rip-off. When Brown was still there it produced a report, in December 2005, called *A Vision for the Common Agricultural Policy*. The report stated that "economic analysis, even on conservative assumptions, suggests the CAP will leave the EU economy around €100billion poorer over the period 2007-13" and "the financial cost to ordinary citizens is much greater – €100billion each year according to OECD estimates... This is an average cost to an EU family of four of... €950 a year", a figure that "has been estimated to be equivalent to a value added tax on food of around 15 per cent"[164].

Surely the Commission itself is a fan? You'd think so but Dalia Grybauskaité (former budget commissar) has said, "In reality our CAP today is a more protectionist policy than a market-oriented policy and, because of this, we pay, all of us, all consumers, two to three times more for food than we would pay without this policy."[165] The Treaties say: "The objective of the Common Agricultural Policy shall be to ensure that supplies reach consumers at reasonable prices"[166].

In 2006, Oxfam estimated that British households pay an extra £832 a year in grocery bills because of the huge EU subsidy system, which also deprives tens of

---

[163] *Open Up: Why The EU Must Reform To Survive*, October 2005, available from www.openeurope.org.uk
[164] Quoted by Christopher Chope in *Hansard (Commons)*, column 1201, 20 June 2008
[165] *Commissioner slates EU budget efficiency of CAP* in *The Irish Times*, 13 November 2008
[166] TFEU 39(1)(e)

thousands of African farmers of their livelihoods. Everyday goods such as bread, milk, sugar and chicken are all more expensive because of the payments made to British and European farmers. At the same time, dumping of subsidised produce in African countries forces local producers out of business. Claire Godfrey, the charity's trade-policy adviser, said: "Not only does the CAP hit European shoppers in their pockets but it strikes a blow against the heart of development in places like Africa. The CAP lavishes subsidies on the UK's wealthiest farmers and biggest landowners at the expense of millions of poorest farmers in the developing world"[167].

In a letter, dated 13 May 2008, to the finance minister of Slovenia (which held the rotating EU presidency) ahead of an Ecofin meeting, then chancellor Alistair Darling wrote, "The EU has a clear responsibility to play a full role in the international community's collective efforts to address the consequences of spiralling food prices by tackling the causes, but it also has responsibility to its own citizens to ensure that its own policies do not unnecessarily inflate the cost of food within the EU. It is therefore unacceptable that, at a time of significant food price inflation, the EU continues to apply very high import tariffs to many agricultural commodities. The Commission should give urgent consideration to extending the [December 2007] suspension of import tariffs on [most] grains, and to reducing or suspending the import tariffs that apply to other agricultural commodities." Darling also called for a "phasing out of all elements of the Common Agricultural Policy that are designed to keep EU agricultural prices above world market levels – such measures cost EU consumers €43billion in 2006".

The chancellor was admitting that the UK had no control over how much its own citizens pay for food staples. We consumers (and those in Africa and elsewhere) are in a headlock. What's more, our elected politicians can do nothing about it except write letters to Slovenia that are leaked but otherwise ignored. The CAP has its own section later, in "The neighbourhood".

Slapping 16.5 per cent on children's shoes from China is another cost of the customs union. The EU taxes clothing and food imports most heavily despite the fact that the two consume a huge part of the income of the EU's poorest people. In an article for the *Financial Times*, Open Europe's chairman, Lord (Rodney) Leach, wrote, "If Europe's trade barriers were brought down, the poorest tenth of people in Britain would see their disposable income rise proportionately six times more than the richest tenth."[168] Likewise, the poorest fifth of Britons spend 16 per cent of their income on food while the top fifth spend less than half that.

---

[167] *The Independent*, 16 May 2006
[168] *The Financial Times*, 19 October 2005

Is this one of the implied benefits that we supposedly receive when we act as part of a huge bloc and have a single voice at World Trade Organisation meetings? Or are we in fact ripping off our own consumers with regressive tariffs – while also denying access to farmers from the developing world? Where is the added value for us or the rest of the world?

Before Halloween in 2008, Sainsbury's wrote on its website, "We have been struggling to fit a square peg in a round hole for too long now when it comes to conforming to the more controversial elements of EU regulations. We're not allowed to use up to 20 per cent of what's produced in this country and in the current crunch climate, we cannot continue to waste this much food before it even leaves the farms. Buying wonky veg would have saved cash-strapped Britons up to 40 per cent on some items such as carrots. It not only saves money, it also reduces waste and supports our British farmers." It had been spurred on to strike a eurosceptic pose when it discovered that a plan to sell "zombie brains" cauliflowers, "witches' fingers" carrots and "ogres' toenails" cucumbers, as alternatives to sweets and chocolate at Halloween, would have resulted in individual employees, rather than the FTSE giant itself, being prosecuted under EU regulations[169].

Fearing bad PR in a time of cost cutting, the EU moved "quickly". However, as is the nature of being governed remotely, the relaxed rules would not come into effect until July 2009, quite some time after Halloween. Besides, although it let 26 types[170] of fruit and veg to be sold as they were born, the EU continued to control other types – including apples, all citrus fruits, kiwi fruit, lettuce, peaches and nectarines, pears, strawberries, sweet peppers, table grapes and tomatoes – which account for three quarters of the market. But, bananas and cucumbers were set free to be imperfect again.

Dr Helen Szamuely wrote at the time of the amnesty for strange fruit:

"In July 2005 I wrote about the Fragrant Commissar, Margot Wallström, going on her fact-finding missions and also explaining the need for yet another rapid-rebuttal unit. The Commission simply had to deal with all these nasty rumours the evil eurosceptics were spreading:

'Among the measures are plain-language summaries of the benefits of European policies and a rapid rebuttal unit to counter false claims. This team would be able to fend off outlandish stories about the

---

[169] *EU zombies react to credit crunch*, openeuropeblog.blogspot.com, 3 November 2008

[170] Apricots, artichokes, asparagus, aubergines, avocados, beans, Brussels sprouts, carrots, cauliflowers, cherries, courgettes, cucumbers, cultivated mushrooms, garlic, hazelnuts in shell, headed cabbage, leeks, melons, onions, peas, plums, ribbed celery, spinach, walnuts in shell, watermelons, and witloof/chicory

effects of Brussels regulations, which have famously included claims that smoky bacon crisps faced a ban, or cucumbers had to be straight.'

"At the time I pointed out that before they started rebutting, the team might like to have a look at Commission Regulation (EEC) 1677/1988, which lays down quality standards for cucumbers, mentioning among other multitudinous matters:

"Cucumbers are classed into the four classes defined below:
(i) 'Extra' class
Cucumbers in this class must be of superior quality. They must have all the characteristics of the variety.
They must:
– be well developed
– be well shaped and practically straight (maximum height of the arc: 1cm per 10cm of length of the cucumber)
– have a typical colouring for the variety
– be free of defects, including all deformations and particularly those caused by seed formation.

"Not a straight cucumber directive then but a regulation, which is directly applicable to member states without the least necessity to go through the legislature."[171]

The last line of Roger McGough's poem *The Icing-Bus* is: "You can't taste shapes." Perhaps not but you can sure have fun making laws about them. When the latest EU pesticide directive lays waste crop after crop, consumers will be grateful for any shape of fruit or vegetable that has made it to their plate without being nibbled.

There are some surprising indirect membership costs for the UK, too. Remember the euro? Blair was convinced we'd all love the new "notes 'n' coins" when they were introduced into the eurozone in 2002. Eighteen months later, his chancellor, the Clunking Fist, decided he'd rather keep a fistful of sterling and ruled out UK membership. However, *The Bumper Book Of Government Waste (2006)* noted: "By the end of March 2004, the total spend on public-sector euro preparations had run to £43million. Of this, £20million had been forked out by the Inland Revenue, £8.8million by HM Customs & Excise, and £9.7million by the Department for Work and Pensions." It wasn't until 2010 that preparations were wound down.

There are too many indirect costs to list. Some of the more absurd include the fact that over 60,000 British ex-pats must receive winter-fuel-allowance payments despite living in far warmer countries such as Italy and Greece. Under EU law, anyone who was eligible for the payment when they left the UK is still

---

[171] *As problems go*, brugesgroup.blogspot.com, 13 November 2008

entitled to claim it while living inside the European Economic Area (the EU plus Liechtenstein, Iceland and Norway).

Rather more alarmingly, "When Alan Johnson, as pensions minister, looked into a New Zealand-style citizens' pension – whereby everyone over a certain age gets a fixed, low allowance, thus incentivising private provision and eliminating the means test – he was told that all EU nationals would be entitled to claim it, regardless of whether they had worked in the UK."[172] In 2010, the ECJ ruled that the UK government could not block benefits payments to the families of those suspected of terrorism. One can argue whether this is right or wrong but the law underpinning the decision is now beyond the reach of our parliament.

If someone needs to ask how much the EU costs, they probably can't afford it. Who can?

---

[172] Daniel Hannan's *Ici Londres* column, www.thefirstpost.co.uk, 10 November 2006

Value Added Tax (VAT)

On 25 March 2007, accompanied by many fireworks – not the only time in its history that money has gone up in smoke – the European Union turned 50. To put it another way, which would appeal to the project's vanity, reflect its often unorthodox accounting systems, as well as recognise its most famous revenue stream, it turned 42.55 (plus VAT)[173].

Income tax was first foisted on the UK in 1799, to pay for the war with France. PAYE, its grasping child, first dipped its hand into our pockets 145 years later, in 1944, to pay for the war with Germany. VAT, the only everyday tax introduced when we were not at war, was first levied in the UK in 1973 as a condition of our joining the EEC. And, not without irony, it helps to finance an organisation formed to keep the peace between France and Germany.

The member states are currently subject to the Sixth VAT directive (dating from 1977 but revised by directive 2006/112), which states that VAT rates throughout the EU must be between 15 per cent and 25 per cent. The UK's rate has reduced only once – from 17.5 to 15 per cent, for 13 months from 1 December 2008. Otherwise, it has only risen. Thatcher had raised it early in her reign to 15, in order to comply with the minimum specified in the directive, and John Major raised it in 1991 to 17.5 per cent. George Osborne raised it to 20 per cent in his first budget.

On certain goods, the rate can be reduced to 5 per cent. This group, which is dictated by the Commission and the Council Of Ministers (*not* by our own chancellor of the exchequer or parliament), includes several far from luxurious toiletries, such as prophylactics and women's sanitary products. Why they should be taxed at all is a question for Commissioner Šemeta and his colleagues. The UK has been granted some VAT exemptions – known as "zero-rated" goods – on quite a few famous "luxuries", including children's clothes, tickets on public transport, food (though not on processed foods such as crisps, or meals eaten in restaurants and sandwich shops etc), prescription charges, newspapers and books. These are all red rags to the bull of "harmonisation"[174].

When a High Court judge rules that Jaffa Cakes are cakes, not chocolate-covered biscuits, and so should not attract VAT – or when an Appeal Court judge finds for HMRC and declares that Pringles (42 per cent potato) are crisps and so should attract VAT – it makes for a jolly story in the papers. What's less jolly is that the decision to tax – or not – these items, and many, many others,

---

[173] At the UK's then rate of 17.5 per cent
[174] It has never been satisfactorily explained how the third word in the European Union's (unofficial but widely disseminated) motto – "Unity In Diversity" – squares with harmonisation

was *never* ours to make, a point almost always missed in the reporting: His or Her Honour is interpreting EU not UK law. VAT is explicitly an EU tax, one of thousands of conditions of our membership. But, like the forgotten injury behind the scar on a loved one's face, people no longer think of its cause – or even notice it much (except the people and businesses who have to levy it, acting as unpaid but highly scrutinised tax collectors).

The Commission's refusal to modify VAT rules has meant that the magic roundabout of "carousel" fraud (or "missing trader intra-community" fraud) persists. This scam involves the import of (usually) small, high-value goods such as computer chips and mobile phones. Under EU rules, a company importing the goods does not have to pay VAT. Instead, the tax is charged to the company that finally sells the goods to the consumer. So, the (crooked) importer sells the goods (plus VAT) to an unsuspecting firm and then disappears without paying HMRC the VAT liability. The more brazen scammers sell the items, reclaim the VAT from HMRC, then re-import the same items without VAT, over and over again: this is the carousel[175]. When a simple way of eliminating the carousel was suggested – refund suppliers only at the point of sale, ie not to any middlemen – the EU declined it. According to the BBC, the con has cost the UK Treasury £8billion per annum recently, making us the biggest victims in the EU[176]. The Treasury itself estimates that it lost £7billion of VAT in 2005-06 and £14.5billion between 2005 and 2008[177].

---

[175] Keen students of EU scams might be reminded of the enterprising farmers who herd the same livestock across the same borders over and over again for multiple export restitutions, or of the ship owners who unload a boat one end and stock it again with the same goods at the other, for the same reason
[176] BBC news online, 22 September 2006,
news.bbc.co.uk/1/hi/business/5369776.stm
[177] *Measuring Indirect Tax Gaps*, HMRC Report, November 2008, page 6, quoted in *The EU's Credibility Crunch* by Damon Lambert, December 2008, available from www.brugesgroup.com

Structural and cohesion funds

The biggest share of the budget (about 35 per cent) after the Common Agricultural Policy are structural funds or "Brussels money", the apogee of pork-barrel politics, which are administered by the Committee Of The Regions.

In doling out funds, the EU is often guided by where wealth is produced rather than where it's consumed, and is further confused by the varying size of the "regions". This leads to all sorts of anomalies, such as Lunenburg, a rich part of Germany, receiving a mammoth €900million in the 2007-2013 budget. As a dormitory town, its income looks low because its commuters are trousering their colossal wages in Hamburg banks. A Commission spokesperson argued that whatever method is used there will always be "grey areas".

The pro-EU *Economist* saw another reason for giving to the rich: "Euro-officials talk of the need visibly to spread largesse to every corner of the EU. People in rich regions must also see the fruits of cohesion spending, the argument goes, or they may resent sending money to poorer neighbours and come to see the EU as nothing but a machine for emitting annoying rules and regulations. Danuta Hübner, [then] EU commissioner for regional policy, says her funds shored up a sense of European 'solidarity' across the EU. 'Frankly speaking, this is a policy that is sometimes the only proof that Brussels exists, if you go to the regions that are quite far from national capitals.'"[178] Indeed so: Guadeloupe, a French department, is in the Caribbean, which is really quite a long way from Paris. Nevertheless, the group of islands has received almost £20million in regional funds to renovate its swimming pools. Hübner said that the "investment" there was intended to help to "develop a charming hotel industry" and to promote Guadeloupe's "potential and culture".

In December 2007, Open Europe published a report about the Structural and Cohesion Funds (SCF)[179]. The SCF are worth £7.2billion to the UK during the current budget round (2007-2013) and the report argued that as little as 10 per cent of the funds would be spent in the poorest 20 per cent of the country. It also found that the bureaucratic way in which the funds are administered leads to huge administrative costs – simply running the funds costs the UK £670million a year. Because of EU rules that say that regional authorities must spend money or lose it, the focus is on "getting the money out of the door"[180]. This and other

---

[178] Charlemagne column, *The Economist*, 26 July 2007. It concludes: "Bribery of the rich is wrong – and no number of smart EU billboards advertising such bribery can change that"
[179] *Why the EU should not run regional policy*, www.openeurope.org.uk
[180] This is the EU's "N+2" rule (funds must be spent within two years or the money will be cancelled), which makes for hurried rather than considered spending in the "regions"

factors lead to the commissioning of wasteful projects that do not boost growth or employment, including roving "city clowns" in Finland, conceptual projects to turn Barnsley into a 'Tuscan hill village' (and create a giant lake in Bradford city centre), and a mobile burger van intended to lecture building-site workers on sustainable development. While the UK and other member states have argued for control of such spending to be returned to the national level – as mentioned, even Gordon Brown understood this, back in 2003 – this was rejected by other member states.

The free school dinners of the EU are:

The European Social Fund (for the unemployed and the young)
See "Propaganda" for the EU's actual attitude to minors and for more on all of these funds. In July 2008, the EU Ombudsman found that the Commission was late in paying 22 per cent of its 2007 Social Fund commitments, the average delay being 48 days. In 2007, according to the Commission, "irregularities" in the Social and Cohesion Funds were up almost 20 per cent on 2006, to 3,832 cases.

The European Regional Development Fund
The original fund, it was instigated by us in 1975 when we realised we were soon to be robbed of our fish. The ERDF gives money to areas hit by industrial decline. As such it's an occasional opportunity to get a few pence in the pound back from the morass, but usually it's a subsidy for our economic rivals. Above all, a costly and bureaucratic way of robbing Peter to pay Paolo. Of the 44 regions granted Objective One status – the neediest group – in 1989, 43 were still eligible for funding 14 years later. (It's rumoured that one country keeps its GDP under the 75 per cent average of the EU so as to remain eligible for this fund.) In 2010, the UK was fined £150million for not displaying the EU flag prominently enough – for instance on a permanent plaque and on letterheads – during the previous seven-year budget round. Offending recipients, including the Eden Project in Cornwall and the King's Dock in Liverpool, had received money from the European Regional Development Fund but had not credited the wasteful middleman sufficiently gratefully.

The European Agriculture Guidance And Guarantee Fund
This one's concerned with the Common Agricultural Policy.

The Fisheries Guidance Instrument
This one's concerned with the Common Fisheries Policy.

The Cohesion Fund
This is another child of the Maastricht Treaty and was designed for the then

"Poor Four" of Spain, Portugal, Ireland and Greece (which had threatened to veto the Iberians' 1986 accession if its own handouts were reduced). However, the 12 most recent accessionists are giving these countries a run for the EU's money.

The Cohesion Fund ostensibly doles out money for infrastructure so that a single currency might work in a hopelessly lopsided collection of countries. The EU sign by the road will tell you that the flyover or whatever is a recipient of EU cash. Since we are a net contributor, it's not EU cash, it's our cash. And if we hadn't had to give the money to the wasteful and corrupt EU in the first place, the flyover would have cost you and me less, with money to spare to reduce the deficit.

Perquisites and emoluments
I don't mind if I do...

The problem for MEPs is that 90 per cent of them give the rest a bad name. Until the 2009 Euro elections, the headline salary for an MEP used to be the same as that of a domestic MP: about £64,000 in the UK, only about £11,000 for Lithuanian MEPs and as much as £110,000 for Italians. Since the 2009 elections MEPs can opt instead to be paid €91,980 (worked out as 38.5 per cent of an ECJ judge's salary) by the parliament itself (but don't forget who gave it to the parliament), and be taxed at the Belgian rate of around 20 per cent. Any MEPs who were doing better before could opt to stay on their old rate.

The exchange rate at the time of the 2009 election was £1=€1.11, which meant that the British MEPs' new salary of €91,980 was equivalent to a pay rise of 43 per cent (only six Britons, two of them Ukip, declined the new rate). Because British MEPs are no longer paid by the UK parliament, they are even likelier to "go native"; the complaint that MEPs tend to represent the EU in their UK "regions", rather than vice versa, will become more common.

Countries are allowed to tax their own MEPs to bring their MEPs' tax take up to domestic levels (eg up from the Belgian 20 per cent, which that country keeps, to the UK's 40 per cent, or 50 per cent if the MEP has enough other income). At the time of writing only the UK and Sweden had done so.

As with Westminster's notorious £24,000-a-year Additional Costs Allowance (ACA) and other expenses, MEPs' allowances are a tax-free, taxpayer-funded *pay supplement* dressed up as "expenses". The fees offices in both parliaments are party to the scheme, helping and advising members to claim the maximum from the system, instead of merely helping only to reclaim outgoings incurred in the course of one's work. Westminster MPs are powerless in the face of EU legislation and cannot reasonably argue for far higher salaries – most of their work has been outsourced. This is why, instead of pay rises, they get the ACA (after producing irrelevant, though often hilarious, invoices). The ACA was introduced in 1971 when Ted Heath was well on his way to ruining the economy. A salary increase would have caused riots, so the ACA acted as a backdoor pay rise (just before UK accession to the EEC). Thatcher and Blair both enlarged the ACA, and MPs found that they had, by virtue of EU treaties that offered up more and more competences to the EU, even less legislating to do in Westminster. No wonder they dreamt up funnier and funnier ACA claims – there was precious little else to detain them, except voting against giving the UK a referendum on the Lisbon Treaty.

Brussels MEPs are as powerless as MPs, but in a different way: they cannot, unlike MPs, initiate legislation. As with MPs, it's not the headline pay that makes MEPs rich, it's the allowances. As in Westminster, look on the salary as an opening offer: there's plenty more available. However, MEPs are far better rewarded for their impotence: their version of the ACA is a black American Express card compared to Westminster's electricity top-up card. The spring 2009 revelations about Westminster politicians' expenses may have looked like the high-water mark for the tide of greed. No way.

Open Europe has found that in total MEPs are entitled to expenses and allowances of £363,000 a year, including a €298 (£260) daily subsistence allowance and £45,648 in general office expenses even though they are provided with offices in Brussels and Strasbourg. This equates to £1,816,250 per MEP over a five-year term – and no receipts are required. This comes on top of around £83,282 in salary, £29,309 in pensions and £41,641 in transitional payments (demob money). In contrast, MPs can claim up to only £144,000 in expenses.

Most people would consider MEPs a waste of money, for they cannot initiate legislation. Money went literally down the drain on installing £7,000 showers in the office of every MEP in the Strasbourg parliament (no building in the world has more). And what a shower most MEPs are. Draft figures for the European parliament's 2011 budget show that each MEP will cost £2.15million per annum. The assembly's budget will rise to £1.6billion (up 6.5 per cent on 2010). Coming in at about 22 per cent, this breaks a 1988 pledge that the European parliament's kitty never exceeds 20 per cent of the EU's overall spend on admin. Astonishingly, visitor groups to the various parliament sites will in total be given £26million – without receipts – in 2011, up from £21.4million in 2010, as "going home" presents[181]. That's £500,000 per week in brown envelopes.

The goodies available to MEPs and Eurocrats are many but highlights include[182]:

Travel: getting to work from, say, Tallinn is only part of this cost. Decamping to Alsace every four weeks is another part. Every MEP used to be reimbursed for first-class travel, plus a little extra, even if he or she travelled economy, although this abuse – the "kilometrage" scam – ended after the 2009 election, after which the EU asked for receipts. In 2004 only 37 of 732 MEPs gave back the difference – as much as £500 each way. Counted as expenses rather than income, it's tax

181 *The Daily Telegraph*, 22 March 2010
182 This section draws on the website of the campaigning Austrian MEP Hans-Peter Martin (www.hpmartin.net), which includes the full tariff for the MEPs' trough; *The Bumper Book Of Government Waste* (2006); and private information from British and other MEPs

free. Nick Clegg, who at the time of writing was deputy prime minister, admitted that when he was an MEP he used excess "kilometrage" to fund his office. This was well within the rules. (He had previously been a Commission official in Brussels.)

The 2007 Court Of Auditors report for the financial year 2006 stated: "In various cases, travel expenditure was refunded on the basis of handwritten travel agency invoices always showing the same amount. In the context of an ex post-verification procedure, the committee's administration found that this amount was on average 83 per cent higher than the price charged by the airline for the ticket used. There was no evidence of the actual administrative cost invoiced for the purchase. The committee's administration carried out a broad investigation into the matter, which was completed in July 2007. In the Court's opinion the results of this investigation do not demonstrate that the amounts paid for administrative costs were justified."

In April 2008 Giacomo Regaldo, who was previously the head of Ecosoc's employers' section, Group One, was alleged to have been recompensed by Confcommercio, the Italian trade, tourism and services confederation, for travel expenses between Brussels and Italy. The problem was that he had already been reimbursed by Ecosoc. It's a standard scam, known as "double reimbursement". He had once been touted as a possible future president of Ecosoc (but not, as you would be forgiven for thinking, by virtue of this creative habit). A 2005 investigation by Olaf concluded that there was strong prima facie evidence that he had double claimed. The Belgian prosecutor called for him to be jailed for two years, fined €10,000 euros and ordered to repay €45,000. Regaldo denied any wrongdoing, and his lawyers said that the system for claiming expenses from the Ecosoc was far from clear and may have contributed to the mistake. Ecosoc lifted his immunity from prosecution and a month later he was given a five-year suspended prison sentence by a Brussels court, which found him guilty of obtaining money fraudulently from public bodies. Why should a high-up in Ecosoc have the book thrown at him for travel expenses fraud while MEPs do not?

A clutch of MEPs had long campaigned for "kilometrage" to end. One was Daniel Hannan: "Year after year, I and a group of Scandinavian MEPs put down an amendment calling for reimbursement at cost; and, year after year, we lost. Then, to our astonishment, the parliament agreed to the change. Judging from their expressions when the result was flashed up, some of those MEPs who had voted with us were even more astonished. In an elaborate piece of game theory, they had wanted to vote for reform, but lose. When the numbers were declared, they realised to their horror that everyone else had made the same calculation. Still, at least the change was made."[183] The Swedish MEP Jens Holm claimed on his blog that he had given away about €70,000 in surplus allowances to charity. From 2006 to 2008, Holm said, he had received €158,708 in travel expenses from the European parliament although his true costs were only about €88,000.

Now, therefore, MEPs really do fly first class (and no taxpayer money has been saved). They might as well, because they can no longer pocket any surplus. Poor old easyJet. (Or is it? On the evidence so far, it would not be beyond the wits or beneath the morals of an MEP to buy an expensive ticket, get reimbursed for it, then swap it for a cheaper alternative.) MEPs can also claim a "duration allowance" of up to £257 per journey that reimburses them for the time spent travelling between their homes and European parliament buildings. (Every Christmas, the EU pays for employees' travel home. In 2008, the European Commission and Council spent just under €47million on Christmas travel arrangements.)

There is also usually a security guard by the cashiers' office – where MEPs happily went with their boarding cards (not receipts) to claim back their flights etc – to deter filming. But it was the unaudited per diems or "subsistence allowance" of €298, nicknamed "siso" ("sign in, sod off"), which first gave rise to filming MEPs. So unpopular with the EU was this awful, cruel blood sport that the parliament did the only humane thing – it banned TV cameras. A memo written by the authorities after the "siso" scandal broke provided new rules "to clarify the areas where filming and photographing is, or is not, permitted" and to allow these activities only when "MEPs are acting in their official capacity" (ie not when they're submitting boarding cards or clocking in). A code of conduct mentioned "acceptable behaviour which TV crews are expected to display, notably when filming members" and provided the power to "apply proportionate sanctions in cases of inappropriate conduct, including removal and exclusion for subsequent periods"[184]. Much of the same meeting (those quotes are from its minutes) was spent debating whether to ban journalists altogether. There's CCTV in the corridor outside the cashiers' office now in order to, er, stop filming: cameras to counter cameras. (Be sure to clock in between 7am and 10am to get your allowance.)

Despite this, in June 2008, the German TV channel RTL filmed several MEPs clocking in at 7am with their suitcases, ready to leave for the weekend, but rushing for the lift when they knew they were being taped (see YouTube). RTL's crew and presenter were thrown out. In 2004, Austrian MEP Hans-Peter Martin documented 7,200 cases of false allowances (including Glenys Kinnock using

---

183 *The Daily Telegraph*, 7 June 2008
184 *The Sprout*, volume III issue 6, p 23

"siso": her office correctly said, "She's broken no rules"), and in 2008 Paul Van Buitenen discovered that MEPs' assistants had faked their bosses' signatures. In 2009, the European Policy Centre, a Brussels think tank, launched votewatch.eu, a site which showed how (and if) MEPs voted (an earlier site with a similar aim, run by the assistant of an Italian MEP, had been sued). As "Brussels Sprouts" in *Private Eye* noted, MEPs must be worried that someone would now compare records of siso payments with voting records.

A leaked October 2008 note from the parliament vice-president Diana Wallis (British Lib Dem) showed that more than 60 MEPs sign in to be present for the monthly session in Strasbourg on Fridays, although the EP never sits on Fridays. The "Friday reimbursement" cost the European parliament about €820,000 between 2004 and 2008.

Such scams are of course not unique to Brussels – our MPs have had problems with disclosure of expenses and explaining precisely the overlap of their staffing arrangements with their list of dependents. But neither excuses the other. In January 2008 Derek Conway, a backbench Tory MP in Edward Heath's old seat, made the news. Though supposedly a eurosceptic, Conway was previously best known, if for anything, as being a government whip (together with David Davis) who had used almost any means necessary to get the Maastricht Treaty through the Commons.

Fifteen years later he himself lost the party whip when it was revealed that he had put several family members, as well as a friend of one of his sons, on the public payroll (£374,401.73 since 2001) for no obvious return. After castigation – he was ordered to repay some of the cash – he said he would not stand at the next general election. A few months later, 177 British MPs, including three cabinet ministers, volunteered that they, too, had employed family members, usually spouses, but in return for rather more work. That's only just over a quarter of all MPs, though full disclosure might well have raised the figure. In July 2008 the figure for all 200-odd Tory MPs was about 30 per cent. Less than a year later, a newspaper revealed that scores of MPs had been on the take, usually via the second-homes allowance. As mentioned, their efforts were amateur.

Conway was small beer by Belgian standards. In Brussels there is an unaudited secretarial allowance for MEPs of €19,040 per month (up from €17,540 – to cope with the "extra work" dealt them by the Lisbon Treaty) on top of the office allowance of €45,468 per annum. In 2005, only six of out of 78 British MEPs (be they Labour, Ukip, Conservative, whatever) *didn't* give this to either their spouse or another family member. When Lord Kinnock's wife Glenys was an MEP, for instance, she employed their daughter Rachel as a researcher in 2006. By the by, their son Stephen's first job after Cambridge University was as a research assistant to an MEP; he later worked for the British Council while his father headed it. Stephen's Danish wife Helle was an MEP from 1999 to 2004.

By January 2009, "only" 16 out of the 27 Tory MEPs employed their spouses. A French MEP once said to a (blameless) British MEP, "What is it about you English? You employ your wives and you sleep with your staff."

This secretarial allowance is meant to be at arm's length from the parliamentarian. Each MEP is supposed to pay an assistant directly or designate an intermediary, either a "service provider" or "paying agent". This can be a professional accountancy firm or other professional bookkeeper. Many MEPs have had problems with this guidance. On 28 September 2007, in an interim verdict on a case brought by a Maltese journalist arguing against the parliament for greater transparency, the EU Ombudsman recommended that MEPs should reveal details about money they receive from the EU budget, such as their daily allowances and grants for travel or for assistants. "MEPs have to be aware of the public interest in their use of public funds," he said in a statement.

In February 2008, the EU parliament's internal auditor, Robert Galvin, carried out 167 spot checks on the activities of 40 MEPs to ascertain how they were distributing this staff allowance. He wrote that his researches gave "rise to a presumption of the existence of possible illegal activity" and that there was "extensive, widespread and criminal abuse" of staff allowances. Many MEPs, whose identities he knew, were employing family members for no obvious return, others did not even have staff but still claimed the sum, sometimes channelling it to their political party. He identified abuse of funds totalling £98.4million per year, or about £125,000 for each MEP on average. There was even a "service provider" who traded in timber, and payments to ghost employees.

His 92-page report had been shown only to MEPs on Cocubu, the parliament's budgetary-control committee – who could make no notes or copies and had to read the document alone, except for a guard, in a windowless room protected by biometric locks. And the MEPs had to sign a confidentiality agreement. The recipe for Coca-Cola is more public. An MEP who read the report said, "Some service providers simply do not exist. Others are individuals that work for or are dependent on the MEP." One of the British MEPs on Cocubu, the Lib Dem Chris Davies, recommended that Olaf should become involved. Herbert Bösch, the Austrian chairman of Cocubu, refused a demand from 11 of his colleagues for the report to be published. "I made it available to members of this committee. I did my job. I will refuse any demands to have a look at my journeys and trips," he said. "Some things should not be published."[185]

In one case, Davies said, a staffer had received a "Christmas bonus" that was 19 times an assistant's monthly salary. On the *Today* programme, he said, "Maybe when some MEPs are named, exposed for defrauding the European parliament and the public, and are sent to prison a more acceptable approach will be adopted."

The Court Of Auditors, in a separate report a few days later, said that 66 per cent of the £100million budget for MEPs' staff was paid without receipts: "There is not sufficient documentation to demonstrate that the MEPs have actually employed or engaged the services of one or more assistants, and that the duties or services mentioned in the contracts signed by the MEPs have been really carried out."[186] As so often, the COA was ignored.

The other report was not, and so the EU parliament moved quickly. "As the internal auditor's report has not revealed any individual cases of fraud, he has not recommended referring his findings to Olaf," an EU parliament statement said. There was a good reason for there being no "individual cases of fraud": the names of the MEPs in the report had been anonymised. A press officer explained: "This report is not secret. It's confidential. It can be read by certain approved MEPs on [Cocubu], in the secret room but not generally. That is not the same as a secret document nobody can read. This is a technical decision not a political one because it was taken by the auditor himself. The decision was not taken by the president or secretary general." All clear?

On 22 April 2008 MEPs really outdid themselves. Sitting in Strasbourg, they voted not only to keep the report secret, they also "discharged" or approved (by 582 votes to 77, with 18 abstentions) the EU's 2006 accounts, which, of course, the Court Of Auditors had not seen fit to pass the previous November. But that's not all. They also voted to increase pay for their assistants (money that they would usually be managing) but agreeing to a non-mandatory (later made mandatory) undertaking not to employ family members (MEPs elected for the first time in 2009 are banned from hiring relations, but those already employed can stay on until 2014. How long before MEPs work out that they can "employ" each other's spouses?). The parliament also voted, in defiance of advice from the EU Ombudsman, to keep secret the names of the 407 MEPs who receive a second voluntary pension (ie in addition to the one they receive from their home government; only Italian and French MEPs have pensions paid by the EU, the rest are paid by national governments).

---

[185] *The Daily Telegraph*, 27 February 2008
[186] *The Daily Telegraph*, 26 February 2008

These 407 MEPs put €1,194 a month into the pension fund. The contribution is paid automatically from their office expenses into their pot. The next bit is tricky: MEPs are then meant to reimburse the office expenses from their own pocket. Many fail to do so. Once the contribution is made – and whether their office account is repaid or not – it is matched twice (twice!) by the taxpayer, tax-free: another €2,388 a month into the pot! After just one five-year term, an MEP can expect an annual pension, from the voluntary fund alone, of over €16,000. Combined with their standard MEP pension, they can expect annual payments of over €30,000 after just one term.

The voluntary-pension fund, set up in 1989, has been continually criticised by the Court of Auditors. In their November 2008 report, the COA said that the parliament should have "clear rules to define the liabilities and responsibilities" of the parliament, and members of the scheme, in the case of shortfalls. (After much criticism, the scheme was not made available to MEPs new to the trough in 2009.) Several MEPs are challenging the parliament's decision to raise the age, from 60 to 63, when MEPs can take this "second pension".

When the voluntary pension was publicised in Germany in 2006, one of her MEPs, Markus Ferber, promised to reform the system. His critical report was emasculated for suggesting that perhaps taxpayers shouldn't have to fill a €28.9million black hole in the already overgenerous scheme (they did so anyway – just as UK taxpayers had plugged a £25million hole in MPs' pensions in 2003). Three MEPs thought they had a better idea than Ferber: not to reform the system. So they tabled an amendment to keep open the option of a taxpayer-funded bailout, thereby eliminating a provision that would mean MEPs had to pay out of their own pocket, not out of their allowances. And those three MEPs were Brits: Terry Wynn (Labour)[187], James Elles (Conservative) and Bill Newton Dunn (Lib Dem). The last of these said, "We are public servants, and just as if Westminster were to run a deficit on its fund, it is up to the taxpayer to help out" and defended the system, saying "This was originally set up for the convenience of the parliament, on the basis that honourable members could be trusted to repay the money. We have no evidence that our colleagues are not doing the right thing."[188]

The Ombudsman has repeatedly ruled that beneficiaries must be identified but has been ignored. In 2009, a brave German journalist, Hans-Martin Tillack (see "Fraud and whistleblowers"), published the names of the (by then) 478 MEPs – as well as hundreds of ex-MEPs – in the scheme. At around the same time, up to €120million (separate from the replaced €28.9million) was found to have been lost from the fund – £50million had been invested with disgraced American

---

[187] The same MEP who serves on the Commission's ethics committee
[188] *The Daily Telegraph*, 14 September 2006

financier Bernie Madoff, perhaps the only person more corrupt than the EU itself. Discussing the shortfall, a leaked internal memo from the European parliament's office stressed that the "parliament will assume its legal responsibility to guarantee the right of members of the Voluntary Pension Scheme to the additional pension, even when the fund is empty". Soon after, MEPs voted against bailing out their fund with taxpayer money. It was, of course, a show vote, designed to shore up their own votes before the 2009 Euro elections: the "promise" that taxpayers would not make up the shortfall could be made only after a unanimous vote by all 27 member states at Council level. The reality was that the message of the phrase "parliament will assume its legal responsibility to guarantee the right of members of the Voluntary Pension Scheme to the additional pension" was unaltered by the MEPs' vote and they knew it. Cynical is too weak a word.

But back to MEPs' families. On 11 May 2008, the *News Of The World* revealed that Tory MEP David Sumberg had paid "wife Carolyn almost as much as he earns himself!" She received, the paper said, up to £60,000 a year – it was later lodged in the register of interests as £54,000 – for her services as a "secretary/assistant… our records show in 2002 there were payments of £7,922.22 a month in her name. That's £95,066.64 a year". Sumberg said that his wife worked for him full-time. It later emerged that he had been receiving more than £40,800 a year, the standard allowance for keeping an office in one's home country, despite having no office in his constituency[189]. He did not contest the 2009 election.

The piece had led with an undercover interview with MEP Tom Wise, once of Ukip, who said, "It's cushy – £60,000 a year! Thank you very much indeed! What have we got to do for it? Not a lot!" The article then described a typical day in his diary and it did indeed amount to "not a lot". He was also quoted saying how he pocketed the travel surpluses and other legitimate expenses. Later, he was arrested by Bedfordshire police on suspicion of obtaining money by deception. In 2009 he was convicted, in the UK, of false accounting and money laundering of expenses worth £39,000 and jailed for two years. Nigel Farage, Ukip's leader, told the *Daily Telegraph* that parliamentary officials had at first exonerated Wise. "The parliament looked into it and he was cleared. Obviously, the parliament suppressed it because of the fear that it was happening in hundreds of cases. There have been changes to the expenses system since then but they are cosmetic and I suspect there are still many cases of fraud."

Another Ukip MEP, Ashley Mote, had been found guilty, also in the UK, of eight charges of false accounting, eight of obtaining a money transfer by

---

[189] *The Sunday Times*, 23 November 2008

deception, four of evading liability and one of failing to notify a change of circumstances, relating to a period in the 1990s, before he was an MEP, when he had resumed work after unemployment but continued to claim welfare payments. His parliamentary immunity from prosecution had been waived by the European parliament, which looks after only fellow travellers. Nevertheless, when Mote retired in 2009, he had an MEP pension pot of £174,968 and he received a "transitional payment" of £32,382. Wise's pension pot when he stood down in 2009 was £235,000 and he also received the £32,382 demob payment[190]. As with other retiring MEPs, he also received up to £55,000 to close his office.

In the same article, the *News Of The World* revealed that Giles Chichester, the leader of the Tory MEPs, had employed his wife part-time for up to £30,000 per annum. He had also put £445,000 of expenses through the family firm, which had been founded by his famous yachtsman father Sir Francis to make maps. As a director of that firm, he was in breach of the parliament's rules: a "service provider" must be at arm's length. In a TV interview on 4 June Chichester appeared to make light of the situation, calling his transgression "technical" and telling ITV West Country: "It is embarrassing, *not least because I have introduced a new code for my Conservative colleagues for expenses.* Here I am leading that process for the last couple of months and – whoops a daisy! – I am shown up to have made a mistake. OK, hands up, mea culpa, and I will put it right." [Emphasis added.]

On 5 June 2008, he stood down as leader of the Tory MEPs but stayed on as an MEP. His statement said: "I personally sought a meeting yesterday with the European parliamentary services to clarify the situation. At this meeting I was informed that there had been a change in the rules relating to service providers, a change that took effect in 2003. This had not been brought to my attention when I renewed the contract in 2004... As a result of this information, I immediately cancelled the contract with the company. I will now work with the parliament services to provide a detailed breakdown of all monies received and expended since 2003 which will demonstrate they are fully accounted for... At all times, I have acted in good faith within the original parliamentary rules, and what I believed the current rules of the European parliament still to be. I recognise that it was my responsibility to have learned about the change in rules. I confirm that there has been no misappropriation of any funds..."

By chance, on the same day as the *News of the World* article appeared, the *Sunday Independent* revealed, in an article about MEPs going on jollies provided by sectors they were supposed to "regulate", that Chichester "is also president of the European Energy Forum, which promotes the interests of the oil, gas and

---

190 *The Times*, 2 June 2009

nuclear industries. In May 2007, he was the guest of nuclear company Areva at the America's Cup race off Valencia. Mr Chichester says the trip had no bearing on his long-held pro-nuclear views."

In September Harald Rømer, the secretary general of the European parliament, not only exonerated him but also apologised for the delay in bringing the matter to "a positive conclusion". He wrote to Chichester: "I can inform you that I have come to the conclusion that although your contract with that company constituted a potential case of conflict of interest, you have had no personal financial benefit from that contract, and that no conflict of interest has ever materialised... I am content that there was no personal gain arising out of a conflict of interest in breach of the relevant rules and that the use of the money received from your parliamentary assistance allowance has been fully justified..."

Another Tory MEP, Caroline Jackson, was a rapporteur on the Waste Framework Directive, which would dictate, among other things, how much rubbish can be incinerated, buried and burnt etc (see "Landfill"). The draft directive reclassified incineration as "recovery" if some energy is generated. This would be a boon to incineration firms, including one called Shanks, on whose board sat Jackson (for a fee of £6,000 per annum). Her spokesman said that the MEP, who had not declared her seat on the board before she was made rapporteur, found "it useful to see things from the industry side as well". Her husband, the former Tory-turned-Labour MP Robert Jackson, had been involved with a similar firm until 2006[191]. A year later, it was discovered that Dr Jackson, presumably to keep him out of trouble in retirement, had paid her husband £22,500 to help to write a 15-page leaflet on waste management. She failed to list the fee in two of her "declarations of interests" before finally listing it in a footnote as three payments of up to £10,000 for "consultancy fees"[192]. Standing down in 2009, she had amassed a pension pot of £1million (after 25 years' "service") and received the maximum "transitional allowance" of £129,528[193].

Warming to its theme, the *News of the World* revealed on 8 June 2008 that Conservative MEP John Purvis had siphoned off up to £120,000 per annum into his own firm, Purvis & Co, of which he was a paid partner, also contravening the 2003 rule. "I consider myself completely a victim in this whole thing," he later told the *Courier*, a Scottish newspaper. The same *Sunday Independent* piece on potential conflicts of interest had noted that Purvis, "vice-chairman of the influential committee on economic and monetary affairs, is a

---

[191] *Brussels Sprouts* column, *Private Eye*, 11-24 July 2008
[192] *The Sun*, 26 May 2009
[193] *The Times*, 2 June 2009

non-executive chairman of Belgrave Capital Management, a recruiting arm of a Swiss company that invests in hedge funds". Five years earlier, it went on, he was the parliament's rapporteur and had proposed a "light-handed EU-wide regulatory regime" for the hedge-fund industry. He told the paper he saw no conflict of interest: "The whole of my career has been in banking and finance, so at least I know something about it." Also in the *News of the World* in June was Sajjad Karim, the Lib Dem who had defected to the Tories in 2006. He had paid his wife £26,000 a year to act as his assistant – while she was apparently also working as a teacher in Blackburn.

For some weeks – since before any of the *News Of The World* and other stories – Open Europe had been asking the UK's 78 MEPs some questions about their secretarial allowances, such as whether they were paid to family members etc. At this stage, only 13 out of 28 Conservative MEPs had replied. With Labour, the figure was four out of 19. The Lib Dems could boast three out of 11. Nine out of 10 Ukip members replied. There was a strong correlation between the likelihood of a candid reply and that MEP's distaste for the great "project" (most Tory MEPs favour deeper EU integration – Daniel Hannan, one of the Tory respondees, is more eloquent than he is representative of his colleagues).

Sir Robert Atkins, a Tory MEP, had employed his son James until 2004 on a handsome retainer – £2,513.23 per month. James would later become a Brussels lobbyist. The England Expects blog noted that Atkins's claim that he paid his son a slightly lower rate than other parliamentary assistants "isn't quite true. I was working as a parliamentary assistant at the time and you would have been lucky to make 2,513.23 in euros, let alone in sterling." The author also looked at allegations about payments to Sir Robert's wife, Dulcie: "Well, there does seem to be a discrepancy between what was reported in *Stern* magazine on 18 March 2004 by Hans-Martin Tillack and what was reported in the *News of the World*. *Stern* had it that he was paying her €8,332 per month whereas the *NoTW* claims only 'over 30,000' [per annum]. Quite a lot over it seems."[194] Lady Atkins, a professional secretary who has been her husband's assistant since at least 1980, ran her husband's constituency office (based, legally but unusually, in their Lancashire manor house) while also discharging her duties as a borough and town councillor and carrying out charitable and other community work.

Den Dover was removed as the Tories' chief whip in 2008 when it was discovered that he had since 1999 put £760,000 through a firm run by his wife Kathleen and daughter Amanda. They had as directors been paid £271,692 in that time. Unlike Mr Chichester, he had broken no rules; he was not paid by the firm and was not a director. The accounts of MP Holdings Ltd revealed that it

---

[194] englandexpects.blogspot.com, 15 May 2008

had spent £32,462 on repairs, widely presumed to be on the family's Hertfordshire home. A further £56,411 went on motoring costs and £75,397 on postage and stationery[195]. In 2007, 57 per cent of the company's "tangible assets" were cars, worth £63,517. A Herts neighbour told the *Daily Mail* that "Since he became an MEP you could immediately tell he [Dover] was more affluent. He changed his car and he and his wife started going on holidays to tropical islands. He has a large blue BMW and his wife drives a top-of-the-range silver BMW 4x4."[196] Electoral Commission figures showed that MP Holdings had given the Chorley Conservative Party £1,200 in December 2007.

Dover defended the employment of his wife – on between £20,000 and £30,000 as a part-time parliamentary assistant – and daughter: "They get market rates but they put in two or three times the number of hours. They just never stop. Therefore I am totally innocent of any charges." The *Telegraph* discovered that the European parliament's register of assistants showed that neither woman was accredited to enter or use official buildings in Brussels or Strasbourg[197]. Furthermore, Dover's daughter worked four days a week as a travel agent in Hertfordshire. The parliament's register of interests, written by the MEP, says that both Amanda and her mother "are required to work very unsociable hours". Perhaps if Amanda didn't work four days a week for a travel agency then the hours she devoted to her father's MEP business might have been more sociable.

In November 2008, the parliament decided that Dover had breached its rules on expenses and demanded that he repay just over £500,000 and Cameron expelled him from the Tory party for "gross misconduct". However, when he stood down as an MEP in May 2009, Dover was entitled to six months' pay (which with allowances could be stretched to £79,000) and a pension pot estimated at £235,000 (after 10 years' "service"). His "transitional allowance" was £59,367.

Dover even filed a case with the ECJ asking that demands for repayment "be suspended, in the light of the serious and irreparable harm that he would suffer if he were required to pay the sum of £538,290 by 25 April 2009". The ECJ disagreed and devised ways to claw back some of the cash. It judged that Dover should lose £60,000 "being 50 per cent of the general expenditure allowance, the whole of the extra month's half-allowance payable at the end of the applicant's term of office, together with the end of service allowance and the entire capital of the life assurance from which the applicant stands to benefit at the end of his term of office". The remainder of the cash would be sought by the

---

195 *The Sunday Times*, 8 June 2008
196 *The Daily Mail*, 9 June 2008
197 *The Daily Telegraph*, 7 June 2008

EU through the UK's civil courts[198]. A month after the judgment he attended a ceremony for retiring MEPs at which the European parliament "expresses its gratitude to the members who, throughout their term of office, have placed their talents and their commitment at the service of citizens and the European project". Tom Wise, who had by then been charged in the UK, also collected a medal and framed certificate, which a parliament spokesman said were "for being an MEP... not about anything else that an MEP might have done"[199].

By now, with the press in pursuit, British MEPs swiftly amended their register of interests, which were held in a grey filing cabinet in a room on the second floor of the European parliament (as well as online). "As the scandal broke and awkward demands for transparency and accountability came from London party leaders, new pages were being hurriedly (and, one imagines, reluctantly) submitted for inclusion in the cabinet's four blue folders. 'They are literally arriving by the hour,' the female bureaucrat in Room A-20 said," reported the *Daily Mail*'s Richard Pendlebury[200].

Michael Cashman revealed, in this new though unscheduled spirit of glasnost, that his civil partner had been paid £30,000 per annum from the public purse. His register of interests had previously shown nothing more interesting than a set of *Lord Of The Rings* stamps signed by Sir Ian McKellen. Richard Corbett, a Labour MEP for Yorkshire & The Humber, also didn't use the word "wife" in the register. In the first declaration that he employed her, on 13 March 2008, he submitted to the register that he had a part-time secretary "related to me by marriage"[201]. (He meant his wife, not – say – her father or sister.)

The following year, the *News Of The World* found that Labour MEP Stephen Hughes had claimed his full £42,000 office allowance, despite his office rent being just £1,642. He had also paid his wife, a local councillor, £40,000 to be his "chief of staff"[202]. Again, no rule had been broken: the EU permits claims for the full amount regardless of need, as per the old "kilometrage" scam/scheme. It was unclear for how long Mr Hughes had been claiming the full amount. He had led the parliament's unsuccessful 2009 campaign to end the UK's opt-out from the 48-hour week. He had, therefore, wanted to deny his constituents (and others) the right to supplement their wages through overtime. Did he know of a better way of supplementing one's wages?

---

198 *Den Dover owes the taxpayer £538,290* on blogs.telegraph.co.uk/bruno_waterfield, 15 June 2009
199 *The Daily Telegraph*, 15 July 2009
200 *The Fatcat Parliament: How MEPs pocket a staggering £630,000 a year*, Richard Pendlebury (and Ian Drury) in *The Daily Mail*, 14 June 2008
201 Richard Pendlebury and Ian Drury, *The Daily Mail*, 14 June 2008. Corbett lost his seat in 2009 but is now employed by Herman Van Rompuy
202 *The News Of The World*, 22 March 2009

Chris Davies told *Newsnight* on 5 June 2008 that even he had claimed excess travel expenses – "we get a ridiculously generous travel allowance" – and paid it to his party. Between July 2003 and April 2004, he gave the Lib Dems £22,000. He suggested such practices were widespread, but said it was "completely wrong" that it was allowed. He blamed "the culture of the European parliament, which allows what most people would regard as unacceptable, unethical behaviour to be treated as normal." He said the problem was that Italian and Greek MEPs and the majority always vote against reform: "The European parliament may be incapable of reforming itself."

The Lib Dems confirmed in June 2008 that Andrew Duff, the Lib Dem leader, Fiona Hall, Bill Newton Dunn and Sarah Ludford paid the party, as their service provider, a fee for payroll and other administrative services, but insisted that funds were kept entirely separate from party finances. However, eight of their 11 MEPs had donated £86,000 to the party over the previous seven years (MPs had also been making party donations from allowances). Duff denied that any of the cash had come from travel surpluses.

In early June 2008, Cameron sent Andrew Robathan MP, the deputy chief whip, as well as his probity enforcer or "head of compliance", Hugh Thomas, a former director of global compliance at Deutsche Bank Private Wealth Management, a qualified barrister and former Church of England vicar, to read the 28 Tory MEPs the riot act. The next month, Cameron ordered a "deep clean" of expense claims by his MEPs. He said that anyone refusing to sign up to a new code on allowances would be deselected. He ordered all MEPs to make public their expense claims twice a year, from 2009, or face expulsion from the party. Also, he said that Tory MEPs would in future be barred from employing family members (a ruling that the parliament had already made, but it sounded good to say it for those who didn't know it was on its way anyway). As mentioned, there's no way of stopping X's spouse from "working" for Y, and vice versa. After the 2009 election, it was revealed that at least 17 British MEPs were making the most of the "British clause", which allowed employment of relations until 2014[203]. Although eight of them were Tory (including Atkins and Chichester), Cameron made no comment.

Amid all the expenses fervour, there was still time for news from the jollies front. On 18 May 2008, the *News Of The World* reported on a separate study from Open Europe which estimated that overseas excursions by MEPs had cost £3.1million since 2004. On one nine-day trip to Australia in 2007, just 18 hours were spent on official business, while the nine MEPs had five days set aside for cruising on a yacht, watching *La Traviata* at Sydney Opera House, touring

---

[203] *The Daily Telegraph*, 17 October 2009

vineyards and visiting Uluru/Ayers Rock. "After an 'informal' lunch, they toured Uluru Kata Tjuta National Park, before a slap-up dinner with Australian politicians at the award-winning open-air restaurant Sounds Of Silence. With grotesque irony, the official report noted that the MEPs were 'afforded an opportunity' to discuss the plight of Aborigines while stuffing their faces." Giles Chichester had led the £110,000 trip, and had been on the Delegation for Relations with Australia and New Zealand group's 2005 fact-finder to Oz – as well as a 2006 trip to New Zealand. In February 2009, he defended a planned trip to Australia by a group of nine MEPs, whom he led, as "an important delegation which does good work".

The Labour Party is also concerned about the underprivileged. Two years earlier, the *News Of The World*'s stablemate reported that "Glenys Kinnock, champion of the Third World poor, is to lead 70 members of the European parliament to a Barbados resort for a conference debating development and deprivation. During the five-day trip, costing taxpayers more than £200,000, the MEPs will meet politicians from some of the world's poorest nations. The official agenda is to address water shortages, aid and EU trade policies, but away from the conference hall delegates will indulge in some of the island's luxurious recreations. Kinnock, who co-chairs the African Caribbean Pacific-EU joint parliamentary assembly (EU-ACP JPA), will be offered accommodation in the island's exquisite hotels, including the Amaryllis Beach, Tamarind Cove and Turtle Beach. Many MEPs will be 'slumming it' in the Colony Club, a luscious resort that offers poolside suites with four-poster beds and four freshwater lagoons. The former gentleman's club is billed as the perfect honeymoon location and its website portrays a tempting picture of 'seven acres of palm-filled gardens on a glorious stretch of Caribbean beach'. Normal rates range from $357 to $657 a night…"[204]

In April 2008, she led a team of MEPs to the Seychelles, again for EU-ACP JPA, to study the islands' tuna industry. The visit cost £28,000. On 25 May 2008, she told *Wales On Sunday*: "I was not lying on a beach getting a suntan. I work very hard and take my job extremely seriously. I would never do anything irresponsible that would not give the [EU-ACP JPA] the respect and status that it deserves [continues]." Between 2004 and 2009 she would clock up 143,033 air miles while on EU business, making her the best-travelled MEP, according to Open Europe. The biannual ACP conferences have, since 2004, met in a variety

---

204 *The Sunday Times*, 12 November 2006. For another view of her work as an MEP, see *When will Glenys keep her promise?* in *The Sunday Telegraph*, 21 June 2009, by Christopher Booker. He urged her to ensure that justice is "very belatedly done" to the many Botswanans and Kenyans whose health and livelihood were "destroyed" by a botched EU-funded infrastructure project that she had initially at least promised to "pursue"

of glamorous capitals, such as Port Moresby (Papua New Guinea), Prague, Rome, Vienna and Cape Town. There is no good reason why the ACP-EU cannot meet in EU buildings in Brussels or Strasbourg.

You'd think that the Tories might have reined in their jollies after all that embarrassment. Not a bit of it. On 29 June 2008, the *Sunday Times* reported that 200 MEPs from the EPP grouping, including several Tory MEPs, were to go on a three-day trip to Paris, costing taxpayers up to £200,000. The trip, described as "study days" to discuss security issues and an opportunity for MEPs to leave their normal Brussels working environment, included dinner at the Palais De Versailles, cocktail lunches and a champagne boat trip down the Seine. Details of the trip were not available on the EPP website, but a leaked agenda revealed that they would spend most of their time sightseeing. Having debated security policy for a few hours, they were whisked by police guard to the Elysée for a drinks party hosted by Sarkozy. The guests were told that "you may wish to bring a sun hat".

The following year a delegation of MEPs visited China and wrapped up each day's meetings by 11.15am, leaving them free to sightsee. A trip to Japan included only two hours and 45 minutes of meetings.

Anyway, on with the timetable for the gravy train:

On top of the per diems for MEPs are €50 per week for taxis – payable only after the event so do remember to have a credit card or an account with the firm.

An "information fund" of €10,000 per annum to spend on newsletters, websites, lunch with journalists, etc. Warning: this needs receipts.

There is also something called Budget Line 3701, for promotional activity. Each MEP gets €55,738 per annum for this, so long as the material carries the European parliament's logo, a variant of the ring of stars.

€4,202 per month for office expenses in one's "region" – not to be confused with the secretarial fund for the EU parliament – and domestic travel (ie around the "region" that you represent).

€4,148 per annum for discharging one's duties around the globe[205].

All of these sums, including the secretarial allowance, are tax-free because they count as expenses rather than income.

---

[205] This is separate from one's duties as, say, chair of the EU-ACP assembly

Language (English, French, German, Spanish and Italian) and computer courses are in-house and free. All of the other EU languages can be learnt where they're spoken, with subsistence, tuition and accommodation included (but there's a €5,885-per-annum ceiling). See how far you can make €5,000 go in Sofia. The computer course checks in at a disappointing €1,500 per annum.

Insurance provides for €250,000 on the death of an MEP, €375,000 if they're maimed, and €7,500 for medical expenses. Life insurance policies mature after an MEP has weathered just two terms (ie 10 years).

The Joint Sickness Insurance Scheme provides for an MEP, spouse and "dependent child" (not necessarily one's own; and up to the age of 26 if still in education), who can all recoup 80 per cent of any private treatment, if it is also available on the state provider. Up to €30,000 each per annum, or get in the NHS queue.

All get deals on glasses: €544 for lenses, €63.46 for the frame; contact lenses attract a €148.75 subsidy; disposables have a budget of €300 every other year. Additionally, "the cost of artificial eyes shall be reimbursed". These can be useful for looking at instances of alleged fraud.

There's also a hearing-aid allowance of €923.41 (plus free batteries); orthopaedic footwear and soles (two pairs twice a year), up to €359.96 per pair. The following are provided at cost: maternity belts; knee bandages; ankle supports; lumbar girdles; artificial limbs and segments of same; crutches; walking sticks; wheelchairs.

There's post-op nursing allowance (€85.75 per diem), available at home; convalescence allowance of €29.16 per diem, for up to 28 days; thermal bath allowance of €20.21 per diem (though only three weeks' worth).

Kinesitherapy, anyone? (The "interplay of relaxation and stress", apparently.) MEPs and their families get 60 sessions of medical massage, medical gymnastics, ante- and postnatal gymnastics, mobilisation, rehabilitation, mechanotherapy, traction, mud baths, hydromassage and hydrotherapy. If kinesitherapy is not your thing this year, worry not. There's also electrotherapy (60 sessions per annum), comprising the following: diadynamic currents, radar, ionisation, short-wave treatment and other special currents. Or how about beam therapy (30 sessions; infrared rays and ultrasonics) or acupuncture (also 30)?

In addition, "Treatments with Viagra will from now on be reimbursable." As is methadone, the heroin substitute, for six months' treatment.

For such a toothless body, the attention to dentistry paid by the MEPs' tariff is somehow disproportionate (see Annex IV.I: a whole page of 11pt type). It includes "Richmond crown or ceramic and metal crown, veneer or ceramic and metal bridge tooth element" up to a maximum of €185.92 per tooth and "a full set of dentures, upper or lower (14 teeth, plastic plate)", yours up to a price of €674.14.

Alighting from the gravy train needn't be a wrench. When Lord (Neil) Kinnock stood down as a commissioner in 2004 he received a pay-off ("transitional stipend") of about £272,000 spread over three years, and a pension of £63,900 per annum for life (4.5 per cent of his salary for every year he worked) after he turned 65. It does not affect his pension accrued while in the Commons (at least £25,000 per annum), nor his Lords allowances. And he does not have to declare any of it in the Lords register of members' interests, *even when taking part in debates on the European Union*. However, if an ex-commissar takes any paid work it is deducted from the transition allowance.

When Mandy stood down in 2008, he received a transitional stipend of about £234,000 spread over three years. And when he reaches 65 he will receive an inflation-linked pension of £31,000 per annum (he served only four years to Neil's nine). The cost of such a deal on the private market is about £550,000. However, in addition to the warning in TFEU 245 (see p41), "EU rules show that if he speaks out against the EU he could be stripped of his pension altogether. One of the obligations as a staff member of the Commission is to maintain a 'duty of loyalty to the Communities'. The rules also note that 'an official has the right to freedom of expression, with due respect to the principles of loyalty and impartiality'. If they fail to demonstrate loyalty to the EU, Lord Mandelson can be 'deprived of his right to a pension or other benefits', the rules say."[206] Margot Wallström, who served 10 years, is not likely to do anything to endanger her €113,486-a-year pension. This is all in addition to a host of other perks during their time in office, including residence allowances of 15 per cent of salary (about £40,000) and monthly "entertainment allowances".

The EU's civil servants, the soi-disant Eurocrats, are no less well looked after. One says: "Every month, I look at my payslip, and I try to work out how my net salary can be so much larger than my gross salary."[207] Their pay ranges from €2,556 to €17,697 a month (roughly £28,000 to £193,000 per annum – the average is £70,000). Eurocrats are taxed, like MEPs, at just 20 per cent, the Belgian rate, and there are subsidised skiing trips (and free private education) for Eurocrats' children. There is also a "correction coefficient" that kicks in if one's native state (*never* "mother country" in Commission-speak but "country I know

---

[206] *The Daily Telegraph*, 16 March 2009
[207] *The Daily Telegraph*, 14 August 2004

best" if you must) has a higher-priced living cost – that means another 42 per cent weighting for UK Eurocrats. There are 19 MEPs' researchers earning £75,752 per annum and another 12 on £70,217. The 2010 pensions bill was €1.2billion for the 17,471 ex-Eurocrats aged over 60 (rising to 63 soon) – an *average* of almost €70,000. The Commission has suggested raising retirement ages throughout the bloc to 70, but not of course for its own staff[208].

In December 2009, when many member states had only just emerged from recession, 20 members of the European Council (ie leaders of national governments) voted to halve the 3.7 per cent pay increase going to all of the thousands of Eurocrats, hundreds of MEPs, 27 commissars and the 35 ECJ judges. The annual adjustment, devised in 2004, weighs the Belgian inflation rate and the previous year's civil-service wage settlements in eight of the richest EU provinces. In 2009 it coughed up the figure of 3.7 per cent, way above most states' inflation rates. The Eurocrats went on strike for the other half. The Commission unanimously (ie including our Cathy) decided to pursue the matter in the ECJ because pay was "a matter of law". It was the commissars' money at stake: 1.85 per cent for Cathy is almost another €4,500 a year. So, the EU judges' salaries (as well as those of all of the other EU toilers) were to be decided by... EU judges. The jurists of Luxembourg will almost certainly find for the inflation-mocking booster. At the time of writing, the case was due to be heard in 2011.

The 2010 settlement will probably be a loss in real terms if there's a recovery – it will be based on figures from a recession. And then there'll be another strike. However, all is not lost for the guardians of Europe: much of the pay formula relies on self-reported rents from Brussels staffers, who are assured on the questionnaire that the information is anonymous and goes *only towards working out the next year's pay*. You couldn't make it up. But you can be sure that some Eurocrats do.

All in all not too bad, eh? Because it wouldn't do to say boo to the golden goose, few MEPs or others criticise the system. And such tolerance then extends to the EU's other, even worse wastes of money.

---

[208] *The Daily Telegraph*, 12 July 2010

The euro
The monetary equivalent of Esperanto

When Cyprus and Malta joined the eurozone on 1 January 2008, they became, respectively, the first country to give up the pound for the euro, and the first country whose official language is English to surrender its currency. The good news is that they will also be the last in those two categories. The monarch has consistently been on English and Welsh banknotes since only 1960 but she (and the various Great Britons) will never be replaced by the euro notes' imaginary structures.

In the UK, debate on the euro has been more or less closed since June 2003, when Gordon Brown, then chancellor, ruled out membership, saying the currency had flunked four of his "five tests". But the decision to join was not an economic one but a political one. You can forget, for the time being, about "optimal currency areas" – they're secondary. As Bill Clinton's advisers didn't say to him, "It's not the economy, stupid." Here are some very different people agreeing with one another about this:

"The single currency is the greatest abandonment of sovereignty since the foundation of the European Community: the decision is of an essentially political nature" (Felipe Gonzalez, a Spanish former PM, 1998)

"One must never forget that monetary union, which the two of us were the first to propose more than a decade ago, is ultimately a political project. It aims to give a new impulse to the historic movement toward union of the European states" (Giscard d'Estaing, who drafted the infamous Constitution, and Helmut Schmidt, *International Herald Tribune*, 14 October 1997)

"The process of monetary union goes hand in hand, must go hand in hand, with political integration and ultimately political union. EMU [economic and monetary union] is, and always was meant to be, a stepping stone on the way to a united Europe" (Wim Duisenberg, first president of the European Central Bank)

"Monetary union is fundamentally a political issue" (Eddie George, when governor of the Bank Of England)

"We should be clear that joining is as much about politics as economics" (John Monks, in 2000, when general secretary of the TUC)

"Once EMU has been realised, the realisation of political union will get an extra boost as a logical and indispensable complement of EMU" (Herman Van

Rompuy in 1989, 21 years before he became your president)

"The euro was really adopted for political and not economic purposes, as a step towards the myth of the United States of Europe. I believe its effect will be exactly the opposite" (Milton Friedman, the Nobel Prize-winning economist, in 1997[209])

All sides of the argument are in agreement: the euro is primarily political. This chimes with Sir Arthur Salter's observation that "economic and political rapprochement" are interdependent, or two sides of the same euro coin. (Although the euro is a political construct, it will probably be economics that brings about its destruction. At the time of writing it was still alive.)

If you think of the UK individually as England, Wales, Scotland and Northern Ireland, then sterling itself is a single currency. But let's take the EU's view that the UK is 12 "regions". Only three of these 12 – London, East of England, and the South East of England – bring in more for the chancellor than is spent on them; they subsidise the other nine "regions" – their tax "take" is bigger than what they receive. This is the price of the UK's single currency. A single interest and exchange rate are problematic enough within the UK, where central government is allowed to spray money to struggling "regions", and where people can move freely to find work without linguistic or logistical barriers (despite the EU's "free movement", redundant Greeks cannot easily up sticks to, say, Luxembourg).

In the 16-member eurozone, the rich states are not allowed to subsidise the poor ones. At least those are the rules. However, countries who sleep in the afternoon have received a handout – of which more later – from the earnest BMW makers. The careful Germans, who ate only a starter, resent having to share the restaurant bill with the Mediterraneans, who enjoyed six courses and didn't even save up for the outing.

Of the pre-2004 EU15, only the UK, Sweden and Denmark are not eurozone members. The Scandinavians both voted against membership of the single currency in referendums (2003 and 2000, respectively). The 16 eurozone countries are Spain, Portugal, Ireland, Finland, France, Holland, Belgium, Luxembourg, Italy, Austria, Germany (all 1999), Greece (2001), Slovenia (2007), Malta and Cyprus (both 2008), and Slovakia (2009).

---

[209] Two months later he said, "Europe exemplifies a situation unfavourable to a common currency. It is composed of separate nations, speaking different languages, with different customs, and having citizens feeling far greater loyalty and attachment to their own country than to a common market or to the idea of Europe"

The first 11 of these formed economic and monetary union in 1999, having earlier joined the Exchange Rate Mechanism and kept government spending, borrowing, interest rates and inflation all low for an agreed period[210]. Greece was an eager latecomer with unconvincing credentials: it later confessed to underreporting its deficit by more than 2 per cent of GDP every year since 1997 in order to stir the drachma, the world's oldest currency, which had been mentioned by Aristophanes, into the Frankfurt pot. The Athens government had also included prostitution in its record of income. Apart from desperation, there was nothing wrong with this – prostitution is as legal as panel beating in Greece. The trouble was that the oldest profession was, like the younger ones, not paying its dues to government. And, ostensibly for reasons of security, details of Greece's considerable defence spending were excluded from the "out" column.

Even the Commission would later say that the country, which had enlisted Goldman Sachs to hide some of its debt under the carpet (GS made about 200million in the new money for their legerdemain), should never have been allowed to join but could not now be expelled. There had never been the political will – which as always was focused on "ever closer union" – to confront the economic mess of Greece and so endanger the project.

On 1 January 2002, the 12 countries introduced the euro "notes and coins", which initially at least got on well. The coins are country-specific. The buildings and vistas on the euro notes are all imaginary but the notes also have country-specific markings, denoted by a letter before the serial number more or less in reverse alphabetical order: "Z" is Belgium, "Y" is Greece ("Ellás"), "X" is Deutschland; "W" is reserved for Danmark/Denmark; "V" is España; "U" is France. "J" is reserved for the UK... The euro is used also in Andorra, Monaco, San Marino, Vatican City and two states that have seceded from Serbia: Montenegro and Kosovo (which had used the Deutschmark before 2002). If you suspect that a euro note is a forgery put it under ultraviolet light – if parts of it glow red then it's OK (as it will ever be). The red comes from europium, an element with symbol Eu and atomic number 63, in the ink.

In 1977 Sir Donald MacDougall, a CBI economist who had worked for Churchill during the war, was commissioned by the then EEC to chair an

---

[210] A halfway house for euro membership, ERM II, was established at the same time as the euro. Although Denmark rejected Maastricht, her government signed up to ERM II. Other members include the three Baltic states. Estonia, which in 2010 had a deficit of just 1.7 per cent (and debt of only 7.2 per cent – being a new country it had less time to splurge), is scheduled to join the euro on 1 January 2011. Latvia, pegged to the euro, has had perhaps the worst financial difficulties of any in the 27-member bloc. By summer 2009 she was effectively being ruled by Brussels ("effectively" in the sense of "in practice" or "de facto", rather than "competently")

enquiry into the mooted single currency. Such a project, he reported, would survive only if there were a federal budget of 25 per cent of all states' GDP (the EU enjoys about one twentieth of that) and uniform taxation: in other words, a fiscal union with the Commission holding the tax and spend reins (like the UK Treasury's hold on the UK). The EU picked out the bits it approved of, such as the redistribution of funds necessary for EMU (eg the Cohesion funds), and left behind the politically sensitive but nevertheless essential provisos about a mammoth central kitty funded by centralised tax raising. (MacDougall was luckier than another British economist employed by the Commission, Bernard Connolly, who would be hounded for pointing out the currency's problems.)

Having put the cart of monetary union before the horse of full political and fiscal union (which MacDougall had warned against), the EU elites run the risk of seeing the cart roll back and kill the horse. To avoid strains on the currency, eurozone countries – and the rest of us – must supposedly abide by the EU's Stability and Growth Pact (SGP), which limits national budget deficits (the shortfall between government spending and income) to three per cent of GDP (the total annual value of all the goods sold and all services provided in a country), inflation to two per cent and national debt (a country's total debt) to 60 per cent of GDP. So, even if you halve the deficit, the national debt will still grow. Fans of Charles Dickens might be reminded of Mr Micawber's saying: "Annual income £20, annual expenditure £19 19s 6d, result happiness. Annual income £20, annual expenditure £20 0s and 6d, result misery."

Between 2002 and 2005, when there was still a boom, which country do you think consistently had a deficit larger than the three per cent allowed by the SGP? No, not Greece – it was Germany, supposedly the goody-goody of the eurozone. Between 1999 and 2010, Belgium and Italy (whose debt was well over 100 per cent even in the good times) missed one or both of the SGP debt targets every year. Greece failed every year. Of all countries in the eurozone, only Luxembourg always kept deficit and debt under the limits. All other countries were breaking the pact – including France and the Netherlands. The ECB's French chief, Jean-Claude Trichet, later said that in 2004 and 2005 France and Germany wanted the SGP "destroyed". And what those two countries want, those two get.

The SGP was never officially abandoned, just almost universally ignored. The Commission changed the way that debt was computed by taking perfectly legitimate items (eg defence, aid and education) off countries' balance sheets. Because it wanted deeper integration at literally all costs, in the years of plenty it fiddled the figures and forgave transgressions it couldn't hide.

When the years of plenty came to an end, it was found in 2010 that Greece's budget deficit was 12.2 per cent of GDP and her debt 150 per cent. In 2009 Ireland's deficit was 14.3, the EU record. In 2010, the UK had a deficit of £156billion or 10.9 per cent. On average, the eurozone's 2010 deficit was 6.6 per cent of GDP, with debt at 84.7 per cent, well over the SGP limits. The rules state that during a recession governments can overshoot the deficit target as a "temporary and exceptional" measure. Germany came out of recession in Q2 2009 but it remains to be seen whether she is fined for being in breach but out of recession. The French finance minister does not see France getting back down to three per cent until 2014. However, the Commission has told her, Germany and Spain to bring their deficits under control by 2013. Italy and Belgium have until 2012, Ireland 2014. The UK has until 2015. Greece somehow expects to reach three per cent by 2012.

Try juggling a currency that must simultaneously suit a first-time buyer in Helsinki, a Milanese tailor wishing to export to the US, and a hotel in Ljubljana that wants to attract Japanese tourists. That's what the ECB, in Frankfurt, tries to do, all the while aiming to keep inflation below two per cent. In recent years, interest rates were kept too low for booming economies such as Spain and Ireland (and free-spending ones such as Greece), in an effort to support one particular member state, notably Germany, where politicians wanted low interest rates and used the influence of the Bundesbank in the ECB to get them. Even countries who were not overspending too much at government level were home to individuals and companies that were gorging themselves on money lent too cheaply for the true state of their economy. A strong euro harmed exports and the "Club Med" economies in particular, as well as Ireland, were least well placed to survive under its yoke.

Trichet sets the exchange rate. Reminding people in 2006 of the bank's semidetached status, he told Luxembourg's PM, Jean-Claude Juncker, chief of the 16 eurozone finance ministers, who wanted the ECB to consult more with them over interest rates: "If you check the banknote, you will see it is signed by myself." However, Article 219 of TFEU gives the Council the ability, in extreme circumstances, to set rates. The ECB used to have a degree of independence which disappeared when it became – as a consequence of the Lisbon Treaty – an EU institution, in a move that Trichet said risked making the bank subject to political influence. Well, the currency *is* political. Trichet, a former head of the French national bank, receives a salary of €345,252, over twice what the boss of America's Federal Reserve Bank enjoys but about the same as our Mervyn King, depending on the exchange rate.

Since 1994 the ECB has rented office space in a skyscraper dubbed Eurotower whose basement is home to a nightclub called Living XXL. The club's signage is a reminder to Mr Trichet that many eurozone governments have been living on

XXL portions, paid for with other people's money. Within a fortnight of the announcement of the €440billion bailout fund, the foundation stone for a permanent ECB HQ, on the banks of the River Main in Frankurt's east end, scheduled to be ready in 2014, was laid. The project was three years late and the budget had risen 70 per cent, from €500million to €850million.

The ECB's host, Germany, which had been run with efficiency and low inflation, exported to the less efficient eurozone members, who ran up trade deficits. They could not devalue their currency to make domestic goods more attractive either at home or abroad, and so people were made redundant, making growth and repayment of the fiscal deficit even harder. Without growth, there was also no more money to pay for the German goods and so Germany couldn't export as much and so she too eventually took a step backwards.

Growth was also absent from the euro's forerunners, such as the Snake (1969-1975: Britain lasted six weeks in 1972) and the Ecu currency's parent, the European Monetary System and its Exchange Rate Mechanism, launched by Roy Jenkins (1979-1993: Britain lasted two years, until Black – or White if you see the subsequent 16 years' growth as a blessing – Wednesday, 16 September 1992). It should have been no surprise that it happened a third time.

The euro is a product of the Maastricht Treaty, which contained three stages for economic and monetary union. The UK ducked out of the last stage, which saw, among other things, the abolition of national currencies, the introduction of the currency itself and fixed exchange rates. However, John Major did sign up to the first two stages.

Gordon Brown always maintained that it was coincidence that he – a supporter of monetary union during his first term as chancellor, even selling off the UK's gold to buy up euros – immediately did what the Maastricht Treaty required countries to do before they could join the euro: give independence to one's national bank. Granting the Bank Of England (BoE) independence was widely praised. But did Brown unchain the Old Lady Of Threadneedle Street only in order to obey Maastricht?

The 1997 Labour Party manifesto had mentioned "formidable obstacles" to euro membership but privately Brown, like Blair, was in favour of joining the first stage in 1999, even more so when he heard his enemy Robin Cook warn against it[211]. However, Brown's right-hand man, Ed Balls, was also against joining and his opinion won out. Furthermore, Brown had been opposed to the distraction of a referendum on the single currency, and he began to see that

---

[211] *Gordon Brown: Prime Minister* by Tom Bower (Harper Perennial, 2007)

EMU would not guarantee growth. To top it all, opposition to membership would stymie Blair. In 2001, not long after his second election victory, Blair offered Brown the premiership if he could fudge his "five tests" and say that Britain was ready for the euro. Blair regarded the tests as a sham, and he was right: they were economic tests whereas the primary consideration was political. Brown said the decision was too important for bargains. It's also likely that he didn't trust Blair.

Derek Scott, who was Blair's economic adviser between 1997 and 2003, wrote in 2004: "There was no evidence that Brown thought that membership of EMU was undesirable and no reason to doubt that, if he were to become Labour's next prime minister, he would want to take Britain in, though his strategy and tactics might be different from Blair's. When Labour came to power in 1997 there was little to separate them on EMU. Both saw political advantages in joining, but both were worried about the economics. Over the next few years in government Blair continued to worry about the economics but became more convinced about the political advantages – while Brown still appeared to accept the potential political advantages but became more and more concerned about the economics of entry."[212] As PM, Brown had a playful, limited-edition Justine Smith print of a euro symbol hanging in Number 10 – but no plans to risk a referendum on the currency.

In 2003, the day after Brown ruled out EMU membership, an MP wrote in his column for the *Guardian*:

"Stand by for some baby economics. Brown explained that, today, if UK inflation rises by 1%, UK interest rates would typically need to rise by 1.5% in order to get rising prices back under control. This would deliver a 'real' interest rate increase of 0.5%. Real interest rates are what matters: if inflation and interest rates are both 5%, savers are not getting any real return on their money.

More to the point, if both interest rates and inflation increase by the same amount, nothing changes. The incentives to borrow or save or spend or invest are unaltered. Now for the big question. What if the UK was part of the eurozone and our inflation increased by 1%? Assume inflation in the rest of the zone was unaltered. As we would be a large part of the total, Brown generously said that eurozone interest rates might go up by 0.3%.

Now for the killer punch. If inflation has gone up by 1%, but interest rates increase by only 0.3%, the real interest rate has actually fallen, by 0.7%. Borrowers might as well borrow more, savers might as well start spending again and before you can say 'convergence' the problem that needs to be dealt with is still running out of control. The only way you get things back under control is through what the Treasury like to call

[212] *The Sunday Times*, 19 September 2004

'flexibility'. In English that means 'reducing costs'. In plain English it means sacking people."[213]

Which is what happened in the PIIGS countries (Portugal, Italy, Ireland, Greece and Spain): there were cuts to the three "p"s (pay, pensions, profits) *plus* tax rises and reduced services. The alternatives – their elected leaders devaluing the currency to promote exports, or lowering interest rates to promote growth – were not open to them. And as more people become unemployed, revenues plummeted as the tax base shrank, unemployment benefits went up and so the problem compounded, forcing countries' deficits higher: economic prisoners of a political project.

When Greece (ie the euro) was first bailed out in May 2010, Van Rompuy said: "People are discovering what a 'common destiny' in monetary matters means. They are discovering that the euro affects their pensions, savings, jobs, their very daily life. It hurts. In my view, this growing public awareness is a major political development." He would also say: "Nobody ever told the proverbial man in the street that sharing a single currency was not just about making people's lives easier when doing business or travelling abroad, but also about being directly affected by economic developments in the neighbouring countries."

Not quite. The Scandinavian single-currency referendums of 2000 and 2003 showed clearly that when the proverbial man has the arguments spelt out to him by campaigners, he says no to the euro. And Herman should remember that the euro project was sold, particularly to the German people, with the promise that thrifty Northerners would not have to pay for the Club Med's pool parties (back then it was Italy, not Greece, that was considered the most likely to bomb).

The author of the *Guardian* article was the member for Witney, David Cameron. Earlier in the piece he wrote:

"Everyone knows that the best argument against joining the euro is that a single currency across Europe means a single interest rate across Europe. As I have said to audiences in my constituency with Brown-like monotony: there are times when West Oxfordshire and Westphalia need different interest rates. I feel this with something of a passion. To be frank, I have 'form' on this issue. I was working in the Treasury during our membership of the Exchange Rate Mechanism and was there on Black Wednesday. In my defence I would say that I have learnt the lessons of that humiliating experience: that the UK should never again attempt to fix its exchange rates or join a system that means you lose control of your own interest rates... We should set British interest rates to meet British needs."

---

[213] *The Guardian*, 10 June 2003

The author and commentator Simon Heffer, no Cameron cheerleader, once asked: "What is the point of electing governments, if there are vital policies that they cannot alter? That to me has always been the clinching argument against our entering the single currency. We would be slaves to someone else's economic policy. At present, if the way a government runs our economy is offensive, we can change the government and with it the policy. If we were economically administered from [the ECB in] Frankfurt, simply unelecting one government and replacing it with another would be a footling exercise. The economic policy would stay the same."[214] (He also made the point that, as it stands, our governments cannot change many other policies, eg trade and agriculture.) As Maynard Keynes said, "Who controls the currency, controls the country."[215] The 16 eurozone finance ministers are like toddlers in the back seat with toy steering wheels.

Unfortunately for the euro's fans in Britain, there's no doubt that the UK would have been far worse off in the euro, both before and after the recession. You can hear the lament in a pre-recession comment piece in the *Independent*: "Overall growth in the eurozone has been consistently lower than growth in the non-eurozone EU members since the euro was launched. Worryingly, economic integration within the eurozone does not seem to have brought significant economic benefits. Trade within the zone has grown more slowly than trade between the zone and the rest of the EU."[216] Why "worryingly"? Mr Almunia, who was meant to be enforcing the SGP pact, made the same lament.

Later, the *Financial Times* carried a piece conceding the same point: "There is no evidence that being outside the eurozone has imposed a performance penalty upon the UK economy. Between the first quarter of 1999 and the first quarter of 2008, [the UK] economy expanded by 28 per cent, against 21 per cent in the eurozone as a whole and 16 per cent in Germany... Remaining outside the euro preserves the safety valve of currency flexibility, while losing nothing in

---

[214] *The Daily Telegraph*, 24 January 2008

[215] "The finance of the country is ultimately associated with the liberties of the country. It is a powerful leverage by which the English liberty has been gradually acquired... If the House of Commons can by any possibility lose the power of control of the grants of public money, depend upon it, your very liberty will be worth very little in comparison... That powerful leverage has been what is commonly known as the power of the purse: the control of the House of Commons over public expenditure – your main guarantee for purity – the root of English liberty. No violence, no tyranny, whether of experiments or of such methods as are likely to be made in this country, could ever for a moment have a chance of prevailing against the energies of that great assembly. No, if these powers of the House of Commons come to be encroached upon, it will be by tacit and insidious methods, and therefore I say that public attention should be called to this." William Gladstone, Liberal PM, speaking to the House of Commons, 1891

[216] *The Independent*, 27 September 2006

aggregate economic performance. Being outside has not even hurt London's position as a financial centre."[217] Then came the recession. Even Mandelson said, in 2010, that "sterling's flexibility provided an additional support to demand" during the recession.

Being outside the eurozone, we still have the ability to set our own interest rate. However, we are not as free when doing so as we think. (The treaties state that "member states shall co-ordinate their economic policies".) Although the BoE's Monetary Policy Committee (MPC) is "independent" (because Brussels demands that national banks must be independent – there's irony) and "the pound in your pocket" shows the Queen, interest rates are not determined only by domestic criteria. In December 2003, six months after ruling out euro entry, Gordon Brown, for the purposes of increasing "convergence" (one of the four failed tests), switched the way that inflation was measured to the Consumer Price Index (CPI) from the Retail Price Index (RPI).

The CPI is an EU construct that the ECB, when aiming for two per cent inflation, uses to set its interest rate. It omits all housing costs, such as heating and council tax, not just mortgage payments (which the RPIX rate had also omitted), and so did not and does not include ballooning house prices. Because John Major signed us up to the first two stages of EMU, we are aiming for the same inflation target as the ECB, and the CPI is also the MPC's target when it makes its monthly interest-rate decision. The MPC states that its only job is to control inflation. And because it aimed for such a low inflation figure, it kept interest rates too low during the boom years. If CPI had not been the target, interest rates would have been higher – because RPI and RPIX were higher than CPI, not least because they took note of rising house prices – and there would have been much less easy money available.

In April 2010, it was thought that Greece might need about €10billion to tide it over. Then it was €30billion. A month later, this figure had jumped to €110billion over three years (€80billion from other eurozone members and €30billion from the IMF).

The rules for the euro are explicit about this being illegal. Even in March 2010, Angela Merkel admitted: "We have a treaty under which there is no possibility of paying to bail out member states in difficulty." Anyway, which leader could splash his or her taxpayers' cash on a delinquent neighbour and expect re-election? Won't it encourage others to run up massive debts, safe in the knowledge that the political dream will pay for individual profligacy? Why should the Irish put their house in order if other untidy economies are offered a

---

[217] *Britain is better off outside the euro* by Martin Wolf, *The Financial Times*, 29 May 2008

Teutonic clean-up? This being the EU, however, common sense does not always apply. Fortunately, the Treaties are unequivocal, eg the part of Maastricht that's now TFEU 123: "Overdraft facilities or any other type of credit facility with the European Central Bank or with the central banks of the member states... in favour of... central governments... shall be prohibited, as shall the purchase directly from them by the European Central Bank or national central banks of debt instruments." However, this being the EU, the EU's own rules are routinely broken in pursuit of "ever closer union".

In May 2010 the ECB began to buy eurozone governments' debts (Greece, Spain and Portugal to begin with) indirectly, picking up billions' worth of (junk) bonds from banks, in order to get round Article 123. This is printing money, or "quantitative easing" as the euphemism has it. The UK is allowed to do it, but not the ECB. There were reports in the German and French press that President Sarkozy had leaned on his countryman, the ECB's president, to buy the shabby Greek bonds held by French banks, who were desperate to sell (France was home to the most Greek debt). This allowed Tsarko to offload the liabilities of his private sector on to the ECB – and therefore all EU taxpayers. That is true "European solidarity".

Soon afterwards, Commissar Barnier announced plans to regulate, via ESMA (see below) in Paris, the (American) credit-ratings agencies, which had labelled Greek bonds junk. Yet again, the EU goes after the messenger, not the problem. Standard and Poor's and friends become scapegoats for continent-wide incontinent government spending.

The other famous "no bailout" clause is TFEU 125: "The Union shall not be liable for or assume the commitments of central governments, regional, local or other public authorities, other bodies governed by public law, or public undertakings of any member state... A member state shall not be liable for or assume the commitments of central governments, regional, local or other public authorities, other bodies governed by public law, or public undertakings of another member state, without prejudice to mutual financial guarantees for the joint execution of a specific project."

How could the EU get round that? Well, TFEU 122 states: "Where a member state is in difficulties or is seriously threatened with severe difficulties caused by natural disasters or exceptional occurrences beyond its control, the Council, on a proposal from the Commission, may grant, under certain conditions, Union financial assistance to the member state concerned." This is what insurers call "force majeure" – hurricanes and earthquakes. Does anyone think that a country spending far more than it earns is "exceptional occurrences beyond its control"? Extending the natural-disasters article to cover recidivist fiscal delinquency is a fudge too far. The European Council had previously declared that article 122 should not supersede 123-125 but this was forgotten when the EU got desperate.

On 9 May 2010, exactly 60 years after the Schuman Declaration, the EU announced a backstop with €500billion of lending power. It looked like a treasury, to go with the 11-year-old currency, but no one was crass enough to call it that. When it's in place, will the profligate states continue to order champagne for their end of the table, knowing that someone else will pick up the restaurant bill? This looks like the EU continuing to encourage "moral hazard" (a term defined by the *Oxford English Dictionary* as "lack of incentive to guard against risk where one is protected from its consequences, eg, by insurance").

Already subsidising the former East Germany, Berlin did not really want to subsidise below the olive line as well. Merkel had to cancel tax cuts to pay Germany's share. At the meeting to agree the bailout fund "Sarkozy demanded 'a compromise from everyone to support Greece... or France would reconsider its position in the euro,' according to a source cited by *El País*. 'Sarkozy went as far as banging his fist on the table and threatening to leave the euro,' said one unnamed Socialist leader. 'That obliged Merkel to bend and reach an agreement.' A different source said that 'France, Italy and Spain formed a common front against Germany, and Sarkozy threatened Merkel with a break in the traditional Franco-German axis.' *El País* also quotes Sarkozy as having said... that 'if at time like this, with all that is happening, Europe is not capable of a united response, then the euro makes no sense'."[218]

If all countries had obeyed the SGP, they would not have risked bankruptcy and needed the new treasury – but that is not to say that the treasury does not suit the EU's long-term plans. Knowing since at least the days of MacDougall that a central treasury was a step too far for electorates and the politicians who would have to sell it at home, the euro's architects set up the euro without one – but hoped that a crisis would necessitate one. "I am sure the euro will oblige us to introduce a new set of economic policy instruments. It is politically impossible to propose that now. But some day there will be a crisis and new instruments will be created," said Romano Prodi when Commission president in 2001.

Sceptics always warned that it would come to this: either a eurozone break-up, or full union, with subsidies between members as the norm – although the euro was sold, especially to the Germans, with guarantees that subsidies and bailouts would never happen. The Maastricht Treaty – as quoted – was explicit that this sort of bailout would be forbidden.

---

[218] *The Guardian*, 14 May 2010

Nevertheless, a two-part €500billion sticking plaster was created, in order to support euro governments with payment problems and so try to stem the sovereign-debt crisis. Ministers in the Eurogroup agreed to government-backed loan guarantees and bilateral loans worth up to €440billion from eurozone members, most of whom were in debt themselves. Countries outside the euro, such as the UK, which at the time had a hung parliament and a dead duck chancellor, were not invited to vote even though they might later be on the hook for some of the package's measures and even though measures affecting the EU budget (which would be collateral for some of the borrowing) require unanimity from all members and a vote in the European parliament. It was like tramps promising each other palaces if times got bad. Two countries outside the euro, Sweden and Poland, also chipped in. The €440billion European Financial Stability Facility, based in Luxembourg, is in the form of a "special purpose vehicle", which are often legitimate but were made infamous by Enron's use of them – their responsibilities and liabilities are never quite clear. The IMF added about €250billion (although the US Senate soon after voted 94-0 to think about withholding the US portion of the IMF money to any states with over 100 per cent debt).

It wasn't at all clear that this money was necessarily lying around when it was promised. There were also apparently two secret exit clauses in the agreement: if a country's constitutional court ruled the aid illegal (how could it not?), then that country could opt out of helping. (Several cases were, at the time of writing, being heard in Karlsruhe, the seat of Germany's constitutional court.) And if a country has to borrow at a higher rate than it could lend the money to Greece or Spain or whoever – and is not certain that it will be reimbursed the difference by other eurozone countries – it can also refuse to help.

In addition, a stability fund allowed the Commission to borrow up to €60billion a year on the markets (in addition to €50billion that it already had), using the whole EU budget as collateral. If a country defaults, *all* 27 member states have to repay, meaning that UK taxpayers are pro rata liable for about 13 per cent (or €8billion) of any loss.

Karl Otto Pöhl, a former head of the Bundesbank, said, "The foundation of the euro has fundamentally changed as a result of the decision by eurozone governments to transform themselves into a transfer union. That is a violation of every rule. In the treaties it explicitly states that no country is liable for the debts of any other. But what we are doing right now is exactly that. Added to this is the fact that, against all its vows and against an explicit ban within its own constitution, the European Central Bank has become involved in financing states."[219]

Low interest rates allowed the importing countries to give Germany a huge export surplus, which she is now having to give back to them in cash (having already lent some of it to them in the good times at too-low rates). In the real world this would be like a car company paying off your car loan when you couldn't afford repayments – but you still get to keep the car. Germany can either keep paying off her clients' debts – in perpetuity – or lose its best market when its dependents go to the wall. The first choice, since it uses German taxpayers' money, is electoral arsenic and unsustainable, while the second cuts off Germany's income. (A third option would be for Germany to import more but, souvenirs from Mediterranean resorts aside, she doesn't want enough of her neighbours' stuff.)

The humane exit for Greece would be, wrote Ambrose Evans-Pritchard, to "leave the euro and carry out a controlled default, sharing the pain with foolhardy creditors. The EU is preventing this cure: either to protect bond-holders (eg French and German banks), giving them time to shuffle off their bad debts on to EU taxpayers; or because Brussels refuses as a matter of ideological principle to countenance any step back, ever, in the sacrosanct Project... The North-South divide within EMU has been allowed to go so far that any solution must now be offensive to either side, and therefore will be resisted. The euro is becoming an engine of intra-European tribal hatred."[220]

It wasn't just French banks who were on the hook for Greek debt. As Merkel said, "If the euro fails, it is not only the currency that fails – Europe fails. The idea of European unity fails." At the time of writing, a stronger SGP was planned, with automatic fines as well as cohesion and other funds being withheld (try keeping the French from their agricultural handouts – it's a non-starter). Also being urged, by Herman, was the oversight of national budgets by "peer (p)review" in Ecofin – before national parliaments had seen them, let alone voted on them. So, the Iberian and Greek finance ministers would sit in judgment on the German budget. Until stupid children are allowed to mark their clever classmates' homework, this must be considered lunatic[221]. But it still makes

---

219 *Der Spiegel*, 18 May 2010
220 *The Daily Telegraph*, 24 May 2010
221 "... The EU's budget commissioner will sit around the table with his 'expert team' of civil servants – all well paid and with jobs for life – holding 27 booklets containing the draft budgets of all the member states. They will have no clue about the diverse public sectors of all the different states, but will attempt to give opinions on how many staff the Germany defence ministry should employ, or what costs Italian social security should cover for families with a handicapped member, or how many state schools should be closed down in Poland. Then their

"more Europe", which is the real point. Bolting the stable door long after the horse had bolted (having been set free by most of the members), the economic and monetary affairs commissioner Mr Rehn said: "We want governments to send their budget outlines to Brussels for review before they are approved by their national parliaments. We can then see early whether a country is adhering to the Stability and Growth Pact. If not, we would intervene." As Angela Merkel said at a European Council in March 2010: "I have always said that economic governance for all 27 member states is what we are after."

Just as the independence of national banks is a prerequisite of joining the euro, so is the vesting of the supervision of the banking sector in a separate body. Brown fulfilled this part of the bargain by transferring the regulatory role of the BoE to his new Financial Services Authority (FSA, whose 2,600 employees earned an average £55,000). This body, with the Treasury and BoE, comprised the Tripartite Authorities, none of which was clear about where its jurisdiction started or ended. After the chaos of the 2007 run on Northern Rock, including whether government support for it should have been secret or not, it was regretted that supervision of the banking sector was no longer a matter entirely for the experienced Bank Of England. Poor Gordon – the independence of the Bank had been the one thing he'd done that had been almost universally welcomed and considered brave and wise. Aside from the fact that the decision to grant its independence turns out not to have been his initiative anyway, the BoE's independence – especially the hiving off of the Bank's regulatory duties to the much criticised FSA – caused huge problems, if not the biggest run on the banking sector since the Victorian era. No one in the Tripartite Authorities was sure who should have been keeping an eye on the banks. It was a case of regulatory "underlap".

The House of Lords economic affairs committee said in a 2009 report that the three-way divvy had resulted in "an inadequate definition of roles and responsibilities of the Bank of England, the Treasury and the FSA", causing "failures of regulation and supervision that *contributed to the UK financial crisis*" [emphasis added]. Ben Bernanke, the head of the US Federal Reserve, told the US Senate in 2009 that during "the past few years the government of Britain removed from the Bank of England most of its supervisory authorities. When the crisis hit – for example, when the Northern Rock bank came under stress – the Bank of England was completely in the dark and unable to deal effectively with

---

recommendations would be passed to the Council of Ministers. A curious meeting would then take place when the Greek finance minister would be able to question the British chancellor about how much he spends on equipment for his troops in Afghanistan, or the Portuguese minister might tell the French that they should reduce their unemployment benefit." *As crisis bites, EU grabs for power* by Marta Andreasen in *The Daily Telegraph*, 20 June 2010

what turned out to be a destructive run and a major problem for the British economy." In other words: "The Brits can't blame us for that." Sitting atop this awkward three-legged stool was the EU, which designed the construct.

The tripartite system can also be said to have contributed to the wider financial crisis. The 1997 overthrow of the Bank Of England's sole oversight had made possible a kind of wild west – no single regulator was in charge, in line with EU demands for a regulator independent of the country's central bank. Into this laissez-faire environment came several US banks, who had noticed the "underlap" and took full advantage of the reduced surveillance in the old country. They were particularly happy to find that there was now no UK equivalent of the parts of the USA's Glass-Steagall Act that forbade banks from being involved in a mix of insurance, commercial banking and investment banking. Because so many US banks set up in London, Mr Clinton was forced in 1999 to repeal (the important part of) the Glass-Steagall Act, although he had been lobbied to do so long before Gordon made London a free-for-all.

In opposition, the Tories said that they would abolish the FSA and restore the supervision of the banking sector to the Bank Of England. In office and not being mad enough to join the euro, they abolished the FSA and announced in its place the Prudential Regulatory Authority (PRA), which would come under the BoE and be headed by the BoE's governor. There would also be a Financial Policy Committee to monitor more general trends. It will almost be status quo ante. But there's another three-legged EU stool.

Capitalising on the banking crisis in order to extend its control, the EU botched together a new tripartite system, though at the supranational level. On top of that will be a European Systemic Risk Board (ESRB), to monitor and assess risks to the stability of the financial system as a whole, with the power to demand access to any bank's books. The ESRB, based in Brussels (but in league with the ECB, so hard luck to the countries not in the euro), will look for macroeconomic kinks in the financial sector, and the three new European Supervisory Authorities (ESAs) will monitor, respectively, banks, insurers and securities firms, with the power to overrule national regulators. The ESAs are: the European Banking Authority (EBA, in London); the European Insurance and Occupational Pensions Authority (EIOPA, in Frankfurt); and the European Securities and Markets Authority (ESMA, in Paris)[222].

A Treasury select committee report called the set-up "a recipe for a muddle" – Britain already knew that bad news comes in threes – and warned: "There are concerns that the Commission will have unilateral power to declare a [financial]

---

[222] In 2010, a European parliamentary committee tried to get all of them based in Frankfurt

emergency, which will give ESAs power to direct national regulators still further." The BoE's Financial Markets Law Committee said that the three bodies might create legal uncertainty, which could lead to "systemic failure and widespread market disruption".

The ESAs will work to simple-majority rules (Cyprus has as much of a voice as us), so no vetoes. The Commission proposal for the three ESAs said that they "shall fulfil an active co-ordination role between national supervisory authorities [the UK's FSA or PRA, for instance], in particular in case of adverse developments which potentially jeopardise the orderly functioning and integrity of the financial system in the EU. However, in some emergency situations, co-ordination may not be sufficient, notably when national supervisors alone lack the tools to respond rapidly to an emerging cross-border crisis. The ESAs should, therefore, in such exceptional circumstances, have the power to require national supervisors to jointly take specific action. The determination of a cross-border emergency situation involves a degree of appreciation, and should therefore be left to the European Commission[!]" In short: financial emergencies "should be left" to the people that cannot get their accounts signed off but who did bring you the euro.

One of these ESAs, the EBA, which is perched in the UK capital, can be forced to call on the UK's capital to bail out another country's bank: "[the EBA] shall actively facilitate and, where deemed necessary, co-ordinate any actions undertaken by the relevant national competent supervisory authorities... [when] adverse developments... may seriously jeopardise the orderly functioning and integrity of financial markets or the stability of the financial system in the European Union."[223]

In 2004, the USA, Japan and the EU legislated hastily to guard against a repeat of recent scandals, such as Enron, which had survived as long as it had by inflating its worth. The rules, formulated way above even EU level, were known as the Basel II Accord. The key requirement was something known as mark-to-market rules which maintained that a financial institution must be able to prove its assets at the end of each day's trading. If it could not, it had to cease trading, even if those assets might appreciate greatly in the near future. This is an easy test to pass in a boom. When times are tight and, say, your mortgage book is worth 15 per cent less than a year ago, it is not always so easy to pass – but that does not mean that the company is insolvent or pulling an Enron.

When the financial crisis bit hard in summer 2008, the USA was able

---

[223] How this squares with the "no bailout" rules of Maastricht, now TFEU 123-125, is not obvious – but it's very likely that the elite will interpret the rules in the EU's favour

unilaterally to relax the Basel II requirement, though obviously too late for many firms. The EU member states, however, had to wait for the Commission to suspend Directives 2006/48 and 2006/49, known together as the Capital Adequacy Directive (CAD), and long since implemented by national parliaments. Many companies were banjaxed by a slow-to-legislate Commission; the parliaments in those companies' countries could not unilaterally relax the CAD. By the time that the Commission suspended CAD it was too late for many. Two months earlier, the ECB had even increased the eurozone interest rate from 4 per cent – where it had been unchanged for over a year – to 4.25, just as the USA, which understood which way round to do things, had slashed its rate.

The banking crisis was not a failure to legislate, it was a mixture of lending too cheaply to hopeless cases and too much panicky legislation. The USA soon realised this and shrugged off the Basel yoke. Nor was the crisis caused solely by the USA exporting the financial equivalent of mad-cow debt. Northern Rock, to pick the earliest example of nationalisation, got into trouble all by its greedy self without any help from Uncle Sam. The UK bank with most exposure to the USA – HSBC – seemed to be the UK's fittest. If you lend more than a property is worth and require little or no deposit (or proof of earnings), you will more often than not come unstuck, particularly when interest rates have been set too low as a consequence of aiming for the EU's CPI target.

Northern Wreck, which notoriously offered 125 per cent loans, came unstuck. As a result of strict EU rules on repaying state aid, Northern Rock (NR) also became one of the most aggressive repossessors. And it sold repossessed homes for less than the market rate, depressing the market further. People with a bad credit history could not switch from NR when it became far less competitive (as a consequence of having to comply with EU rules on state-aided banks). When, for instance, in summer 2009 the Bank of England's base rate was 0.5 per cent – and "swap rates", which lenders use to price deals, had fallen from 2.51 to 2.05 per cent in a month – NR was charging 6.29 per cent for its five-year fixed-rate mortgages. Another bank part-owned by the taxpayer, Lloyds TSB, was charging 7.89 per cent for a five-year fixed-rate mortgage. Lenders were making the biggest margins for more than 20 years. Still, at least the EU was happy: the increased margins helped the banks to repay their state aid more quickly. On the deposit side, the EU said that NR could, also for reasons of competition, hold no more than 1.5 per cent of the UK savings market. The bank ended up having to shed a third of its staff and make both its savings and borrowing rates unattractive. The EU also wanted Lloyds to lose a third of its current accounts (it had 30 per cent of the UK market).

In 2008, many other EU members had also bailed out their banks. First had been Ireland, guaranteeing the deposits in her six biggest. Nickel Neelie, the then competition commissar, talked tough: "My people were in Dublin, and returned with positive news that there will be corrections to the plan. They will correct the discriminatory elements which we don't like. You can't introduce something like that, it is not allowed. And a guarantee without any limits isn't allowed either. They will reformulate their plan, after which we can establish together that it is in compliance with the treaty." However, the Greeks soon followed Ireland's lead, as did the Germans, despite having pledged that they would not do so. Denmark then followed suit. National self-interest, for a while at least, looked stronger than EU rules on state aid. Bugger-thy-neighbour was winning the day.

The Commission did, however, ban banks which took part in Brown's bailout from paying dividends to shareholders for five years[224]. And, of course, on top of the provisos already mentioned, Nickel Neelie continually warned the UK that the country's banks would have to dispose of assets if they intended to keep their state aid. She asked the Royal Bank of Scotland to rein in its lending to small businesses just as the UK government, which owned 70 per cent of it (later 84 per cent), was urging it to lend more to SMEs. RBS chief executive Stephen Hester said, in August 2009, "It's our job to support our customers. Anything that disrupts our ability to do that is not good for the UK economy and that is being taken into account in our discussion with the EU." Despite Mr Hester's protest, RBS's share of small-business lending fell from 30 per cent to 20. A few months later, he would say, "The combined impact of the EU and the decision on bonuses has reduced the value of the bank by 40 per cent."

The subsequent EU-mandated massacre of RBS led to 3,700 job losses and the sale of 318 retail branches. In addition to turning banks into wine bars, RBS had to sell its investment-banking operations and insurance businesses, such as Churchill and Green Flag. It also found £3billion by selling Asian retail and commercial banks to HSBC. Lloyds had to sell 600 branches, including its Cheltenham & Gloucester branches as well as the TSB brand and its telephone bank, Intelligent Finance [sic].

Two years later, the financial crisis leapt from the corporate level to the national level and the European Union itself was endangered, at which point it became even less keen to stick to the rules.

The EU's protectionist hedge-fund directive, Alternative Investment Fund Managers Directive (AIFM), will, unless greatly amended, see an exodus from

---

[224] Separately, the EU later ruled that bankers had to defer 40 to 60 per cent of their bonuses for between three and five years, and half of any upfront bonus had to be in the form of shares or other securities linked to their employer's performance

the City (to anywhere outside the EU but mostly Switzerland). The AIFM will also deprive "third country" start-ups of funds from the EU, thereby choking global enterprise while preventing EU investors from profiting from the next Google. Pension-fund managers throughout the EU's provinces have warned that AIFM will smash the nest eggs of several generations – the Dutch estimated that their sector alone would be €1.5billion a year worse off. Charities, too, will have fewer places to invest. However, hedge funds can find (though not create) a currency's weak spots: Juncker has said that the EU has "torture instruments in the cellar" to use against anyone speculating against the euro. He may very well have meant the destructive AIFM, which can only leave all EU citizens worse off. But at least the euro is cosseted. However, in a rapidly ageing continent it might be wise not to choke pension funds.

In 2001 "most of the 12 euro countries supported a transcontinental competition called 'Be A Euro Superstar', a euro-knowledge contest for schoolchildren... The first prize didn't seem terribly appealing – it was a trip to Frankfurt to spend New Year's Eve with Wim Duisenberg, then head of the ECB – but the bank said millions of children took part," wrote TR Reid in *The United States Of Europe*[225]. In the next section, the EU's other approaches to children are looked at.

---

[225] *The United States Of Europe* (Penguin, 2005)

Propaganda

We know that the EU, via lobbyists and NGOs, likes to talk to itself. But it also likes to talk *about* itself. A lot. It's been estimated that it spends €2.4billion per annum on advertising[226] but almost all of its budget is propagandistic.

Where does so much of your money go? A leaked 1993 EU report[227] on propaganda urged the targeting of young people because "it is strategically judicious to strike where resistance is weakest". It also suggested targeting women, who are "more intuitively inclined"[228]. Can you imagine if your government wrote something like that? It did – for the EU is our true government – and did so again in 1998, when another report explained "[the] education system – and teachers in particular – will have a major role to play in forming and communicating with young people. Children can perform a messenger function in conveying the [euro] message to the home environment. Young people will often in practice act as go-betweens with the older generations, helping them familiarise themselves with and embrace the euro"[229]. To think that the children would be more enthused by a trip to meet "Dim Wim", the first head of the ECB, than almost anything else is part of the great disconnect between the EU and its citizens.

To help children to "perform a messenger function in conveying the [euro] message" and other integrationist ends, there have been several child-unfriendly publications put out by the EU:

Captain Euro, in which the hero, with the help of his Yellow Agents, fights the evil "Dr D Vider", a shamed financier turned terrorist who believes in national boundaries (nice conflation, Brussels). His henchpersons include a former human cannonball who totes a yo-yo (possibly a reference to fluctuating currency rates experienced by those "unfortunate" enough not to be in the eurozone) and another ex-circus star – a female trapeze artist who wears hotpants and "Chanel

---

226 *The hard sell: EU communication policy and the campaign for hearts and minds*, available from www.openeurope.org.uk. The authors estimate that the EU spends more than Coca-Cola on advertising. In an earlier interview, one of the authors, Dr Lee Rotherham, said, "Much of this [material aimed at children] is outrageous propaganda cynically trying to brainwash the young into thinking the EU is an essential part of their lives. This stuff is relentlessly positive about the EU's work, with only the tiniest, if any, mention of the counter-arguments or any dissenting voices. Brussels realises it is losing people's hearts and minds and so it is spending more and more of our money on marketing material and hordes of press officers to champion its existence"
227 *De Clercq Report for Comité des Sages*, 31 March 1993
228 The 1998 *Pex Report* said women should be targeted because "they manage the finances of the family, go shopping"
229 *Report of the Working Group on Euro-Education*, EU parliament, January 1998

No 13". It is unfair to paraphrase these characters, do pay a visit to www.captaineuro.com – after all, your sterling has paid for it.

L'Europe, Mon Foyer [*Europe, My Home*]. Ten thousand copies of this book, which features "Papa Houpette", a dwarf who's one foot tall in his socks and wears a natty moustache and red waistcoat, were distributed to primary-school children in Belgium. The book's aim is to tell children how marvellous the European Union is – and it also informs them, in the words of the *Guardian*, that "the EU is a necessity, that the Common Agricultural Policy is an unalloyed good, and the European Constitution essential"[230].

The Raspberry Ice-Cream War, in which our teen heroes travel back in time to tell their ignorant forebears that divisions between countries cause war: "A peaceful Europe without frontiers – Christine, Max and Paul take it for granted. Until a mysterious home page on the internet pitches our three heroes into a land long before our time. Here, there are still guards at the city gate and every summer the raspberry ice-cream war breaks out anew. The people in this country need a good lesson in democracy and Europe. Christine, Max and Paul arrive just in time to help." ("A good lesson in democracy"? Such as how to accept the odd yes vote but ignore all of the no votes?)

Had the young shavers not heard of Yugoslavia (or even the EU's own seat, Belgium, which can barely keep itself in one piece, let alone most of a continent)? Conversely, if the EU itself becomes a single state, won't the "problem" of nationalism be not only replicated but hugely magnified? You'd need a one-state world if pursuing that logic (and for Tito, or someone similarly cohesive, to live a very long time indeed). As it stands, the democratic nation state, usually in concert with others, is the best defence against rogues and repugnant transnational ideologies, as the United Kingdom showed on 3 September 1939 in an example of *true* European spirit – laying down your life for your neighbours and democracy.

Operation Red Dragon features gorgeous, pouting, fictitious MEP Elisa Correr, who in an average day torpedoes intercontinental trade deals, dodges bullets and wears a dressing gown that does its valiant but unsuccessful best to cover her cleavage. Her photojournalist boyfriend is a Brit called Tony.

---

[230] *The Guardian*, 23 November 2005. The article ends: "... as a pedagogical tool, it [*L'Europe, Mon Foyer*] is shameful: it fails to encourage children to think, only to accept a piece of taxpayer-funded European Commission rhetoric that works by bogus analogy or implausible claim. The noble aim of teaching Europe's children about the EU and getting them to question its institutions has been lost in favour of boring propaganda. Surely such child cruelty should be banned across the EU? But no: from next year it will be offered to schools in all member states"

Elisa seems, in her sub-Lara Croft way, to be a precursor of *Troubled Waters* and its heroine, Irina Vega MEP (also fictitious), who fights companies that pollute rivers (as everyone knows, there was never clean water before the EU) and whose speech bubbles are full of gems such as: "I seem to spend my whole life on the train between Brussels and Strasbourg, but I'd hate to have to choose between mussels and chips and Strasbourg onion tart!" Jacques Hinckxt (not fictitious), of the European parliament's information team, pointed out that the cost of the initial print run of *Troubled Waters* was a modest €540,000 for 780,000 copies. "You can say it's euro propaganda," he said, "but you can't say it's a waste of money."[231]

Let Me Tell You A Secret About The Environment, which is "the story of Tom, who falls asleep in his favourite cupboard and ends up discovering important secrets, together with his friend Lila the fox. Educational booklet designed to interest children aged 6-10 in environmental questions". Such as how many trees had to die to further the fiction that the EU is good for the environment? (Does CS Lewis's estate know that his Narnia books have been plagiarised?)

See also *Hidden Disaster*, a 2010 comic produced at a cost of £200,000 and circulated in the UK and elsewhere which told the story of two Commission employees. Max and Zana, from the EU's humanitarian-aid department, try to secure emergency funding for a fictional state devastated by an earthquake[232]. A week after the graphic novel was publicised, Chile was hit by a real earthquake. The EU's real Max and Zana, still fresh from criticism of not doing enough for Haiti, were again not seen on the front line of rescue efforts.

Let's Draw Europe Together, a colouring-in book about Europe, which sidesteps those questions you might have – "If the EU has pretensions to statehood, does my child need only one colour for the map? Won't that be a bit boring?" – by asking its junior citizens instead to colour in phrases, such as "Europe – my country". Every school in the UK was also sent something called *The European Union: What's It All About?* which claimed credit, inter alia, for children's future "career opportunities" and "rights to travel". Its suggested further reading was a pamphlet titled according to the laws of Marxist inevitability: *When will the euro be in our pockets?*[233]

The European parliament supplied an "information pack" to UK children in Years 3 and 4 that aimed to show the EU worked, the *Yorkshire Post* reported on 3 January 2007. The eurosceptic character in the worksheets was ageing, non-groovy "Portsmouth plumber Charlie Bolton". Below a chart showing how the

[231] *Reason*, May 2003
[232] *The Sunday Telegraph*, 21 February 2010
[233] Chris Heaton-Harris MEP, *The European Journal*, January 2008

various institutions of the EU interact, Charlie Bolton says: "Europe – it's just faceless bureaucrats – none of them elected. And they impose their laws on us from Brussels whenever they fancy. All that red tape to make our lives harder." As the *Yorkshire Post* went on, "It then guides pupils to reject the notion that the EU is anti-democratic by reminding them of the elected European parliament. 'Do you agree with Charlie? What does the flow chart tell you about how laws are made?' it asks. The teacher is also instructed to show pupils how to counter his argument and to lead the pupils to conclude that he is wrong and that the EU is democratic. The lesson plan reads: 'Discuss Charlie Bolton's attitude to EU legislation. If Charlie knew that the members of the European parliament are elected and that the Council of Ministers represents our governments, do the students think that he would change his mind?'"

In October 2006, the European parliament adopted the Youth in Action (YIA) programme for 2007-13, which was allocated €885m in funding. Ján Figel', commissar for education, training, culture and multilingualism, said that the programme existed "for the defence of cultures, for a future of prosperity, understanding and peace. It fosters the idea of belonging to the European Union". Most notoriously, a coffee house in Finland received YIA funding to sustain its afternoon-nap programme, which in the name of stress-busting offered "everyone the chance to have a sleep for free". Not all of YIA's projects were in the EU: a Serbian venture received £21,000 to show that silent-movie slapstick is a form of "non-verbal communication" and exchange students in Macedonia could enjoy a conference called *Stories And Legends*, which received £18,000.

In 2008, the UK enacted Directive 2005/29 ("concerning unfair business-to-consumer commercial practices"), which was best known for stopping theatre managements quoting selectively from reviews. Its clause 18 states: "… It is therefore appropriate to include in the list of practices which are in all circumstances unfair a provision which, without imposing an outright ban on advertising directed at children, protects them from direct exhortations to purchase." Sure, EU propaganda does not ask children to buy – or pester their parents to buy – anything. But, just as certainly as tears precede bedtime, those children are being asked by EU propaganda to buy *into* something.

The EU's website is named after Europa. In *Europe: A Concise Encyclopedia Of The European Union*, Lord (Rodney) Leach writes: "With their unique gift for imagery, the ancient Greeks symbolised Europe in the myth of Europa, the lovely daughter of the king of Tyre, who was abducted by Zeus after he had taken the form of a bull. She later married the King of Crete and bore him a son, King Minos, who built the notorious labyrinth. Thus, within a single story, Greek mythology perfectly captured Europe's abiding beauty, its propensity for political rape, its descent into labyrinthine bureaucracy and the ambiguity of its eastern borders." The labyrinth, like the EU, contained a lot of bullshit. Schoolchildren in the EU are provided with the "Europa Diary". It has been sent to 1.2million pupils in more than 9,000 schools across the EU and includes such neutralities as "the EU has improved the quality of people's everyday lives". In the Dutch version, the EU parliament is described as the "most important multinational organ in the world"[234].

In summer 2009 a Swedish think tank called Timbro produced a report on EU propaganda. It included the fact that schools who wanted to benefit from Brussels's €69million a year "free"-milk scheme must display an A3 poster outside their canteens showing the EU flag and stating that EU money paid for the drink[235]. The EU also sends 600 officials a year into schools as part of its "Back To School" programme[236].

Socrates is a €250million programme that promotes ideas of EU citizenship from the kindergarten upwards. But the UK often needs no encouragement. Geoff Hoon, when Europe minister, tried to get lessons on the benefits of the EU introduced into classrooms[237]. Our own British Youth Council (BYC), in contravention of the 1996 Education Act[238], teamed up with the European Commission to promote a competition in UK schools to design a poster promoting the virtues of further integration[239]. The prize was a trip to Brussels. (At the time the chairman of the British Council, effectively the financial parent of the British Youth Council[240], was ex-EU commissar Neil Kinnock but this really was no more than a coincidence; his role did not extend to micromanagement of the BYC.)

In 2006 the British Council won the contract to process Lifelong Learning (see below) payments, worth £5million over seven years, from the EU Commission on behalf of all UK higher-education institutions.

---

234 *The Sunday Telegraph*, 1 July 2007
235 *EU Observer*, 29 July 2009
236 *There's more*, openeurope.blogspot.com, 14 August 2009
237 *The Guardian*, 1 August 2006
238 Schools are required under the Act to forbid "partisan political activities" for junior and older pupils and to ensure that, where political issues are discussed, a "balanced presentation of opposing views" is offered (Education Act (1996), Articles 406 (1) & 407 (1)). The EU, by virtue of its ability to legislate, is a political entity, albeit not party political (there's no opposition party), and it fools no one when it pretends its one-sided and tendentious bumf is "information".
The European parliament's outpost in the UK runs the "free, open and impartial [sic]" euroacademyonline.eu "for the benefit of teachers and pupils who are studying the European Union and the European parliament in secondary schools"
239 *The Sunday Telegraph*, 26 March 2006
240 *Hansard* (Lords), 27 January 1999, column 1091

In a 2008 article, *London Student* wrote of delays in payment to students, not unlike the delays from Defra in paying Single Farm Payments: "The University Study Abroad Offices across the UK have slammed the British Council for not employing enough staff to process the [EU] payments on time. *London Student* also understands that the staff employed by the British Council were not suitably qualified for the job. There has been criticism of the British Council's communication with individual institutions. University of London colleges were unable to provide struggling students with a fixed date for the payments, with University College London's (UCL) year abroad office informing worried students that they 'should probably reckon on it being at least another month'. UCL said it had lodged a strongly worded complaint with the British Council stating that the delays were causing 'anxiety, worry and financial hardship' to many of its students… A BC spokesperson refused to apologise, stating only that: 'The British Council regrets any hardship or inconvenience caused to students whose grants were delayed.' They also flatly denied that the first payment was late… The British Council has assured *London Student* that the problem will not be repeated: 'We now have staff who are all now fully trained and knowledgeable about the new programme.'"[241]

Would it not be simpler – and cheaper – if the money never went on its own Belgian exchange, travelling as it does from the pockets of these students' parents to the Treasury, then to the EU Commission (Lord Kinnock's employer, 1995-2004) and then back to the children, via the British Council (chair: Lord K, 2005-9)?

As children turn into teenagers, they often turn to activism. Learning about the EU's protectionism and environmental snafus from the beastly media, they are now the age group least likely to be "good little Europeans". To counter such independence of mind, the EU has scores of Jean Monnet professors waiting for them when they arrive at university. The EU's 2009 budget included "Budget Line 150209: subsidy for College Of Europe [where many Eurocrats are schooled] and 'European integration in universities'" (£22.5million) and "Budget Line 150222: includes Jean Monnet programme, to 'support institutions active in the field of European integration'" (£779million)[242].

These Jean Monnet profs in their "Centres Of Excellence" do not, as might be guessed, trumpet the advantages of the UK remaining outside the eurozone – after all, their funding started life in euros. The Bruges Group describes the situation: "In the name of the battle for the minds of tomorrow, money is made

---

[241] *Les Miserables: British Council errors leave Erasmus students destitute*, 15 September 2008, www.london-student.net
[242] *A Rough Guide to the EU Budget* by Chris Heaton-Harris MEP, on conservativehome.blogs.com, 29 August 2008

available to universities for the establishment of academic chairs, named after the father of Europe, Jean Monnet, for projects which 'must deal specifically and entirely with the issue of European integration'. Since 1990 over 2,000 projects have received support in over 800 European universities and by May 1998 there were 409 Jean Monnet chairs across the EU. In the 1990-98 *Directory Of Jean Monnet Projects*, the list of UK courses ran to 38 pages, and 23 per cent of the projects were UK-led. With five establishments being classified as European Centres of Excellence, the UK had the most of any member state. The Centres of Excellence require a higher level of European consciousness within the university and a determination to carry on with the scheme *after the funding runs out* [emphasis added]."[243] The literature states that Jean Monnet professorships "stimulate excellence in teaching, research and reflection", although such excellence is to be promoted solely "in European integration studies in higher education institutions". It is not there to spread best practice in teaching, or anything other than to spread the word of European integration as a purely good thing[244]. In addition, the Commission routinely offers its staff to speak, free of charge, in universities on topics such as "climate change", the "Lisbon Treaty" and "careers in the EU institutions"[245]. There is not a chance that these speakers are impartial: the Commission is the guardian of the Treaties.

The 2008 budget for the 13 free EU schools in seven countries, including the UK, that privately educate the children of Eurocrats working there was €144million, up 11 per cent year on year. The EU said that the schools were "a vital element in attracting and recruiting staff of the highest calibre"[246]. In 2010 another school was added, and by 2011 the bill for the schooling of 22,500 Eurocrat children will be €175million. It will be €195million by 2013, when British taxpayers will be paying £22million per annum of the total[247].

The Commission's Lifelong Learning Programme, which has a €7billion budget for 2007-13, has four parts: Comenius for schools[248], Erasmus for higher education (best known for student exchanges which, of course, predate the EU by years if not centuries), Leonardo for vocational training, and Grundtvig for adult education. Euroscola exists to show students around the EU parliament. Six million children and young adults will be enrolled in the first two

---

[243] *Propaganda: How The EU Uses Education And Academia To Sell Integration*, The Bruges Group, available from www.brugesgroup.com
[244] Chris Heaton-Harris MEP, *The European Journal*, January 2008
[245] *EU Commission officials – coming to a uni near you*, openeurope.blogspot.com, 13 August 2009
[246] *The Times*, 3 May 2007
[247] *The Daily Telegraph*, 20 July 2010
[248] Its 2003-6 programme included a module called Democrisis, devoted to "studying the lack of, and threats to, democracy in different parts of the world". Chris Heaton-Harris MEP, *The European Journal*, January 2008

programmes during the current budget round. Cash is also made available to other youth organisations, such as in the UK the Girl Guides and YMCA, so long as they can prove they "pursue an objective which is part of an EU policy" and "exist as a body pursuing an aim of general European interest".

In January 2008, the NSPCC spoke in favour of the Lisbon Treaty while it was being "debated" in the Commons; David Miliband, then foreign secretary, mentioned this in one of those debates – "The NSPCC pledged its support, as have One World Action, Action Aid and Oxfam". The NSPCC had, of course, received funds from the EU over the years but had not revealed this when making its political intervention. One can only guess at how much more funding the charity might have received if the money had come to it straight from HM Treasury rather than first travelling through the Brussels cloaca.

Daniel Hannan asked the Commission how much EU funding the four charities mentioned by Miliband had received. A lot: in 2007 ActionAid, the NSPCC, One World Action and Oxfam received, between them, €43,051,542.95.

It was the same when the EU confected the Constitution. The Convention On The Future of Europe took soundings from "civil society". Its working group called for "the government of the Union to be in the hands of the Commission, which alone was capable of representing the common interests of its citizens". The *Economist* noted that "five NGOs on this working group were invited to deliver this message directly to the Convention. But all five – including the Young European Federalists (YEF), the Federalist Voice and the Active Citizenship Network – are financed, directly or through EU-funded members, by the Commission. It is hardly surprising that they are eager for their paymasters to become the government of the Union. The YEF, which styles itself as an autonomous youth organisation campaigning for 'the creation of a European federation', has received €466,000 from the Commission since 2000, accounting for at least 50 per cent of its funding[249]. And this is just one of hundreds of NGOs funded by the Commission."[250]

---

[249] "The Commission will in 2010 pay €6.7million in subsidies to a group of think tanks and NGOs... The top recipients are: the Platform of European Social NGOs on €700,000; Notre Europe €605,000; the European Council on Refugees and Exiles €500,000; the European Movement International €430,000; Association Jean Monnet €250,000; the Council of European Municipalities and Regions €240,000; the Association of Local Democracy Agencies €209,000; the Lisbon Council €200,000; the Fundacion Academia Europea de Yuste €195,000; and Friends of Europe €192,000. The money is part of a larger €30million a year pot in the Commission's education and culture department, which pays for a scheme to promote 'common values' and to get ordinary people interested in politics" *EU-funded think tanks defend their credibility* in *EU Observer*, 29 January 2010
[250] *A rigged dialogue with society* in *The Economist*, 22 October 2004

International News Service reported that "the Centre for European Policy Studies, a think tank which claims to be independent, was on the take through the Commission of some €6.1million [in 2007] of taxpayers' cash. Indeed, the Brussels undergrowth is thick with such bodies – all 'thinking', but who never seem to produce any monographs of intellectual distinction by comparison with their Washington counterparts. The difference is that such USA bodies are privately funded – not subsidised by the authorities they are supposed to be examining."[251]

Conscious that Tony Blair had in April 2004 granted a referendum on the Constitution, the Commission said that it would not campaign in the UK (the Treaties do not allow it to anyway) but would continue to "provide information" about the supranational monster: "We have every right and obligation to promote information about our activities, and we will continue doing that. We are not going to shy away from our duty," said a spokesman at the time.

And they sure didn't shy away from or shirk their duty. The *Times* reported on 5 February 2005 that "[the Commission] gave €10,551 to Hull University to 'raise awareness and understanding' of the Constitution, and €25,000 to Liverpool Hope University College, to help school pupils and students to find out about the Constitution. It gave the Foreign Policy Centre €38,318 for a conference on the Constitution, and €48,601 to the Institute for Citizenship in London to hold a series of seminars on it. Grants to public authorities include €27,291 to Yorkshire Forward, the regional development agency [one of those quangos that maintain offices in Brussels and more glamorous places], to pay for a conference called Europe Alive with Opportunity. It also paid €18,233 to Europaworld, a non-profit company in Wales, to set up a website to educate people about the Constitution and send information to secondary schools. The Federal Trust, a British think tank, was paid €42,005 to promote the enlargement of the EU, including the production of 100,000 'information' cards... The Commission will continue to fund the Europe Direct Information Network in Britain, which costs €840,000 a year, to 'raise local and regional awareness of the Union's policies and programmes'. And it will continue the 'Spring Day for Europe' to celebrate the constitution in British schools."

As adults, we are no less bombarded, mostly by ambient advertising. Our driving licences, number plates, twinned towns[252], passports and flyovers carry the 12

---

[251] Quoted by Open Europe's newsletter of 6 August 2009
[252] "The Commission makes cash available for joint projects in return for which it urges the [two] mayors to swear an oath in favour of European unification. The suggested wording is: 'We, the mayors of [X & Y] confident that we are responding to the deeply felt aspirations and real needs of our townspeople... and believing that the work of history must be carried forward in a larger world... Give a solemn

gold stars on the blue background, as if we first gave Brussels these everyday items and it then returned them to us gift wrapped – for a stonking fee – in its emblem. At some stage we are going to have to question the wisdom of sending off £10 notes and receiving beribboned €5 notes in return. "Brussels takes 'visibility' seriously," noted the pro-Brussels *Economist*[253]. "The rules for regional funds include instructions on the design of those European billboards that so irritate eurosceptic motorists [and pedestrians and bus users etc]: at least one quarter of the sign must be taken up with the EU flag and the name of the EU fund involved, and preferably the slogan 'Investing in your future'. In addition, every regional or central government body that manages EU-funded projects must mark Europe Day (May 9) by flying the European flag outside its premises for a week."

The familiar "CE" marking is on many of our goods but its authority was in doubt even before the recall of millions of Mattel toys in the UK in the summer of 2007. Despite small loose parts and a possible excess of lead paint, these toys literally sailed into the market from China, their "CE" markings – certified by the manufacturer – acting as passports as well as guarantors of safety[254].

Not only is the EU a project in search of a purpose, it is in perpetual search of popularity. As mentioned in "What the EU isn't", it has tried to muscle in on popular sports and other diversions, including football. It got its wish in the Lisbon Treaty, which gave the EU the ability to legislate for sport (TFEU 165). Propaganda produced for children deliberately confuses football teams that happen to be based in Europe – Arsenal, say – with the EU itself, carefully avoiding mention of famous non-EU teams such as Red Star Belgrade (winner of the 1991 European Cup), Galatasary and Spartak Moscow. The 1992 Olympics in Barcelona opened with a £8million firework display making the 12 stars, but a plan to have the then 12 EC countries compete as a single team was banned by the International Olympic Committee[255].

---

pledge to foster exchanges... in every area of life so as to develop a living sense of European kinship... And to join forces to help secure, to the utmost of our abilities, a successful outcome to this vital venture of peace and prosperity: European Union'" "Twinning" in *Europe: A Concise Encyclopedia Of The European Union* (Fourth edition, Profile Books, 2004) by Lord (Rodney) Leach

[253] Charlemagne column, *The Economist*, 26 July 2007

[254] If national parliaments still had responsibility for toy safety this might well have never happened. As it stands, domestic safety checks have been phased out, their funding withdrawn. So much for economies of scale in safety. Better give the children some EU colouring-in books instead...

[255] "Specific criticism is levelled [in a Court Of Auditors report] at the Commission's decision to spend 12.5million ecus to promote the idea of the EC as host of the 1992 Olympic Games at Albertville [French Alps, venue for the Winter Games] and Barcelona [Summer Games]. It also found irregularities in the way the contract had been awarded to an advertising agency involved. The report says the

A "Treaty Of Rome" yacht has competed in round-the-world races but the only sport the EU has properly managed to commandeer is golf. The Ryder Cup, which has since the 1970s allowed Europeans other than Brits to compete against the USA, is nowadays festooned with the 12-star flag as well as the stars and stripes, even though half of the victorious 2006 European team was British and only three of the other 24 EU countries were involved.

Jim Dougal was head of the EU Commission in London. In an article headlined *Why I ran away from the rulemasters of Brussels* in the *Sunday Times*, he wrote: "When I resigned as head of the Commission in the UK, I walked away from a secure job with private health insurance, an excellent pension scheme [no kidding] and superb colleagues. So why did I leave? Because it had become intolerable for me to work in such a bureaucratic nightmare. The reality of working in the Commission is, I am afraid, not far from what its greatest critics claim: that Brussels does indeed control each country of the European Union with stupefying one-size-fits-all rules… People are being regulated into paralysis. As a result, the battle for hearts and minds is being lost… The European Commission, of course, does a great job in preaching to the converted. It provides money to organisations that hold seminars preaching the European dream. In the main, the people who attend these events already know what they think – they are in favour. But the Commission cannot reach people with eurosceptic views. *As a pro-European, I wish it could* [emphasis added]."[256]

But still it tries. In recent years the budget has been spent on posters promoting the EU in which, for instance, the Queen was mocked up in a *ménage à trois* with Blair and Bush and splashed across Austrian billboards; a television station, EuroNews, which doesn't even go through the motions of impartiality – when asked if the Commission funded it, the then head of the Commission, Romano Prodi, answered yes but that "such grants in no way restrict the editorial freedom of the beneficiary, who must, however, respect the image of the European institutions and the raison d'être and general objectives of the Union"[257]. The EU gives it €10.8million per annum. By March 2009, the EU was referring to EuroNews as "corporate communication" in policy documents.

Commission paid a third of the costs of the opening ceremony at Albertville and half at Barcelona. But 'the idea of dual loyalty on the part of athletes and of using the Community flag when medals were being awarded came to nothing when some of the national Olympic committees refused to participate'" *The Financial Times*, 17 November 1993

The COA report also said: "As the Olympic Charter did not permit any overtly political demonstration, the visual presence could only be a symbolic one... The programme for the Community's participation in the Olympic Games proved not totally appropriate"

[256] *The Sunday Times*, 18 July 2004
[257] Daniel Hannan newsletter, 28 April 2004

On 1 May 2008, the Spanish newspaper *El Mundo* reported on plans to promote the EU through the European TV network in order to try to encourage and distribute EU-related programmes and so reverse public apathy about (and antipathy towards) Brussels. The article noted that the EU Communications Directorate spent €81million on "information" activities and had 665 people involved in communication roles. Those staff are assisted by yet more in the EU member states – in the case of Spain, 50 people work in Barcelona and Madrid. In London, the Commission spent £24million on the Tories' old London base, 32 Smith Square, after the landlord of a previous property that the Eurocrats had had an eye on would not let them fly the 12-star flag from it. About 70 staff will pump out the message from number 32's eight floors. Commission documents revealed that first there would be renovation work costing at least £5.2million, which seems rather a lot for taking down some pictures of Margaret Thatcher and replacing them with ones of Ted Heath.

In September 2008, the EU launched EuroparlTV (EPTV), a web-based channel showing action from the "debating" chambers of the EU. A private company charged €45million for the four-year contract. Or about €14,000 per MEP per year. The EU has refused to say how many visitors EPTV enjoys but a German newspaper reported that the site had received just 120,000 hits by the end of 2008[258]. The *Daily Telegraph*'s Bruno Waterfield discovered that the site attracted fewer than 1,200 viewers a day. Its draft budget for 2011 is £8million. Undeterred, in 2010 the EU produced an online simulator of its parliament.

The BBC has specific and pronounced problems with bias. One of these biases – seemingly unwavering support for the EU – cannot be helped by the fact that it borrows money from the European Investment Bank (EIB), which describes itself as "an autonomous body set up to finance capital investment *furthering European integration* by *promoting EU policies* [emphasis added]"[259]. Since 2002, "Auntie" has had a £141million credit facility with the EIB and has also received grants

---

[258] *Die Welt*, 17 January 2009. The EU Commission also has a channel on YouTube
[259] In the UK, its intermediaries include Barclays and The Prince's Trust. Just 14 per cent of EIB loans go to the small firms that make up 99 per cent of the EU's businesses: *The Daily Telegraph*, 3 June 2008.
The Brussels Sprouts column in *Private Eye* (7-20 August 2009) reported that the EIB lent to companies in tax havens, just as the Commission announced initiatives to close down tax havens.
Furthermore, senior EIB officials often sat on the boards of the companies receiving money. The article also mentioned that EIB money given for development assistance was used to support tax evasion: "In June [2009] the EIB agreed a $15million loan to Shorecap International Limited, a private-equity outfit specialising in microfinance... Cyrille Arnould, the EIB's head of microfinance, is one of Shorecap's directors... Arnould is also on the board of Africap, a Mauritius-based investment company, which received €5million from the EIB in 2007"

totalling £1.4million[260]. In July 2006 Mark Thompson, BBC director general, dismissed claims that this would lead to biased BBC reporting. He said, "I can give an absolute assurance that I have no doubt that the BBC's impartiality is unaffected by this." You might be rude about your bank in public but the nation's broadcaster is more polite about its soft-loan provider.

As we know, the EU can decide how much state aid Northern Rock, for example, can enjoy so as not to disadvantage others in the same sector. The same principle applies in broadcasting. The EU decides how much state aid (eg licence fee, which has been classified as a hypothecated tax since 2006) a nation's broadcaster may receive – because any sum disadvantages commercial broadcasters, who must compete for money. In the hands of the unskilled, this proviso might make for rather partial reporting of certain subjects, such as the EU.

In January 2008, the Commission announced that it would be looking at the future of state broadcasters. In short, it doesn't like them – they remind the peoples of Europe of their nationhood, as national railway companies and such like once did. The Commission said in a statement that it hoped the review would be able to define clearly what a public-service mission was and limit state aid to "what is necessary for the fulfilment of this mission"[261].

When the EU announced these check-ups, which included a look at the BBC, the blog EU Referendum observed: "Of course, while the BBC devoted many broadcast hours to discussions on the last licence-fee settlement [conducted by the UK government's Department of Culture, Media and Sport], you can bet that it will give no time at all to this far more important 'consultation' [by the EU's competition commission], not daring to admit that the real power to determine the whole framework in which it operates is held not by our provincial government in Whitehall but by our real government in Brussels. But this does to an extent explain why the BBC is so deferential to the EU and so quick and constant in relaying its propaganda in the most favourable of terms. It is not the British government that decides on the BBC's longer-term future but the Eurocrats in Brussels, so the BBC is merely acknowledging where the real power lies, keeping in with its true masters."[262] How impartial can one expect the Beeb to be when reporting on the EU?

---

[260] *The Guardian*, 11 July 2006, and *The Sunday Times*, 27 January 2008, which reported on the letter written by BBC finance director Zarin Patel in reply to a parliamentary question from Dr Bob Spink MP
[261] *EU Observer*, 11 January 2008
[262] *The true masters of broadcasting*, eureferendum.blogspot.com, 10 January 2008

Anyone who thinks this is an exaggeration should see the EU Commission's own website's section on state aid. Under the heading *State aid to TV2 Denmark*, Brussels lets us know that there was once something rotten about state aid in Denmark: "In May 2004, the European Commission ordered the Danish public broadcaster TV2 to pay back excess compensation for public-service tasks. It had initiated this investigation following a complaint from a commercial broadcaster operating on the Danish market, claiming that TV2 received state aid to finance its public-service tasks. The investigation showed that the total amount of state aid TV2 received exceeded the costs of accomplishing its public service mission by €84.4million. TV2 could use the excess compensation to finance its commercial activities, unduly favouring it over competitors that did not receive state funding. In order to restore competitive conditions in its commercial activities, the Commission ordered TV2 to refund the excess compensation plus interest."[263]

The Spanish state broadcaster, RTVE, has recently abandoned advertising (or, perhaps, advertising has abandoned RTVE) and has opted instead to shake down private broadcasters for a three per cent levy. Mentioning France, which has switched to a similar model for its state broadcaster, the Commission said that it doubts "whether the new taxes are in line with EU rules on electronic communications networks and services"[264].

The Beeb has no intention of handing back, as TV2 did, any of its licence fee, hence the flattering EU reports. In 2008, the European Commission banned the UK government's proposed £14million bung to Channel 4 to help to meet the costs of both its switch to digital and its public-service broadcasting remit; Neelie Kroes, then competition commissar, wrote to David Miliband, then foreign secretary, to say that the funding would be incompatible with state-aid rules[265]. She suggested that the channel of *Big Brother* (not her exact words) had enough reserves and revenues to pay for its digital expansion. Now *that's* remote control of TV.

The same principle of monitoring state aid in arenas where there are commercial players applies to city-wide free Wi-Fi (wireless broadband). Several cities in the 27-state bloc – including Dublin and Prague – have been told by the EU Commission that they cannot lay on this service because it would disadvantage existing internet service providers in the city. That may well be so but is it not a decision that should be taken as closely to the people as possible? Shouldn't city councils themselves decide whether or not free broadband for

---

[263] web.archive.org/web/20080601062151/http://ec.europa.eu/comm/
competition/consumers/stateaid_en.html
[264] *The Guardian*, 7 December 2009
[265] *The Guardian*, 6 October 2008

their citizens is a universal right, or a commercial opportunity to be protected? But such thorny questions need not be debated by those whom we can elect at Westminster level or council level: the European Commission has spoken. When campaigning to be London Mayor in 2008, Boris Johnson stated that one of his aims was "free Wi-Fi" everywhere. All that time on European standing committee B wasn't enough to show him that his scheme would have been disallowed by our Bruxellois masters.

In the mid 1990s, two thirds of the 800-strong Brussels press corps were directly or indirectly funded by the EU (often they were employed on the side to write or edit EU newsletters), and most of the French and German correspondents gave the parliament copy approval. Even now, the EU asks pliant journalists to edit its journals. The press corps, though essentially "embedded", no longer has to get copy approval. The notoriously inaccessible Strasbourg parliament even pays for 60 journalists to cover its "deliberations", routinely offering first-class return train tickets or economy-class plane tickets to the city from any of the then 25 EU countries as well as a daily allowance of €100 to cover hotel, food and entertainment over two days. One TV journalist, when asked by his editor to cover the story of MEPs' perks, had to decline because he was, he reckoned, feeding from the same trough[266].

Two months before the 2008 Irish referendum, the Commission presented *Debate Europe*, part of Commissar Wallström's ongoing "Plan D" ("D" being for "democracy, dialogue and debate" or, as it turned out, "denial" of those things), which aimed to make the EU more popular and increase the involvement of its citizens after the double whammy of the 2005 French and Dutch no votes. Among other things, the project was designed to establish "European public spaces", including regional and local exhibitions, debates, seminars and training sessions involving EU officials and citizens. The budget was €7.2million. Her country's *Svenska Dagbladet* quoted her as saying, "It may seem like a lot of money, but it's really expensive to pay for translations and travel expenses in cross-border projects like these." The piece also noted that at the press conference "Wallström had difficulties giving examples on how the proposals from citizens' meetings had led to any concrete proposals from the EU Commission."

By 2014, there will be a museum or "House Of European History" in Brussels. The old saying that the victor writes history has often been found to be untrue but it will surely be tested to destruction here. The contentious museum was the brainchild of Hans-Gert Pöttering, the German ex-president of the European parliament. Already there have been disagreements over coverage of the role of

---

[266] *International Herald Tribune*, 5 April 2006

the USA in ending World War II. Adam Bielan, a Polish MEP and vice-chairman of the parliament, raised concerns about "serious omissions and misinterpretations" in the 28-page document setting out the museum's topics. In a letter signed by 12 other MEPs, Mr Bielan criticised language that implied "the outbreak of World War II was Hitler's success", and also objected to wording that stated "the last Polish resistance was snuffed out in 1939"[267]. (Polish resistance certainly looked healthy enough 70 years later.) The document also said that exhibitions should make it clear that, in a world of progress, "a united Europe can live together in peace and liberty on the basis of common values". Included in exhibits charting European history from the 5th century AD to the present day will be "questions for Europe's Future" designed "to prompt greater citizen involvement in political decision-taking processes in a united Europe". Examples of suggested questions for the public include: "How should we react to the referendum defeats on the EU Constitution?" Whenever there has been "greater citizen involvement in political decision-taking", it has invariably led to setbacks for the EU project, such as "referendum defeats on the EU Constitution".

In the next section, the saying that "All publicity is good publicity" is examined.

---

[267] *Anger at plans for 'official' European history* in *The Daily Telegraph*, 3 January 2009

Fraud and whistleblowers

"The more laws and order are made prominent, the more thieves and robbers there will be." Lao-tzu

"Just whistle while you work
And cheerfully together we can tidy up the place"
from Walt Disney's *Snow White And The Seven Dwarves* (1937)

Brussels remains far from "tidy", despite some fairly valiant whistleblowing.

One of the more famous episodes in whistleblowing came courtesy of Paul Van Buitenen, who was even knighted by the Dutch queen for his efforts[268]. In 1999, when he was a Eurocrat (he would become an MEP), he caused the fall of Jacques Santer's entire Commission, having exposed its many sins of commission and omission.

His devastating dossier about the irregularities in the department of a French commissioner, Edith Cresson, triggered the Moonie-style mass professional suicide. A woman of some arrogance, Cresson was a former PM who had served under Mitterand in a number of positions. She once asserted that a quarter of English men were homosexual. The scandal started when she employed her 66-year-old live-in "dentist" (who was also her sometime astrologer) on a two-year contract worth £100,000 to research Aids, a disease he knew next to nothing about. During his tenure he produced 24 pages of notes deemed worthless by experts. The cover-up, fraud, nepotism, mismanagement, misuse of the security service for dirty tricks against whistleblowers, and lack of accountability caused the exodus of every commissioner, just as asbestos had evacuated the Commission's HQ, Berlaymont, eight years earlier. All of the commissioners resigned rather than face a vote of confidence by the parliament, very possibly because that way they would be allowed to keep their pensions. In July 2006, the ECJ decided that Mme Cresson should not be punished further and should keep her full pension. The newspaper coverage of her disgrace, the Court decided, was punishment enough.

On 15 March (the Ides) 1999, a five-man committee of "wise men", appointed when Van Buitenen's allegations could be suppressed no longer, produced its report into the Commission. Its executive summary baldly stated: "The responsibility of individual commissioners, or of the Commission as a body,

---

[268] For a first-hand account of the EU machine turning on an employee, see *Blowing The Whistle* by Paul Van Buitenen (Politicos, 2000). Like most EU whistleblowers' stories, it's a frightening tale of sustained EU vindictiveness – and of the victim's eventual vindication

cannot be a vague idea, a concept which in practice proves unrealistic. It must go hand in hand with an ongoing process designed to increase awareness of that responsibility. Each individual must feel accountable for the measures he or she manages. The studies carried out by the committee have too often revealed a growing reluctance among the members of the hierarchy to acknowledge their responsibility. *It is becoming difficult to find anyone who has even the slightest sense of responsibility* [emphasis added]. However, that sense of responsibility is essential. It must be demonstrated, first and foremost, by the commissioners individually and the Commission as a body. The temptation to deprive the concept of responsibility of all substance is a dangerous one. That concept is the ultimate manifestation of democracy."

Despite this verdict, four of Santer's 20 commissioners were reappointed to the Prodi Commission of 1999-2004. Among them was one singled out to combat fraud. It must have been a very dark day indeed for Neil Kinnock to be mistaken for a white knight, but it was he who was given this brief (vice-president, administrative reform)[269]. Blair had pressed for his reappointment "because he was untarnished by the Santer years", an opinion seemingly at odds with that of the "wise men". Several honest people would seriously rue Mr Blair's victory.

Whistleblowers were ritually victimised during Kinnock's reign, despite his initial assurances that they would be protected. Van Buitenen said, "The whistleblowing facilitation procedures put in place by Commissioner Kinnock were almost a criminal offence as they were fundamentally wrong and deliberately did not work."[270] Another (now retired) MEP, the Dane Jens-Peter Bonde, said, "Kinnock brought in rules that would have got Paul Van Buitenen sacked, had they been in place then."

The lessons of the Cresson scandal, for which the "wise men" thought that Kinnock as a commissioner and so part of the "Commission as a body" should bear "responsibility", were not heeded by everyone. In 2002 yet another EU scandal blew up, this time in Eurostat, the outfit's number cruncher, probably best known in this country for once producing a map of the EU that didn't include Wales.

---

[269] When Neil Kinnock arrived in Brussels he bought the house where Boris Johnson, then the Brussels correspondent of the *Daily Telegraph*, had been living (76 Rue van Campenhout). For a long time, the Kinnocks claimed a housing allowance on top of their respective incomes (he as a commissar, she as an MEP), even though they both lived in number 76. Over a decade, according to Open Europe figures, this entirely legitimate claim would have netted them around £600,000

[270] Speaking to the NUJ (Brussels)'s *Whistleblowing and Institutional Accountability* conference, at the International Press Centre in Brussels, 30 September 2004

The later scandal, which investigators would describe as a "vast enterprise of looting", had started in January 2001 when Dorte Schmidt-Brown, a Dane who had worked at Eurostat since 1993, noticed that there were several suspicious contracts. Some had been awarded on the basis of favouritism, and payments had been made for work that was never carried out. Also, £1million of work had been unfairly handed to a British-based company run by a former Commission employee.

Like the next victim in a bad horror film, she unwittingly confided her fears to someone who was complicit. Ignored, she then took her criticism higher up, but was again turned away and told to keep quiet. Eventually, she went directly to Cocubu, whose Danish vice-chairman, Freddy Blak, took up her case publicly. Kinnock rejected Blak's allegations. Schmidt-Brown, sidelined by her department, became ill and was treated as an outcast: "It got to the point where I was unable to enter my own place of work without my legs physically shaking. People often ask me if it has all been worth it and, from a personal point of view, you have to say, on reflection that, no, it hasn't. But if you ask, if I would do it all again, I wouldn't hesitate to say that I would."[271]

When an internal audit in 2002 confirmed the extensive fraud, the Commission and Kinnock promised to come to her aid, but it was too little, too late, and too cynical. Nothing Schmidt-Brown said has ever been disproved. She now lives on a €35,000-a-year invalidity pension. She did, however, receive a public apology from Kinnock for the Commission's handling of her complaint.

Jens-Peter Bonde: "There is a letter signed on the 7th of January 2002 by vice-president Neil Kinnock concerning an investigation into the affairs of one of the sub-contractors involved in the Eurostat fraud. It shows the commissioner was aware of part of the problem. But at a [Cocubu] meeting on 16 July 2003 this vice-president pronounced, 'I was not aware that there had been an internal auditors' report into Eurogramme or indeed into anything about Eurostat.'"[272]

Britain had another commissioner in the Prodi Commission: Chris Patten, who knew a thing or two about ceding British sovereignty, having delivered Hong Kong back to China. He said of the Eurostat scandal, which involved millions of euros: "It doesn't appear that any of the money went towards mistresses' furs or villas in the south of France. That doesn't of course excuse it."

One cannot say if the money went on "mistresses' furs" or Riviera properties

---

[271] *Accountancy Age*, 17 November 2003
[272] From Bonde's site, www.bonde.com, in the section *The Eurostat Affair*. He gives a good account of the myriad EU scandals in *Mamma Mia* (2004), available as a pdf from the same site (under "Books")

because no one knows for sure where it went. It had been alleged that Eurostat's director general, Yves Franchet, and director, Daniel Byk, had squirrelled away about a million euros in a Luxembourg bank account, but they always denied this. After being investigated by Olaf, no charges were brought and a 2003 report said merely that there had been "failings" at Eurostat. Nobody resigned.

In July 2008, the ECJ awarded Franchet and Byk €56,000 for being "confronted with feelings of injustice and frustration" and because they had "suffered damage to their honour and professional reputation...". The blog EU Referendum reported that "the pair had taken the Commission to the ECJ, claiming that both Olaf and the Commission had breached procedures, and their human rights. The court agreed, finding that, when it 'disclosed various pieces of information in the context of the investigations at issue', the Commission had behaved unlawfully, failing to maintain a fair balance between the interests of Mr Franchet and Mr Byk and those of the institution. As a result, 'the Commission committed sufficiently serious breaches of the principle of presumption of innocence to render the Community [the EU] liable.'"[273]

One morning in March 2004, a German journalist, Hans-Martin Tillack, who had been covering the EU in Brussels, was hauled out of his bed by Belgian police. At a press conference he would say, "I am a pro-European. I want the EU to be closer to the citizen. But when their [sic] police were dragging me out of my bed, I felt they were getting too close to this citizen."

He would later write, "I wrote quite a few... stories about Mr Brüner [the head of Olaf] for the German magazine *Stern* in Brussels from 1999 to 2004. These were stories for which I had proof – stories about him and about the then EU [budget] commissioner, Michaele Schreyer. I was the first journalist to reveal, basing my stories on internal EU documents, that there were serious problems with fraud and possible corruption in the EU Commission's statistical agency, Eurostat. I was also able to prove in several cases that Commissioner Schreyer and Mr Brüner seemed not to treat internal EU fraud cases seriously. Mr Brüner, for example, flatly refused to forward evidence about a possible case of fraud to the Belgian public prosecutor in October 2003. I wrote that Mr Brüner might act like this because he did not want to anger mighty politicians and EU officials who had to decide on his future career at the helm of Olaf... Never did Mr Brüner claim that any facts I mentioned were wrong. Still, Mr Brüner and Ms Schreyer were pretty unhappy about my reporting."[274]

Olaf had sent the Belgian police a file that stated without any evidence that Tillack, long a pain in the Commission's side, had paid EU officials €8,000 for

[273] *But, if you are guilty...*, eureferendum.blogspot.com, 12 July 2008
[274] *The Wall Street Journal*, 9 October 2006

information. Acting on Olaf's tip-off (which in law carried no more weight than a tip-off from a member of the public but in reality was treated rather more respectfully) that he was bribing officials, les flics seized four mobile phones, two laptops, a collection of business cards and his address books. And, from Tillack's office in the press building where the police then marched him, they took 17 boxes of documents as well as all of his personal bank statements. Tillack was then interrogated about his sources for 10 hours, without a lawyer, and was not allowed even to make a phone call. According to documents seen by the *Daily Telegraph*, Olaf had requested urgent "simultaneous searches" by the Belgian and German police[275]. (The Hamburg prosecutor did not, as requested, authorise a raid on *Stern*'s HQ.) Tillack was then continually libelled by Brüner, who as an EU servant had immunity. Brüner repeated the entirely unsubstantiated hearsay from Schreyer's spokesman, Joachim Gross, that Tillack had been buying up EU employees' stories. The employees were singing because they wanted to. Gross would change the identity of his "source" several times.

The Belgian courts, in the first action that Tillack brought, said that they did not need to check the evidence that was delivered by Olaf and dismissed his complaints against Gross, the Commission and Belgium (ie her police). The German courts, in another action that Tillack brought, said they had no jurisdiction over Tillack's compatriot Gross while the latter was in Belgium.

In May 2005, the EU Ombudsman criticised Olaf for giving him "incorrect and misleading information" about the Tillack case. Nevertheless, in October 2006 the Court Of First Instance (the ECJ's lower court) rejected Tillack's claim that the Commission had punished him for exposing the Eurostat fraud by using the Belgian police to arrest him and take his files. The Court also cleared Olaf of allegations of smearing Tillack's name with bribery allegations between 2002 and 2004. Tillack responded: "It's a licence for Olaf to lie. It's astonishing that the court allows an EU institution to present rumours as facts. This is damaging to journalists' rights and to the rights of European citizens as well." In the same *Wall Street Journal* article he wrote, "The European Court of First Instance ruled… that Olaf should get away with presenting wrong and misleading facts about me in order to spark a police action against me and to get to my sources inside Olaf."

In February 2006, the European Commission had to appoint a new head of Olaf. Under the rules, it had to consult the EU parliament and member states, which it is then at liberty to ignore. And ignore them it did. It reappointed Brüner, who had been one of 180 candidates for the post. This was after he'd been criticised by Ombudsman Diamandouros for his handling of the Tillack

---

[275] *The Daily Telegraph*, 8 July 2004

case. And he'd been in charge when leaked Olaf documents said that the agency conducted "fake investigations". He'd also been criticised for his handling of the major Eurostat scandal. Commission spokesman Johannes Laitenberger argued that Olaf should be "a special case", exempt from the principle that top Commission officials should be rotated every seven years.

In July 2007 Brüner was questioned by MEPs over allegations of conflicts of interest and irregularities in the way Olaf operated[276]. He was asked why applications for the job of director of investigations were screened by a pre-selection panel that included an official who was herself being investigated by Olaf at the time. (Van Buitenen said that an internal candidate for the job tried to block disciplinary follow-up against the female official, in spite of the "seriousness" of the case.) Eventually, she was removed from the panel. Van Buitenen also alleged that Olaf's investigations were influenced by pressure from national public prosecutors and argued that Olaf should not investigate allegations of fraud concerning its own funds. He said, "There are problems with the European anti-fraud office. The reforms of Olaf that were recommended by a committee of experts in 1999 after the fall of the Commission have not been implemented."

In November 2007 the European Court of Human Rights (not of course an EU institution) in Strasbourg ruled that Belgian police had violated the right to freedom of expression of Tillack by raiding his home and office on the basis of "vague unsustained rumours". The kingdom of Belgium had to pay Tillack €10,000 for moral damages and €30,000 in costs. He had lost twice against Olaf in the European Court Of Justice, despite the fact that the EU Ombudsman had ruled in his favour against Olaf[277]. Therefore, the EU itself never had a blow landed on it in this matter, either for smearing a journalist, or for doing nothing to pursue the fraud he had pointed out to it and his readers. It did manage, however, to distract attention from what the journalist had been writing.

Tillack wrote again for the *Wall Street Journal*, this time after the ECHR ruling: "During my years in Brussels I was able to study quite a number of secret Olaf reports. Therefore I can compare the considerable energy the EU investigators committed to my case with the relaxed attitude Olaf officials often have toward, well, real cases of institutional fraud. These do not concern journalists doing their jobs but powerful EU officials and politicians abusing theirs. Olaf was set up in the summer of 1999 after [all] 20 EU commissioners had to resign en masse following allegations of serious fraud and nepotism. The antifraud office was given an annual budget of €50million and nearly 400 staffers. An October report by Olaf's own supervisory committee paints a depressing picture. The

276 *The Financial Times*, 6 July 2007
277 See ombudsman.europa.eu/recommen/en/042485.htm

committee voiced its astonishment about Olaf's often sloppy work style – Olaf would deliver reports on cases without mentioning such basic information as the date of the suspected infractions... An internal paper for the committee back in March 2003 concluded that Olaf was incapable of conducting anything more than 'simulated investigations'. Officials were going through the motions of an investigation without trying to gather evidence of criminal or irregular behavior."[278]

Tillack also referred to a July 2005 report from the Court Of Auditors that said: "[Olaf's] files take a very long time to process, the reports submitted are inconclusive and the results are difficult to identify. In the area of internal investigations, little progress has been achieved since 1998 with regard to sanctions imposed."

It emerged in April 2008 that a director at Olaf had requested access to Tillack's files, which were held by the Belgian authorities. However, Brüner and Commissioner Kallas (then Barroso's anti-fraud man) had always denied that such a request had been made, including in evidence to both the European parliament and the Court Of First Instance (eg August 2004: "Neither Olaf nor any other Commission staff have ever contacted juge d'instruction Franzen" [for access]). How had it come out that a request had in fact been made? That job of director of investigations at Olaf, which initially had the amazingly conflicted selection process, was eventually filled – by a Mr Thierry Cretin, who reviewed the Tillack case. He found that his predecessor, Alberto Perduca, had in fact requested Tillack's file from the Belgian police. Mr Brüner apologised to journalists, in an email sent by a flunkey to Associated Press International, for this oversight, admitting "one element" of his story had not been quite correct. No such apology was received by the two EU institutions he had fed the same lie. Only in January 2009 did the Belgian prosecutor decide there was no case against Tillack. That was 13 months after the ECHR had ruled in Tillack's favour.

In January 2010, Brüner died unexpectedly. A couple of months later, the final Olaf report into the affair confirmed that there never had been any evidence that Tillack had bribed officials. *Private Eye*'s Brussels Sprouts column reported: "[Olaf] had said that they would not access files confiscated from Tillack by the Belgians until various court proceedings had finished. Oops! The report shows Olaf was exchanging details from Tillack's files with [the Belgian police] throughout 2005 and 2006, while court cases continued. Documents thus obtained were returned by Olaf to the Belgian authorities only at the beginning of 2009, long after the November 2007 ECHR ruling in Tillack's favour."[279]

---

[278] *The Wall Street Journal*, 10 December 2007
[279] *Brussels Sprouts* column, *Private Eye*, 19 March-1 April 2010

Marta Andreasen was hired as the EU's chief accountant in 2002. The polyglot, a naturalised Spaniard who had a French mother, Danish father, Argentinian husband, exemplary American qualifications, and Price Waterhouse and the OECD on her CV, would have made a terrific poster girl for the European Union. She headed a 130-strong team and, surprisingly, was the first qualified accountant to hold the post (actually, it's not that surprising, is it? Her predecessors included an engineer and an architect – no, really). There was a problem, though: she refused to sign off 2001's accounts, having noticed a £170million-shaped hole in them. She found herself on the end of a disciplinary charge for "defamation", was smeared in a whispering campaign, and suspended. Kinnock called all of this "entirely fair procedure"[280].

Her claims – that 95 per cent of the accounts were "an open till waiting to be robbed", that accounting practices, including an absence of double-entry bookkeeping (invented in Florence in the 13th century), were "worse than Enron's" – turned out, of course, to be true. "I was a Euro-enthusiast when I joined the Commission and I was proud to contribute to the project," she said. "But my experience has led me to conclude that it is a project of a political elite that runs things in its own interests far from the interests of its own citizens."

In 2006, when Günter Verheugen found himself in the papers, she said that he was being dragged through the mud because of his complaint that "too much is decided by [EU] civil servants on spending in a non-accountable way" and that she had received internal emails which warned "We have ways of breaking people like you". She would later notice intimidation: "Every time I left the building, they followed me. There were usually two of them, one just in front and one behind, and they made it so obvious." She has written about her time in *Brussels Laid Bare*[281], which includes details of her home phone being bugged and ends with the words "I know where the bodies are buried".

In December 2004 she wrote for the *Times*: "Opportunities for fraud are open and they are taken advantage of. The most elementary precautions are neither taken nor even contemplated. People such as myself who attempt to bring openness and accountability to the system are pursued, suspended and dismissed. I drew attention to the inadequacies; I refused to sign accounts that I

---

280 "However, without having any contact with me to understand the issues I was raising, Mr Kinnock led the Commission to decide on 22 May [2002], about the withdrawal of my responsibility as Accounting Officer... Mr Kinnock has put all his effort into preventing me from being heard by the Cocubu [the EU parliament's budgetary control committee], as soon as he learned that I had put a petition to the relevant committee. He even requested legal advice to do so" Marta Andreasen, speaking in the Strasbourg parliament, 25 September 2002
281 *Brussels Laid Bare* by Marta Andreasen (St Edward's Press, 2009). She blogs at martaandreasen.com

believed unreliable; for two years I was suspended from my job, obliged to live in Brussels yet forbidden to enter any EU building; and in October I was dismissed."

The stakes for the EU were high – the budget then was about €100billion, with the auditors continually unable to clear as much as 95 per cent of it. The blame was plain to the Commission's former chief accountant: "The primary weakness is a computer system that leaves no trail of changes made on registered transactions... too many people can access the system without being authorised. We, the accountants, who are supposed to verify those budgets, are left in the dark... Neil Kinnock was appointed vice-president in charge of administrative reform. He was not then new to Brussels: he had been an insider for five years by then. Here was a wonderful opportunity. But when I joined, I was astonished to find that he had not addressed the problem of the computer system. At first I could not believe it; then I witnessed the state of denial of what the real problem was. The sole action that the Commission took was to proudly announce a new accounting system for 2005. From then the EU proposes to use Accrual accounting, a worldwide standard. [It is not certain that this was ever done.]"

There are other ways in which the EU is different from the rest of the world, continued Andreasen: "In any normal company, alarm bells ring if auditors refuse to pass the accounts. If nobody knows where the money is going, shareholders are up in arms, contributors cease contributing, the negligent or incompetent are dismissed. But EU taxpayers have no say in where their taxes are spent. In Brussels and Strasbourg there is no tradition of accountability. Instead, when evidence of massive fraud becomes too great to ignore, the practice is to blame others."

The checks and balances do not work, she said: "MEPs continue to give discharge [approval of the accounts] to the Commission on its financial responsibility, in the knowledge of the vulnerability of the system to fraud and the lack of action to resolve this situation for the past ten years. The leader of the Liberal group at the European parliament, Graham Watson[282], even praised Signor Prodi for my dismissal... The [Commission] officials who recommended dismissing and prosecuting me are the same ones who have been managing the funds entrusted to the EU without control for years... The new constitution will do nothing to combat the Brussels culture of graft, secrecy and corruption that so tarnishes the European dream."[283]

[282] A British Lib Dem, who once said that national politicians should be more honest with the public about where real power lies: "Let the national political class be honest that nearly 70 per cent of the laws they pass now start in Brussels." *The Times*, 15 June 2004
[283] *The Times*, 6 December 2004

Jules Muis, the former head of the World Bank, was hired by the EU in 2000 as chief auditor. The Dutchman had warned Kinnock that Andreasen was "factually and substantively correct", and that she was fighting a culture inimical to transparency. To sack her would be "a serious blow to reform, sending a signal that the old ways of keeping things from happening still work". He was ignored. Chris Heaton-Harris, a Tory on Cocubu at the time and later, wrote: "Mr Muis claimed the Commission's accounting control systems were 'rudimentary', and complained there were hardly any checks made on the quality of statements made by each department head, which 'repetitively opens the Commission to a high level of reputational risk'. The Commission's budget department was described as 'severely under-resourced' and the weakness of the budget control systems was a cause of 'major concern'. In another he said that the Commission should start reforming its accounting practices only 'if it has a commissioner... who has the stamina and spine to take a lot of shit and see it through consistently'."[284]

Muis left the EU in 2003 in disgust, expressing his frustration at the impossibility of conducting sweeping audits: he had been "steered into the trees" and was "spinning [his] wheels"[285]. On resigning, he said, "I look forward to the Commission [defining] what it wants with the Internal Audit Service, because that is not clear even to me." He said the EU seemed unable to break free from a culture of waste. Though there had been improvements there had not been the fundamental reforms required: "We are trying to discover why we can't get out of the doldrums in terms of the present too-low quality of controls within the Commission." Muis also said the problems of fraud and waste were deep-rooted in the EU's culture and that its accounting was "chronically sordid". He told the EU parliament that pledges of reform were not always matched by action. "It is one thing to have a good language of reform. It is another thing to implement it."

In 2007 Andreasen became treasurer of Ukip, which is quite a volte-face for someone who was once pro-EU. Shortly afterwards, in November of that year, the EU's civil service tribunal rejected her bid to have her dismissal annulled and it upheld, in a 55-page judgment, every complaint made against her by the Commission. "It is unbelievable for me that the judges would find it admissible that the chief accountant of the Commission can be sacked merely for stating clearly what the Court of Auditors has done every year for more than a decade," she said and vowed to appeal[286]. Weeks later, the Court Of Auditors refused to sign off the accounts for the 13th year in a row. In the 2009 Euro election, she

---

[284] *A Beginner's Guide to the Discharge of the European Budget* by Chris Heaton-Harris MEP on conservativehome.blogs.com, 20 March 2009
[285] *The Sunday Times*, 13 July 2003
[286] *The Daily Telegraph*, 9 November 2007

was second on Ukip's list of candidates in the South East "region" and duly elected.

Soon after arriving back in the Belgian capital for her second stint, in July 2009, she was serving on Cocubu – but was blocked from becoming its vice-chair by an unprecedented secret ballot (20 votes to 9) of MEPs, proposed by the Tories' old grouping, the EPP, and the socialists. Chris Davies, a Lib Dem MEP, said: "The message [this] sends to the public is that anyone who speaks out against malpractice in Europe risks being excluded from office." She herself told the Press Association: "What are they scared of? If they have nothing to hide then they would have supported my candidacy. This underhand and childish reaction just shows us how scared they are of the truth. I will not be going away. I intend to use my position to act as a particularly sharp thorn in the side of the EU accounts. It can be no surprise that the accounts are never signed off when they act like this." After blocking her from the Number 2 job, the leaders of the MEP groupings celebrated with champagne, and a parliament official joked that "Marta is still the martyr". Inge Graessle, a German CDU MEP, admitted that Andreasen had been opposed because of "the role she played in the past; what I feel was a certain scandalising of issues is not really one we want endorsed by her becoming vice-chairman"[287]. A short while later Andreasen resigned as Ukip's treasurer to concentrate on her work in Cocubu.

Because of the bountiful and virtually bulletproof terms of employment it is often difficult for EU institutions to dismiss staff whose opinions they do not care for. In earlier times, such thorns could be extracted from the EU's side with the aid of a hefty early-retirement package. Nowadays, original or honest thinking among the apparatchiks summons the clipboards and tilted heads of psychiatrists, who pronounce the whistleblower to be mentally ill. You don't have to be mad to work for the EU but it will say you are if it wants rid of you.

One victim was Jose Sequeira, a Portuguese diplomat who joined the Commission in 1987 and ended up in its Ministry for Development. Not only should Kinnock's supposed amnesty have protected him but he had no knowledge of any fraud and was therefore not even planning to blow any whistle. Nevertheless, his personnel file said his behaviour "sowed doubt regarding the state of his mental health" and he was diagnosed by a

---

[287] *The Daily Telegraph*, 21 July 2009.
A month earlier Graessle had produced the Graessle Report into conflicts of interest within the Commission, as a result of Mandy's yachting with Oleg Deripaska: "The interpretation of the code of conduct's gift policy as covering other hospitality was not applied to hospitality received by former Commissioner Mandelson," it said (quoted in *The Daily Telegraph*, 15 June 2009). Andreasen backed the report, calling it "fundamental". A few weeks later, Graessle would block Andreasen from the second-top job. Funny old world

Commission-appointed psychiatrist as suffering from "verbal hyperactivity" and speech lacking in "conceptual content"[288]. Many disinterested people (as well as the tabloid press, which gave him the unshakeable "Welsh Windbag" moniker) believe that Kinnock suffers from "verbal hyperactivity" and that his speech lacks "content" – "conceptual" or otherwise – but look how far he went.

Sequeira told the *Sunday Telegraph*: "They offered me early retirement in February 2004 and I refused. The medical service then began to call me straightaway asking me to come in for consultations, which I thought was strange. A month later I received notice that I had been placed on compulsory medical leave for psychiatric reasons but told that the Commission would drop the issue if I agreed to early retirement. I protested, and a few days later the doctor came to my desk with security guards to physically remove me from the building. There is a system of psychiatric trials in place in the Commission and I am a victim. I am not the only one, but the first to decide to fight the system."[289]

Somewhat hypocritically, the Commission's personnel department had earlier accused him of "megalomania and paranoia". He had no knowledge of fraud in his department, but his department heads *thought* he was about to publicise a fraud in their department. Who sounds more paranoid? He saw eight independent psychiatrists, all of whom passed him mentally fit. The Commission rejected their opinions because none was on its list of accredited mental-health professionals. This did not impress Paul Van Buitenen. He tabled a parliamentary question: "Following his refusal to accept early retirement the official was forced under duress to consult a psychiatrist, even though he had just received the results of his [EU] biannual medical examination, which made no mention of any anomaly or pathological condition." In December 2006, a tribunal found against the Commission, saying it had had been wrong to brand Sequeira mentally unstable and place him on indefinite sick leave. Paul Maloney, president of the EU civil service tribunal in Luxembourg, annulled the Commission's decision to bar Sequeira from work. He also reversed the Commission's move to place him on indefinite sick leave and ordered it to pay his costs, ruling that the decision had been taken not on purely medical grounds but in part because of his behaviour. Sequeira had been denied access to his medical file, as well as the defamatory dossier he allegedly compiled on his colleagues, a decision the tribunal condemned. The tribunal found that Serge Dolmans, head of the Commission's medical service, acted above his station when he recommended Sequeira be banned from all Commission premises[290].

---

[288] *The Sunday Telegraph*, 13 November 2005
[289] *The Sunday Telegraph*, 13 November 2005
[290] *The Financial Times*, 14 December 2006

Sequeira's defence team called the Commission's abuse of the psychiatric profession "worthy of the KGB"[291]. In Tom Stoppard's play *Every Good Boy Deserves Favour*, a dissident, Alexander, is imprisoned by the KGB. He has been falsely accused of mental illness and complains to his doctor: "I have no symptoms. I have opinions." The doctor replies: "Your opinions are your symptoms. Your disease is dissent. Your kind of schizophrenia does not presuppose changes of personality noticeable to others. I might compare your case to that of Pyotr Grigorenko, of whom it has been stated by our leading psychiatrists at the Serbsky Institute that his outwardly well-adjusted behaviour and formally coherent utterances were indicative of a pathological development of the personality."[292] The play is dedicated to Vladimir Bukovsky, the Soviet dissident who spent 12 years in Russian labour camps and psychiatric prisons, including Serbsky, for defending human rights. He has lived in Great Britain since 1976 and is also a persistent and vocal critic of the European Union.

Ataide Portugal, another Portuguese Eurocrat, suffered treatment similar to his countryman after a long-running dispute: "They said that if I wanted they would declare me unfit to work as a way of solving my problems." He chose to self-declare[293].

Such smears are, of course, far from unknown in the UK – for example, Alastair Campbell's description of Gordon Brown as "psychologically flawed". A former Number 10 spokesman, Tom Kelly, repeatedly described the late Dr David Kelly as a "Walter Mitty figure". Mo Mowlam also was briefed against in this way. Edith Cresson, too, similarly smeared Paul Van Buitenen, saying he had psychological problems because he had not been promoted[294].

The Prodi Commission had been a fresh mandate, a new chance for the EU. Britain had two commissioners in it, one Labour and one Tory, who had both been mostly released from domestic duty by the results of the 1992 general election. The one with the specific task of promoting best practice tried to shoot the messengers and bury the problems deeper, while the other wasn't as troubled by scandal as he might have been. Again, it's a mistake to see the EU or its (mis)management as a wholly foreign construct – British input has been almost constant and usually enthusiastic.

---

[291] The Commission president when Sequeira's problems started was Romano Prodi, who the Russian dissident Alexander Litvinenko claimed had been a KGB agent. Before he was murdered, probably by the KGB's successors, Litvinenko had not substantiated this claim
[292] *Every Good Boy Deserves Favour* by Tom Stoppard (Faber and Faber, 1977)
[293] *The Sunday Telegraph*, 13 November 2005
[294] *Algemeen Dagblad*, 17 March 1999, quoted in Van Buitenen. He didn't have any such problems, and was promoted

Want to feel prouder of our involvement in the EU? Britain can claim the first ever EU whistleblower: Bernard Connolly, a very high-flying economist in the Commission, who was later labelled "out of touch with reality" by it. After he told the truth about the euro's forerunner, the Exchange Rate Mechanism – "economically perverse and politically perverted" – in a book[295], his house was staked out at night whenever he was away, in an obvious attempt to frighten his wife. We can also boast other whistleblowers of note, as if in atonement for some of the UK's commissioners.

In 2002, Dougal Watt, an official at the Court of Auditors since 1995 and an A Grade staffer since 2001, alleged corruption and mismanagement against several EU institutions, including the Court Of Auditors, the Commission and Olaf, which he said misled the European parliament about the circumstances of the death of the head of the tobacco division of the agriculture directorate. Watt claimed that foul play may have been involved in the 1993 death of Dr Antonio Quatraro, who had fallen from the sixth floor of a Commission building in Brussels while the subject of a corruption investigation. Belgian police classified the case as an unsolved murder. Having gone public, Watt stood for election to the staff committee. About 200 of his 500 colleagues voted for him but he was nevertheless sacked in 2003. Two years later he was interviewed by Emma Hartley for her book *Did David Hasselhof End The Cold War?*[296]. Watt had just sold his car to make ends meet. "It has been a very difficult time. And it wasn't much helped by the fact that they tried to classify me as a nutcase. If you have spent your working life trying accurately to describe reality – which is what an auditor does – it doesn't make you happy to see things deliberately obscured. A lot of my former colleagues regard what I did as extreme, because essentially I was blowing the whistle on things that they already knew about. But – and I think this is important to understand about the way things work – whereas many of them had families to think of, I did not. A lot of people who work at the Court of Auditors feel that, yes, some of their findings are twisted, obscured and hidden. But as long as some of their work gets through it allows them to sleep at night."

Another Briton, Robert McCoy, had been a loyal Eurocrat for 30 years until irregularities under his nose in the Committee Of The Regions (COR), where he was an auditor, prompted him to go public. "I have to admit that the campaign of isolation, vilification and character assassination is taking its toll on me," he said at the time. His colleagues took to calling him "Gestapo". His "offence", in 2003, was to discover, investigate and then seek to correct a series of financial irregularities in the COR's budget, including £250,000 printing contracts being awarded without tenders. He was rebuked privately and in a global email by the

295 *The Rotten Heart Of Europe* (Faber and Faber, 1995)
296 *Did David Hasselhof End The Cold War? 50 Facts You Need To Know About Europe* by Emma Hartley (Icon Books, 2007)

secretary general of the COR for requesting spot checks for signatures on sign-in rosters[297]. A year later, the parliament demanded that the COR should apologise to McCoy but it has never done so. In 2009, the Commission's staff union wrote that the COR had been guilty of trying to restrict McCoy's "independence as an internal auditor" and was also guilty of "acts of intimidation". Even Olaf confirmed McCoy's reports and said that the COR had been involved in "systematic and flagrant incompetence" regarding "the essential rules of tendering procedures" (eg printing contracts).

In April 2008, the *Sunday Times* reported that another Briton, Terry Battersby, faced losing his job after whistleblowing. He was, said the paper, "removed from his job as head of information technology at the Brussels-based Centre for the Development of Enterprise (CDE)", which manages about £14million per annum in EU funds to support the private sector in developing countries. He was placed on a short-term contract after he had "uncovered evidence that the agency's former director, Hamed Sow, who is now Mali's energy minister, approved the award of lucrative EU contracts to a company in which he had a financial interest"[298]. When at the CDE, Sow was alleged to have arranged for it to back a loan of nearly £3million from the European Investment Bank to a textile company in Mali, without disclosing that he owned up to 20 per cent of the African company and was receiving payments from it.

In May 2009, Open Europe, citing the England Expects and Berlaymonster blogs, wrote that 14 EU civil servants investigated for suspected benefit fraud had each been *awarded* €3,000 from the EU, after it transpired that Olaf failed to tell them that they were to face criminal proceedings in Italy. In a 2002 audit, 230 officials at the Joint Research Centre in Ispra in Italy – 20 per cent of all staff – were found to be claiming a disability benefit, and 43 employees had apparently suffered nine or more accidents each between 1986 and 2003. A total of €5.7million was disbursed between 1996 and 2002, an average of €25,000 for each employee (although evidence of disability was slight, 23 staffers had received more than €50,000 in that period, two got €300,000 and eight others received €80,000). Olaf said that this "could appear, at first sight, suspect, and should be the object of an in-depth review". However, on referring the case to the Italian judiciary to conduct an investigation, Olaf neglected to inform the civil servants. The EU civil service tribunal then ruled that this was in breach of their rights of defence, and awarded the 14 who brought a complaint (for making baseless accusations that attacked their reputations, and for depriving them of a right to defence) €3,000 each in damages, as well as annulling the Italian investigation into them.

---

[297] *Design For A New Europe* by John Gillingham (Cambridge University Press, 2006)
[298] *The Sunday Times*, 27 April 2008

Investigations into Olaf itself are perhaps not the height of irony. The Belgian police officer who would be assuming control of the executive board of the European Policy Academy during the Belgian EU presidency in the second half of 2010, Eddy Muylaert, was himself found to be a corruption suspect; the public prosecutor had started to investigate him in 2008 over alleged kickbacks from a consultancy firm and the case was ongoing. A Belgian paper quoted a police trade-union official saying that "apart from the [alleged] corruption, he bears responsibility for a department that has been administered in a bad way for years."[299]

Not long after that, José Da Mota, the Portuguese head of Eurojust (an EU outfit that seeks judicial harmonisation), resigned. He had been suspended by his country's chief prosecutor for 30 days for putting pressure on lower-ranking Portuguese prosecutors to stop a corruption probe involving prime minister José Socrates. In 2002, when the PM had been minister of environment he had allegedly allowed the construction of a shopping mall on protected land, supposedly in exchange for kickbacks. At the time, Da Mota was his country's rep in the newly formed Eurojust, which is based in The Hague (he would get the top job five years later). Two magistrates dealing with the "Freeport affair" – named after the British-built mall, which had been opened by Prince Edward and his wife in 2004, who Buckingham Palace would neither confirm nor deny held shares in it – accused Da Mota of having tried to persuade them to sideline the investigation at the request of the PM, who had been a ministerial colleague of his in Lisbon in the 1990s.[300]

The standard corporate defence when corruption is exposed is statistical: some people are dishonest and so any big organisation is likely to employ several "bad apples" ("A big institution cannot escape having a bad employee. The EU has many big institutions. Therefore..."). The expression "a bad apple" means "a bad or corrupt person in a group, typically one whose behaviour is *likely to have a detrimental influence on his or her associates* [emphasis added]". The point is that mould spreads throughout the barrel if the bad apple is not removed promptly. The EU tends to leave the bad apples in situ and punish those who point them out, often calling them mad.

Will Brussels ever rid itself of grift? Don't hold your breath, however bad the stench of corruption gets. If MEPs can vote overwhelmingly to keep secret a report into their own finances, the chances are very poor indeed.

---

[299] *De Morgen*, 3 September 2009
[300] *Eurojust chief embroiled in Portuguese corruption scandal* in *EU Observer*, 13 May 2009 and *Eurojust chief quits over power abuse scandal* in *EU Observer*, 17 December 2009

CHAPTER 4: THE NEIGHBOURHOOD

The EU was formed to stop Germany invading France again. Now that, thanks to Nato, several decades have passed with nothing more serious than a French schoolchild being jumped on by the German exchange, there is some question as to what the EU is for. So it is trying to refashion itself as "the Environment Union". David Miliband, when he was environment minister, said that "the environment is the issue that can best reconnect Europe with its citizens". The environment (as a cause and as an earner) has a far, far better chance of saving the EU than vice versa, though neither is worth a bet.

You can tell that our Bruxellois masters *really* want to be champions of the environment. In the summer of 2007, the EU publicly mooted letting its male staff in Brussels go tieless – so that its many buildings could reduce their aircon. Two years later, a Commission document outlined a plan to mug EU taxpayers to cover half of the commuting costs of its many Eurocrats (who were already well paid, lightly taxed and full of perks): "The creation of a specific appropriation for reimbursing public-transport season tickets is meant to be a small but crucial tool to confirm the EU institutions' commitment in reducing their own CO_2 emissions, in line with agreed climate change objectives."[301] You see, the EU *really is* on the side of the environment. And if you are against the EU, you are against the environment.

The problem with all of this is the EU's CV. Mr Barroso used a Volkswagen Touareg 4x4 SUV but said, in March 2007, that it did not conflict with the Commission's plans to limit CO_2 emissions from cars to 130 grammes per kilometre[302]. The Touareg manages 265 g/km. Mr B explained that the Volkswagen was used mostly by his wife. So what did he use? Er, a top-hole Mercedes with CO_2 emissions of 270 g/km. "I never see myself as an example. A moralistic approach is not mine. We are setting public targets and should avoid giving certificates of good behaviour to individuals," he said.

A month later, in answer to Tory MEP Roger Helmer, Commissar Kallas announced that the average emissions from the Commission's own fleet of cars had been 271 g/km in 2006. In November 2007, the Ministry Of Defence

---

[301] *The Daily Telegraph*, 30 September 2009
[302] From 2015 (until the economic crisis it was 2012) there will be an EU levy of €20 per g/km per car over this limit, whether the manufacturer is EU-based or not. The target is staggered: 65 per cent of new cars must average 130g/km by 2012, 75 per cent by 2013 and 80 per cent by 2014. By 2020, carbon dioxide emissions must be reduced to 95g/km.
In July 2009 Commissar Dimas proposed a CO_2 emissions limit on all commercial vehicles of 175 g/km from July 2013

confirmed that all 3,000 of the army's next generation of armoured fighting vehicle, the FRES utility vehicle, would have to comply with EU rules on limiting CO_2 emissions. But Mr Barroso's 4x4 and Mercedes happily billowed out 270g of CO_2 per kilometre. Thus, the British army, which is usually trying in the long term to install or restore democracy in countries, is subject to stricter rules on the exhausts of its vehicles than the EU Commission, which infamously prefers to ignore or discourage democratic acts, such as referendums.

There are many good reasons why the EU has rather sheepishly stopped noisily claiming credit for cheap flights. Prime among these is "the environment". There are others, too, such as the fact that the EU did not make cheap flights possible; the budget carriers did. All the EU did was foist fines on late departures and arrivals – thus threatening the whole spare-change enterprise – and then tried to disallow, in the name of competition, the generous subsidies that regional airports paid to the low-cost carriers who were bringing in tourists. The EU had also previously insisted airlines had to take off from or land in the country they were headquartered, thus very effectively keeping competition out of air fares and so keeping prices high. For the EU ever to claim credit for easyJet is like a man releasing his grip from another's throat and then trying to claim credit for the man's recovery. But the EU is embarrassed about the role it once claimed.

Here are things it really does have responsibility for, almost all of which should engender feelings not just of embarrassment but shame, and should prove that the EU is not suited either to guarding or mending the environment.

Genetically modified (GM) food
The EU has "competence" over GM food. So, licences to grow Frankenfoods/the planet's saviour (delete according to taste) are nothing to do with Westminster. For a long time, the EU couldn't make its mind up whether or not to allow the commercial production of GM crops throughout the 27 provinces. It was torn between its commitment, enshrined in the Lisbon Agenda[303], to make great strides in science and a desire to please its client base, such as Friends Of The Earth Europe and Oxfam etc.

---

[303] In March 2000, at a European Council in Lisbon, the bloc's leaders promised that the EU would become "the most dynamic and competitive knowledge-based economy in the world capable of sustainable economic growth with more and better jobs and greater social cohesion" by 2010. The text was full of references to the USA (boo) but the word "China" (who?) did not appear once. The Lisbon Agenda (not to be confused with the Treaty signed in that city seven years later, when Portugal again had the EU presidency) is now a reminder of how the guff spouted at European Councils so often fails to translate into results. The Lisbon Agenda never had a chance when the largest share of the EU's budget remained agricultural spending rather than, say, research and development. It was succeeded by the "EU-2020 Strategy", another 10-year plan with no hope

In March 2010 the Commission allowed the cultivation of GM potato and the use of three types of GM maize (for food and animal feed) in the member states[304]. Who can say what the impact on the environment will be? Might conditions be different from one country to the next? Might there be more risk of contaminating traditional crops in some areas than others? Is having an area of commercial GM production near non-GM crops like having a "Urination Allowed" area in a swimming pool?

The European Union also has the final say on whether bacon, beef and milk etc produced from cloned animals can be sold within its 27 provinces. Its European Food Safety Authority has decided they can be. Will you want cloned meat on the same supermarket shelf as natural beef and veal? What will happen if a country refuses to allow imports of cloned meat? It will be taken to the European Court Of Justice and lose the case. There's nothing that our Food Standards Agency – especially the Food Standards Agency, which is merely a substation of the European Food Safety Authority – can do about it.

The WTO ruled that the EU had illegally banned GM products between 1998 and 2004. In March 2009 an Agricultural Council voted overwhelmingly to allow Hungary and Austria to keep their bans on certain types of GM maize. The UK (Hilary Benn) had been one of four countries unsuccessfully siding with the Commission against the two.

Fortnightly rubbish collections
If you put rubbish into the EU, you get rubbish out. According to the "one size must fit 27" method of legislating, the Landfill Directive (1999/31) was drafted (we threw away responsibility for waste disposal when we signed the Single European Act). The directive sets targets for reducing landfill that are appropriate for Holland, which lobbied for them because landfill there can interfere with the water table and Dutch politicians wanted the EU to pass the law so that they didn't have to.

The UK must achieve a 25 per cent reduction on 1995's landfill levels in 2010 (ie down to 13.7million tonnes). Three years later landfill must not exceed 9.2million tonnes and finally there must be a 65 per cent cut by 2020 (ie down to 6.3million tonnes). In May 2007, the *Independent* reported that the European Commission was already undertaking legal action against 14 member states for failing to enforce landfill regulations, with large fines expected to follow[305]. The previous year, in a now forgotten report, the National Audit Office said that taxes would have to rise if we did not meet EU targets under the landfill directive

---

[304] *The Guardian*, 3 March 2010
[305] *The Independent*, 25 May 2007

– local councils would face fines of up to £180million a year, it said, if they failed to reduce the volume of landfill.

The 2007 Defra waste strategy (Defra can do little other than what Brussels tells it) for England aims to reduce "Municipal Solid Waste". Part of this strategy is "an increase in the landfill tax escalator handed down to local authorities: the standard rate of tax will increase by £8 per ton per year from 2008 [when it was £32] until at least 2010-11 [actually 2013, when it will reach £72 per ton] to give greater financial incentives to business to reduce, reuse and recycle waste". And if Ireland does not reduce its annual landfill from 1.4million tons (in 2006) to 970,000 tons in 2010 it can expect to be fined €500,000 per day by Brussels[306]. It is not a sum the country can afford.

As EU Referendum puts it, "Landfill tax… is entirely a child of the EU. It was devised by the British government as a means of forcing local authorities to recycle and thus to avoid the swingeing EU fines that will accrue if we do not cut landfill. But, with it standing at £32 per ton [in 2008], councils are potentially spending an extra £6.4million sending recycling to be dumped. Since landfill tax will rise to £40 per ton in 2009, the potential cost spirals to £8million. Thus, we are in a classic EU vice. If we do not recycle, we pay massive fines to the EU. But since we cannot recycle, because the bottom has dropped out of the market [as a result of the recession, not least in manufacturing], we pay massive amounts for recyclable waste to be collected, then we pay silly amounts to have it stored and then, when the storage space runs out, we pay the landfill tax when it has to be disposed. Then we also pay massive fines to the EU."[307]

In the UK, fortnightly rubbish collections are suffered by most council taxpayers, despite a suppressed £27,000 UK government report from Central Science Laboratory which said that fewer collections would "significantly alter the pest infestation rates and hence the disease transmission at source", while vermin and insects could be "encouraged into the home environment". The World Health Organisation has also recommended that rubbish should be collected at least weekly in a temperate zone such as the UK.

"Alternate weekly collections" are a wrongheaded local attempt to encourage recycling and so comply with the EU diktat, even though landfill is often the "greenest" solution for this country: we can, for instance, reclaim wasteland and old quarries and mines with it – yes, land can be recycled! – while also capturing methane. Christopher Booker noted that "We are repeatedly told that we are 'running out of sites for landfill', when every year we quarry 110million cubic metres of soil and rock, more than the refuse we produce. We are told that

---

[306] *The Independent (Ireland)*, 7 October 2008
[307] *Any which way, we pay*, eureferendum.blogspot.com, 20 December 2008

incineration is cheaper than landfill, when it fact it can cost as much as £190 a ton, as opposed to a maximum landfill cost of only £62."[308] And when Brussels fines councils, it's the businesses and householders who will pay.

The intrusive and expensive methods by which councils are now dealing with domestic waste mostly started life in a Dresden University Of Technology research paper entitled *Variable Rate Pricing Based On Pay As You Throw As A Tool of Urban Waste Management*. In answer to a parliamentary question, the UK government conceded that this was its waste bible.

Discovering this, Richard Littlejohn wrote: "The Eurocrats admit bin charges are a 'politically sensitive issue', and warn of 'uncertain and perhaps uncontrollable citizens' response'. But the handbook stresses 'this lack of consensus should not be allowed to intimidate us into avoiding innovation'. They acknowledge that higher charges, tougher rules and fortnightly collections will be unpopular and will lead to an increase in littering, fly tipping and dumping of waste in other people's bins and recycling containers. To combat this, it urges the 'disciplining of citizens' by 'intensive observation of illegal waste disposal through patrol and special task forces'. Councils should set up a 'police department' to sift through rubbish to search for the addresses of 'offenders' in discarded mail, and issue fines of up to £400. All those stories about people being punished for leaving the lid of their bin open, putting out the 'wrong' kind of rubbish or dropping an old gas bill in a public litter bin can be traced back to this sinister document. They weren't isolated incidents, or the result of over-zealous enforcement by bloody-minded local officials – they were part of the great masterplan. Thought those reports of councils installing microchips [2.5million and counting] in wheelie bins was localised madness? Think again. It's all outlined in this handbook. The eventual aim is for every dustbin to have an 'individual identification code' using either 'transponder chips or barcodes'. Dustcarts will be fitted with tracking devices, which explains that story about York City Council spending £40,000 fitting sat-nav systems to all its refuse lorries, complete with maps of the whole of Europe."[309]

Households contribute just nine per cent of the country's total refuse. That hasn't stopped councils, including Islington in London, the bleeding heart of New Labour, from sifting through the rubbish of 1,000 homes to see – anonymously, for research purposes, it said – how much people were recycling. Brussels's preferred means of waste disposal is, in order: produce less in the first place (difficult when the EU mandates so much packaging on food); recycling; incineration; and, as a last resort, landfill. This is why councils now burn waste much more often, spending millions on polluting incinerators. Or they can

---

[308] *The Sunday Telegraph*, 24 August 2008
[309] *The Daily Mail*, 20 May 2008

express their creativity, as the *Sunday Times* discovered: "… the scheme is seriously flawed because waste collected by the private sector is not usually included in the scheme. It means councils can legitimately raise their prices for collecting commercial waste in the knowledge the private sector will step in and landfill the rubbish for them 'off the books'"[310].

As Booker wrote: "Much of the waste nominally collected to meet EU recycling targets ends up either being shipped off to China or quietly landfilled when no one is looking."[311] Somewhere en route to China the spirit of the law falls overboard, perhaps where the ship crosses the slipstream of a ship coming the other way and bringing all that often unnecessary packaging to the EU in the first place.

Because cheap Chinese goods are no longer pouring into the UK in such numbers, there are fewer empty ships to take our rubbish (which is good also for ballast) on the return journey. And the demand for recycled material has collapsed because the recession has throttled manufacturing demand. Instead, old airfields are now harbouring the loo rolls and washed-up yoghurt pots; they are giant repositories for items that *Blue Peter* could make use of but the rest of us have shown that we cannot.

The transport, sorting, washing and processing costs of recycling often greatly exceed the environmental or other advantages. For example, even washable nappies harm the environment more than disposables, according to a government report hushed up because ministers were embarrassed by its findings. Defra instructed civil servants not to publicise the conclusions of the £50,000 study and to adopt a "defensive" stance towards its conclusions[312]. Many of today's recycling drives are as futile as the UK's World War II campaign – "Saucepans For Spitfires" – which urged civilians to donate kitchen utensils so that the aluminium could be melted down and made into fighter planes (the poster showed an overflowing bin and commanded Brits to "Help put the lid on Hitler – by saving your old metal and paper"). All along, the government had plenty of the metal but wanted people to think that they were helping to "biff the Boche". The campaign was for morale, to make people think

---

310 *The Sunday Times*, 10 June 2007
311 *The Sunday Telegraph*, 30 December 2007
312 "Washable nappies… have a higher carbon footprint than their disposable equivalents unless parents adopt an extreme approach to laundering them. To reduce the impact of cloth nappies on climate change, parents would have to hang wet nappies out to dry all year round, keep them for years for use on younger children, and make sure the water in their washing machines does not exceed 60C…" *The Sunday Times*, 19 October 2008

they were doing their bit. Only certain metals are always worth recycling, many other materials are a Pyrrhic victory environmentally and economically[313].

The same directive has confused the distinction between waste and recycling so that it has become virtually impossible to recycle waste oil, and Scottish Power is no longer allowed to use processed sewage to make electricity[314]. Similar problems have been encountered by people who wish to use grease from chip shops to power cars. That scheme is forbidden by the EU as well, even though it's about as "green" an idea as any.

Batteries Directive

The car batteries directive, whose costs and red tape shrank profit margins for recyclers so much that reuse of all spent car batteries dropped in this country from 95 per cent to under 60, killed an industry, reduced battery recycling and encouraged fly tipping.

Fridge mountains

In 2002 the UK was covered with discarded fridges after Regulation 2037/2000 made recycling them illegal. Part-exchange disappeared, as did the sale of refurbished fridges to the developing world.

End Of Life Directive

That of cars, not humans (although the output of crematoriums has been suggested for inclusion under the ETS scheme – see below). Just when the nation's hedgerows had been partly cleared of fridges, along came the bangers. Enacted in 2003, this directive saw the business of licensed scrapyards plummet as car owners decided that the costs and burdens of the new bureaucracy were not worth the candle and so disposed of their cars in other ways[315]. Before the directive was law, two million cars passed through the system every year. In 2006, only 900,000 cars received an official "certificate of destruction" and so many were disposed off the books, often hazardously, and usually by being abandoned. (The "cash for bangers" scheme in 2009 improved the numbers.)

Waste Electrical and Electronic Equipment Directive (WEEE)

Since July 2007, owing to domestic implementation of Directive 2002/96, any business making or importing goods containing electrical circuits, wiring or

---

[313] *Recycling Is Garbage* in *The New York Times Magazine* by John Tierney, 30 June 1996, argues this point persuasively

[314] From eureferendum.blogspot.com's Myth Of The Week, *The EU is good for the environment*

[315] See the 31 August 2006 post *Love is blind* on eureferendum.blogspot.com, which includes details of a US incentive in which vehicular write-offs receive a tax write-off if given to charity

batteries has had to pay for some of the costs of recovering and recycling these goods when they are disposed of. Retailers have either to accept old goods – anything from mobile telephones to electric toothbrushes to washing machines – from consumers free of charge or pay for councils to upgrade their facilities to take the separate waste. Shops also have to display recycling information at the point of sale to discourage consumers from dumping unwanted electrical goods into household wheelie bins – although this is not yet illegal[316]. If the WEEE directive were properly enforced, our hedgerows would be strewn with old computers, electric toothbrushes and, as the *Sun* newspaper gleefully confirmed, devices that are sometimes marketed as "neck massagers".

Reach

At 849 pages long, it is possibly the most tortuous and unnecessary EU legislation yet, which is a distinct achievement in an overpopulated field. Supervised by the European Chemicals Agency, Reach ("Registration, Evaluation and Authorisation of Chemicals") requires the individual registration, evaluation and authorisation of tens of thousands of chemicals and chemical compounds in use in everyday items such as paint and shampoo.

The research is likely to cost billions and it is impossibly bad news for the denizens of Watership Down, who are going to have a lot of compounds to test. It will be the largest testing programme in this planet's history. In a paper for the journal *Nature*, a toxicologist who supported the aims of Reach, Thomas Hartung of the Johns Hopkins Bloomberg School of Public Health, estimated with his colleague Constanza Rovida that before 2020 as many as 101,000 chemicals would have to be tested, claiming the lives of 54million research animals at a cost of €9.5billion.[317]

The EU is interested in all chemicals first used before 1981, when more stringent checks came in. The legislation ignores the fact that the compounds have been used safely for at least a generation.

Water Framework Directive

Compliance with this legislation (Directive 2000/60) means that water companies have little money left over with which to secure canals and repair infrastructure. Although water bills have risen steeply in recent years, most of that money has been spent not on repairs to avoid floods and provide us with extra water and lower bills, but on complying with directives on water purification. Continual roadworks, with signage that doesn't tell the whole story ("Replacing London's Victorian water mains"), are the least of it...

---

[316] *The Daily Telegraph*, 20 March 2007
[317] *EU chemicals law "spells surge in animal testing"*, Reuters, 26 August 2009

Just before the UK's 2007 floods, Booker said that "capital spending on water is skewed by the need to comply with three EU water purification directives. On 24 April, Lord Pearson of Rannoch pointed out in the Lords that, up to 1997, we had spent £48billion on complying with the often absurdly over-the-top requirements of these directives (the companies had to spend over £3billion, for instance, on 'denitrification plants' to solve a problem that turned out not to exist). Lord Pearson asked the minister how much more money had been largely wasted on these directives since 1997, and how much had been spent on the infrastructure needed to improve the efficiency of our water supply and sewerage systems. In a letter, Lord Rooker, as 'minister for sustainable farming and food', has now given the answer. Spending to comply with the directives now totals £65billion. Only £14billion has been left for infrastructure."[318] When the Biblical rains came a few weeks later, it was obvious that money hadn't been spent by the water companies on flood prevention.

Almost all problems are better dealt with locally (ie nationally). Those problems that do not respect borders – industrially produced acid rain, say – can be managed through ad hoc treaties. When Britain's factories caused acid rain to fall on Norway (never an EU member), treaties were signed which ended the problem. There was no need for a huge, power-hungry body to extend its reach into our lives, just a cordial bilateral agreement respected by two neighbours[319].

Renewables Obligation
By 2020 we in the UK must, says the EU, derive 15 per cent of our energy from renewable resources (excluding nuclear). The EU as a whole is aiming for 20 per cent by the same date.

The original EU target that Blair agreed, at one of his last European Councils, was that 20 per cent of all – including our – energy should be provided by renewables by 2020. Perhaps the grandees were attracted to the soundbite snappiness of those three "20"s. However, the target is pie in the sky and no closer to reality than a perpetual-motion machine.

The UK civil service tried to get Gordon Brown to backtrack from this target almost as soon as he took over. In August 2007, the *Guardian* splashed with the news that "government officials have secretly briefed ministers that Britain has no hope of getting remotely near the new EU renewable energy target that Tony Blair signed up to in the spring – and have suggested that they find ways of wriggling out of it. In contrast to the government's claims to be leading the world on climate change, officials within [DBERR] have admitted that under current

---

318 *The Sunday Telegraph*, 13 May 2007
319 From eureferendum.blogspot.com's Myth Of The Week, *The EU is good for the environment*

policies Britain would miss the EU's 2020 target of 20 per cent energy from renewables by a long way."[320] The leaked paper said that the UK would probably be told to aim for 16 per cent, but the best it could hope to be awarded would be nine. It asked ministers to examine "what options there are for statistical interpretations of the target that would make it easier to achieve" and suggested a more flexible interpretation of the target, including counting nuclear energy as "renewable". Presciently, the paper also saw that any target would be incompatible with the UK's participation in the Emissions Trading Scheme (see later). The contradiction between the two pledges, the paper said, would be a key element in persuading Brussels to grant greater flexibility.

The same paper reported two months later that Malcolm Wicks, the then energy minister, said Britain would after all source up to 15 per cent of her power from renewables by 2020, but that did not mean the UK was backing away from the EU-wide target of 20 per cent by the same date[321]. Of course not. The 20 per cent figure had been an EU average, Wicks explained, and the UK had now been handed a 15 per cent target. Germany attempted 27 per cent.

The same paper, on 29 March 2008, reported that the UK would try to introduce flexibility into the reduced commitment too. At an Energy Council, the then business minister, Lady (Shriti) Vadera, proposed that British investments in renewable energy *anywhere in the world* should count as part of the UK's effort. In a speech that "astonished" European renewable-energy companies, environment groups and other EU energy ministers, she said: "It is imperative that cost-efficiency is at the heart of our approach... Demand for renewable-energy projects outside the EU should be considered [part of the UK's 15 per cent target]." Displaying a flair for the "statistical interpretation" that the civil servants had advocated, Vadera proposed that power generated by coal plants fitted with carbon capture and storage should also be classified as renewable (although such technology is still a long way from being ready, tested or even proven worthwhile).

On 18 June 2008, the *Guardian* reported that Britain could invest more than £100billion in renewable energy over the next decade and *still* fail to meet an EU target on "clean" technology. This, it said, was according to the government's own renewables advisers. The Renewables Advisory Board, made up of senior figures from across the industry, said that the best the UK could realistically hope for was to generate 14 per cent of its energy from sustainable sources by 2020. Recognising that the transport and heating sectors would not be able to help in achieving the target, the report put the responsibility on the electricity producers, saying that there needed to be an eightfold increase in their

---

[320] *Revealed: cover-up plan on energy target* in *The Guardian*, 13 August 2007
[321] *The Guardian*, 24 October 2007

use of renewable sources – up from 4 per cent to 32. The final bill for Britain's required renewables revolution, the report noted, would be "expected to exceed £100billion". The *Guardian* noted that it was not clear from where this money would be found, but that a large proportion of the investment could be passed on to consumers as higher energy bills.

At the end of the month, Ernst & Young said the same thing in a report entitled *Costing the earth?*. It also priced the commitment at £100billion and estimated that households would need to pay £213 a year more to energy providers to meet EU targets. Reporting this, the *Independent* added that "Ofgem, the energy industry regulator, said existing efforts to reduce emissions were already adding to household bills, though few consumers realised this was the case. It said the cost of carbon credits that power companies have to buy to meet their pollution caps translates to a £31 annual addition to the average bill [see "Emissions Trading Scheme" later]. A government initiative to force suppliers to install more efficient appliances in customers' homes adds a further £38, while requirements for more renewable power sources tacks on another £20. Increases in transport tariffs had added another £3 to customer bills."[322]

Ofgem was always more willing than the government to warn, if indirectly, that chasing targets would increase fuel poverty. In March 2008, Alistair Buchanan, the chief executive of Ofgem, said, "Over the next 12 years, the government [he meant the one in Brussels whether he knew it or not] has said that it wants to increase energy consumption from wind power from 2.5gigawatts (GW) to 30GW. Most of these wind farms will be built in inaccessible places. We will need to develop the network to connect to these places. We want to ensure that, if prices go up on the 25 per cent of the energy bill that we regulate, customers do not feel they are being ripped off."[323]

A household is suffering "fuel poverty" if more than a tenth of its income is spent on energy. In 2008 there were 5.4million households (a fifth of them) in this position, a figure which had doubled since 2003 and can only increase if £100billion of spending is shared out (that's £4,000 per household before 2012). The Labour government gave itself a legally binding target of eliminating fuel poverty by 2016. That is impossible. The Office for National Statistics stated that the "excess winter death rate" in 2008 was 25,300, a 49 per cent rise on 2007. Once again, the poor are paying the most – some of them the ultimate price – for an inefficient ideology. In August 2009, the UK's Department of Energy and Climate Change conducted an "impact assessment" of the Renewables Obligation and discovered that it would cost £4.2billion a year, against benefits of £300million. This strategy would, it said, add an average of

---

[322] *The Independent*, 30 June 2008
[323] *The Daily Telegraph*, 7 March 2008

£75 to domestic electricity bills and £172 to domestic gas bills by 2020, an increase of 15 and 23 per cent respectively.

In 2007, Ofgem called for the Renewables Obligation to be scrapped: "It is a very expensive way of providing support for renewables," said Andrew Wright, its MD.

Professor Sir David King, who was the UK government's chief scientific adviser between 2000 and 2007, including when the European Council made its crazy promise, said in a documentary, "If we overdo wind we are going to put up the price of electricity and that means more people will fall into the fuel poverty trap... These are difficult numbers to estimate but numbers around half a million are not at all unrealistic." He said that leaders at the EU Council in spring 2007 had not properly understood what their pledge entailed: "I think there was some degree of confusion at the meeting dealing with this. If they had said 20 per cent renewables on the electricity grids across the EU by 2020, we would have had a realistic target but by saying 20 per cent of all energy, I actually wonder whether that wasn't a mistake. I was rather surprised when I heard what the decision was."[324]

How would the increase in renewable power be achieved and how would the £100billion be spent? In June 2008, John Hutton, the business secretary, outlined plans for a massive shift away from fossil fuels to wind, solar and tidal power. He called the plan the biggest shake-up in Britain's power generation since the Industrial Revolution and warned that it would need £100billion, leading to five years of higher gas and electricity bills from about 2015. "We think there will be a cost," he said[325].

At the beginning of 2008, the UK had 2,000 wind turbines, which together produced about 2.5GW or 1 per cent of our electricity – less than the output of a single conventional power station. According to the government target quoted by Alistair Buchanan, to reach 30GW we would need to build 22,000 more by 2020. However, the government implicitly admitted its failure by unveiling plans in June 2008 for only 7,000 offshore plants and 3,500 of the inland subsidy magnets – fewer than half the number required. Booker calculated that "to build those offshore turbines alone would mean lowering 7,000 colossal steel structures into the seabed, each the size of Blackpool Tower, at a rate of more than two every working day between now and 2020"[326]. In a separate piece he noted that "the world has only five of the giant barges that can install monster turbines offshore – and for more than half of the year our weather conditions make

[324] *The Investigation*, Radio 4, first broadcast 8pm, 4 September 2008
[325] *The Times*, 26 June 2008
[326] *The Daily Mail*, 26 June 2008

installation impossible anyway"[327]. He also worked out that "for the sum of £100billion which the government plans to spend on the new turbines we could buy 37 'carbon-free' nuclear power stations at current prices, permanently supplying enough electricity to cover all our current needs". Those nuclear power stations would also provide four times as much electricity. But nuclear cannot be included in the 15 per cent EU target.

The wind turbines are not without huge environmental cost themselves: each bird killer[328] needs 100 tons of concrete for anchorage. Because of their intermittency, they need constant back-up from conventional power plants when the wind doesn't blow (or blows too hard). Switching on and switching off back-up power stations wastes more energy than a windmill could ever produce anyway. To say that wind farms are "green" is like saying that a free-wheeling motorbike is as green as a bicycle. At some point the motorbike will need back-up from a two-stroke engine (fossil fuel), just as a wind turbine continually needs back-up from coal-fired power stations (fossil fuel again). In 2010 Ofgem calculated that most of Britain's onshore wind farms provide only a quarter of their potential, some just 4.9 per cent. In England, only eight out of 104 managed 30 per cent or more of their potential. But all got hefty subsidies.

The most exposed areas, which are best for wind farms, tend to be on Scottish and Welsh peatlands. Before those 100 tons of concrete are poured into the countryside, the peat must first be dug up, releasing CO_2 into the atmosphere which had been locked up in the soil for millennia. Then there is the connection to the national grid, service roads to be built, etc. (And the back-up from fossil fuels or nuclear.) No one has ever proved that turbines recoup the energy and materials expended in their production, siting, maintenance, connection and back-up. They themselves also use electricity, to keep their blades turning when there's no wind so that they do not weigh down the rotor shaft and warp it.

In June 2008, the Renewable Energy Foundation (REF), a body opposed to wind schemes, commissioned an independent consultancy to report on wind power. Using wind-speed data from the Met Office, the report's authors found that in January 2008, when UK demand for electricity was at its highest, wind farms often failed to produce enough electricity, sometimes dropping to four per

---

[327] *Look out, Mr Cameron, or we'll all be in the dark* in *The Sunday Telegraph*, 29 June 2008

[328] There is strong evidence that wind farms kill even more bats than birds – the mammals are particularly susceptible to the changes in air pressure around windmills and often suffer collapsed lungs. *Wind farms put pressure on bats*, BBC news online, 26 August 2008

Of course, bats are protected by EU Habitat directives – building work can be held up for months while the creatures are rehoused at a cost of tens of thousands of pounds. But the bats are not safe from the effects of other EU policies

cent of maximum output[329]. (The same was true in January 2009 and January 2010 when even southern England experienced temperatures of -11ºC but no wind at all.) Back-up fossil-fuel plants would need to be switched on and off to make up the shortfall, a highly inefficient process that negates any other savings. The report went on: "Wind output in Britain can be very low at the moment of maximum annual demand. These are times of cold weather and little wind. Simultaneously, the wind output in neighbouring countries can also be very low, and this suggests that intercontinental transmission grids will be hard to justify." Conversely, electricity (whether conventionally generated or at the expense of birds, peatlands and vistas) cannot be efficiently stored; the grid responds in real time to demand. This means that wind power very often has to be wasted even when it does materialise, because it is surplus to requirements.

The demand peak for 2006 was at 6pm on 2 February, the report found, when wind farms would have been able to provide no power at all. The man who led the investigation, James Oswald, an engineering consultant who'd been head of R&D at Rolls-Royce Turbines, said, "Wind power does not obviate the need for fossil fuel plants, which will continue to be indispensable. The problem is that wind volatility requires fossil fuel plants to be switched on and off, which damages them and means that even more plants will have to be built. Carbon savings will be less than expected, because cheaper, less efficient plants will be used to support these wind fluctuations. Neither these extra costs nor the increased carbon production [when conventional plants kick in as back-up] are being taken into account in government figures for wind power." Or perhaps they're being ignored. Dr John Constable, director of REF, said the wind target was "not feasible" and that "the government was being insincere. They know they won't be around in 12 years when this fails"[330].

Booker quoted Paul Golby of E.On, the energy giant, which supplies most of Europe's wind power and a huge amount of its conventionally derived electricity. Golby is not, then, a cynic. Booker wrote: "The [UK] chief executive of the German-owned E.On came up with the shattering admission that the back-up needed for our new wind turbines would amount to 90 per cent of their capacity. This alone would mean building scores more gas- and coal-fired power plants, to guarantee continuous supply during those times when the wind is not blowing and therefore the turbines are not generating any electricity."[331] So, wind farms are responsible for the construction of the very things they are meant to replace; they necessitate the very things they are meant to obviate. And the infrastructure needed to connect them to the grid ravages some of the most beautiful countryside.

---

[329] News report, *The Sunday Telegraph*, 29 June 2008
[330] *The Daily Telegraph*, 26 June 2008
[331] *The Daily Mail*, 26 June 2008

Booker estimates that the UK would need another 20 conventional power stations to cover for the proposed wind farms "at a time when, by 2015, we already stand to lose 40 per cent our existing generating capacity through the closure of almost all our ageing nuclear power plants and half of our major coal- and oil-fired power stations (due to the crippling cost of complying with an EU anti-pollution directive)". Of that directive, more later.

In July 2008, the BBC, the *Guardian* and others reported that DBERR had again tried to dilute the obligation's rules. "[The department] is trying to change a line in an EU Directive which mandates that energy sources such as wind and wave should get priority connections to the grid. Problems with getting electricity grid connection to windy sites is one of the biggest reasons for the UK failing on its current renewables targets... DBERR's attempt to weaken the terms of the mandate was revealed in a leaked document. It wants to change the phrasing from 'shall' to 'may' get priority on the grid. DBERR's argument is that you cannot give total priority to renewables because new gas plants will be needed to back up wind farms when the wind is not blowing"[332]. Not everyone in government is stupid, then.

Dominic Lawson met Golby and wrote: "... Oil and gas provide domestic heating at between a fifth and a half of the cost of energy from renewables. Golby explained to me that, because it was hard to envisage much contribution from renewables for energy used by transport, we would need to generate about 45 per cent of our domestic electricity bills from such sources – principally wind – in order to conform with the Renewables Obligation. According to him, meeting such a commitment will involve an increase in electricity-generating costs of about £10billion per year; equivalent to almost £400 per household – or, in the roughest terms, an increase of about 40 per cent in electricity bills."

No one can forecast totally accurately when the wind will blow, but Lawson predicted that an ill wind would blow: "Mr Golby told me: 'The politicians have not been entirely honest about the cost of our renewables commitment, and so the public don't really know what's coming their way.' I told him that I thought he was being somewhat naive if he genuinely expected any government to volunteer to the public that it was responsible for a swingeing increase in energy bills, especially if it thought it could get away with blaming the increase on anyone else – such as Mr Golby and his colleagues. So far, the likes of E.On – perhaps because they also stand to make what amount to large heavily-subsidised revenues from wind power – have been careful not to blame the government. I forecast that this gentlemanly conduct will not last."[333]

---

[332] BBC news online, 23 July 2008
[333] *The Independent*, 22 April 2008

In October 2009, Wulf Bernotat, the global chief executive of E.On, said that government plans to generate 30 per cent of UK electricity from renewable sources by 2020 were doomed to failure.

Until common sense returns, wind farms are a windfall for investors. A typical 330-foot high turbine will, if it doesn't snap or catch fire, earn around £500,000 a year for its owners. This is why energy firms, which are obligated to buy wind power, find that prices are twice those charged by other means. The consumers pick up the difference, while taxpayers – usually the same people – pay the subsidy to the wind farms. Energy expert Peter Atherton, of financial analysts Citi Investment Research, famously said of wind farms, "It's a bonanza. Anyone who can get their nose in the trough is trying to."

Even the Crown Estate is indirectly benefiting, making £211million profit in 2007. Much of this came from owning miles of the UK's coastal shelf, whose value leapt 10 per cent in anticipation of the subsidies offered by those 7,000 offshore windmills[334]. A year later, according to the *Guardian*, the Crown Estate "helped to trigger a resurgence of interest for wind projects in the deep waters off Britain by promising to invest in [them]… The decision by the Crown Estate to pay up to half of all pre-construction development costs has brought a huge surge in applications for the latest round of licensing, with almost 100 companies wanting to build wind farms far into the North Sea"[335].

In 2008, Scottish Power Renewables offered farmers "the chance to make millions": for each 2MW windmill on their land they would earn £10,500 per annum; for a 25-year-term, that's £262,500. Elsewhere, firms were offering £17,000 per annum for one turbine. That might sound generous but each turbine would earn its owners £425,000 per annum: £230,000 from the (guaranteed) sale of electricity to the energy companies, and £218,000 in subsidy[336].

In May 2008, half a million UK homes lost access to electricity because of the EU's Large Combustion Plant Directive (LCPD; Directive 2001/80), which restricts the use of coal- and oil-fired power stations. The *Times* reported that "industry sources say that a key factor [in the blackout] was the European Union's LCPD, which sets strict limits on the number of hours that some of

[334] Her Majesty derives no income from the Crown Estate – it goes to HM Treasury not HMQ. However, she does quite well from the CAP (see later) – the search bar on www.farmsubsidy.org even offers "Windsor" as an example of a beneficiary to look up. In 2008 her Sandringham Farms received £473,500. Prince Charles's Highgrove also does well
[335] *Queen of green: Crown Estate's offer fans interest in wind farming* in *The Guardian*, 21 October 2008
[336] *Down On The Farm* column, *Private Eye*, 11-24 July 2008

Britain's largest and most heavily polluting coal and oil-fired power stations can operate before they have to close in 2015. The time is measured in 'stack hours' – the length of time that chimney stacks, rather than individual generation units, are in use. For power stations that have more than one burner, this has created a clear economic incentive for plants to be switched off unless they are being operated at full capacity, or until wholesale power prices increase enough for them to be economically viable to be turned back on. Power-industry executives said that the rules had contributed to mounting instability on the network because increasing numbers of power stations were not being run at any one time, reducing the margin of spare capacity and the ability of the National Grid to boost supply rapidly at times of crisis. 'The concern is that it is driving more volatility,' said a senior executive at one British power company, who added that it was also affecting wholesale prices and, in turn, retail prices. 'You don't want to turn these plants on unless prices are high enough to justify firing them up. It's another factor that is affecting the quality and reliability of the system.'[337] It is these types of power plant that must be switched on when the wind is not blowing...

By 2015, nine coal- and three oil-fired power stations, which together provide 13GW of electricity, will have closed because of the LCPD. On top of that, most of our seven nuclear power stations, which together provide 10GW, will soon be obsolete and their replacements, despite Gordon Brown's emergency planning legislation, will not be ready before we need them. Together, these various plants generate about 40 per cent of the production needed to meet minimum peak demand (currently around 56GW). The government can either outlaw the making of cups of tea during the ad breaks in *Coronation Street* or it can repatriate energy policy from the EU. Something has to give. As it stands, it will be the lights. It's impossible not to think of Sir Edward Grey's "The lights are going out all over Europe". A keen ornithologist, Grey wouldn't have approved of turbines either. Statistics from the Department of Energy And Climate Change showed that in the first quarter of 2010 renewable electricity was 6.2 per cent of the total supply. It had been 6.7 per cent in the same quarter the year before.

The wind-farm scheme neatly illustrates the meaning – and etymology – of the word "quixotic". The *Oxford Dictionary* says that "the character of Don Quixote [who tilted at windmills] is typified by a romantic vision and naïve, unworldly idealism". It's difficult to say which is crazier – to legislate to impoverish the neediest in society by driving more people into "fuel poverty" in exchange for no environmental saving, or upping our reliance on unreliable yet oil- and gas-rich countries, at least in the short term.

---

[337] *The Times*, 16 June 2008

Emissions Trading Scheme (ETS)
This book will take the United Nations' Intergovernmental Panel on Climate Change (IPCC) and others, including the EU, at their word when they say that "carbon" (the stuff of life, the stuff of diamonds) is an enemy of the planet which causes "climate change". "Carbon" makes people think of horrible, dirty charcoal but is not quite the right shorthand. What is really meant is CO_2 or carbon dioxide, the stuff of fizzy drinks, the stuff we all continually exhale, the odourless and colourless gas that plants and trees depend on for photosynthesis. The rights or wrongs of seeking to reduce the volume of this gas in our atmosphere, as well as the science, can be left to one side.

In the 1990s, both Enron and Lehman Brothers were interested in formulating a market for CO_2. They cannot be with us today, but other brokers soon filled their shoes. And those brokers very soon got down to filling their boots. Open Europe found that the two largest carbon-trading exchanges – Bluenext, which includes Barclays, JP Morgan, Merrill Lynch and Shell, and the European Climate Exchange – had 92 per cent of the ETS market and traded permits worth on average about €364,547,223 a day in 2009. For this they earned a combined average of about €245,000 a day in transaction fees[338]. (Each side in the transaction is charged.) Even the scientist who has done most to sound the alarm over CO_2, Professor Jim Hansen, director of Nasa's Goddard Institute for Space Studies, opposes schemes such as the ETS, saying: "The corporates see emissions trading as a huge opportunity to boost profits." In 2009 the right to emit CO_2 was worth $126billion across the world.

Under the Kyoto Treaty of 1997, the EU promised to reduce by 8 per cent its CO_2 emissions by 2012, compared to 1990. The EU later unilaterally committed the bloc to going 20 per cent under 1990's level by 2020 (or 30 per cent if the rest of the world pledges the same) – as well as producing 20 per cent of energy from renewables by the same date.

As part of the UK's own Climate Change Act – passed in 2008 when it was snowing in Westminster in October for the first time in over 70 years – Gordon Brown committed the UK to cut "carbon" emissions by 34 per cent of 1990's levels by 2020, and down to a Bronze Age-beckoning 80 per cent by 2050. This will hamstring the UK's heavy emitters, particularly manufacturers and power suppliers, whose European "partners" have a much lower target.

The EU plan, known as "cap 'n' trade" elsewhere, to reduce emissions might

---

[338] Open Europe press release, 14 December 2009, with figures gleaned from the EU's Community Independent Transaction Log, which shows the trade in permits (EUAs or EU Allowances). National "carbon" registers have also been hacked: in January 2010 the German one lost about £2.5million

look great on paper but it's rather useless in the atmosphere. Like a very expensive leaf blower, the ETS at best merely pushes CO_2 emissions elsewhere, reducing employment in the bloc as jobs (and "carbon") move away.

The basics of the scheme are as follows: each of the UK's "polluting installations" (steelmakers, hospitals, factories, etc) are given vouchers – each one representing a tonne of CO_2 – after the government has agreed a national allocation with the EU Commission. Companies that use less than their quota – which has often been agreed after the concern has threatened to relocate outside the EU – can sell to those who need more. The idea is that the Commission allocates fewer and fewer permits in each phase – like a limbo-dancing competition for CO_2 – until it becomes too expensive not to reduce emissions. To prevent "carbon leakage" (firms relocating outside the EU) free permits are planned for manufacturers of chemicals, iron and steel, cement, and lime. The price of a voucher – there are two billion in the EU – fluctuates, from over €30 to under €10.

Because of the scheme, our hospitals, for instance, must often buy permits in order to operate without being fined. That these vouchers often come from foreign energy companies means that the NHS is buying "permits to pollute" from oil companies such as Shell (which has made £20.7million from sales), Esso (£17.9million) and BP (£17.9million). Castle Cement, which makes a quarter of all UK cement, has an annual surplus of 829,000 permits. The carmaker Ford has about 80,000 spare permits each year. Heathrow Airport, Toyota, Astra Zeneca and Thames Water all have permits to sell. Meanwhile, Leeds Teaching Hospitals NHS Trust – with an annual deficit of 5,800 – needs to buy permits[339].

The steelmaker Corus produced an average 26.5million tonnes of CO_2 between 2005 and 2007 (the first phase of the ETS). For 2008-2012 (the second phase), however, it secured 34.5million vouchers per year. Then in 2009 the recession depleted its order book by a third, giving it 7.5million spare credits (worth about £100million at €14.55 per voucher). This meant that Corus would need even fewer vouchers than in 2005-7 – but it could make money from selling them[340]. .

In 2009, 15 per cent of all the EU's surplus permits were held by the UK's richest man, Lakshmi Mittal[341]. By the end of that year, Mittal and his steel business ArcelorMittal sat on a potential windfall of €1billion from the second phase of the ETS[342], thanks to some shrewd lobbying and heavy hints to the

[339] *Britain's worst polluters set for windfall of millions* in *The Guardian*, 12 September 2008
[340] Brussels Sprouts column, *Private Eye*, 23 January-5 February 2009
[341] *The Guardian*, 9 September 2009
[342] *The Sunday Times*, 6 December 2009

Commission of 90,000 EU-based jobs "carbon leaking". His firm had originally been given 90million tonnes' worth of vouchers per annum in phase 2, more than any other outfit, but it used only 68million in 2008. A year later it was estimated that ArcelorMittal emitted just 43million tonnes (like Corus, its orders were down). An ArcelorMittal spokesman said: "ArcelorMittal's surplus carbon credits are an asset which will only grow in importance."

In 2005, the first phase, 2.5 per cent more vouchers were printed than there was CO_2 produced, and only four of 25 countries reduced emissions[343]. This was equivalent to 63.7million tonnes of the gas. The *Financial Times* reported: "…companies and government bodies in relatively strict countries such as Britain have been forced to buy pollution permits from countries such as Germany that had successfully argued for a more generous allocation. So the overall effect has been to punish financially countries that are curbing pollution and to reward those that are not."[344]

Open Europe discovered that the NHS had spent the equivalent of 309 nurses' salaries on vouchers in 2005-6, the first two years of the scheme[345]. In a 22 June 2006 article in the *Guardian*, Geoff Hoon and David Miliband (then the Europe and environment ministers) wrote that "the EU's emissions trading scheme" is "the most innovative and efficient method yet invented for reducing carbon emissions", and in the same month Miliband told MPs that "our system has worked well: all but the electricity supply sector are living within their allocations".

Whether Miliband knew it or not, this wasn't true. If it had been, it would have come as news to many NHS trusts, including one whose emails were obtained under the Freedom Of Information Act by Open Europe. The *Sunday Telegraph* took up the story: "Rupert Hughes, of Epsom and St Helier NHS trust, complained in an email to Lorraine Brayford, the programme manager of the Department of Health's estates and facilities division, on June 29 [the same

---

343 *Environmentalism is the last refuge of the europhile*, on conservativehome.blogs.com, 28 March 2007. The piece repeats the dangerous syllogism beloved by politicians and known to viewers of *Yes, Prime Minister*: "Something must be done [about the environment]. This [the ETS] is something. Therefore, we must do it"
344 *The Financial Times*, 28 November 2006
345 Open Europe's August 2007 report *Europe's dirty secret: Why the EU ETS isn't working*, which concludes that "far from creating a credible basis for EU-level action on climate change, the ETS has instead established a web of politically powerful vested-interest groups, massive economic distortions and covert industrial subsidies, which will be of little environmental value", is available from www.openeurope.org.uk
Its July 2006 report, *The high price of hot air: Why the EU ETS is an environmental and economic failure*, is equally damning

month that Miliband was telling *Guardian* readers and the House Of Commons of the ETS's efficiency]: 'I'm not sure where David Miliband gets his briefings. I've just paid £23,000 to make up our shortfall for the year 2005 plus our projected shortfall for 2006. This can hardly be called living within our allocation. It all seems to be getting more and more remote… yet it gets potentially more and more costly.' Brayford replied: 'The education sector also feel aggrieved.'"[346] (The Department Of Health had claimed that it did not hold figures for how much its various arms had paid for permits in 2005, despite having been provided with a spreadsheet by the NHS's Purchasing And Supply Agency showing exactly that information.)

Five months later, in evidence to the House Of Commons environmental audit committee, which was discussing "The EU ETS: Lessons From Phase 1", the Environment Agency (EA) was unable to name any individual case in which a firm had reduced emissions, saying "it's not clear whether we're seeing any environmental benefits as yet". The committee asked whether the ETS had had any effect in reducing CO_2 emissions. The EA answered: "We have not been aware of any significant impact." There had, even then, been a significant impact of another type: the ETS had already cost UK businesses £500million – but the UK installations covered by the ETS scheme emitted 3.6 per cent more CO_2 in the first phase than they had before it.

In April 2007, the EU's CO_2 figures for 2006 were published. They showed that in the second year of ETS the bloc's emissions had grown by between 1 and 1.5 per cent. Because too many free permits (about 90 per cent) had been allocated and so firms polluted up to their normal levels, and then sold their spares to cancer hospitals and others. Shamelessly, the then EU energy commissar, Stavros Dimas, according to the *Guardian*, on the same day that the figures were released, told the UN's IPCC that "only EU leadership can break this impasse on a global agreement [to find a successor to 1997's Kyoto Agreement, which expires in 2012] to overcome climate change"[347]. The piece went on: "What Mr Dimas knew – but did not tell the scientists, apparently – is that the EU's programme for cutting carbon, its two-year-old ETS, remains in disarray." The paper also alleged that Dimas and the Commission chose to release the incomplete figures – covering only 93 per cent of CO_2-emitting installations – so as not to repeat the "debacle" of the previous year, when the release of the consolidated emissions figures caused an overnight collapse in carbon prices. Mr Dimas also found time to criticise Australia for not ratifying the Kyoto Agreement. The then PM, John Howard, countered that his country's emissions were dropping while those of the EU bloc were rising.

---

[346] *The Sunday Telegraph*, 5 November 2006
[347] *The Guardian*, 3 April 2007

The most famous Kyoto refusenik was America. (It's often forgotten that it was Clinton, not Dubya who took office only in 2001, who first failed to implement the treaty.) Between 2000 and 2004, America's emissions grew by 1.3 per cent, the EU's by 2.4 per cent. What those figures don't say is that the American economy was then growing far faster than the EU15's[348].

As ever, it's the customer who pays for the useless grandstanding. The *Sunday Times* reported in June 2007: "Britain's power generators have made £2billion in windfall profits by passing on charges to customers under a scheme which was introduced to combat climate change. They are charging customers for the notional cost of carbon credits – the right to emit greenhouse gases – even though the credits were given to them for free... Critics are now accusing the electricity companies of unfairly exploiting customers. Steve Smith, managing director of markets for Ofgem, the electricity regulator, said: 'In essence rather than the polluter paying, the polluter is actually getting paid. It is a straight transfer [of cash] from customers to generators' shareholders.'"[349] Mr Smith wasn't the only one who suspected that the cash was going to shareholders rather than green alternatives. The House Of Commons environmental audit committee's report found that the sector was "broadly holding on to its profits rather than investing them in low carbon energy technology". Nor was the sector using money to lower domestic electricity bills, which had risen over 18 per cent in the previous 12 months.

In May 2008, the CO_2 figures for 2007 were released in Brussels. The British increase was 2.2 per cent and there was an overall increase in the EU of 0.68 per cent, or 16million tonnes of CO2. Emissions rose in 10 of the EU's 27 countries, including Germany and Spain[350]. How could Dimas spin that? He said that the rise in emissions was below the 2.8 per cent rise in Europe's GDP that year and that "emissions trading is yielding results. Studies show that emissions would most likely have been significantly higher without the EU Emission Trading Scheme". Factories covered by the ETS saw their emissions drop by 3.06 per cent in 2008. However, during this period factory output itself dropped by far more than that (because of the recession) so it's not obvious that the CO_2 drop had anything to do with ETS. In 2009, the overall drop was 11 per cent, also a result of the recession.

No fundamental reform of the €90billion EU system can happen before the third phase starts in 2013. By 2020, the Commission wants 21 per cent fewer permits in circulation than in 2005. However, in the current phase, countries can unilaterally import credits from outside the EU. "Certificates of emission

[348] *The Independent*, 5 June 2007
[349] *The Sunday Times*, 3 June 2007
[350] *The Times*, 27 May 2008

reduction" (CER) are produced by the UN's Clean Development Mechanism (CDM) fund. The CERs are issued to companies investing in "clean" energy projects around the world – or for forgoing, say, the building of a "dirty" power station. A country can submit plans for six coal-fired power stations and then build only two, earning CERs for the four never built, which can be enough to pay for the two "dirty" units (which might be as many as were really ever planned anyway). The CERs, which represent notional savings, can then be sold as "carbon offsets" to credulous Westerners, with a broker taking a slice from both sides. (The CDM fund is similar to the EU's compensation scheme for not growing crops.) The CERs, which are generally cheaper than the ETS permits, make even more of a nonsense of the ETS. In 2009, EU firms spent €860million on them in order to meet their obligations.

Thanks to the EU, consumers, NHS patients, taxpayers and others are burdened with this century's version of "pardoners" peddling indulgences in the churches of the later Middle Ages. At least the Church sold them as a means of atoning for past sins – the current contract forces us all to say our very expensive Hail Marys before even committing the "sin".

In the third phase of the ETS, from 2013, national governments will be able to sell 100 per cent of their allocations. The Commission devised its own auction house to do this, wanting to sell all of the permits itself on behalf of all of the member states. However, Poland, Spain, Germany and the UK, among others, preferred to keep their auctions national. Ms Hedegaard, the "carbon" commissar, lamented that the Commission's "single platform" would – for the time being – be voluntary and not the only trading floor for the gas.

Currently, the UK sells only about seven per cent of its EUAs, receiving about £500million per annum. By 2020, it's estimated that the UK will bank about £40billion a year from the ETS. That's one reason why governments do not find "climate change" altogether unwelcome. And there is nothing to stop this money being spent on "carbon intensive" things such as new coal-fired power stations[351].

National CO_2 allowances have been tested in the ECJ: Poland and Estonia won their challenges. As Bloomberg reported on 23 September 2009: "The European Court of First Instance said that the Commission has 'very restricted' authority to review national plans for allocating CO_2 permits in the EU's ETS, the world's biggest greenhouse-gas market. The Commission had exceeded its powers when it awarded only 73 per cent of the permits sought by Poland and just 52 per cent of those Estonia requested for the five years to 2012, lawyers for the countries'

---

[351] *Cash from EU green plan "to fund dirty coal plants"* in *The Independent*, 27 April 2010

governments told the court… The rulings may open the way for more challenges by EU countries to the limits set by the Commission." Indeed, Berlusconi wrote to Barroso almost immediately after the verdict requesting that Italy be given more permits.

To complicate matters even further, the price of a permit fluctuates wildly, making it difficult for companies and hospitals etc to budget. When factories stop making things – during a recession, say – they sell off their permits and flood the market, killing the price. In the first phase, overallocation meant that the price collapsed almost to zero. Because of the fluctuating price, firms are reluctant to commit to building replacement power stations. Analysts suggest that unless the price climbs to €40, investment is too risky.

The permits have also been instruments of "carousel fraud". In 2009, seven people were arrested in England in connection with a £38million scam. None was charged. Wisely, the UK (as well as France and Holland) later "zero rated" the permits so that they did not attract VAT and, therefore, the notorious "missing traders". Of course, ETS permits are a tax on "pollution" so it was a bit much to put a further tax – VAT, a consumption tax – on them in the first place. Much later, the Danes had to introduce similar reforms because of a rampant scam in its ETS scheme. In Denmark, VAT is the maximum rate – 25 per cent – making the place doubly attractive after the Netherlands, UK and France made themselves no longer scammable. Embarrassingly, the Danes had to announce the emergency measure on the eve of the Copenhagen UN "climate change" jamboree, which was intended as a roadshow for emissions trading on a global scale. A Dutchmen and three Brits were charged in January 2010 with a £2.7million ETS fraud by the Belgians, where VAT is 21 per cent.

According to Europol, the EU agency based in The Hague, fraudulent trading may have accounted for up to 90 per cent of all activity in the ETS market in some countries, mainly the UK, France, Spain, Denmark and Holland, with criminals making an estimated €5billion. Europol's Rob Wainwright, the director of its serious-crime squad, said that "these criminal activities endanger the credibility of the EU Emission Trading System and lead to the loss of significant tax revenue for governments"[352]. That's how to rip off a rip-off.

Commercial airplanes, which contribute just 3 per cent of the EU's CO_2 emissions, will be included in the scheme from 2012. All aircraft taking off or landing in the 27-nation bloc, including those based in "third" countries, will have to buy 15 per cent of their "permits to pollute" in ETS auctions. In summer 2009, the EU published a list of the 4,000 airlines – and air forces – that will

---

[352] Europol press release, 9 December 2009

have to sign up to the ETS to avoid penalties when flying into Europe. Included on the list were Lufthansa, United Airlines, the US Navy and the Russian air force.

From 1 January 2012, the cap will be set at 97 per cent of average emissions levels compared to 2004-2006, and reduced to 95 per cent between 2013 and 2020. In its impact-assessment report, the Commission acknowledged that the consumer would end up paying: "Fully passing on costs to customers would mean that, by 2020, airline tickets for an average return journey could increase by €4.60 to €36.90 depending on the journey length." That's for the commercial outfits. For the national air forces of various countries, the taxpayer will of course pay the tax. It is not known if the beneficiaries of Mr Tajani's "right to tourism" will have to pay this levy.

As a UK newspaper, one of many that ran adverts from the government's Carbon Trust, chirruped: "Airlines could almost double their profits on the back of carbon trading if they succeed in passing on the full price of emissions permits to their customers, according to the Carbon Trust. It estimates that the worst-performing airline will see up to 80 per cent lower profits than the best-performing airline as a result of the system. In total, passengers flying to and from Europe will pay an extra €23billion to €35billion on the price of their tickets between 2012 and 2020 based on an estimated carbon unit price of €25, its new report will say. This would compensate the aviation companies for the amount of permits they will have to buy if the heavy emitters do not switch to greener fuels. However, the sector is given 82 per cent of its permits for free – and could see huge windfall profits if it adds the value of these free allowances on to ticket prices."[353]

Biofuel Directive
The road to hell is paved with dangerous intentions and driven on by food-powered cars

By 2020, biofuels must satisfy at least 10 per cent of our overall transport needs, or 25 times what they were when the EU decreed this target.

Biofuels had seemed to the Commission to be a terrific opportunity. First, they offered the prospect of earning countless greenie points, which would offset several embarrassingly public environmental disasters, such as the Common Fisheries Policy (see below). Also, they served to keep European farming afloat, by providing – in the times before a global cereal shortage – farmers with something to grow that people wanted or at least their governments told them

---

[353] *The Daily Telegraph*, 5 December 2009

that they did[354]. Therefore, not only would biofuels atone for the Common Agricultural Policy (see below), they would replace the need for it. Brilliant!

But, among many considerations, it ignored the fact that ethanol, made from corn, was considered by many to be nearly as CO_2-intensive as petrol once the cost of production and transport are taken into account. A University Of Minnesota report found that biofuel production was responsible for the emission of between 17 and 420 times more CO_2 than it saved because of the disturbance of huge quantities of the gas locked in soil.

It wasn't difficult to discern, though, whether the Commission's priorities were the environment or the farmers. If the priority really were saving the world from CO_2 emissions at any cost, you'd expect the Commission to lower the common external tariff for US biofuels, making imports cheaper. But that wasn't the priority: US biofuels were highly taxed to protect EU farmers. You can pretty soon smoke out the EU's true motives when its environmental "concern" comes up against a cheap foreign solution.

The same hypocrisy became obvious when the Commission laid down the law on light bulbs, phasing out traditional incandescents and promoting "compact fluorescent" (CFL) bulbs, such as those made by the Dutch firm Philips and the German firm Osram. Consumers know as well as anyone that CFL bulbs from China, Vietnam, Pakistan and the Philippines attract a 66.1 per cent tariff when coming to the EU. If there's a straight fight between, on the one hand, a Commission policy on the environment and, on the other, the interest of EU members, particularly founder members, bet the subsidised farm on a win for the latter. (Similarly, in March 2008, at a European Council, Gordon Brown proposed EU-wide VAT cuts for "environmentally friendly" products. Few ideas, said Jonny Dymond on the *Today* programme, had ever been shot down so quickly.)

By early 2008, biofuels were widely nicknamed "deforestation diesel" as developing countries such as Indonesia cleared trees in order to plant subsidy-rich biofuels, anticipating huge demand from the EU (and USA). Much arable land worldwide had also been given over to the crops, causing or at least exacerbating a global cereal shortage that provoked riots and toppled at least one government. The UN's rapporteur on "the right to food", Jean Ziegler, said that biofuels were a "crime against humanity". Biofuels became known as A Bad Thing. People nodded sagely and said that The Law Of Unintended

---

354 "The EU's ambitious but realistic 10 per cent target will provide the market pull stimulation that these farmers need to face a future market-based agricultural economy and less dependence on EU subsidies" Blog entry, Andris Piebalgs, then energy commissioner, 28 March 2008

Consequences had struck. Except it hadn't: many economists and others had foreseen just such consequences.

In early 2008, Friends Of The Earth Europe (FoEE) was continually trying to persuade Commissar Dimas to back down over EU biofuels targets, while receiving money from his directorate. According to Internet Archive, the acknowledgment of this cash appeared in mid April 2007, a month after FoEE and Greenpeace had jointly criticised Mr Kallas's Transparency Initiative for lobbyists for not going far enough, but before he had revealed that the Commission part-funded FoEE.

Anyway, the stance of Friends Of The Earth UK (FoE) had been rather different in 2004: "The [UK] government should introduce a Biofuels Obligation, to stimulate a UK biofuels industry – as a lower carbon alternative to conventional transport fuels. The obligation would require that a proportion of all road transport fuels in the UK should be sourced from accredited renewable sources."[355]

In 2005, FoE said: "Friends Of The Earth welcomed the [UK] government's promise today (Thursday 10 November) that biofuels will form five per cent of transport fuel sales by 2010, helping to tackle transport's contribution to climate change... Friends Of The Earth also welcomed the government's proposed assurance scheme 'to ensure that biofuels are sourced sustainably'. But they warned that without strong safeguards the proposed Obligation could encourage biofuel producers to damage the countryside by intensifying production at the expense of wildlife, destroy rainforests through imports of palm oil or harm wildlife overseas by using oils derived from GM-crops."[356]

All this time, Directive 2003/30 ("Done at Brussels, 8 May 2003") had been published, like all EU legislation, in the EU's *Official Journal* and online. It stated (Article 3(1a)): "Member states should ensure that a minimum proportion of biofuels and other renewable fuels is placed on their markets, and, to that effect, shall set national indicative targets" and 1b(ii): "A reference value for these targets shall be 5.75%, calculated on the basis of energy content, of all petrol and diesel for transport purposes placed on their markets by 31 December 2010"[357].

---

[355] *Climate Change and the Budget*, November 2004, page 19:
www.foe.co.uk/resource/briefings/pre_budget_nov_2004.pdf
[356] *Cautious welcome for biofuels obligation*, 10 November 2005 (which at the time of writing was still listed in FoE's archive of 2005 press releases, but with a dead link)
[357] The May 2003 mandate was a result of a 7 November 2001 Commission proposal – "Communication of the European Commission of 07/11/2001 on an Action Plan and two Proposals for Directives to foster the use of Alternative Fuels for Transport, starting with the regulatory and fiscal promotion of biofuels"

The 2003 directive was not a secret. Why was FoE campaigning in 2004 and later for something that had already been publicly mandated over a year earlier by the EU for introduction into member states? When the wind changed, FoE reversed its position in a press release of 11 September 2007: "Friends of the Earth called on the EU to scrap its 10 per cent target for using plant-based biofuels for transport, after a leaked paper revealed that the Organisation for Economic Co-operation and Development has grave concerns about their social and environmental effects."

In 2007, Booker did the arithmetic for the 10 per cent obligation: "The UK's current wheat production is 11million tons (against our consumption of 10million). To meet the 10 per cent target by 2020 from wheat alone would require us to grow 14million tons of wheat a year, three million more than we currently grow. World demand for wheat is rising so fast that, in the past two years, a global surplus has become a deficit. Soaring prices have already doubled. Yet it is at this moment that the EU decides we must either turn our entire domestic wheat production into fuel (thus needing to import 13million additional tons from the world market), or devote similar amounts of our farmland to growing other fuel crops."[358]

By January 2008 even the Commission's own scientists at the Joint Research Centre advised, in an unpublished but leaked report, that the 10 per cent target for transport fuel use should be abandoned and that "the uncertainty is too great to say whether the... target will save greenhouse gas". In March, Defra's chief scientific adviser, Professor Bob Watson, warned that biofuels might aggravate rather than arrest climate change, saying, "If one started to use biofuels... and in reality that policy led to an increase in greenhouse gases rather than a decrease, that would obviously be insane. It would certainly be a perverse outcome." A month later he said that using food crops for fuel was "environmentally, socially and economically unacceptable"[359]. The House Of Commons environmental audit committee called for "a moratorium on current targets until technology improves, robust mechanisms to prevent damaging land use change are developed, and international sustainability standards are agreed."

Andris Piebalgs replied that "the Commission strongly disagrees with the conclusion of the report, where it says that the overall environmental effect of existing biofuel policy is negative. On the contrary, it is delivering significant greenhouse-gas reductions, compared with its alternative, oil." Then another EU body, the European Environment Agency, said the target of 10 per cent could deprive millions of people of food and lead to environmental damage[360].

---

[358] *The Sunday Telegraph*, 22 July 2007
[359] *The Daily Telegraph*, 22 April 2008
[360] *The Financial Times*, 11 April 2008

On 15 April 2008, the Renewable Transport Fuels Obligation came into force in the UK. It decreed that all petrol and diesel must include 2.5 per cent biofuels, in an attempt to be en route to complying with the 2003 EU directive which stipulated that 5.75 per cent of all petrol and diesel sold by the end of 2010 was from "renewable" sources. Professor Sir David King, who had just stepped down as the government's chief scientific adviser, said that quotas should be put on hold until the UK's Renewable Fuels Agency (RFA) reported. He said, "What is absolutely desperately needed within government are people of integrity who will state what the science advice is under whatever political pressure or circumstances." When Ed Gallagher's RFA reported, it suggested slowing the introduction of biofuels and concentrating on fuel from agricultural by-products, such as crop waste, known as "second generation" biofuels, that do not compete with food production.

The Commission decided to tough it out. In March 2008, Mr Barroso himself defended the 10 per cent target, saying that "some of the arguments that have been advanced about the rise of food prices coming from biofuels are really exaggerated… The problem of hunger in Africa has nothing to do with biofuels. The idea that, if you have more production of food near you, you can eat better is a complete mistake"[361]. Stavros Dimas's spokeswoman, Barbara Helfferich, said at a press conference on 14 April, "There is no question for now of suspending the target fixed for biofuels."

Meanwhile, the European Environment Agency, the Organisation for Economic Co-operation and Development, the Food and Agriculture Organisation, the World Bank, the International Monetary Fund, and the United Nations High Commission for Refugees, among others, called for a halt on biofuel production. On 18 April 2008, even Mandelson (then still in Barroso's first Commission) told the *Today* programme that the EU needed to "carefully reflect" on the policy. But on 6 May, at a press conference, Mariann Fischer Boel, then Agriculture commissioner, tried, as her boss had done, to separate soaring food prices from biofuel use: "Biofuels have become a scapegoat. The media storm has become so intense that it's hard to hear the real debate." What was her contribution to the "real debate"? Crassly, she said that long-term high prices – "not an entirely bad thing" – might help farmers in the developing world, forgetting that others in the developing world would be further priced out. She also defended the 10 per cent target. A week later she would be copied in when Alistair Darling wrote that impotent letter to the Slovenian finance boss. If she had got to the end she would have seen his final point: "We need a close examination of the direct and indirect effects of EU biofuels policy, including a full assessment of its effect on food prices, now and in the future." The UK energy minister Malcolm Wicks

---

[361] *The Times*, 13 March 2008

said, "It would be ridiculous if we fill up our cars with 5-10 per cent biofuels if the consequences are that somewhere else in the world people are not being fed."

On 4 July 2008 the *Guardian* published a secret World Bank report, suppressed since April, which said that biofuels had driven up global food prices by 75 per cent. Dismissing the effect of several failed Australian harvests, the report said that the EU and US[362] drive for biofuels had by far the biggest impact on food supply and prices: "Without the increase in biofuels, global wheat and maize stocks would not have declined appreciably and price increases due to other factors [higher fertiliser costs, for instance] would have been moderate." Professor King had found his "people of integrity who will state what the science advice is under whatever political pressure or circumstances" and he told the paper, "It is clear that some biofuels have huge impacts on food prices. All we are doing by supporting these is subsidising higher food prices, while doing nothing to tackle climate change." The World Bank had previously estimated that the rising food prices – not quite all of which could be blamed on biofuels – had pushed a further 100million people below the poverty line. At around the same time, the IMF estimated that biofuels had been responsible for 20 to 30 per cent of 2008's global spike in food prices after 125million tonnes of cereals had been diverted to fuel tanks[363].

At an Energy Council in Paris the day after the *Guardian* had published the World Bank report, the bloc's ministers said that they had perhaps misread the Commission's 10 per cent target. By 2020, they said, a tenth of transport energy should come from any renewable source, not necessarily crop-derived ones. But offficially the 10 per cent biofuels target remained. By 2010 the charity ActionAid (a recipient of EU funding) was warning that, to meet just the EU target, the land area required to grow biofuels in developing countries would rise to 68,000 square miles (over eight times the size of Wales). For the EU targets, said the charity, additional land would also be required in developed nations, displacing food and animal-feed crops on to land in new areas, often in developing countries. By 2020, ActionAid estimated, 600million more people would go hungry as a result of global biofuel use.

Three months after that Energy Council, the Commission amended its values for

---

362 Other countries, including India, Canada, Brazil and China, also have biofuel-use targets.
About 10 per cent of the EU biofuel market is "splash and dash", which is the name given to the unscrupulous practice of some European producers who sail to America, "splash" some US biofuel into their homegrown stock in order to claim the 11p-per-litre US subsidy on the entire consignment, and then dash back to the EU, undercutting fellow EU producers
363 *The Guardian*, 3 June 2008

the amount of greenhouse-gas emissions that biofuels were permitted to release during their manufacture, so that certain fuels produced in the EU that previously had not met "green" thresholds approved by MEPs could do so. Biofuels must, said the EU, release no more than 65 per cent of the carbon dioxide that the same amount of fossil fuels would release when burnt. The change, based on new data from car manufacturers, oil companies and the Commission's own researchers, was a convenient U-turn for the EU's biofuels industry. It might look self-serving for the Commission to "reassess" the threshold – using unpublished data prepared by the Joint Research Centre, its own in-house scientists – but whacking even higher tariffs on third-country biofuels (such as the USA's) would have looked even worse.

In addition, Nusa Urbancic, of the European Federation For Transport And Environment, a Brussels-based lobby group (part funded by the EU: in 2006 it derived over a third of its income from the European Commission), told *EU Observer* that it was unfair that the Commission could include fresh, unpublished data that favoured the EU biofuels industry "at the drop of a hat while they continue to refuse to incorporate scientific paper after scientific paper on the far more profound impact of indirect land-use change [from food production or grazing to biofuels]... It is right that the EU takes on board the latest science regarding greenhouse-gas emissions from biofuel production but the fact that the Commission and Council are still ignoring the absolutely critical issue of indirect land-use change shows that they are being selective about the science they take on board. The timing and lack of transparency surrounding these new figures raises serious questions about how the biofuel lobby has been able to influence the debate."[364]

This unpublished research was, of course, carried out by the same Joint Research Centre that had already, in January of that year, said that the plan to increase the use of biofuels to 10 per cent of all transport fuel use should be rejected. That earlier study – unpublished but leaked – argued that "the costs [of the target] will almost certainly outweigh the benefits". It claimed that taxpayers would face a bill of between €33billion and €65billion from 2008 to 2020 and said: "The uncertainty is too great to say whether the EU's 10 per cent biofuel target will save greenhouse gas or not."[365] And then, a few months later, the same body was revising upwards its estimates of the savings of EU-produced biofuels (so that they could meet the green threshold and therefore repel imports) – having already dismissed *the entire scheme* in January!

Four environmental groups, including Urbancic's, took the Commission to the ECJ's lower court in 2010 for not disclosing all of its research into biofuels. They

---

[364] *European biofuels win last-minute reprieve* in *EU Observer*, 29 October 2008
[365] *The Financial Times*, 18 January 2008

were successful and parts of the research were released: it showed the Commission still thought that biofuels should play a (reduced) part in people's fuel tanks.

In late 2009, another group of white coats was giving the Commission the truth. As the *Guardian* reported, Heinz Ossenbrink, of the EU's Institute Of Energy, said that research increasingly pointed to a long-term problem with large-scale biofuels use, specifically the emission of nitrous oxide, which is about 270 times more potent than CO_2 as a greenhouse gas and is released through the use of fertilisers to grow biofuel crops. "Some of the older studies don't take that into account," Ossenbrink said. "We have now come to less positive values for biofuels."[366] Nitrous oxide is laughing gas. Food shortages are less funny.

By February 2010, another EU report into biofuels had made its way into the papers against the Commission's wishes. In a leaked copy, Jean-Luc Demarty, an official in the Agriculture DG, had made notes in the margin suggesting that there appeared to be evidence that biofuels grown in the EU, particularly on land converted and ploughed for the purpose, failed the "35 per cent fewer carbon emissions than fossil fuel" threshold test. The evidence, he thought, "would kill biofuels in the EU"[367]. A few weeks after this report came to light, it was reported that the UK's Department of Transport had found fossil fuels to be more "carbon efficient" than biofuels; palm oil was responsible for 31 per cent more emissions than petrol[368].

The *Times* story reminded readers that "it takes up to 840 years for a palm-oil plantation to soak up the carbon emitted when the rainforest it replaced was burnt". However, in Indonesia, Malaysia and elsewhere, the hefty EU subsidies meant that it made better sense economically to chop down trees, even vast areas of forest – which absorb carbon dioxide – to make way for biofuel crops that save far less in carbon dioxide. Environmental correspondent Geoffrey Lean discovered that "the European Commission wants to use a scandalous sleight of hand to justify felling tropical rainforests to make way for oil-palm plantations. A leaked document from the Commission… proposes getting round measures to limit the use of biofuels from deforested land by classifying dense oil-palm plantations as 'forests', thus pretending that no destruction has taken place. 'This means,' it says frankly, 'that a change from forest to oil-palm plantation would not per se constitute a breach of the [sustainability] criteria.'"[369]

---

[366] *The Guardian*, 8 December 2009
[367] *Questions about biofuels' environmental costs could alter Europe's policies* in *International Herald Tribune*, 11 February 2010
[368] *Green fuels cause more harm than fossil fuels, according to report* in *The Times*, 1 March 2010
[369] *EU raises biofuel threat to rainforests* in *The Daily Telegraph*, 6 February 2010

That passage was absent from the final text, released in June 2010. The document was intended to define the Commission's criteria for "sustainable" biofuels but it failed to address biofuels' role in food-price inflation and the extra carbon dioxide emitted because of indirect land-use change. It also did not dare to question the system whereby biofuel producers commission their own auditors for "sustainability" certificates.

If the biofuels directive proves successful, it will hugely depress the price of carbon vouchers and so ruin the ETS scheme, meaning polluters can pick up vouchers for next to nothing, making even more of a nonsense of the ETS. Just as our civil service predicted in the document leaked in August 2007. These ideas for saving the planet must sound great at European Councils but they often contradict other grandiose schemes.

As mentioned, hope has been placed in so-called second-generation biofuels, which are made from non-food material such as chaff. Grasses have also been considered, despite the fact that the majority of these still need land that is currently either forested or used for food production. There have also been warnings that many supposedly suitable species are Triffid-like and likely to be "invasive"[370].

"Were we directed from Washington when to sow and when to reap, we should soon want bread," wrote Thomas Jefferson in his autobiography. Change each "when" to "what" and you have the problem with biofuels – in America, the EU and elsewhere.

The Nobel Prize-winning economist Amartya Sen's observation that "No substantial famine has ever occurred in any independent and democratic country with a relatively free press" made the point that *starvation is manmade*. The manmade rush for biofuels – plunging millions more into food poverty – concurred with his point. If Sen is right that democracy makes famine impossible (he is), you have to wonder about the EU's admitted "democratic deficit", which is widening. The absence of democracy does not make starvation inevitable – but why take the risk? The world can feed itself and only a lack of democracy ever stops it doing so.

You may have thought that would be quite enough "unforeseen" consequences. The *Times* reported the possibility of increased motoring costs as well as fears that biofuels could corrode engines: "The UK Petroleum Industry Association (PIA) said that drivers of cars built before the year 2000 would be worst hit because they may have to buy a more expensive type of fuel to avoid damaging

---

[370] *New biofuel sources may not be food, but they could prove invasive* in *International Herald Tribune*, 20 May 2008

their engines. All drivers will have to fill up more often because biofuels produce fewer miles per gallon... The PIA said that warranties might be invalidated if drivers bought petrol or diesel with more than 5 per cent biofuel." In 2009, diesel contained about 5 per cent biofuel and petrol 1 per cent. In the same year, 127million litres of palm oil were sold as diesel on UK forecourts. However, forecourts do not have to reveal the biofuel content if it is 5 per cent or under.

The article pointed out drivers were mostly unaware of the dangers. "Many drivers do not realise they already have biofuel in their tanks... Malcolm Watson, PIA's technical director, said that drivers of older cars would have to buy 'super unleaded', a higher-octane fuel that costs about 6p more per litre, or £3.60 extra to fill a 60-litre tank. He said oil companies would increase the biofuel content of unleaded to 10 per cent, while keeping super unleaded at a maximum of 5 per cent, and said that new cars had fuel systems able to cope with higher levels of biofuel but there could be problems with older cars. The AA said that ethanol, the biofuel added to petrol, could perish rubber seals, corrode metal components and block filters. It said the first sign of a problem would be the engine spluttering, possibly followed by a complete loss of power. Paul Watters, the AA's head of transport policy, said: 'Government and industry have failed to explain how much extra people will have to pay and what the risks are to their cars.'"[371]

In 2009 the Commission mooted taxing fossil fuels used for transport, in order to promote biofuels which would be exempt.

However, the EU's two most notorious – and entirely avoidable – environmental disasters are:

The Common Agricultural Policy (CAP)
How agriculture bought the farm

"How can you defend the CAP and then claim to be a supporter of aid to Africa? Failing to reform the CAP means being responsible for the starvation of the world's poor." Tony Blair to Jacques Chirac, October 2002[372].

However, Blair himself failed to reform the CAP during the UK presidency of the EU three years later, waiving £7billion of our rebate in return for nothing, having said that he would never give anything away without CAP reform. "The UK rebate will remain and we will not negotiate it away. Period," he had said on 9 June 2005. (He was right: he did not negotiate it away, he simply gave it away.) Then he said that it would be surrendered only if the CAP were "got rid of"

---

[371] *The Times*, 16 April 2009
[372] *The Guardian*, 5 April 2004

entirely. The CAP, unfortunately, is safe until long after this budget round, which ends in 2013.

A year before, in 2004, Gordon Brown told the Labour Party Conference: "In the years to come the test that the British people will apply to [the EU] is that it embraces reform, resists federal fiscal policies, rejects tax harmonisation, and tackles, root and branch, the waste and excesses of the Common Agricultural Policy". In a January 2005 speech he said, "Ending the EU's agricultural barriers and subsidies could raise the income of farmers in developing countries by more than $8billion each year." And just months before the Blair giveaway, he told delegates at the 2005 Labour Party Conference: "Because if we are to make poverty history, we must make the scandal and waste of agricultural protectionism history. Let us make agricultural export subsidies history. Let us seek to make the excesses of the CAP history." In the Nigerian capital of Abuja, he made several speeches in May 2006 demanding that France retreat on the CAP. A month later he wrote a piece for *Newsweek* which said that in order to revive the Doha round of the World Trade Organisation talks, "[the EU] should indicate that when it comes to review its budget and its agricultural policies, the essential element of both will be a radical reform of the Common Agricultural Policy and a timetable to end all forms of agricultural protectionism." One might have expected him to keep that theme in his speech to the 2006 Conference, exactly as he had done in 2004 and 2005. But, in his last speech to the Labour Party Conference as chancellor he made no mention of protectionism, the CAP or the EU. He didn't want to scare the horses before he assumed the premiership. Was that because he had finally decided that the problem of French farmers was intractable or because Africa was second to his ambition?

In the debate on the EU (Finance) Bill in January 2008, which approved the rebate surrender, the Lib Dem Treasury spokesman Vince Cable said, "The outcome of all this is a rather unfortunate one – that the government will have made a substantial concession in respect of the rebate, it will continue to be party to a European Union that is not reforming the European agricultural policy at anything other than at glacial speed. We may well be confronted in the next few months with a collapse in international trade negotiations caused at least in part by the intransigence of European agricultural interests and the British government will have absolutely no leverage whatever in preventing any of those things happening." For the Tories, Philip Hammond, the party's Treasury spokesman, said: "The government first promised us that Britain's rebate was non-negotiable. Then they said they would only negotiate it away if the Common Agricultural Policy was reformed. But instead Gordon Brown, at a time when government borrowing is soaring and public sector pay settlements are having to be staged, has given away £7.4billion of our money without any guarantee of reform."

A year after the 2005 Live8 concerts, Bob Geldof said, "You can largely lay a lot of the blame [for the deadlock in the Doha round of the WTO talks] at the European door." America had been refusing to budge on subsidising her farmers – because the EU, larger by far, would not do so. The OECD noted in 2001 that Australia subsidises fewer than 5 per cent of her farmers, New Zealand *none*, the USA 20 per cent, and the EU 35 per cent. (Geldof has also said that, in the fight against hunger and Aids in Africa, "the Bush administration is the most radical – in a positive sense – in its approach to Africa since Kennedy. The EU has been pathetic and appalling"[373].) In July 2006, then Australian PM John Howard, discussing Doha, said, "The big stumbling block is the intransigence of the European Union." In an article for the *Sunday Times*, Irwin Stelzer wrote: "the EU contented itself with such ludicrous offers as reducing tariffs on high-quality beef from an eye-watering 80 per cent to a still-trade-blocking 61 per cent, while retaining bogus health restrictions[374] should any imports manage to climb the tariff wall... rich French farmers shot down a deal that the World Bank has been saying is crucial if poverty in underdeveloped countries is to be relieved"[375]. As it stands, the EU's common external tariff is a third higher than America's. The West once enslaved Africa in order to enjoy cheap sugar and tobacco. Nowadays, the West impoverishes Africa through trade tariffs – and then whacks huge mark-ups on those same imported goods so that its own consumers can enjoy impoverishment as well.

In February 2007, the World Trade Organisation found that "agricultural products are the most tariff-protected" of all in the EU. Its report noted that the average duty on farm goods was 18.6 per cent, up from 16.5 per cent in 2004. For some meat products the tariffs exceeded 400 per cent. In that letter to the Slovenian finance minster, Alistair Darling said that the CAP "cost EU consumers €43billion in 2006".

---

373 *The Independent*, 5 June 2007
374 More bogus restrictions: on 12 May 2008, the *Financial Times* reported that European poultry producers were using a chlorine-washing process on exported chicken, even though the same cleaning method was prohibited on imported chicken and had led to a ban on American sales in the EU. The paper quoted a senior Commission official who said, "The French use [chlorine washing] for exports to Saudi Arabia. This fact has been concealed. Not once has it been mentioned in all the Commission meetings on this subject. This is all about protecting vested interests... The European Food Safety Agency [sic] has determined that chlorine washing does not raise safety concerns. The EU chicken import ban on US chickens based on the proposition that chlorine washing damages health therefore breaches World Trade Organisation rules. The hypocrisy of the EU agricultural lobby in hiding behind phony phytosanitary arguments while defending or even trying to augment protectionist barriers, is breathtaking"
375 *The Sunday Times*, 30 July 2006

In December 2006 David Cameron travelled to Brussels to tell his MEPs that "last year the EU made helping lift Africa out of poverty a priority. But many of the EU's policies are making poverty in developing countries worse. The EU remains committed to a largely unreformed CAP, an economic and humanitarian disaster which pushes up food prices for the poorest people in Europe and helps lock the developing world in poverty. And the EU still has higher trade barriers against poor countries than it does against rich. That's not good enough and it needs to change... It's because we want to see a future for the EU and believe in a strong Europe that we want to make the EU confront its failings."

The journalist Johann Hari, a supporter of the EU, wrote: "The most urgent challenge is to dismantle the CAP. Does anyone think it is sensible that in 2007, more than half of the EU's budget is spent on agriculture, when fewer than 3 per cent of EU citizens rank it as one of their top priorities [actually, the CAP had accounted for 46.7 per cent of overall allocated EU expenditure in 2006 and 46.2 per cent in 2005]? This policy is one of the biggest factors in the starvation of Africa, smothering Africa's agricultural industries in their cot by making it impossible for poor farmers to sell competitively in the most enticing markets. For every euro we give to Africa, the EU takes away seven euros in thwarted trade."[376] Redirecting the CAP budget for one week a year would double EU aid to sub-Saharan Africa.

To approve of the EU, but not the CAP, is like approving of France but not the French; financially, the CAP *is* the EU (and the biggest share of the CAP, almost 20 per cent, goes to France). Taking almost half of the not inconsiderable EU budget and most of the mickey, the CAP was designed to keep farmers in work when postwar subsidies produced a food glut. De Gaulle feared that his country's farmers – a quarter of her workers – would give up farming, leave the land and swamp the cities looking for non-existent jobs. France already operated subsidies to prevent this but was running out of money to pay for them. Fortunately, a contrite neighbour – Germany – was around to fund CAP, the successor scheme. In Sir Humphrey Appleby's view, the French joined the EEC in order "to protect their inefficient farmers from commercial competition"[377]. This is not true. The CAP is not a scheme to subsidise inefficient French farmers. It is a scheme to subsidise *efficient* French (and German) farmers.

The CAP, therefore, was designed not to stimulate production, but to do the opposite: its job was to maintain prices in the face of abundance. The scheme's

---

[376] *The Independent*, 19 March 2007. A British diplomat in Brussels has also argued this, saying: "You cannot spend 45 per cent of the EU budget on 5 per cent of the population who produce 3 per cent of the EU's output"
[377] *Yes Minister*, series 2, episode 5

guaranteed prices gave rise to the infamous "butter mountains" and "wine lakes" (which took product out of the market so as to inflate the price). Now, the EU dumps a little less of its overproduction on poor countries, which has always been one way of undercutting "third countries" (often developing countries) while also destroying their native markets so that they can't sell their produce at home either. The 2005 UK Treasury report quoted in "Costs" also said that "global income could increase by $290billion by 2015 if trade-distorting policies... were eliminated" and that "removing market price support would bring a one-off reduction in inflation" in the UK of "0.9 per cent".

One reason that production decreased was the famous "set aside", a 1988 refinement to the CAP, which for a compensatory fee took a minimum of 10 per cent of a farmer's land out of food production. But this land was still allowed to be used for biofuels (wheat included), animal feed, flowers or textiles etc; set aside rarely meant a scrappy fallow field of thistles. There were EU funds available to convert land from cereal production to non-food use. Now, with global grain shortages (for humans and livestock), the EU has ended the minimum for set aside but many farmers have contracted land to non-food use and can't easily revert to producing food. It's no surprise that the CAP, an instrument designed for a glut, is worse than useless in times of dearth.

In 2002 "decoupling" was introduced. This is the term for the fact that a farmer's CAP payments are no longer linked to output but to acreage, which he or she must "steward" responsibly. Essentially, one is paid for what one owns (or farms) not what is produced; it's like paying someone a salary based on their IQ or potential rather than by what they achieve. Decoupling is nothing to do with trains, except of course those of a gravy flavour.

Predictably, there have been problems, which the Court Of Auditors has pointed out. The *Guardian* reported: "Rules linking payment of subsidies to farmers with protection of the environment are poorly managed and enforced... Farmers who receive cash from Brussels to grow crops must comply with various environmental laws designed to keep farming land, and the countryside, in good condition. If they fail to adhere strictly to a list of EU standards in environment, food safety and animal health and welfare, they can quickly lose funding. Meeting the obligations is called cross-compliance – the key environment element in the reform. [The COA] said that while cross-compliance was a vital element of EU farm policy, it was not particularly effective due to the way it was being managed by the European Commission, and implemented by EU countries. There was too much red tape, and the objectives and scope of cross-compliance were not at all well defined, making it unclear what it is designed to achieve, the report said. In addition, penalties applied were often too low and did not act as a deterrent: '... the objectives of this policy have not been defined in a specific, measurable, relevant and realistic way, and that at farm level many obligations are still only for form's sake and therefore have little chance of leading to the expected changes,' the court said in its report. When there were cuts in subsidies, they were often not based on the cost of compliance or on the consequences of non-compliance, the report said... Information provided by EU countries to the Commission was unreliable, the court said, while the Commission itself was failing to monitor the policy properly or stipulate how the reporting should best be done."[378]

According to a written UK parliamentary answer, it cost an average of £742 in 2007-8 to administer each UK claim made under the scheme. (The same answer revealed that there were 14,645 UK claims for under £400 in the period.) However, in October 2009, the National Audit Office said that the average cost of Defra's Rural Payments Agency (RPA) processing a claim in England, Wales and Northern Ireland was £1,743, "a masterclass in maladministration". The House of Commons public accounts committee called this "unacceptably high" and said that Defra's own estimate of £742 was an unconvincing "smokescreen". The PAC described the management of the £2billion-a-year scheme as "a singular example of comprehensively poor administration on a grand scale".

Decoupling allows city dwellers to make huge profits from the CAP without ever setting a gumbooted foot on a farm. Since 2005, the CAP has been funnelled through the Single Farm Payment Scheme, which is paid to the farmer if he or she is not also the landowner. The failure of quondam agriculture secretary Margaret Beckett to distribute this money to farmers promptly, via the RPA, meant that Defra was fined £305million by Brussels, a sum that Defra clawed back from its rivers and floods budget – just before the Old Testament-style floods of summer 2007.

The loophole allows investors to become classified as farmers, and they are then eligible to receive EU subsidies. Scottish landowners are now leasing out more than 200,000 acres of rocky highland for as little as £5 an acre per year. For each acre leased, annual subsidies averaging £100 an acre can be bought, but these can rise to over £1,000 in some places. Giles Lane, of C&D Property Services, which brokers the rights to farm subsidies, said: "You don't need a farm to claim the entitlements. Sitting in your living room in London you could be claiming them. There has been a lot of interest. Anyone who bought entitlements last year was laughing all the way to the bank. You'd get your money back in three years." One buyer said, "You can play this game like a stock market. What I would say is that we shouldn't be here doing this; it is a

---

[378] *EU watchdog says agri-environment policy badly run* in *The Guardian* (Reuters), 9 December 2008

crazy world."[379] Entrepreneurs can potentially increase their capital fivefold in five years. In 2007, an Open Europe researcher went to Inverurie in Scotland and paid £562.82 for a subsidy entitlement on three and a half acres that will pay out £306.87 a year until the CAP is reformed (2014 at the very earliest).

In 2006, Boris Johnson was delighted to find that his empty paddock was eligible – "By virtue of possessing 0.3 hectares of grass, excluding the dilapidated outside privy, I am apparently eligible for subsidy! You think I am mad; but read the 98-page booklet provided by the Rural Payments Agency... The government – Brussels – the taxpayer – whoever – is seriously going to pay me 10 euros a year merely for being the owner of this blissful patch of grass and rabbits. I don't have to farm it, in any meaningful sense. I don't even have to graze a pony, though I could. I can use it for clay pigeons. I can use it for hot-air ballooning, it says here in the pamphlet" [380]. Unfortunately, he had missed the 2005 registration deadline.

According to the 26 January 2007 reply to a UK parliamentary question, "At the end of the 2006 public storage financial year [30 September 2006], EU public stocks were 13,476,812 tonnes of cereal, rice, sugar and milk products and 300,529,002 litres of alcohol/wine." One imagines that even the EU could organise a piss-up with 300million litres of booze. Or perhaps not: most of these supplies were sold soon after because the Commission wrongly anticipated a bumper 2007 harvest. Grain mountains – stocks it had bought from its own farmers to guarantee prices – had been poisonous PR for the EU for years and it had jumped at the chance of a sale. However, as everyone discovered, there was a worldwide dearth of cereals in 2007. As a result, the EU became a net importer of cereals that year, suspending import tariffs on most crops, and was forced to buy in 18million tons of wheat for twice the price it had sold the same crop just months earlier. All the while, of course, it was encouraging biofuel production.

In January 2009, the EU was again spending your money to ensure that your food would cost you more: it spent £237million on 139,000 tonnes of dairy products. Between 1 March and 31 August 2009, it was the sheepish owner of 30,000 tonnes of butter and 109,000 tonnes of skimmed-milk powder, all paid for at above market cost. "We are not anticipating a return to the old days of butter mountains and milk lakes. This is a temporary crisis situation on the market," said a Commission spokesman[381]. Five months later, the Commission had bought a total of 81,000 tonnes of butter and 203,000 tonnes of skimmed-milk powder. It was thought then that it would have to buy another 31,000

---

[379] *The Times*, 13 March 2007
[380] *The Daily Telegraph*, 11 May 2006
[381] *The Daily Telegraph*, 23 January 2009

tonnes of butter and 50,000 tonnes of skimmed-milk powder. By January 2010 hoarding of cereals (mostly barley) was back: Germany had 850,000 tonnes in store, France 390,000, Poland 230,000 and Finland 216,000.

The late Screaming Lord Sutch and his Monster Raving Loony Party used to promise in their manifestos free skiing on EEC butter mountains – and water skiing on the wine lakes. Such thinking is sensible next to the enslavement of the developing world and paying farmers to create a stock market in "naked acres". One year, a business that supplied airlines with sugar managed to rake in £500,000 from the CAP because it could argue that it was "exporting" the sugar sachets served on flights with your coffee[382]. Ligabue, an Italian caterer serving luxury cruise ships and airlines, received €148,000 of export subsidies in 2008 for the dairy and creamer sachets consumed by international travellers[383]. In December 2007 the British Sugar factory in York reopened for 48 hours only in order to claim £60million from the EU.

Reporting on the statistics for 2008 subsidies, the *New York Times* wrote on 7 May 2009 "that an elite class of beneficiaries got more than 700 payments of at least €1million. The largest payment, €140million, went to the Italian sugar company Italia Zuccheri. An Italian bank, ICBPI, got more than €180million in five payments. The list shows that an Irish agribusiness called Greencore, which produces Weight Watchers meals, received more than €83million in 2008, the fourth-largest subsidy. The French chicken giant Groupe Doux earned almost €63million." Haribo, the German makers of Gummi bear sweets, received €332,000.

The campaigning group farmsubsidy.org (even it receives EU funding) compiled a list of the top countries by number of recipients of €1million or more. Italy was top with 189, followed by Spain (174), France (149 – though she had the most euros), Portugal (40), Belgium (23) and Britain sixth with 22. The website also revealed that Tate & Lyle received £357million per annum from the CAP (in the UK alone it received €134million in 2007). Nestlé UK had to manage on £38million. In 2009, the top-earning fifth of UK CAP claimants received 73 per cent of all payments – including Tate & Lyle etc there were 29 CAP "millionaires" – but 20,000 small-holdings received less than £300 apiece.

In October 2009, the Commission decided, after pressure from 21 member states, to grant EU dairy farmers an extra €280million in aid. Agriculture commissar Fischer Boel warned the 21: "You have killed the goose that lays the golden eggs... That's it, there's no point in coming back for a single euro more." The payout had been opposed by the UK and the Netherlands but not France,

---

[382] *The Bumper Book Of Government Waste (2006)*
[383] *The Daily Telegraph*, 18 July 2009

Germany or 19 others. These direct market interventions were meant to have been abolished in return for Blair's surrender of our rebate. Well, it's no use crying over spilt milk.

It was Mariann's job to respond to the Court Of Auditors' annual reports, which usually find myriad frauds – and sachets of airline sugar – in the CAP budget. In November 2007, she was riled. At a press conference she confronted the fact that farm payments were going to golf clubs, saying it was a "stupid message... I was disappointed, then surprised, then I became angry to see the Court of Auditors say we paid money for golf courses. It's a pity that all the efforts, and all the improvement that we have made in agriculture to secure that money is duly spent, is totally overshadowed by a history of golf courses. And that's why I'm pissed off with that discussion." Not half as pissed off as most of the EU and the rest of the world is with the CAP itself.

Her husband, of course, had received €136,914 in CAP payments in 2006. In 2009, the 27-year-old daughter of Bulgaria's deputy agriculture minister received almost €700,000 from the CAP. Other recipients that year included a Swedish accordion club (€59,585); a Danish billiards club (€31,515); an Estonian school alumni society (€44,884); a Dutch iceskating club (€162,444); a Dutch amateur football club (€354,567) and Amsterdam Schiphol Airport (€98,864)[384].

In a June 2010 ECJ judgment, the UK's advocate general, Eleanor Sharpston, said that it was an infringement of the rights of CAP recipients to publish their names and addresses. (It was she who, when based in Britain, had prosecuted the Metric Martyrs for selling fruit and veg only in pounds and ounces.)

Mariann's fellow commissar, Dalia Grybauskaité, has already been quoted as saying that the CAP doubles or even triples prices for EU consumers. At the same time she said that the CAP doesn't even do much for the small-holder. According to her, "three quarters of the beneficiaries in the EU15 receive less than €5,000 a year or just 14 per cent of the budget. The rest goes to very large farms or industries". She continued, missing the point of the CAP: "Agricultural output or input gives about 5-7 per cent of GDP in each member state and we pay 40 per cent out of the EU budget. Is it proportional?"[385].

The CAP was created 50 years ago, shortly after the EEC itself, to guarantee the French rural way of life in the face of competition from increased global productivity, and was paid for by the Germans. Now, it punishes the developing world and ensures EU consumers pay once for the subsidy and twice for the levy

---

[384] *EU Observer*, 5 May 2010
[385] *Commissioner slates EU budget efficiency of CAP* in *The Irish Times*, 13 November 2008

on non-EU food. It was designed for "seven years of plenty" (guaranteeing French farmers a living in the face of depressed prices) and is entirely inappropriate – before one even considers its effect on the rest of the world – for the "seven years of dearth" that we seem to be living through. It must go. But the French will see to it that it does not. For as long as we 27 countries are all artificially yoked together this will be the case. And while that is the case we – and Africa and other poorer areas of the world – will be at the mercy of the intransigents.

Before he was president, Sarkozy called for a return to "community preference". He argued: "Controlling globalisation means re-establishing the community preference principle, which has been neglected. This does not mean a return to protectionism... Europe must buy European... A Europe without borders, that has trade agreements with China, Brazil and India that are sometimes more advantageous than those with countries in our immediate surroundings, is not what we want. We want a Europe with borders."[386] By 2010 he was saying, "When it comes to the CAP, my margin of negotiation is nonexistent."

Dominique Bussereau, when French agriculture minister, said that France wanted to maintain the CAP budget: "Spending 0.5 per cent of European GDP to ensure the quality and quantity of our food security is not an expensive price to pay. In any case, France is willing to continue to pay this price, including after 2013." Dismissing the concerns of several other continents as well as those of his own, he reiterated that France would prefer "no agreement [in the Doha round] rather than a bad agreement leading to the end of the CAP"[387].

A month later, Mr Mandelson offered a 54 per cent cut in import tariffs (subject, of course, to the "bogus health restrictions" that Stelzer spotted) at the WTO. France said that it wanted to go only to 39 per cent; there was no deal. Afterwards, Bussereau said, "We are not defending this position because we are in a pre-electoral period, but because we always defend it: 14 per cent of French workers depend on the agricultural sector." His successor, Michel Barnier, now a commissar again, said, "The CAP is the primary economic policy of the Union. We need others for energy, research and industry, but we must not break up that one, we must adapt it. That is where my vision differs from the Anglo-Saxon."[388] (That's the first time that Kenyans, among countless others in Africa and elsewhere who find the CAP abhorrent and want it abolished, have been called "Anglo-Saxon", but never mind.)

Barnier's successor, Bruno Le Maire, told the French National Assembly in

---

[386] *European View*, 6 January 2006
[387] *Agence France Presse*, 14 December 2006
[388] *Le Monde*, 4 September 2007

October 2009 that "the biggest support to French agriculture is the European Union. In addition, France is the main beneficiary of the CAP; it is essential to guarantee that it will continue to benefit from it since the CAP constitutes France's principal means of getting its contribution back from the European budget." Two months later, he organised a meeting of 22 EU agricultural ministers to "reflect on the future" of the policy: the UK, Holland, Sweden, Denmark and Malta were not invited. Le Maire said that he wanted to produce "a battle plan to defend a strong common agriculture policy, to support a renewed CAP [after 2013]. Work on this has to start as quickly as possible. The whole point of this meeting in Paris is to show our attachment to the CAP, our attachment to the tools of European regulation that are the only thing capable of guaranteeing the future of European agriculture, and to show that we are capable of imagination and daring."[389]

Rightly, the French, the EU's biggest agricultural producer, are held most responsible for maintaining the iniquitous CAP but they are not acting alone. In the summer of 2007, Germany's agricultural minister Horst Seehofer said that Angela Merkel's government would not support CAP reform before the end of the budget round: "My position is that neither the basics nor the financing of the CAP must be changed up to 2013." He said that Merkel supported him, calling her "a great friend of German agriculture". Before an Agriculture Council in January 2008, Seehofer said that he would resist reforms, such as capping payments to the largest farms. "Of course we have to be willing to compromise. But we are going to fight very, very hard for our corner," he said. In April 2008, justifying his decision to back France's proposal to maintain direct payments to farmers, Seehofer said, "We have to make sure that we can provide this continent with food sustainability and make sure that we produce enough to combat poverty in the developing world. In the future we will have food conflicts... and we have to make sure that the population here is fed at prices that are affordable. Food security is a demand of our population," which cannot be satisfied "by taking away subsidies from European farmers"[390]. This did not ring true at a time of record cereal prices.

However, after the Agriculture Council a month earlier, Agence France Presse reported, on 18 March, that the EU's food ministers had rejected that same Commission proposal to cap some CAP subsidies for larger farms. Germany and the UK, the paper said, had helped to raise a block against any reforms. While we may rejoice for once at not being outvoted in the Council Of Ministers, can we be sure we were on the right side? (It was Hilary Benn, by the way. He continued to show that he had not inherited his father's admirable principles on the EU.) Two months later, then chancellor Alistair Darling attacked the CAP in

---

[389] *The Sunday Telegraph*, 7 December 2009
[390] *The Times*, 24 April 2008

that sorry letter to his Slovenian counterpart. In the spring of 2009, the Swedish government announced that its presidency of the EU (July-December) would try to alter the CAP. For Germany, Gert Lindemann said his country's government opposed the plans and that "farmer subsidies should remain as high as possible".

The protectionist CAP has indirect social costs everywhere. Colombia's foreign minister, Jaime Bermudez, has argued that reforming the CAP, and thus giving South America access to the EU market, could strike a fatal blow against the cocaine trade: "Every inch that we add to legal cultivation and legal activity [in coca-growing countries such as Colombia] is an inch we take away from drug traffickers and terrorists. That's the reason why we need full access to the European market. The sooner the better, for both Europe and Colombia."[391] This echoed what the country's vice-president, Francisco Santos Calderon, had said a few months earlier: "If our farmers and our peasants were able to export to the European Union without the tariffs and without the barriers, we would have a farming sector that would be more competitive and a lot of peasants would not go into drug growing." Of course, we can't trade on our and Colombia's terms with Colombia so we are stuck with the status quo. And because Colombia is not a former French colony, it is not an ACP – African, Caribbean and Pacific – country and so does not enjoy preferential tariffs. For that reason, its farmers grow coca for cocaine. And so cocaine is what we get instead of sugar. Unless you're a coke-snorting and figure-conscious socialite, you might think that we have got the two white powders the wrong way round.

The CAP also supports licit drugs. The EU itself funds anti-smoking advertisements on British television (which cost about £50,000 per 30 seconds in prime time) and bans cigarette advertising and sponsorship throughout its 27 provinces. However, the CAP also subsidises the crops of about 200,000 Greek and Italian tobacco growers – which are of such poor quality that not enough people in the EU want them – to the gasp-inducing tune of €300million per annum, which is €5,250 per hectare, or over 20 times the subsidy for cereals. Remember poor old Antonio Quatraro, who had fallen to his death from a Commission building? The wicked weed and its subsidies had been his remit. Once more, as with biofuels, as soon as principle meets European agrarian interest, the former comes off worse. Guess who, in 2004, said, "The EU's support of the tobacco industry is subject to serious double standards. The EU spends large sums of money to support both the tobacco industry and anti-smoking campaigns."[392] Yes, Mariann Fischer Boel, when she was Denmark's agriculture minister. In May 2008, the European parliament voted to extend the EU's tobacco subsidy regime until at least 2012.

---

[391] *The Daily Telegraph*, 13 October 2008
[392] *Politiken*, 1 June 2007

In 2005 the House Of Lords EU select committee said: "Questions of how far to subsidise one's farmers or how much to pay for protecting the rural environment fall naturally to nation states... it seems strange to demand that the answers should be identical both for a relatively poor country such as Poland, and a richer one such as Denmark... We are not persuaded by the view of the Commission that they are better placed than member-state governments to lead regional development projects..." However, in November 2008 Michel Barnier asked, "Why do countries which have the same geographical coherence as us not do what we Europeans have been doing for 50 years with the CAP?" Why indeed.

And from turf to surf...

The Common Fisheries Policy (CFP)
The fish rots from the head down

The CFP is a quota system whereby half, but often as much as 90 per cent, of an EU fisherman's catch must be thrown back into the sea to rot as "discards" because accidental or "by" catches cannot be taken into port once one's quota has been reached; it's a criminal offence to land over one's quota (or to land fish for which one has no quota). To adapt *The Tempest*: "Full fathom five thy fishing lies/ Thy catch was slightly oversize." This is why Iceland, Norway and Greenland – all outside the EU – have thriving fish stocks and fishing industries whereas we do not.

Discards equate to 880,000 tonnes of fish on the seabed every year. Or 2,410 tonnes a day. Dutch sole fishermen in the southern North Sea use a fine mesh that allows young sole to escape but it is too fine for plaice or cod – meaning that up to 80 per cent of their catch is thrown away. Fishermen also argue that the strict time limits at sea, which have been imposed by Brussels, give them little choice but to discard low-value fish, crabs and shellfish so as to leave room on the boat for more lucrative catches[393]. The average worldwide discard rate outside the EU is about 8 per cent. Scottish fishermen, adhering to EU law, must discard 49 per cent of their total whiting catch. What is on supermarket shelves is half of what was landed: there should be a sign saying, "Buy one, know that another was dumped at sea". And the more that the quota is reduced, the more discards there are.

Trawler skipper Phil Walsh told BBC News in November 2007 that he had landed all of the cod he was allowed by June. Since then, he had been fishing for prawns and dumping prime whiting, haddock and cod, which would fetch as

---

[393] *The Times*, 29 March 2007

much as £30 per pound on a supermarket shelf. "I can't describe the feeling really," he said. "It's your livelihood and you spend your life trying to catch it and then you have to throw it back over the side [dead]. It's an impossible situation and, unless it is sorted out soon, we will all be finished."[394] In the same month, Greenpeace estimated that of the 186million fish caught in UK waters in 2006, 117million (63 per cent) were discarded. The EU itself conceded that in the North Sea trawlers were discarding between 40 and 60 per cent of all catches.

What did the last fisheries commissioner Joe Borg (Malta) have to say? Commenting on the EU's quota system, which encourages trawlers to throw back discards as well as smaller or younger fish of little commercial value, he declared, in February 2007, "It is damaging the environment. It is morally wrong to literally dump fish back into the sea. We are wasting a precious resource... every fish should be landed and when a quota was fulfilled the fishery shut."[395] A month later he called for an end to this "un-ecological, uneconomical and unethical" practice, which is "a real waste"[396]. In November 2007 he again said it was "immoral". In April 2009, the Commission admitted that 88 per cent of European fish stocks are overfished, compared to 25 per cent in the rest of the world's seas. Almost a third of managed fisheries are "outside safe biological limits, they cannot reproduce at normal because the parenting population is too depleted. Yet in many fisheries we are fishing two or three more times more than what fish stocks can sustain", said the EU research paper

The CFP was concocted late, in 1970, so that the Six could "share" the waters of Britain, Denmark, Ireland and Norway when those countries joined the EEC in 1973. Norway ran a mile (well, 200 miles, which is what the international maritime exclusion allows when there is no median with another country). The keen sailor Edward Heath, notoriously, did not run from these terms. A 10-year derogation for the UK, designed so that our fishing industry had time to prepare for the legitimated piracy, expired in 1983 and we then found that our fish -- from six miles out but still more than two thirds of the EEC's total – belonged to all 10 EEC countries. Our seas had become a "common resource".

Who has access to this "common resource"? There are 80,000 EU vessels. Spain has the biggest fleet in terms of tonnage, but only 11,350 boats to Greece's 17,350. Italy has 13,700, France almost 8,000. Britain has 6,763 boats, according to a 2007 survey (compared with 8,458 in 1997)[397].

---

[394] BBC news online, 20 November 2007
[395] *The Financial Times*, 20 February 2007
[396] *The Times*, 29 March 2007
[397] *The Times*, 23 April 2009

The ruin of our fishing industry and fishing stocks – in 1970 the UK had 21,443 fishermen but by 2007 it had 12,279[398] – are exactly what Norway foresaw for herself. In 2007, Norwegian PM Jens Stoltenberg, talking about the two referendums in his country against EU membership, said, "We have a strong economy, low unemployment, and high economic growth... The people on the coast are afraid of a common fisheries policy. Norway has proven very clever in managing our fish resources. We have not had what we have seen in many other countries – where they have destroyed their fish resources."

Also in 1983, Total Allowable Catches (TACs), species quotas (some countries' governments are more diligent than others at enforcing these) and minimum net sizes were introduced as our grace period ended. None of the measures helped Britain. In 1991, the ECJ ruled that "quota hopping" (whereby you can register boats in different EU countries to hoover up – sometimes literally – more quotas) was lawful.

Every December, the TACS are set for each state in the Fisheries Council; we currently get 28 per cent by volume, or 18 per cent by value. Either way, not quite two thirds of the stocks we initially at least provided. Brussels allows the French to catch 3,377 tons of cod each year in the English Channel, against only 366 tons for English fishermen, forcing them to dump most of what they catch[399]. Students of fairness might also be surprised to know that the CFP does not apply to the same extent in the Baltic and the Mediterranean, whence hails Mr Borg. (A fisheries commissar from a landlocked country cannot be far off.) Bruno Waterfield wrote that "The CFP is run for the administrative convenience of national and EU officials who use fishing industries as chips in negotiations... [It is about] bureaucratic trade-offs, often bringing entirely unrelated side deals on CAP and structural funds into the picture." Most infamously, this was true when Ireland and the UK acceded in the 1970s, forgoing most of their stocks for the "privilege" of joining the EEC.

As Adam Smith, star of the £20 note, observed: "If you gave a man a freehold on a patch of desert, he would turn it into a garden, but if you gave him a seven-year lease on a garden, he would turn it into a desert." And, as Aristotle (who wasn't the first) pointed out, "For that which is common to the greatest number has the least care bestowed on it." Rather more recently, the economist Larry Summers remarked that "No one ever washed a rented car." That is why the "common resource" is now so low on resources: those who should be – and

---

398 UK Sea Fisheries Statistics 2007, Marine & Fisheries Agency, quoted in *How Much Does The European Union Cost Britain? (2008)* by Gerard Batten MEP, available from www.brugesgroup.com
399 *The Sunday Telegraph*, 25 November 2007. Booker's article also explains how the rest of the world avoids committing this "crime against nature"

historically were – its guardians no longer own it or manage it. In 1968 there was a particularly widely read article in the journal *Science*: Garrett Hardin's *The Tragedy Of The Commons*. Published two years before the CFP was devised, it discussed the short-termism that can destroy the long-term prospects of common resources. In his article, Hardin invented the example of a piece of common land used for grazing by several herders; the more each man uses the land, the more he and his herd will benefit – but the sooner the grass will be eaten and the sooner no one will have any grazing land. Hardin even extended the metaphor to cover fish stocks: "The oceans of the world continue to suffer from the survival of the philosophy of the commons. Maritime nations still respond automatically to the shibboleth of the 'freedom of the seas'. Professing to believe in the 'inexhaustible resources of the oceans', they bring species of fish and whales closer to extinction."[400] There was no excuse for the CFP.

In September 2009, it was reported that Borg had been pressurised by his own country not to ban the sale of bluefin tuna, a severely depleted Mediterranean stock[401]. Since 1955, bluefin populations there have shrunk by 75 per cent, with the most dramatic reduction since 2002. And since 2001 the average mass of the fish has halved. Spain and Italy were also against the move. However, the UK, Germany, France and the then environment commissar, Mr Dimas (opposing his own country, Greece), were in support of cutting off the lucrative market, in order to allow the bluefin to recover from serious overfishing. Back home, in Borg's Malta, a thousand jobs in a market worth €100million annually depended on selling the half-tonne fish, mostly to Japan. Might that fact have influenced his decision to want to stay a ban (made, let's not forget, on behalf of the whole of the EU)? He was at the time hoping to be re-nominated by politicians in Valletta to be EU fish commissar. Borg then unexpectedly agreed with Dimas and argued for a ban. However, there was then another U-turn: France joined Spain, Italy, Malta, Greece and Cyprus in opposing a ban. And so the bluefin was not protected after all. Luckily, nor was Mr Borg: he also became "discard" (soon after changing his mind yet again). Then in 2010 the new fisheries commissar said that the EU would after all ban bluefin catches, from 2011 – but "traditional" boats (no concrete definition was offered) would be exempted. It should be no surprise that in 2010 the Commission's restaurant was still serving bluefin tuna.

At the end of 2009, an EU parliamentary question revealed that between 2000 and 2008, the EU had been subsidising Mediterranean tuna fishers with €33.4million of handouts, which had gone towards 121 new boats and modernisation for another 481. Only nine vessels were scrapped with the cash.

---

[400] *Science*, 13 December 1968
[401] *Political infighting threatens survival of the bluefin tuna* in *The Independent*, 5 September 2009

Spain had received more than half of the sum, with the French and Italians the next biggest beneficiaries. Cyprus, Malta and Greece had also been given money. In 2010, fishsubsidy.org (a sister organisation of farmsubsidy.org) cross-referenced the EU register of handouts with the register of fines, discovering that French and Spanish recipients of EU largesse were often found in possession of illegal catches: Spain's Vidal Armadores firm, for example, received at least €2.8million between 2004 and 2005 but had been caught with a contraband catch of 24 tonnes of Patagonian toothfish[402]. Subsidies had been facilitating piscine theft.

Having mismanaged its own "common resources" to the point of ruin, the EU has since 1979 leased on behalf of its 80,000 fishing vessels the waters off north-western Africa, as well as countries as far away from the EU as Mozambique. While the practice deprives thousands of African fishermen of a living, it also drives down the global price of fish because so many more are landed: under the "fisheries partnership agreements", there are no quotas – EU vessels, which are licensed by tonnage, can take as much as they want from the waters of 20 or so African states.

The sums offered are nearly impossible for a poor country to decline: in July 2006, Mauritania received £516million; its annual budget had been just twice that. The €7million that Guinea-Bissau earned in 2009 was a third of the country's budget. Cirilo Vieira, her director of fisheries, lamented the waste of the EU vessels, which never land in Guinea-Bissau: "An EU vessel that catches 2.5 tonnes of prawns per day can dump 25 tonnes of [other] fish! Fish that we need for human consumption."[403] In October 2009, Sierra Leone's president Ernest Bai Koroma gave a speech in which he noted, "I'm sure you will agree with me that it remains a travesty that Sierra Leone is banned from exporting fish to the EU, when fish illegally caught in our waters [mostly by Asian pirates] and repacked elsewhere [transferred to ships that have EU permits] are ending up on kitchen tables throughout Europe, costing our economy an estimated $30million a year."

Stelzer's "bogus health restrictions" apply also to fish. Hygiene qualifications for processing plants mean that the Senegalese and others cannot sell to the EU the few fish that the EU's hoovers have missed.

In 1976, Mauritania and Morocco annexed what's now Western Sahara. A few years later, Mauritania withdrew, leaving Morocco to rule the region, although the USA and UN continue not to recognise the administration. Nevertheless, the EU signed a €144million-per-year deal with Morocco in 2006 that gave it fishing

---

402 *Brussels Sprouts* column, *Private Eye*, 25 June-8 July 2010
403 *The Times*, 24 October 2009

rights until 2010 not only off Morocco but also in the waters of Western Sahara. (Only Sweden and Finland of the EU25 had opposed the deal.) According to the *Observer*, "in 2002, the year an EU report revealed that the Senegalese fish biomass had declined 75 per cent in 15 years, Brussels bought rights for four years' fishing of tuna and bottom-dwelling fish on the Senegal coasts, for just $4million a year... It's estimated that [such] deals have put 400,000 West African fishermen out of work."[404]

Finding there is nothing left to live on or to make a living from, the local fishermen often transform their boats into makeshift ferries for themselves and their families but also for others, paying or not, to make the trip to the Canary Islands and mainland Spain. According to the UN, about 6,000 people (out of 31,000) died trying to make the trip to the EU in 2007[405]. Those who remain to try to fish the leftovers from their pirogues – canoe-like boats carved from a single piece of wood – are often drowned by the giant "factory ships" of nearby EU states.

There's a particularly vicious and ironic circle here, noted by Felicity Lawrence in her book *Eat Your Heart Out*[406]. Many African farmers found in the 1990s that dumped EU food surpluses made it impossible to make a living from the land, so they were pushed into fishing. In the Atlantic, they encountered Euro hoovers, with which they could not compete, so they sailed to Europe to find work. The easiest work to find was in, you guessed it, agriculture. So they got to work on a CAP-subsidised farm, the produce of which would be dumped on Senegal, which etc...

Over the last three decades fish stocks off West Africa have halved. Absenting itself from this disaster by ignoring the fact that the drop coincides exactly with the period since 1979, the EU Commission describes the African nations from whom it has leased fishing rights as "woeful managers of their own fish stocks"[407]. If the EU had not been such a "woeful manager" of its own stocks, it would have had no business poaching Africa's.

Dr Richard North wrote: "The problem [in EU waters] is the EU itself, which insists on quotas as the only fisheries management system that it is capable of operating from Brussels – despite the devastating environmental impact. The alternative is a 'days at sea' regime, where boats are licensed to fish in certain

[404] *The Observer*, 11 May 2008
[405] *Europe Takes Africa's Fish, And Boatloads Of Migrants Follow* in *The New York Times*, 14 January 2008
[406] *Eat Your Heart Out: Why the Food Business is Bad for the Planet and Your Health* by Felicity Lawrence (Penguin, 2008)
[407] *The Wall Street Journal*, 18 July 2007

areas for a specified number of days, a regime in which discards are banned and fishermen must land all they catch. But this must be combined with a highly responsive system of closed areas, where feedback on fish stocks can be used to close down areas where the number of juvenile fish being caught is excessive, that in itself requires good local enforcement and strong peer pressure amongst fishermen – which only works within a framework of national control. There is also a need for much more work on selective fishing techniques – which would be driven by a discards ban as fishermen would not want to waste valuable days at sea hauling in fish they cannot market."[408]

If fish are thrown back as discards, it becomes difficult to gauge how healthy stocks are; no one is keeping count of everything caught because it is not all landed. This compounds any problem and makes effective husbandry almost impossible. Quotas can work in areas with only a single species, but they are not suitable for mixed-fish seas such as those found around Europe. It is easier to track stock levels if you land everything. Then you can impose "days at sea" limits if necessary. By autumn 2009, even Borg was conceding the need for something like a "days at sea" scheme.

The Court Of Auditors damned the CFP in a November 2007 report. A press release accompanying the report starkly said: "Lower catches and overexploitation of fishery resources have been observed for many years. These findings are now widely shared and represent the failure of the Common Fisheries Policy."

The EU plans to extend the CFP to recreational marine anglers, who in the UK catch about one per cent of UK (OK, "common resource") fish. Those fishing from piers or rocks are exempt but those fishing from boats are included and must log their catches and register what they land against the national quota – regardless of where the fishermen hail from. Cormorants and gannets are not included in the legislation even though they tend to present very, very little of what they catch.

At the final Fisheries Council of 2009, when TACs were allocated, the UK (abetted by Denmark and Germany) proposed CCTV for boats. Now, if fishermen allow three closed-circuit cameras on their vessels – to monitor stocks and to see what the fishermen are up to – they will be allowed to catch five per cent over their quota. Proving they didn't understand that smaller quotas mean more discards, ministers cut TACs for haddock, sole and cod by between 20 to 25 per cent (but increased hake catches by 15 per cent).

In September 2006, at the Labour Party conference – the one at which Brown

---

[408] *Unfinished business*, eureferendum.blogspot.com, 20 November 2007

did not criticise EU agro-environmental policy, because he could finally see power, or at least office – David Miliband, then environment minister, told a Greenpeace event that "the European Union needs to be stronger if we are going to respond to the climate change challenge. In my view you cannot be an environmentalist if you are a eurosceptic. The European Union of the future needs to be an environmental union that wins and mobilises its support by its engagement with environmental issues."

The environment gives the EU plenty of scope to legislate 27 nations into one (always its primary purpose). And it offers the chance of a direct revenue stream, perhaps a carbon tax (separate from the ETS) levied directly on the EU citizen, bypassing national treasuries. But it would be obscene to give the EU more power to wreck the environment. Its "climate change" remedies exacerbate or even cause environmental damage (increased deforestation to chase palm-oil subsidy, or birds and bats killed by wind farms, which unearth vast quantities of carbon dioxide and despoil the countryside), while pauperising hospitals and people. The central planks of its environmental approach, the Common Agricultural Policy and Common Fisheries Policy, have been described as the miracle of the loaves and fishes – in reverse.

In the next chapter, the EU helps itself to more of its neighbours' resources.

CHAPTER 5: THE NEIGHBOURS

Trade and aid

Although our aid budget still mostly goes through our own Department for International Development, a quarter of it is administered for us by Brussels.

As might be expected, distribution does not always run smoothly. The Echo, Phare and EuropeAid programmes are all synonymous with grift, and when the 1999 Commission fell it was discovered that 10,000 aid programmes were incomplete and awaiting funds.

In 2006, the €7billion Tacis programme (Technical Assistance for the Commonwealth of Independent States) for 12 ex-USSR countries was examined by the Court Of Auditors. Almost three quarters − or €5billion − had been misspent since the fund was set up in 1991. The auditors investigated 29 projects in Russia, the main beneficiary, and found only nine achieved the objectives for which the EU thought it was paying and, in total, only five projects had any lasting impact. The examples of waste included: fitness equipment intended for children had been taken by Russian soldiers; a heating and power project for a city that did not want it; a scheme for harmonising road standards between the EU and Russia that failed because the EU itself had no such common standard; and technical equipment sold off by the recipients because they did not know how to use it and did not have the necessary internet connection[409].

In summer 2008 there were even problems with aid to EU members. Freezing €486million in aid to Bulgaria because of its failure to combat corruption, organised crime and abuse of EU funds, the Commission said, "High-level corruption remains a serious problem. It has not yet been effectively tackled by the administration and the judiciary. The Bulgarian authorities have not applied the law in such a way to reduce corruption in state institutions." It also warned that Structural Funds worth €6.85billion in the current budget round were at risk if the country did not clean up its act (only €288million out of €1.03billion of EU funds available under the European Regional Development Fund between 2007 and 2009 were given to the country). With an entirely straight face, the Commission also castigated Romania, noting "the lack of sanctions being taken against public officials who commit acts of corruption".

In 2010, the COA criticised the opacity of the relationship between the EU and the United Nations: "Aid implemented by the European Commission through

---

[409] *The Times*, 21 April 2006

UN organisations amounted to over €1billion in 2008. The Court has examined whether decisions to channel aid through the UN have been the result of a transparent and objective selection process and whether monitoring arrangements provide adequate information on the achievement of objectives and the robustness of financial procedures. The European parliament has questioned why the Commission channels funds through the UN, and encouraged more direct management by the Commission. It has expressed concern at the lack of transparency and visibility concerning Commission funding through the UN and has requested assurance on the adequacy of the management of these funds. Regarding the process for deciding to implement aid through the UN, the Court concludes that the strategic and legal requirements to select partners in an objective and transparent way are insufficiently translated into practical criteria to support decision-making. The Commission does not convincingly demonstrate, before deciding to work with a UN organisation, that it has assessed whether the advantages offset any disadvantages."[410] The EU and UN are perfect bedfellows – they both work over the heads of member states and accountability is not always foremost in their minds.

There have also been problems when only EU-based suppliers can be used for aid projects. Aside from providing jobs for the boys, EU aid is showy benevolence, which is grimly ironic when it leaves communities stranded and far worse off than before. Examples include a Kenyan village whose water supply was cut off when work on a road was started – and not reconnected when the EU-based firm left as soon as its funding ended[411].

Other avoidable disasters include the EU's ban on DDT, in the face of World Health Organisation advice, which has led to the deaths of many Africans, particularly Ugandans, from malaria.

Peter Mandelson has said in private that aid to Vietnam is useless while trade tariffs exist[412]. Another to make the point is South Africa's foreign minister,

---

[410] *EU assistance implemented through United Nations organisations: decision-making and monitoring* (ECA/10/05), The Court Of Auditors, 13 January 2010. On the same day, in a separate announcement (ECA/10/02), the COA criticised EU aid to Turkey: "On the evidence of its audit, the Court concludes that there was insufficient direction and a lack of specific criteria to determine the priorities to which the EU assistance should be allocated. Specific and measurable objectives for that assistance were not set and the timescales to achieve those objectives were not realistic. The Commission did not have sufficient information to demonstrate the effectiveness of the pre-accession assistance as there was not a sound basis for monitoring performance, including value for money"
[411] *When will Glenys keep her promise?* in The Sunday Telegraph, 21 June 2009
[412] *The Daily Telegraph*, 31 August 2006

Nkosazana Dlamini-Zuma, who says that the cost of the EU's regulations to the whole of Africa "is almost double what the EU gives in aid"[413]. After the Asian tsunami in 2004, the Thai government – as well as Oxfam – told the EU that it would prefer reduced tariffs instead of money and dumped agricultural surplus. But, as we know, the EU will never relinquish the CAP or protectionism.

The think tank Civitas says: "Imports most heavily taxed by the EU tend to be from poor countries. For countries with a GDP per capita of under £5,000 per annum the average tariff is 6 per cent, compared with 1.6 per cent for countries with a GDP per capita of over £15,000 pa."[414] Open Europe's 2005 figures concurred: "Malawi, with a per capita income of less than £100 a year pays an average 12 per cent tax on its exports to the EU. Lesotho, Namibia and Swaziland face a tariff of over 20 per cent"[415].

Aid from the EU does not come with strings attached so much as a cat's cradle. In 2006, the Commission proposed something called Economic Partnership Agreements (EPAs) for African-Caribbean-Pacific (ACP) countries, where most of Europe's former colonies lie. (The previous ACP-EU arrangements had been ruled illegal by the World Trade Organisation in 1996.) The prospective signatories were soon sceptical about whether the €2billion in aid was new funding – and whether it would arrive on time. "The track record of the European Commission in terms of disbursement of EDF [European Development Fund] funds is not good," Daniel Moroka, the trade minister for Botswana, told the *Financial Times* on 8 November 2006.

In May 2007, an Open Europe survey[416] found the EU's war on want was, er, wanting. Having interviewed recipient countries, the report's authors documented how 21 per cent of EU aid money arrives more than a year late, compared to just three per cent from other aid donors. The survey also found that, while just over 7 per cent of the total EU budget is spent on overseas aid, aid programmes account for 21 per cent of all fraud investigations by Olaf, making aid fraud even likelier than the already stratospheric Brussels average. Fraud aside, the report argued that, far from delivering economies of scale for member states, delivering aid through the 118 Commission delegations represented a wasteful cost. Closing the delegations and scaling back on admin would release huge sums for real aid, potentially over €1billion per annum. The report also argued that the wrong conditions were attached to EU aid. Although the EU pushed EPAs, which require ACP counties to 'open sesame' to EU

---

413 *The Sunday Telegraph*, 9 April 2006
414 Civitas's set of fact sheets has been refereed by both sides of the EU debate and is available from www.civitas.org.uk/eufacts
415 Neil O'Brien, *The Spectator*, 8 December 2005
416 www.openeurope.org.uk, *EU aid: is it effective?*

imports rather more quickly than might be in their interest, the EU continued to give unfettered aid to countries such as Cuba, North Korea, Uzbekistan and China, despite their open disregard for human rights.

By October 2007, resistance to EPAs had became more than vocal. The Kenya Small Scale Farmers Forum (KSSFF) and Kenya Human Rights Commission (KHRC) asked the country's high court, which can stop the country signing agreements that might infringe the rights of its subjects, to block EPAs. They said that the EPAs could force hundreds of thousands of Kenyans into joblessness and deeper poverty owing to undercutting European imports. The executive director of the KHRC, L Muthoni Wanyeki, explained the action in a newspaper article: "A study commissioned by the ministry of trade and industry and carried out by the Kenya Institute of Public Policy Research Analysis – the government's own economic think tank – shows that EPAs will bring about a revenue loss of between Ksh6billion (£60million) and Ksh9billion. They will reduce national output by between 0.6 and 1 per cent and result in the loss of at least 3,000 jobs. The EPAs will also drive intra-East African Community trade down by about 15 per cent. As a result, Kenya will either be forced to expand its tax base or seek increased external revenues. For members of the KSSFF, EPAs will pose significant challenges to the continued domestic production of food commodities – from maize, rice, sugar and wheat staples to dairy and meat products."[417]

A few weeks later the Kenyan trade and industry minister, Dr Mukhisa Kituyi, said, "The impression I get is that the European Union wants to use this deadline to arm-twist for more concessions on market access from our countries... It is not acceptable that we have less than two months to the end of the current trade and tariff arrangement, and there isn't sufficient signal of solidarity to assure our exporters that there will be no tariffs that can cost contracts in the European markets."

The country insisted that it would not sign an EPA without a 25-year transition period. The EU wanted 10 years. The next day, trade union leaders in Ghana, Zimbabwe, South Africa, Zambia, Botswana, Niger, Burkina Faso and Kenya urged their countries' leaders not to be seduced into signing EPAs in Brussels. A joint statement said, "As the deadline looms and our ministers meet in Brussels we urge them to withstand any pressure they may be subjected to sign a deal which leaves the workers of our countries worse off." What could go wrong when dealing with Peter Mandelson, then trade commissar?

---

[417] *The East African*, 29 October 2007

A week later, the EU gave the East African Community (Kenya, Uganda, Tanzania, Burundi and Rwanda) another year to sign up and also offered the 25-year concession. But the scope and terms of this interim deal or "framework agreement" were criticised by many. "Both the deal on the table now and the dirty tactics employed by the EU in the negotiations process represent a step backwards for the region's development. East African countries stand to lose $162.5million every year in government revenue from signing an EPA," Ruthpearl Ng'ng'a of the charity World Accord, told Agence France Presse[418]. On the other side of the continent, Senegal's President Abdoulaye Wade stated: "I say that Senegal will not sign these accords." The draft EPAs had already been rejected by the 15-strong group of the Economic Community of West African States (ECOWAS), of which Senegal is a member.

Rebuffed, the EU sought to forge bilateral deals but President Wade said, "I will not sign a separate pact", proving himself more aware of the EU's own rules than the EU itself was. Another African who saw the EU's hypocrisy in trying to deal bloc-to-nation rather than bloc-to-bloc was Tetteh Hormeku, a leading lawyer at advocacy group Third World Network Africa. In an interview he said, "The EU delegation shouldn't have come here to Ghana. ECOWAS had set up a negotiating team. The EU knows that and yet it comes to Ghana and goes to the head of state. This would be like bypassing Peter Mandelson [EU trade commissioner] by going to Gordon Brown [then prime minister of Britain, whose trade policy is decided in Brussels]. It would be like saying to Brown, 'We have a problem with Peter Mandelson, you have to intervene.' This exposes the cynicism of the European Union. First, they are saying an EPA is for promoting regional integration. But when they are not getting their way, they behave in a way that undermines our own regional integration."[419]

In Brussels, Luis Morago, the head of Oxfam's EU office, said, "Developing nations have been placed under enormous pressure to sign. Despite concerns raised by many, including the IMF, the Commission has ignored possible alternatives and insisted on the deadline. This agreement will oblige the East African region to remove 80 per cent of its tariffs on EU goods over 15 years, possibly more quickly, which could lead to unemployment and loss of vital government revenue that might otherwise be spent on health and education."

In December 2007, South Africa and Namibia rejected the new agreements, saying that they would compromise their sovereignty. According to the *Financial Times*, both wanted to avoid guaranteeing the EU equal terms with any trade deals negotiated with other parties in future – the so-called Most Favoured Nation (MFN) clause. Hanno Rumpf, Namibia's EU envoy, told the newspaper

---

[418] *Agence France Presse*, 20 November 2007
[419] Inter Press Service, 20 December 2007

"the MFN clause… is very disturbing" [420]. Faced with such poor terms – and Mandelson – it was no surprise when agreement couldn't be found. A week later, President Wade declared that the EPAs would not be imposed: "It's clear that Africa rejects the EPAs. We are not talking any more about EPAs… We're going to meet to see what we can put in place of the EPAs. It was said several times during the plenary session and it was said again this morning: African states reject the EPAs." [421] The *Financial Times* quoted him as saying that EPAs would amputate state budgets and ruin African industries by dismantling tariff barriers [422]. The president of the African Union Commission, Alpha Oumar Konaré, said, "No one will make us believe we don't have the right to protect our economic fabric." Back in Brussels, Oxfam's spokeswoman on trade, Amy Barry, said, "It is astounding that the Commission is prepared to push through such highly inequitable deals that will hurt poor farmers and undermine future development." One of those who found the EU's EPA offer possible to refuse was Zambia, whose president, Levi Mwanawasa, pointed out that EU health-and-safety controls cost his country as much in lost trade as it receives in EU aid.

By the end of 2007, 35 ACP countries, including 19 in Africa, had signed "framework agreements" with a view to signing full EPAs in 2008. Unease persisted: in April 2008, South Africa's deputy minister of trade and industry, Dr Rob Davies, said that EPAs would not deliver the benefits they claimed, adding that "the devil is in the details of the agreements". Like Mwanawasa, he had spotted the 'elf and safety provisos for exports. Using stronger language was Malawi's President Bingu wa Mutharika. He said he would not sign an EPA on current terms because it would not benefit Malawians, and he criticised the EU's strategy of using aid as a lever to cajole developing countries into signing. "This is imperialism by the EU, which we must fight against because the [aid] funding has nothing to do with EPA conditionalities. [The EU is] doing this in order to punish those that who are not signing their agreements," he said.

The unease over the "framework agreements" was also felt across the Atlantic. Quoted in the same Agence France Presse article, Guyana's ambassador to the EU, Patrick Gomes, said, "We are really uncomfortable, feeling the pressure of the deadline. Given the level of complexity, we need more time." Eventually, the country did sign "but with strong reservations after being threatened with being kicked off the EU's list of countries with market access" [423].

Of the 19 African countries that signed "framework agreements" by the end of

---

[420] *The Financial Times*, 4 December 2007
[421] *The Guardian*, 10 December 2007
[422] *The Financial Times*, 10 December 2007
[423] *Zambia, Comoros refuse to sign EU trade accord at last minute* in *EU Observer*, 31 August 2009

2007 deadline, only six had signed full EPAs by mid 2009. About 40 African countries were still unwilling to meet the EU's terms.

When Mandelson returned to the UK in 2008, the *Guardian* looked at his record: "Governments in the Caribbean are signing an EPA with the [EU], one of the few free-trade deals that this 'brilliant' negotiator actually clinched. Enormous pressure was put on Caribbean nations to cross what they considered red lines. This was especially so with the inclusion of a 'Most Favoured Nation' clause... Junior Lodge, the chief negotiator for the Caribbean, had stated that he was 'violently opposed' to the EU's demands for this clause – which others have described as an affront to the national sovereignty of the countries concerned. Yet because of Mandelson's bullying, his region eventually had to capitulate."

The bullying was explicit: "The Caribbean was told that if it did not accept EPAs, higher tariffs would be imposed on its exports. Shortly before he left Brussels, Mandelson reiterated that threat to Guyana... Imposing increased trade taxes on Guyana would deprive it of some €70million per year, a huge sum for a small economy where the national income per capita is only about €7,000."

And hidden in the EPAs were clauses perhaps more harmful than the MFN: "There are also chapters on competition, investment and public procurement. Known as the Singapore issues, these topics proved so contentious during the Doha round of world trade talks that developing countries insisted that they be taken off the agenda. Unable to get its way in a quasi-global forum, the EU is now reintroducing these measures – aimed at giving multinationals unimpeded access to wherever they wish to do business – through the backdoor."

As if that weren't enough, the EU had devised a way of protecting patents in these territories after expiry: "Stringent rules relating to pharmaceutical patents are likely to mean that people with life-threatening diseases will no longer be able to afford cheap generic versions of medicines... EU officials want this agreement to serve as a model for similarly comprehensive ones they are hoping to reach with over 60 countries in Africa and the Pacific. Diplomats from these countries do not share Brown's view that Mandelson did a 'brilliant job'; some have described the EPA talks as the most painful experience of their careers."[424]

It is hoped that Mr De Gucht, the current trade commissar, will not bully countries hotter than his own.

---

[424] *Not such a 'brilliant job'* by David Cronin, on guardian.co.uk/commentisfree, 15 October 2008

Enlargement

When trying to propound the benefits of the EU – after having not convinced even themselves that Italian restaurants in High Wycombe and Dutch footballers in the Premier League are a result of our membership of the European Union – europhiles go for the "soft power" argument[425]. The gist of this is that the prize of EU membership forces applicant countries to raise their "standards" – not least by taking on the acquis communautaire (like a goose learning how foie gras is produced). The desirability of uniform "standards" imposed throughout a bloc of 27 interestingly differentiated peoples is not obvious to all. Besides, there's a mountain of evidence to suggest that once countries are admitted to the EU they revert to bad ways. "With anti-corruption reform faltering since EU accession, the cases of Bulgaria and Romania show that EU membership is no magic bullet," Transparency International, the anti-corruption campaign, said in July 2008 when, as already mentioned, even the Commission criticised those countries[426]. Many candidates for accession behave beautifully before joining and afterwards do not – like cars slowing down before a speed camera and racing away again when they've passed it.

So, who will be next to join? In order to avoid an awkwardness in the 2005 vote on the Constitution, President Chirac promised the French people that the EU would not again enlarge after the 2007 accessions without a referendum in France. This was code for "You can have the final say on Turkey but please don't sink the Constitution". The bribe didn't work, and a vote is hypothetical anyway – it will never get to that stage. (Sarkozy later repealed that part of the French Constitution.)

Just as turkeys are reluctant to vote for Christmas, so Christians seem reluctant to vote for Turkey. Despite Nato membership since 1952, Istanbul being the heart of the later Roman Empire, Turkish Council Of Europe membership since its inception, and Ankara applying to the EU in 1987 (having had an associate agreement since 1963), acceptance of Turkey is not likely soon. Cyprus's veto alone would see to that. The fact that 40 per cent of Turkey's workforce (pop: 70million) is involved in agriculture might jeopardise the CAP for, to pluck an example from plein air, the French (Sarko is really not keen on Turkish accession). Other countries not in favour include the Netherlands, Austria and Germany (Angela Merkel, December 2007: "We are, have been and will remain in favour of a privileged partnership with Turkey, but we are against full

---

[425] There is a "Chinatown" shop-and-restaurant quarter in many major Western cities, including London, but China is not saddled with EU membership; EU footballers are not the only foreigners playing the game in the UK; rumours abound that there were French restaurants in the UK before 1 January 1973
[426] *The Guardian*, 24 July 2008

membership"). In 2009 Barroso said that Turkey's entry into the EU "will not occur during the next Commission mandate" (ie not before 2014).

The Turkish PM, Recep Tayyip Erdogan, did his country's cause no favours in February 2008 when he said that the cultural assimilation of Turks in Germany was a "crime against humanity", nor a year later when he criticised the appointment of the Danish PM as head of Nato – because he had not prosecuted those sections of the press in Denmark that had printed the infamous Mohammed cartoons.

Before the 2009 Euro elections, Merkel tried to tone down her anti-Turkish rhetoric. The *New York Times* reported on 1 June: "As citizens across Europe prepare to vote this week for a new European parliament, Angela Merkel's conservative bloc has abandoned its attempt to create a wedge issue out of Turkey's potential entry into the European Union. The change in approach is an acknowledgement... that they have more to gain by appealing to Germany's 690,000 Turkish voters than by alienating them with blunt talk about the political and cultural differences separating Turkey and the rest of the EU. The conservatives view the parliamentary balloting as a barometer for the federal elections and realise that they need every vote they can get. Though she spoke out against Turkey's EU ambitions as recently as last month, the bloc has since refrained from making Turkey's entry, or EU enlargement in general, a major issue in the campaign."

Eight of the 35 "chapters" required for Turkish accession have been satisfied. Another eight have been frozen since December 2006 because of continued disagreements over Cyprus. Problems concerning the judicial system and freedom of expression and of religion dog the other 19.

Sweden, Spain, Slovenia and Britain are in favour of Turkish membership. In September 2007, foreign secretary Miliband visited the country, saying, "It's great that Turkey has broken through the barrier that says Islam is incompatible with democracy and a secular public realm... My job as a politician is to win the argument that Britain is better off with Turkey in the EU." Eight months later, he dragged the Queen there to say much the same thing.

If a common foreign policy is indeed possible, how is it possible to have only one EU embassy in a "third country"? If France is hostile to Ankara's ambition to join the EU and Spain is not, which view prevails in the EU embassy in the Turkish capital? Whatever line is toed will be determined by qualified-majority voting.

Despite Turkey's key importance in the proposed Nabucco gas pipeline, which the EU is keen on developing "as quickly as possible" in Barroso's words (the organisation's EIB and other bodies are trying to find a quarter of the €11billion price tag) so as to avoid reliance on Russia, she has no chance of accession. Any dialogue with the EU about joining is just that: talk. Perhaps knowing this, Turkey is also co-operating with Russia, her biggest trading partner, on a rival system, the South Stream gas pipeline.

Croatia will join the Enron-style boondoggle next, having already swallowed a lot of the acquis. In November 2006, the Croatian minister in charge of negotiations with the EU, Vladimir Drobnjak, said that negotiations had been more difficult than expected: "To enter the EU, the UK had to implement 30,000 pages of EU legislation. We, 30 years later, have to implement more than 100,000! To respond to the demands of the Commission, we have produced in one year no less than 20,000 pages of documents, and 2,000 people are dealing with the negotiations in our country." He also said that it was "incontestably" harder for his country to enter the EU than it had been for the 10 accessionists of 2004.

Not understanding quite what the Common Fisheries Policy entailed (ring up Norway!), Croatia planned to create a protected fishing zone in the Adriatic to prevent overfishing by the Italians. Enlargement commissioner Olli Rehn suggested that this would have "negative consequences for the country's accession process"[427]. A few months later, in March 2008, the Croatian parliament dropped plans for the 30,000 km² area. However, it still has an ongoing border dispute with Slovenia, who might yet block accession.

In April 2008, Serbia achieved candidate status, signed a Stabilisation and Association agreement and has since intensified attempts to arrest General Ratko Mladić, the war-crimes fugitive, the most important precondition set by the EU for granting it pre-membership status. The capture of Radovan Karadžić in July 2008 helped her cause, and she applied for full membership in December 2009.

The EU's Javier Solana had previously urged Montenegro – which has filed a membership application that Germany and the Netherlands blocked – to secede from Serbia, which it did. (Solana had been secretary general of Nato when it bombed Yugoslavia, especially Serbia, to smithereens in 1999.) And, of course, Kosovo, another secessionist from Serbia, is run by the EU's EULex service. Another former Yugoslav state, Macedonia, also has candidate status, but Greece refuses to recognise her name, for historical reasons. Bosnia-Herzegovina signed a pre-accession agreement in December 2007 after Muslim, Serb and Croatian parties adopted an "action plan" for police reform in the country. It later signed a full Stabilisation and Association agreement. Quite why all those

---

[427] BBC news online, 31 December 2007

fractious former Yugoslav states, which spilt so much blood so recently in order to be autonomous, want to unify once again – with Slovenia – is unclear.

Albania has "candidate" status, having signed a Stabilisation and Association agreement in June 2006, and applied to join in April 2009.

Iceland's parliament voted in 2009 by 33-28 to "explore" the idea of applying for EU membership. Sometime after the vote, Iceland's minister for agriculture and fisheries, Jón Bjarnason, said at a conference in Biarritz on coastal fisheries: "Iceland is a small island in the middle of the Atlantic Ocean with just over 300,000 inhabitants. The foundation of our livelihood lies in our natural resources; we must maintain sovereignty over our most valued assets, our economy, our culture and our future generations are depending on it. We can enjoy wide-ranging international co-operation without being tied up in the EU framework. Given these circumstances, it is my firm belief that the future of our country is will be much better off outside the European Union than inside." When Iceland has recovered economically, her citizens (and perhaps her politicians) will "do a Norway" and stay out.

Foreign policy

According to legend, the EU has always been stung by Henry Kissinger's reasonable question – "If I want to ring 'Europe', whom do I call?" The comment was used as a spur to action by proponents of a uniform foreign policy and deeper integration. In fact, Kissinger never said it. Well, he said it long after he was first supposed to have done so and only after it was quoted to him[428]. The fact that Kissinger had not said it until then did not matter to those who wanted to form a single polity; if it helps the cause to invent a quotation, invent a quotation.

Now, post Lisbon, it seems that having a president of the Commission (Barroso), a high representative (Ashton), a president of the Council of the European Union (leader of whichever country has the increasingly marginalised six-month presidency), a president of the parliament (some MEP or other, it doesn't matter) and a president of the European Council (Herman) has only deepened confusion over whom to call. So muddled was Barack Obama that he used the institutional chaos as an excuse to cancel an EU-US summit.

The Maastricht Treaty created a Common Foreign and Security Policy and we have ceded 28 foreign policy areas to common action since.

---

[428] EuroNews interview with Kissinger, 31 March 2007

One of these areas is Zimbabwe, which means that we cannot take any action against that country without unanimity in the Foreign Council, despite the fact that it was in the Commonwealth until recently.

Another area of foreign policy we have ceded is dealings with the constituent parts of the former USSR. Forty years to the month after rolling into Czechoslovakia in August 1968, the Russians set the satnavs in their tanks for Georgia, a former USSR state. The UK's response to the most frightening territorial crisis in a generation was of no worth. The then president of the European Council, Mr Sarkozy, spoke for us all, cobbling together a sketchy peace plan that had loopholes big enough to drive a tank through, which the Russians duly did. Just over a year later the French sold the Russians amphibious assault vehicles which would have, according to the Russians, got the Georgian job done "in 40 minutes rather than 26 hours". It was the first such sale to Russia by a European state since the end of the Cold War.

An unequivocal EU message would have been impossible anyway: Britain, Sweden, and the east Europeans – who reacted to the invasion like villagers discovering that the local burglar had been let out of jail – wanted sanctions, whereas the Germans in particular had no desire to antagonise their gasman, who they realised would be increasingly important to them as they closed their nuclear power stations at the same time as the EU mandated ever more useless windmills in their country.

Foreign policy is often energy policy in a different envelope, especially if you forgo nuclear. Which is why Germany – so heavily reliant on Russian gas – ensured that the Bear was not castigated by the EU after it had invaded Georgia. Although the EU recognised Kosovo, which had seceded from Serbia, it couldn't bring itself to recognise South Ossetia and Abkhazia. As mentioned, the EU also flashes a leg at Turkey, pretending Ankara has a chance of membership when that country is the only one in the world to recognise Northern Cyprus, which is part of an island whose lower extremity is in the eurozone. If none of this makes sense, that's because sense cannot be made of the EU's position. If foreign policy is actually a combination of foreign policy and energy policy – and the EU is nice to Turkey only so that its Russia-avoiding Nabucco gas pipeline has a chance, although Turkey would understandably rather act as a middleman between Asian suppliers and the EU rather than as a conduit – then you have as many as 54 policies trying to fit into one policy.

At the time of the Russian excursion into Georgia, Vaira Vike-Freiberga, who was Latvian president when her country had joined the EU and Nato, said that she was "surprised and frustrated" that the EU "was unable to come up with a united, co-ordinated and condemning" stance against the Kremlin. Poland sympathised with her, as did another 2004 entrant, the Czech Republic, whose Prague Spring had been ended by Russian hardware 40 years earlier.

Foreign policy first became an EU competence as a consequence of the Single European Act and it fell further into Brussels's maw with the second half of that treaty (Maastricht).

The Amsterdam Treaty created a "High Representative for Foreign Affairs", a post filled until 2009 by Javier Solana, a former secretary general of Nato. Until 2009, the EU also had a commissioner for "external relations and European neighbourhood policy", Austria's Benita Ferrero-Waldner. On top of that, the foreign secretary of the country with the EU presidency was primus inter pares. (There is also, of course, still a foreign secretary in each of the other 26 provinces.) The Lisbon Treaty provided a unifying panjandrum, a job first filled by Britain's Cathy Ashton, whose remit is on p78.

As Daniel Hannan wrote, "When is the last time you can remember the UK acting wholly independently in foreign affairs? All right, we can still decide the absolutely critical things for ourselves: whether to invade Iraq, for example. But most issues – selling arms to Beijing, funding the Hamas regime, sucking up to the ayatollahs in Teheran, sponsoring a ceasefire in Georgia – are now determined by Brussels. British politicians still talk quaintly of the pros and cons of a common European foreign policy, as if the idea were being newly proposed. In fact, a common foreign policy is up and running. The EU has its foreign secretary [then Javier Solana], its embassies, its diplomatic training college, its External Action Service. It's true that this last body has no legal base without the ~~European Constitution~~ Lisbon Treaty. But it has been conjured into being anyway, along with much of the rest of the text. Eurocrats don't let little things like 'No' votes put them off."[429]

The embassies are part of the EU's €3.9billion External Relations service. In June 2010 *Der Spiegel* reported that the EU's office in Addis Ababa had paid out €65million incorrectly and was unlikely to see the money again. Lax budgeting aside, the EU has a property portfolio outside the EU worth €63million (the Tokyo office accounts for €34million of this, while the one in Abuja cost £4.1million in 2005 and the Chinese base is worth £2.8million[430]) and representatives in over 130 countries, where its ambassadors can earn up to €240,000 in salary and perks[431]. These reps – pushing the message of the EU as

---

429 *Don't let the EU speak for Britain in the Caucasus*, 17 August 2008, on blogs.telegraph.co.uk/politics/danielhannan
430 *The Sunday Times*, 22 November 2009
431 *EU Diplomats*, September 2009, by Dr Lee Rotherham, available from www.taxpayersalliance.com

well as its interests regardless of the interests of the UK, whose taxpayers fund them but cannot hold them to account – are in competition with not only Her Majesty's ambassadors but also, in the larger countries, the reps from our beloved 12 regional development agencies (or whatever they're called this week).

Getting 27 countries to agree on foreign affairs is an obvious non-starter – the EU15 was split by Afghanistan and the 2003 Iraq war. Before that the bloc had stood by while Yugoslavia (an immediate neighbour, part of which is now in the eurozone) and Rwanda tore themselves apart (as well as when Cyprus was invaded). To believe the EU can throw its weight around the world stage – in one direction at a time – is hopeless. But there is a blind desire to act like a state, whatever the contradictions, unwanted spending priorities and fatal delays (Indian Ocean tsunami, Haiti earthquake) that entails.

At a July 2006 Foreign Council, the Israeli-Lebanon conflict came up for discussion. We and Holland were said to have blocked a proposal by France, Italy, Spain (whose PM was later photographed in a Lebanese *kufia* or scarf) and Belgium to demand an "immediate and unconditional ceasefire". The Council met again two months later. This time, we and Germany refused to call for an immediate ceasefire. The Finns, who held the presidency, wanted a watered-down declaration such as a call for an immediate cessation of "hostilities" that everyone might agree on. France and others had wanted the word "ceasefire". The Finnish presidency could say only that "This crisis is now a test of whether – and how well – the EU can act and exert influence." The Israelis and Palestinians themselves could have reached agreement sooner. In March 2007, a Foreign Council discussed a possible resumption of direct EU aid to the Palestinian Authority (PA), which had received €120million the previous year after its election. However, the EU had recently legislated against financing terrorists and had placed Hamas, which ran the PA, on its list of proscribed organisations. The resumption was supported by France, Spain and Italy but not by us and Germany. The following year the EU again ignored its own rules, giving over €256million to Hamas.

The EU was still unembarrassed by this gross double standard in January 2009 when Hamas, after shelling Israel, cried foul when Israel invaded the Gaza Strip. Whose side would the EU back? Hamas, to whom it gave money? Or would it chastise Hamas, whom it proscribed? It being January, the rotating EU presidency had just been passed on, from France to the Czech Republic. In the old days, in January people would forget to write the new year on their cheques. In January 2009, Sarkozy "forgot" that he no longer held the EU presidency and freelanced in the Middle East, undermining the EU-Czech representation that was also there. So, there were two official EU positions on Hamas (forbidden yet indulged) and two EU six-month presidents (one ex and one incumbent) in the

Middle East. As well as that, there was Tony Blair – representing the "Quartet" of the EU (yet more representation), Russia (the same country that had done to Georgia what Israel had done to the Gaza Strip), the USA and the UN (40 per cent of whose permanent security council are EU members: France and the UK).

Just seven months earlier something called the Union for the Mediterranean had been created in Paris by Sarkozy. An extremely awkward collection of countries, it squashed together the EU27 plus 16 others such as Israel, Albania, Turkey, Jordan (Red Sea), the Palestinian Authority, Mauritania (Atlantic) and Egypt. Almost half the members, including the UK, had no coastline on the sea that the organisation was named after. It was little heard of after January 2009's events. Although it was not an EU body it might as well have been. The Israeli blockade of Gaza also divided the 27. In 2010 a plan to lift it was presented by the Spanish foreign minister, whose country had the rotating EU presidency, but not by Ashton, who refused to be drawn on what she thought of Israeli plans to investigate the nine deaths in a Gaza-bound flotilla that the Israelis had intercepted.

A recap shows the impossibility of a common EU foreign policy:

Back in August 2006, France had refused to negotiate with Syria. However, the Finnish foreign secretary was saying that Mr Solana must hold "dialogue with everyone, including with Syria".

In November of that year, France, Austria, Greece and Cyprus wanted to stymie Turkey's accession talks because of a trade dispute with Cyprus. Other states didn't want to.

In December 2006, Hungary and Italy (as well as America) wanted to reopen accession talks with Serbia. This would have been fine if we, France, the Netherlands, Germany and Finland hadn't wanted to.

Later that month, the EU's head of mission in Afghanistan was, with his UN colleague, expelled from the country for holding an illegal meeting with members of the Taliban and also of offering them money. An Afghan official wondered, "It is not clear whether they were supporting the insurgency or not."

Also that month, the Portuguese PM, Jose Socrates, looked ahead to the EU-Africa summit that would be held during his EU presidency 12 months later. He called for Robert Mugabe's visa ban to be withdrawn to allow the Zimbabwean tyrant to attend. In August 2007, the Tories' last foreign secretary, Malcolm Rifkind, a europhile, wrote a newspaper article saying that Brown should boycott the summit if Mugabe attended: "If the EU fudges this, we not only betray the brave people of Zimbabwe; we say goodbye to any prospect of a meaningful European foreign policy."[432] In October, Angela Merkel said, "The president of the Republic of Germany wanted to invite all African countries to that summit, and it's up to countries themselves to decide how they are going to be represented at the table." In December 2007 the EU welcomed Mugabe to the Africa-EU meeting in Lisbon, ignoring the only part of its foreign policy anybody could remember – that he and his entourage were banned from the 27 states and their designer boutiques. In a rare display of backbone, Gordon Brown did not attend – though he did scuttle into the Portuguese capital the same month to sign the treaty named after it.

In March 2007, Her Majesty's Navy was severely embarrassed when Iran took several British sailors hostage. An EU Foreign Council expressed "solidarity" with Britain but no other EU state would suspend business links with Teheran. (In November 2004 a Belgian firm, Epsi, had sold an isostatic press, which can be used to produce nuclear weaponry, to Iran.) In another newspaper article, Malcolm Rifkind wrote of the crisis, "The members of the EU aspire to having a common foreign policy. What better issue could there be on which our French, German and Italian allies and partners could show solidarity with the UK and demonstrate the benefits of joint action?"[433] At the end of 2008, there was an EU navy – under British command and comprising several frigates – patrolling for pirates off Somalia. Would it have gone to the aid of the British sailors?

In October 2007, there were calls – not unanimous, of course – for Iran to suspend her uranium-enrichment programme; France wanted tougher sanctions but Italy and Germany did not. By February 2009 the pack had been shuffled once more: we, France and Germany (this time) proposed a tough list of sanctions to be imposed on Iran, to support the USA. However, five countries – Greece, Cyprus, Spain, Austria and Sweden – were opposed. By 2010, however, the Foreign Council had finally approved sanctions targeting Iran's oil industry, in attempt to halt its uranium programme.

In 2009, "the European Union demanded the immediate release of Iranian staff at Britain's embassy in Teheran [who were] detained over unrest at the election of President Ahmadinejad. EU ministers warned that 'harassment or intimidation' of embassy staff would be met with a 'strong and collective' response," said the BBC website on 28 June. But no country withdrew its ambassador, for example, in protest. When Ahmadinejad was inaugurated, some member states boycotted the ceremony, others sent "observers", yet others their ambassadors. It didn't look like a "collective" response or a "common front".

---

432 *The Financial Times*, 8 August 2007
433 *The Observer*, 1 April 2007

272

In July 2007, the Foreign Council first asked for troops for Chad. In October 2007 the EU was meant to have sent a peacekeeping force there but two months later had still not collected enough helicopters – even though it needed fewer than a dozen – to support the mission. In the meantime, Chad declared war on the EU, an action with which many of us can sympathise. By February 2008 the EU was almost ready to unleash its peacekeeping force but fighting in the country meant that it would be too dangerous to go in. A renewed rebel offensive in the country had forced the EU to postpone its deployment of advance units of a peacekeeping force, which was intended to protect refugees from Darfur. In other words, war had scared off the peacekeepers.

En route to Chad, an Austrian cargo plane was grounded in Tripoli, while a plane carrying 54 special forces from Ireland was cancelled. A spokesman for Lt General Pat Nash, the Irish commander, said, "The deployment is postponed until the security situation stabilises."[434] A week later, the BBC reported that the 3,700-strong peacekeeping force would not be deployed for at least another month "because of recent violence". Many countries wondered anyway why they were involved in a dispute that seemed to have more to do with French policy (Chad's ruler enjoyed Sarkozy's support against his country's rebels) – she had provided over half the troops for once[435] – than a community interest. This adventure answered a question sometimes posed by those who wonder what the EU can do that Nato cannot: it can try to defend French former colonies even when nearby countries are in greater need of intervention. To dust off an ancient joke: what's the difference between a slice of toast and the EU army? You can make soldiers with the…

And the helicopters? They eventually turned up in autumn 2008, courtesy of Russia. The same Russia that a few weeks before had invaded Georgia and whose troops in that former USSR state were at the time being "monitored" by the EU. Who knows what the EU would be like in a real conflict, but it seems to understand if not acknowledge a conflict of interest: in one part of the world – Georgia – the EU "monitors" the Russian Bear's materiel, in another part of the world (Africa), meanwhile, it is grateful for that materiel and "fights" alongside it.

In December 2007, it looked as if Kosovo would soon unilaterally declare independence from Serbia. Several EU states – including Romania, Cyprus, Greece, Spain and Slovakia – wanted UN approval of the split first, for reasons not unrelated to the fact that many of them had their own separatist elements that they did not want to encourage. However, then foreign secretary Miliband

---

434 *The Scotsman*, 4 February 2008
435 The Francophobe epithet "cheese-eating surrender monkeys" was coined by the Scottish character Groundskeeper Willie in a 1995 episode of *The Simpsons* entitled *Round Springfield*

and his counterparts in Paris, Berlin and Rome wrote to the twitchier states to remind them of their "commitments" to the disputed province.

In foreign policy, the EU cannot agree on anything, not even that America is the Great Satan. (The Poles, the Czechs and quite a few others would rather pick the USA for their team than the EU.) However, a common position on America is the closest to consensus that the EU will ever get in this area…

The EU vs the US

A large part of the EU's raison d'être is to be an alternative to the USA and this attitude will inform its decisions and actions for the foreseeable future. Just as America now likes to forget that the Statue Of Liberty was a present from France, so the EU likes to forget America's postwar helping hand. Although the EEC was a USA-aided bulwark against Russia, the EU now sees itself as a bulwark against America, biting the hand that freed it both militarily and financially. In the eyes of the EU, its relationship with the USA is the Ryder Cup with the gloves off. As a consequence, most of the EU's "grands projets" are in existence solely to counter the "other" united states' version. This desire to best the USA has led to enormous and predictable waste in duplication costs. These projects include:

* The European Space Council: to boldly go where NASA has gone before.

* Galileo: a subscription satellite service in opposition to the USA's free GPS system ("Why pay for Pepsi when Coca-Cola is free?" one commentator asked). It comprises 30 satellites and is meant to be active by 2014. It's not hard to see why Galileo's name has been slapped on this project – he was also propounding someone else's idea. (Galileo was also the name of a 1989 American space probe to Jupiter.)

The project is years behind schedule and dogged by severe funding problems. It was meant to have raised EU revenue from road-pricing programmes (remember that roads and road safety are an EU competence), which might well still happen, despite any number of petitions against them in the member states, including the UK[436]. Galileo is already 50 per cent over budget and when it was short of £1.7billion it was allowed to raid the unspent CAP budget. German objections to this source of emergency funding were dropped when the Commission proposed a change to the tendering rules that would mean German companies having a greater chance of winning Galileo contracts[437]. In 2010, a

---

[436] See pp350-1 for details of several car-tracking schemes
[437] *The Financial Times*, 24 November 2007

German-British consortium won the first major contract, to supply 14 satellites at a cost of €566million.

Gwyneth Dunwoody, the late Labour MP who chaired the UK transport select committee, told the *Today* programme, on 12 November 2007, "This is not one pig flying in orbit, this is a herd of pigs with gold trotters, platinum tails and diamond eyes and we ought to be asking ourselves, 'Where is our common sense? Are we really saying that we are so frightened of the Americans that we must fling gold bars at something that we don't even know is going to work?' The EU now appears to be sleepwalking into a further vast financial commitment to Galileo which is likely to take the public funding for the project to £10billion, without any realistic assessment of its costs and benefits. We must have independent and up-to-date evidence that proceeding with Galileo is worthwhile, and if it can be demonstrated that Galileo offers good value for taxpayers' money. Any decision on funding must be based on sound management of European Union budgets."

Her committee's published report said: "We fear that Galileo's status as a flagship grand projet is clouding the judgment of some in relation to its true, realistic and proven merits. An atmosphere that does not allow the continued rationale for the full Galileo programme to be questioned appears to have enveloped Brussels. But no amount of perceived prestige and status derived from competing in a civilian space race [with the USA, China, Japan and Russia] and no amount of vague but euphoric anticipation of enormous economic and employment benefits can make up for rigorous and balanced analysis of costs and benefit. None of the three key EU institutions has seen fit to cool the overheated atmosphere by ensuring that proper comprehensive analyses and cost-benefit evaluations are undertaken before any further decisions are made. The history of the Galileo programme provides a textbook example of how not to run large-scale infrastructure projects. Many of the problems encountered by the project are not peculiar to the EU and can be observed across a wide range of projects carried out by member states. However, the processes and institutions of the European Union are in danger of falling into disrepute if Galileo is allowed to continue in its present form. The government must work to ensure that common sense and good governance are reinstated. The time has come for the government to initiate a reappraisal of other large EU projects to ensure that the Galileo fiasco is not repeated elsewhere, outside the limelight. It is entirely conceivable that the best cost-benefit solution at this stage might be to scrap the programme entirely, and the government should not resile from that conclusion, if it is where the evidence leads."[438]

---

[438] Her committee's report is at tinyurl.com/26yd6p

Galileo was supposedly a provision only of the failed Constitution but the EU doesn't like to let a no get in its way[439]. Galileo has obvious and acknowledged military uses – a fact which must embarrass the non-EU European Space Agency, which is meant to be civilian. At a press conference on 16 May 2007, Commissioner Barrot said, "You cannot exclude a user because he is military. [Galileo] will be civilian controlled... but there will be military users." In July 2008, the European parliament approved Galileo's military use, by 502 votes to 83.

China had bought a 20 per cent stake in Galileo, which made them partners with the UK in a military project. But the Asians (rightly) became frustrated with the EU's sluggishness, walked away with their capital (plus recently acquired technical knowledge) and created their own satellite system, called Compass, which is already nearer completion than Galileo. Booker reported that the Chinese plan to operate on the same wavelengths as Galileo and, since their satellites will orbit first, they will be able to claim prior ownership, meaning that the EU could use those wavelengths only with permission.

The Court of Auditors also knew a shambles with astronomical costs when it saw one. Its June 2009 report into Galileo said: "The programme lacked a strong strategic sponsor and supervisor: the Commission did not proactively direct the programme, leaving it without a helmsman... Owing to their different programme expectations, member states intervened in the interest of their national industries [who'd have thought?] and held up decisions. The compromises made led to implementation problems, delays and, in the end, to cost overruns." Galileo's former funding model, a public-private plan, was described as "inadequately prepared and conceived" as well as "unrealistic".

* European Rapid Reaction Force: EU forces usually follow Nato troops into battle from a safe distance (about 18 months). The EU likes to claim it has kept

---

[439] Many EU activities were supposedly provided for only by the Constitution. Its failure did not stop those activities (before Lisbon legitimised them). In 2006, Cocubu, the financial watchdog of the EU parliament, pointed out that several budget lines, including Galileo, were provisions only of the rejected Constitution, eg "This budget line has no legal basis. The Fundamental Rights Agency was part of the Draft Constitutional Treaty which has not been ratified. By including this in the budget, the Commission is knowingly bypassing the democratic process and misrepresenting the views of the people of France and the Netherlands, who were asked to approve the Draft Constitutional Treaty as an essential part of the ratification process, and decided instead to reject the document in its entirety – including this budget line. No expenditure on agencies or programmes authorised by the Draft Constitutional Treaty should be included in the Budget until such time as the Draft Treaty has been fully ratified, and therefore obtained a legal base." *Draft Budget Of The European Union For The Financial Year 2007*, EU parliament's budgetary control committee

the peace for 50 years but it did nothing about the genocide on its doorstep in the 1990s, except encouraging the secessionist states by officially recognising them – and then do nothing to help them. Defence procurement has become a transparent attempt to get EU states to buy ordnance from one another, such as the much delayed A400M from the illegally subsidised Airbus. Discussing the European Defence Agency, Gisela Stuart MP said that "[the agency] concerns itself with procurement, rather than with conducting a real audit of the capabilities and shortcomings across Europe, or with setting out who needs to do what… That was not the original idea; the original idea was to make the money spent far more effective by making sure that, when a country purchases something, it fits in with what is needed across Europe. That does not mean that there should be only European purchasing, or that we should become protectionist. The agency regards it as one of its main achievements to have made things much more protectionist."[440]

If we hadn't wasted our defence budget on the outmoded Eurofighter Typhoon, built by a consortium of companies from Germany, Italy, Spain and the UK, we might have been able to replace Trident without fuss. In 2009 the Ministry Of Defence at last succeeded in offloading to Saudi Arabia some of the planes it had ordered. However, the MoD still needed to find £1.6billion to buy 16 of the aircraft for itself, and then buy the 48 remaining aircraft that it had committed to at a later date[441].

* The European Institute of Technology (EIT): like the Massachusetts Institute of Technology but not very good. It must rankle Brussels that 400,000 of America's one million scientists were born in the EU[442]. So, it decided to try to replicate America's research excellence. On 16 February 2007, the *Financial Times* reported that Mr Barroso's plans for his pet project were to be shelved because neither national treasuries nor the various private sectors were keen to provide the €2.4billion backing. Four months later, Agence France Presse reported that the EU itself had found €308.7million for EIT. The plan was to create a network of existing universities and give degrees an "EIT label". Barroso said, "This is a very important step forward, bringing the EIT closer to lift-off." The money from the EU budget would be complemented by a further €2.1billion during the 2008-2013 period from various other sources. Despite having longstanding and justified misgivings, Tony Blair, in one of his last speeches to parliament, said that the UK government was backing the EIT.

---

[440] *Hansard (Commons)*, 6 December 2006
[441] *The Financial Times*, 18 April 2009
[442] *Depicting Europe* in *London Review Of Books*, 20 September 2007 (Volume 29, No 18)

* Quaero[443]: A search engine just like Google, except not useful and a generation behind. Although started by Chirac with €90million of French money, it will spend most of its time searching for users. Quaero is not an EU project but the EU waived state-aid rules to allow it. On 28 December 2006 the *Guardian* reported that the French government would develop "Project Quaero" alone after the German government said it would abandon what was by then a €400million venture. The EU also waived state-aid rules for the German breakaway project, Theseus, which took €120million of government funding and is being developed by Bertelsmann and others. Theseus's goal is to develop an advanced multimedia search engine, creating a set of tools for translating, identifying and indexing images, sound and text[444].

---

[443] Latin for "I seek"
[444] *International Herald Tribune*, 19 July 2007

CHAPTER 6: AFTERMATH

George Orwell famously wrote that at the age of 50 everyone has the face he deserves. When the EU decided to turn 50 its face was still sporting two bruises, from the French and Dutch referendum results two years earlier. The party for its half century, "Europafest", was held in Berlin – Germany then held the six-month presidency of the EU – over the weekend of 24-25 March 2007, the Sunday being the 50th anniversary of the signing of the Treaty Of Rome in 1957. Berlin laid on fireworks, free beer and bratwurst, as well as subsidised minibuses (€12 for an all-night ticket) to transport partygoers between 35 of the city's nightclubs, which between them had 100 DJs; it really was beer and circuses for the people. The 26 leaders and their plus ones enjoyed a "Teutonic-Organic" banquet chez Angela Merkel.

However, "Europe Day" is 9 May, to commemorate the announcement of the Schuman Plan in 1950, which paved the way for the Treaty Of Paris (1951) and the European Coal And Steel Community in 1952. There again, the EEC did not come into being until 1 January 1958 – and the EU was not formed until 1 November 1993. If the EU can't be sure when its birthday is, why should we trust it with laying down the law for most of a continent?

Amid the jollity and jollies in the German capital, a plan was made to resurrect the Constitution. The result of this brazen deafness to democracy was called the Berlin Declaration and it paved the way for the Lisbon Treaty, which was signed – though not ratified – later that year by the 27 heads of state or government[445].

Major events in the EU's history – and indeed prehistory – have usually enjoyed British input. And so, in Berlin, Joe Cocker gave a free concert by the Brandenburg Gate, singing The Beatles' "With A Little Help From My Friends", and Sir Simon Rattle conducted a concert of Italian folk songs. Kim Wilde and Simply Red were part of a concert at Brussels's Atomium building. As well as £180billion there has always been a great deal of British input into the EU, from Jean Monnet's friend Arthur Salter to Lord Cockfield's single market to Sir John Kerr, Giscard D'Estaing's right-hand man when he drafted the Constitution[446]. When the Constitution fell at those two pesky democratic

---

[445] See the Appendix for more on the Lisbon Treaty
[446] Officially, the ex-ambassador to the USA and to the EU was "secretary general of the EU Constitutional Convention". He had previously been a negotiator on the single market and then Maastricht, earning the nickname "Machiavelli" from John Major, who reputedly hid him under the table when negotiating Maastricht, so scared was he of giving away more than he had to.
Now ennobled, Kerr sits on the House Of Lords EU select committee, which is dominated by fellow europhiles. However, because neither the Upper nor Lower House can amend or otherwise change any EU legislation before it reaches our

hurdles, Chris Patten was one of the men whom Romano Prodi chose to help it back on its feet. The efforts of Lord Patten and others, therefore, gave us the Lisbon Treaty. Those who are unaware of this diverse and invaluable British contribution include some of those Britons who are keenest on rule by the EU. They think that because the EU is "foreign" (it is not, it is a system of government that operates through domestic apparatus, and as cannot be stated enough has had British intellectual input from before the start), it is therefore superior to our domestic politics (legally, they're right on that score: EU law enjoys supremacy over our homegrown efforts). To oppose the European Union is not to dislike foreigners, it is about wanting to replace a system of government – which Britons helped to devise and fund – that impoverishes, disenfranchises and enslaves foreigners (and Britons).

When in 2004 the Tories mooted the idea of patients' and parents' "passports" for the NHS and schools, the *Independent*, a proudly pro-EU newspaper, shot the idea down in a leader: "The Tory solution, however, looks suspiciously like a subsidy for wealthier patients. Their 'passport' policy (rather hastily renamed 'right to choose' after confused voters wondered if they had to go abroad to benefit) offers to refund part of the cost of private operations. It is right to try to use the private sector to help reform the public sector. But this assists only those who can afford to pay to go private, while doing little to help the less well-off or to confront the inherent problems of a sclerotic NHS."[447]

But when the same idea surfaced in a draft EU initiative, the Health Services Directive (HSD), which proposed opening up member states' healthcare provision to the market – one reason why British labour unions opposed the Lisbon Treaty – the newspaper welcomed it: "[The EU] is gearing up to challenge the complacency of our monolithic NHS and offering British patients greater freedom of choice in healthcare"[448]. Perhaps the leader writers had had a change of heart, or were new. Or did unconditional love for the EU recommend the idea as soon as it arrived wrapped in a 12-star flag?

The HSD, which seeks only to codify years of ECJ judgments (which it will continue to make), has as good a chance as any of bankrupting the NHS. Patients would, in law, be allowed to receive treatment abroad without approval

---

statute book, the highly partisan make-up of this committee matters less than it might: one can scrutinise Brussels imperatives only in the same way that a fly scrutinises the windscreen of a moving Eurostar train. Many of the House Of Lords select committee receive EU pensions. Others in the Lords also receive EU pensions – for instance, and as already mentioned, Lord (and Lady) Kinnock – but none has to reveal this when speaking in debates on the EU

[447] *The Independent*, 24 June 2004
[448] *The Independent*, 20 December 2007, quoted in *Just add the magic letters 'EU'* on openeurope.blogspot.com, 21 December 2007

from their doctor or health authority (when the Tories called for a "passport policy" they were unwittingly getting to the heart of what the Brussels government would later propose). The danger is not that the NHS would be inundated by Poles – well, no more than it is – but that it would have to spend most of its day writing cheques to people who had been treated elsewhere in the EU. Patients would be reimbursed up to the level of what such treatment costs domestically (the extra, if any, would be borne by the patient). In effect, it's "health tourism" in reverse. The costs, however, are not reversed. The HSD will provide for those who can find enough cash to travel to receive foreign treatment and after care, truly creating a "two-tier" service: one for ordinary citizens, the other for well-heeled queue jumpers. According to the directive, in certain cases patients can get treatment even without paying up front. It will mean that those fit enough and rich enough to travel will get a slice of the NHS budget ahead of those who are bedridden and/or poor. Those not fit enough for international travel will find that their NHS trust has been hobbled by those who can. That might well be contrary to how the budgetary cake should be served.

Ex-health secretary Frank Dobson told the House of Commons during the Lisbon "debate" that "the well-off will be able to pay in advance and wait to be reimbursed, they will be able to pay top-up costs if they need it and they will be able to afford the costs of travel... Badly off people will not be able to do any of those things... If you are getting NHS treatment in Europe you are spending somebody else's money that might have been spent in the NHS" [449]. Two months earlier, when the HSD first surfaced, Nigel Edwards, policy director of the NHS Confederation, told the *Today* programme: "People who are able to travel can go and get their procedure and, because we have a fixed pot of money, that effectively means they get first call on NHS resources. One of the concerns that a number of people – not just in this country – have is the impact that this has on trying to run an equitable system... There could be an effect here where those who are able to travel and pay upfront can to some extent push to the front of the queue... It has a potential differential effect that favours the young, mobile and relatively affluent." [450]

The EU is about to perform open-wallet surgery on the NHS and it will kill it. This is on purpose, for it wants to re-create healthcare at the supranational level. As ever, the poor will be the first to feel its ambition. The 2006 ECJ case of Watts v Bedford Primary Care Trust (Case C-372/04) – in which the Luxembourg lords ruled that a £4,000 hip operation that a British pensioner had paid for in France should be reimbursed by her local hospital – will one day be as notorious as Factortame.

---

[449] *Hansard (Commons)*, 6 February 2008
[450] *Today* programme, 19 December 2007

The HSD was blocked in the Health Council by Spain (a retiree magnet) in late 2009. The UK, apparently, was not against it but Spain found enough allies. However, the Commission promised that the HSD would be back. Most importantly, the ECJ would continue to rule as if the HSD were in force[451]. The defeat in Council meant little: Watts v Bedford (and other cases) had already opened the theatre doors. By June 2010, the directive was indeed back, in a modified form. The EU – intent on dissolving the nation state even at the expense of the disadvantaged – said that patients would need authorisation from their home country's (actually "country of affiliation") PCT for, among other caveats, treatments involving overnight hospital stays. (The Spanish had originally blocked the directive because they were not keen on servicing ageing British gangsters and our law-abiding exports. In the new draft, a Brit in Spain would be reimbursed by Spain, the country of residence, if receiving treatment in, say, Portugal – but Britain would pay if the treatment were in Britain.)

Like many disastrous and inhumane ideas – such as communism and eugenics a few generations ago – the EU tends to attract progressives. It's easy, if you do not look too closely at how it operates, what it does, to whom it does it, and how unfairly it is constructed, to be vaguely and instinctively in favour of the EU. We should co-operate with our neighbours, shouldn't we? The alternative is xenophobia, isn't it? The real alternative to the EU is to be on decent terms with the whole world, not in a Brussels headlock.

Some people are devoted to the idea of the EU because they see it as a sort of cuddly brotherhood of man that melts ancient and rather less ancient enmities. To them, it's a sort of Neighbourhood Watch, with the USA and the strong Asian economies as the hoodies, and it offers the same chance for the retired to look out for the community, albeit with rather better remuneration. And doesn't the EU stop wars? The "EU keeps the peace" argument recalls the apocryphal man seen sprinkling blue powder along a suburban high street. Asked what he is doing, he replies, "Putting down elephant repellent." "But we don't have elephants here," his inquisitor counters. The man replies, "I know, isn't the blue powder magic?" Nato and democracy – for democracies tend not to declare war on one another – stand for the fences and gates of our zoos, the EU the powder.

Does the EU even keep the peace beyond its walls? In 2008 it deemed Chad "too dangerous" to send its own peacekeeping force into and, infamously, stood by while Yugoslavia fought itself in the 1990s. The EU is not an army, it is an army of bureaucrats. Its talent is for interference and legislation, by which it means to turn beautiful variety into harmonised conformity; to season the disparate into the homogeneous.

---

[451] See also the 2010 ECJ case of Antoine Elkhoury, a Swede who travelled abroad for care

The EU is keen on appropriating Greek mythology (but not so fond of another of that country's contributions: democracy, or at least a prototype of it). Its elite cannot be unaware of the story of Procrustes, the robber who, having forced his victims to lie on a bed, then cut or stretched their limbs to fit it[452]. The EU, too, likes to take money, and force its 500million victims to fit in with its prescriptive ideals. The *Oxford Dictionary* defines "Procrustean" as "esp. of a framework or system: enforcing uniformity or conformity without regard to natural variation or individuality". That's exactly apt but is it desirable?

People sometimes ask, "Well, what does the EU do right?" It was admitted in the Introduction that it would take a spectacular amount of churlishness to say that every piece of EU law is without any merit. However, it's the wrong question: the EU should not do anything at all (even if it were a free-trade area – which it is not, never has been and has no desire to be – the World Trade Organisation could enforce trade agreements between its members). There are four main reasons for this.

First, even if the EU passes a welcome law, there's no good reason why member states could not have done the same for themselves; electors pay rather a lot – in salaries, bath plugs and plasma TVs – for domestic legislators and, in the UK, MPs absent themselves for 12 weeks in the summer alone (it was only 11 weeks in 2008). If a law is sensible and desirable – one to end the buying, transporting and selling of slaves, or to clean up the air, or to grant universal suffrage, or to prohibit sending little boys up chimneys – we can pass it and enforce it ourselves. We in Britain have a proud record of doing so. If other countries wish to do the same, all well and good. From a legislative angle, what does the EU confer on us that is otherwise unavailable?

Secondly and more importantly, it's very difficult to change EU law when it ceases to be welcome. Biofuels were once widely (but not universally) seen as A Good Thing, and the Commission legislated to force them on us. Few complained. When opinion changed, the Commission could reverse its policy on them rather more slowly than the proverbial and less damaging oil tanker could perform a U-turn. When EU law becomes objectionable – if it wasn't from the off – we cannot extricate ourselves from the mess as soon as we'd like. In the meantime, we must suffer an inflexible regime whose policies are, anyway, often contradictory. If the EU came close to reaching its insanely ruinous target for biofuel usage, it would depress totally the market in "emissions trading" from which it has tried to derive a sense of legitimacy. Because the EU mandates so

---

452 It was Theseus who eventually killed Procrustes (as well as the Minotaur in the labyrinth that Europa's son had commissioned). The great Athenian's name has been stolen for an EU-sanctioned search engine, while "Europa" is the moribund outfit's website

much unnecessary food packaging, we produce more rubbish than we need to – and then are fined for using landfill when a recession causes the bottom to fall out of the recycling market. The policies of the EU are as disconnected from each other as it is from the people.

Thirdly, there is an opposite problem. Because it is about three times likelier that any new legislation comes from Belgium than Westminster, there's only about a 25 per cent chance that a domestic parliament can make laws in a certain area. Because of the EU's primacy in certain areas (food standards and road safety, for example) we are prevented from legislating even when we want to, because we either fear being overruled later or are told we cannot take such action in the first place. If we urgently want to pass a law – one, say, to ban certain additives in food marketed to children – we must ask teacher and wait for the EU to legislate (or not), because food standards are one of the EU's "occupied fields" (one of many, to which the Lisbon Treaty only added). Before EU membership we could have quickly passed our own law.

A fourth reason that the EU should do nothing is that governments should not be allowed to use it to introduce laws that they know full well they would not get past their own parliaments, let alone their electorates (if in a manifesto). If a country wants a law – a good example is the UK, which lobbied hard for the Data Retention Directive – then it must get it past its own legislature. As it stands, it does not have to do so. (And then the countries that never asked for the law are also saddled with it, which is the nature of horse-trading.)

If the EU put money in our pockets and food in the world's mouth, it would still be wrong in principle. The fact that it does the opposite – it pickpockets all of us and is not, to put it politely, engaged in maximising the growth of food – makes it wrong also in practice.

Increasingly, you cannot elect or eject those responsible for decisions affecting almost every area of life. You might open a newspaper and see stories about embryology; the Royal Mail sell-off; proposals for a minimum price for alcohol or cigarettes; a reduced drink-drive limit; the legality of bank charges; an item about VAT fraud; and a story about wind farms and higher energy bills. In every case there is a major EU dimension, but you might not see that fact mentioned in any more than one of the stories, if at all. If even senior Tories still blame their own party for rail privatisation, which was a result of complying with a 1991 EU directive that explicitly instructed it, how can those not in politics be expected to know about the hidden hand of the EU?

The journalist Anthony Browne, now director of policy for Mayor Johnson, once wrote a paean to Britain in the *Spectator*: "We [Britain] gave the world industrialisation, democracy and football – its economic system, its political system and its fun."[453] He went on to remind readers of, among other things, the harnessing of electricity, the telephone, antibiotics, TV, the world wide web, pneumatic tyres, the drawing of the Greenwich meridian, light bulbs, cloning, trains, etc.

Of those examples, industry is hamstrung by directives and regulations; European democracy, if judged by referendums on the EU, is like that Dorothy Parker put-down – "That woman speaks 18 languages, and can't say no in any of them"; football is slipping into the EU quicksand and has for years been subject to the Bosman and other rulings; the provision of electricity is dictated by the Renewables Obligation; telecoms (eg roaming charges) are interfered with by the Commission for populist reasons that result in higher domestic call charges (and perhaps the loss of free handsets); the NHS is under threat from the HSD and the 48-hour week, while many health supplements have been outlawed; television and TV advertising, including product placement, are subject to the Television Without Frontiers Directive, and the BBC itself exists only on the Commission's say-so; tyres and road safety are a community "competence"; our clocks go forward and back when told to do so by the EU; incandescent light bulbs are being replaced by not entirely ecologically sound CFLs; cloning is a matter for the Commission; train companies had to be privatised, and stock separated from track; etc. There is not much left for Westminster.

The less honest MPs (including D Cameron) say that the EU is way down the list of their constituents' concerns, which start with the economy, immigration and the size of utility bills. Those things are, of course, part of the EU's remit[454]. The MP might list the gripes as schools'n'hospitals'n'policing. Immigration from the EU is far and away the biggest recent pressure on those three. Perhaps when the NHS has been bankrupted – because of having to buy "permits to pollute" from oil companies, as well as paying translators and then agency staff (to comply with the 48-hour week), as well as refunding rich queue jumpers – MPs might just admit that the EU is after all a doorstep issue. Rubbish collection is literally a doorstop issue. Even in education, schools are bound by EU rules on public-sector procurement, having to commission several designs for new buildings so that local authorities have choices.

What is the EU for? One argument trotted out in its favour is that the EU gives us "clout on the world stage". What exactly is this "clout"? What is the benefit of acting en masse, after submitting ourselves to a "common position" in the Trade council? The ability to scupper the Doha round of the World Trade

---

[453] *The Spectator*, 23 July 2005
[454] See the Appendix for details of how the Lisbon Treaty seeks to formulate a common policy for immigration from third countries

Organisation negotiations? The ability to demand a higher tariff on goods from the developing world? The ability to dump surpluses – subject to availability – on those same people, thus ruining their domestic market as well? The ability to charge our poorer citizens more for imported food and goods, such as children's shoes and toys from China?

When Queen Victoria ruled a quarter of the planet, the average Briton was far, far worse off than now: there's no correlation between a country's (or bloc's) political weight or geographical size and her citizens' wealth and way of life. If there were, Russians would be more comfortable than Americans, and the Spanish would be looking down on the Swiss. The emergence of America as a superpower in the 20th century, just as British influence shrank, did not leave the British worse off – quite the opposite. So, why worry now about China or India from an economic point of view? They represent opportunities for export – one of the main reasons why Britons are now better off than in Victoria's day.

If people are worried, however, about Russia or China from a military rather than economic point of view, then they could do better than look to the EU for reassurance and materiel. Nazism was defeated by an ad hoc alliance of governments, not by an inept and cumbersome single administration to which no one feels any loyalty.

It is the EU itself, not its opponents, that is parochial and introspective: it deservedly attracts the nickname "Fortress Europe" for its protectionism, which harms those within its walls – who must pay more for their goods – while also harming those, particularly those from the developing world, who wish to trade with it. There has to be a *very* good reason for us to delegate the power to erect trade barriers against the developing world and for that person or organisation to make those barriers high. The EU is not that reason. "Cui bono?" as they used to say in the home of the Treaty Of Rome and elsewhere in what's now the EU.

Britain's relatively high reliance on food from outside the EU means that we are particularly unsuited to acting in concert with 26 others. But, as a consequence of being tied to import tariffs determined by and for other countries, we contribute 43 per cent of the EU's total take on food tariffs – Kiwi lamb, for example, has a tariff of 173 per cent (although some meat products' tariffs exceed 400 per cent)[455]. It may be that we would maintain such levels against imports. However, if a British trade minister found such discrimination

---

[455] **TFEU 206 states:** "By establishing a customs union, the Union shall contribute, in the common interest, to the harmonious development of world trade, the progressive abolition of restrictions on international trade and on foreign direct investment, and the lowering of customs and other barriers." Really?

repugnant – or if he or she wished instead to raise the tariff – he or she would be free to do so; no one would be setting the level in our name, all the while without the pressure that the ballot box and the spectre of redundancy bring to such decisions. Acting solely in our own interests and making our own bargains and deals, we would rediscover "clout". If a common interest rate and exchange rate are a problem when applied across 16 countries, why should a common trade tariff not be a problem when applied across 27 countries?

To oppose the EU is not to oppose trade deals – it is to be in favour of trading on one's own terms with *the whole world*. Besides, we import from the EU far more than we export to it so it would certainly be in the EU's interest to keep trading with us if we seceded. Since our 1973 accession our deficit with the rest of the bloc is over £50billion. Thanks to the WTO, the EU cannot prevent us from maintaining (or even enlarging) the deficit we enjoy with the 1950s throwback – even if it were malevolent and short-sighted enough to do so, which is unlikely.

So, our trade (gap) would be safe, and we would continue – in effect – to export jobs. If someone says that three million jobs (a number that, strangely, has been static since first being heard in 1975 during the referendum debate) depend on trade with the EU, it cannot be in Britain that they are under threat for we are a net importer. Those supposed jobs don't happen to be British jobs. Or, to be precise for Mr Barroso's sake, they don't happen to be jobs (which are equally open of course to the citizens of all 27 EU countries) based in the 12 Euro "regions" once known as the United Kingdom. A trade war would be bad for Champagne sales, to give an example of something that we could not produce ourselves if forced to give up imports. But such a scenario is unthinkable anyway.

Leaving the EU does not mean severing trade links – so no jobs anywhere would be under threat. The pro-EU group Britain In Europe (you mean we're not in Asia or Africa?) commissioned a study on the effects of secession. Hilariously, the study noted that "Although we find that a large number of jobs are now associated with exports for the EU, there is no a priori reason to suppose that many of these, if any, would be lost permanently if Britain was to leave the European Union."[456]

In the post-EU age we will also be able to administer our foreign aid without the fraudulent and unaccountable middleman of the EU. Our charitable work overseas could again be undertaken in the knowledge that it was not being contradicted by tariffs on imports from those very countries we were trying to help. As it stands, EU aid is a particularly sick joke understood only too well by

[456] *Continent Cut Off? The Macroeconomic Impact of British Withdrawal from the EU* by Nigel Pain and Garry Young, NIESR, February 2000. Quoted by Ruth Lea, *The European Journal*, May 2008

its recipients; it is showy benevolence, usually cancelled out several times over by the EU's own tariffs, if it manages to navigate the fog of Brussels corruption to reach the area of need. Besides, anyone who can tie their own shoelaces knows that government largesse, be it from a supranational or a national government, must originally have come from the pocket of the individual or the balance sheet of a company (which will affect an individual's employment, wages or dividends). It is not, therefore, even the EU's "generosity". But above and beyond that is the fact revealed by the response of the Thai government and aid agencies after the 2004 Asian tsunami: they told the EU that the country would prefer reduced trade tariffs – instead of money and dumped agricultural surplus. It's easy to look a gift horse in the mouth when it is the EU holding the reins.

We know from the examples of Iceland, Norway and Switzerland – all signatories to the Schengen Area of visa-less travel, although none is an EU member – that we could also continue to travel freely throughout the EU (and beyond), but under the colours of our restored navy passports if we wish. Leaving the EU would not lead to "splendid isolation". That's a scaremonger's myth, peddled in the hope that it will find a buyer in a country where a serious newspaper can without blushing carry the headline FOG IN CHANNEL: CONTINENT ISOLATED. Of course, that headline, too, is a myth – it's a cartoon[457].

And we would save over £10billion per annum on membership fees – enough to halve the council tax on every residential property in the UK – let alone the indirect costs, such as higher prices for basic foodstuffs and compliance with kilometre upon kilometre of red tape, which ties up 100 per cent of businesses and individuals although only (at most) 13 per cent of our goods and services are traded in the EU (the vast majority is domestic activity or goes elsewhere on the planet). The EU's own enterprise commissar said that EU regulations cost the EU economies €600billion per annum, while the benefits of the single market amount to not much more than €160billion. Those are the EU's own figures. After a while, the peoples of the EU will start to wonder on what that annual €440billion difference might be better spent. Businesses want competitiveness and flexibility – which are the antithesis of EU regulation – in order to survive, let alone compete, in the 21st century. (By coincidence, €440billion is also the amount that all eurozone countries are on the hook for to keep the doomed euro alive.)

The single market is not attractive even to its supporters. Sarkozy removed the promise of "free and undistorted competition", which had been an EU mainstay since 1958, from the Lisbon Treaty. In July 2006, France faced legal action from

---

[457] First magazine publication not known but first collected in *Round The Bend With Brockbank* by Russell Brockbank (Temple Press, 1948), p13

the ECJ for failing to recover €1billion in state aid from France Telecom. In the same year, the Commission ruled that some of France's major companies profited from illegal government tax breaks. The companies – including Air France, BNP Paribas and Société Générale – weren't ordered to repay all of the funds they'd received because Commission officials had failed to act within six years, despite earlier acknowledging that the tax scheme violated state-aid rules and despite several formal complaints from competitors. Officials were unable to explain precisely why the Commission had failed to act for so long[458].

In August 2007, Sarkozy urged the French company Suez to sell its water-and-waste business and merge its energy division with the state-owned natural gas company Gaz de France to create "a national champion", in order to repel foreign boarders, an act the French called "economic patriotism"[459]. Although not against the rules of the single market, such antics were certainly against its spirit. The Spanish government was found guilty by the ECJ for shielding its energy company Endesa from the attentions of E.On, the German energy giant, and then Enel, an Italian firm. When E.On's bid failed, a Commission spokesman said, "If governments do not follow EU law, there is a danger that the common market will end in chaos."

The spokesman must have been happy with the ECJ's ruling: "The [Spanish] system constitutes a restriction on the free movement of capital in as much as it is capable of deterring investors established in other member states... from acquiring shareholdings in Spanish undertakings operating in the energy sector." Enel now owns Endesa and there are fewer and fewer energy companies in Europe. It's hard to see how the emerging oligopoly helps the consumer. There again, it's not meant to.

In February 2007 the Commission had conceded, in a report on the takeover directive, that the vast majority of member states were exploiting the law's many loopholes to ensure that takeover defences were just as sturdy as before. The report said, "A large number of member states have shown strong reluctance to lift takeover barriers. The number of member states implementing the directive in a seemingly protectionist way is unexpectedly large."[460] In early 2008, liberalisation of energy markets was again being blocked by member states. Eight countries, led by France and Germany, attacked the Commission's main energy-liberalisation measures, which involved forcing the big firms to "unbundle" their transmission networks. The eight, backed by E.On and France's EDF (which

---

[458] *The Financial Times*, 20 December 2006
[459] France would later be found to have unfairly subsidised her vegetable growers for years. In 2009, Sarkozy gave state aid to local newspapers without thinking of EU rules on such funds
[460] *The Financial Times*, 27 February 2007

later snaffled the UK's nuclear power plants), formed a blocking minority in the Council. And that was all well before the recession, when many EU states took their banks to their bosoms, bailing them out with state aid.

At the height of the recession, Sarkozy infuriated east European EU members when he linked €6.5billion of soft loans to Renault and Peugeot-Citroën with a guarantee that the jobs would remain in France and no workers would be laid off, saying, "This does not take away one job from our Slovene friends." (Many French car plants were in Slovenia and he wasn't so much concerned about them and their workers.) In 2010 he was still at it, when Renault (15 per cent owned by the state) decided to make part of its new Clio model in Turkey: "We did not support our car makers with all this money so that all the factories could go abroad. I want to contest, strongly, the idea that large firms, particularly those that are global, no longer have a nationality"[461]. His industry minister later said that "if a car is destined for sale in France it has to be produced in France".

So, the single market is ignored by the big states and costs €440billion per annum. It looks poor value but is still useful to the EU itself. Ostensibly, the "liberalisation" and "unbundling" of energy companies is in the name of "competition" and "customer choice" (not when there are fewer and fewer operators it isn't). But it's really about tugging at the threads of the nation state, to unpick it, so that the EU Commission instead can take control.

As Dr Richard North of EU Referendum put it when writing about the Royal Mail: "The [EU's] intent is to break up national monopolies, not for the sake of it, but in order to re-create them on a European level, under the direct control of the EU Commission. Thus, the attack on national monopolies is not an attack on the monopolies per se but an attack on nationalism – it is an attack on the nation state, an attempt to reduce the power and influence of the member states. As such, the EU has no rooted objection to monopolies – it is, after all, itself a monopoly. Its apparent enthusiasm for 'competition' is simply a smokescreen to gull free-market liberals into supporting its deeper agenda [most notably Margaret Thatcher, who championed the Single European Act in the mid-1980s]. However, the great genius of the Commission is its realisation that it is no longer necessary to nationalise something in order to own it. Basically, it has developed a system of nationalisation by regulation. If you have complete control over an industry, you get all the benefits of ownership without needing the title deeds. So it is with postal services: the EU objective is to break up the national monopolies. As an interim stage, it will encourage 'competition' but it is particularly looking for cross-border enterprises which operate across the EU, in as many member states as possible. That then legitimises supranational control

---

[461] *Commission concerned about French protectionism* in *European Voice*, 15 January 2010

and puts the Commission in the dominant position. Before too long, we will have a European postal service – but it will be messy, delivered by multiple providers, albeit under the control of the EU. The final stage – decades into the future – is then to 'rationalise' and 'consolidate' the market, slimming down the number of providers until a few megaliths service the entire (European) system under the benign control of the Platonic guardians in Brussels." [462]

This is also the thinking behind the Health Services Directive: to destroy the *National* Health Service and then re-create it at the supranational level. (It's why France fosters "economic patriotism" – to try to preserve the national identity it enjoys from national companies.) As well as opening up national companies to foreign takeover, disallowing state aid to them is another tug on the national thread. One way or another, the EU seeks to destroy the symbols of nationhood and thus nationhood itself.

The BBC, our state broadcaster and thus a symbol of nationhood (albeit with quisling tendencies), relies on a hypothecated tax we know as the licence fee and which is viewed by the EU as state aid. However, this "anti-competitive" arrangement is tolerated by Brussels. It's easy to see why: Auntie is very nice about Brussels. If you were in Auntie's position, would your reports query any part of the system that permits you to exist? Not only that, the BBC also borrows at a preferential rate from the EU's bank, the EIB, "an autonomous body set up to finance capital investment furthering European integration by promoting EU policies". The national broadcaster is, then, in debt to the EU three times over: it must toe the EIB's line; it must be grateful for being allowed to receive state aid (the licence fee) and thus not rock the boat; and is literally in debt to the tune of £141million. Many people look to the BBC for impartiality, just as many people look to charities for uncompromised benevolence, but many charities, like the BBC, exist in their current form only on the whim of the EU, whose agenda they, not surprisingly, promote. It is quite brilliant how the EU has taken money from countries and then bribed the constituent parts of those countries – the broadcasters, the charities, the public sector, the regional development agencies, the arts companies, the journalists, the politicians, the schools, the universities, the royalty, the think tanks – to turn against the independence of those countries and their people. Even independent and critical watchdogs, such as farmsubsidy.org, receive EU funding.

To oppose the EU is to advocate and celebrate our and other countries' individuality, it is to campaign for those countries – and us – to be allowed self-governance and the display of cultural, traditional and political variety that the EU's "harmonisation" will otherwise trample over. It is a vote for pluralism. We

---

already have a government, thank you very much, we don't need another one on top of it, especially one that we cannot remove. When did opposing protectionism and a one-size-fits-all system of law become xenophobic?

In years to come, the greatest – yet least deserved – achievement of the EU's supporters will be seen to be the way they painted their opponents as xenophobes or, in the UK, "Little Englanders", a late Victorian phrase that referred originally to those who opposed the expansion of the British Empire, it is now used with no less sneer to describe those who oppose the spread of the EU empire. (Are europhiles "Little Europeans"?) If the UK is not the most tolerant European state, then it has a good claim to being the least intolerant. For this country to be called xenophobic on account of its euroscepticism is a wilful misreading of history. Twice in the last century we sacrificed hundreds of thousands of our number to save our neighbours from the jackboot, and in the century before that we were involved with movements for independence in places such as Greece, Belgium and Italy. And in which European country did the Abolition Of The Slave Trade Act enter the statute book on 25 March 1807 (150 years to the day before the Treaty Of Rome was signed), prompting her to use her navy to enforce this enlightened policy everywhere, on all countries' shipping?

Furthermore, consider the relations between the UK and her former colonies, and then consider the relations between, say, France and her former colonies, or Belgium and hers. Which country looks least insular? Of course, we, like France and the other big colonial powers in Europe, had to sever most of our mutually beneficial trading links with our former colonies when we joined the EEC. That our Commonwealth largely forgave us is greatly to its credit; that it ever had to do so was decidedly not to ours.

If we seceded from the EU we could also control our borders again. Most Britons have nothing against people from Vilnius. But those same right-thinking Brits tend to favour people from Colombo, Adelaide, Bangalore, Wellington and Cape Town above those from Lithuania. We're not "against" any country per se but we are "for" Commonwealth countries. It's ancestral and historical. And moral: what is the Commonwealth Of Nations if it is not an obligation to people from those countries? Their citizens are often directly related to those who fought (2.5million in World War I alone) and died alongside us in countless conflicts, including two world wars to keep this and other continents free. Should they not have first dibs on our finite resources and services, and also enjoy free trade with us? As it is, if they do wish to come here they are sent to the back of the queue – and, what's more, are then queue-jumped by EU nationals. An obvious form of social protectionism is the EU regulation that states that non-EU workers hoping for a highly skilled migrant visa must have a masters degree.

Many lawyers, for example, do not have a masters.

Anglo-Indian relations were particularly badly damaged in early 2008 when thousands of Indian doctors were barred from junior training posts in the NHS so as not to take jobs from non-British EU nationals. The Indians could not understand why we had turned our backs on them. In other words, the UK had given the Indians' jobs to descendants of the people that their forefathers had liberated (or defeated). Later that year, after a German GP on his first shift – who could, by virtue of the free movement of labour, work in the UK without any sort of linguistic or other test – mistakenly gave a Cambridgeshire patient a fatal dose of painkillers, the *Guardian* listed the requirements for *non-EU* GPs in the UK: "[they] must undergo an English test [even if anglophone], complete a three-hour written knowledge exam, in their home country or here, and then face a gruelling day at the [General Medical Council's] clinical assessment centre. The assessment begins with their identity and credentials being checked. Then they have to go through 16 five-minute mini-exams, such as taking a patient's history, or demonstrating communication skills, which may include delivering bad news"[463]. That is social protectionism. Most Indian doctors have far better English than the hapless German, who faced no language tests of any kind. The German doctor would almost certainly never have been needed if UK doctors had been allowed to work their own hours, and not been forced to count their time on call as part of their 48 hours a week. Just remember the mantra: "The EU is not a doorstep issue, the NHS is."

At about the same time that Indian doctors were being sent away, the ancestry visa, designed in the 1970s for Commonwealth nationals to enter Britain more freely, was under threat from a government Green Paper. Austin Mitchell MP tabled a Commons motion to save it. He said, "The dominions sprang to our aid when we needed them in two world wars and since. Their inhabitants are of British descent. They are keen to maintain Commonwealth ties and associations with this country... even to consider getting rid of [the ancestry visa] will produce shock, anger and dismay in Commonwealth countries which fought two world wars shoulder to shoulder with the United Kingdom, and have maintained close relations since." The ConDem coalition's cap on non-EU immigrants, cooked up by a government keener on the EU than it should be, is a squeeze on these very people.

---

[463] *The Guardian*, 24 August 2009. In 2010, similar tests for nurses, such as whether they had even treated people in the previous three years or could speak English, had to be scrapped for men and women from EU states (but retained for Indians and Canadians etc), in case the NHS was sued in the ECJ for blocking the free movement of workers

Such snubs aside, the UK is the most cosmopolitan of nations. Before the recession, it was the world's busiest thoroughfare and busiest financial marketplace. In July 2007 the UK had the most foreign direct investment in Europe, up 17 per cent on the previous year, and was second only to America worldwide. The City Of London is still dominated by foreign banks, and about a quarter of the Square Mile's workforce is non-British. The daily turnover in foreign exchange is more than $1,100billion (32 per cent of the global total), and London has 40 per cent of the global foreign-equity market, while trading 70 per cent of all Eurobonds. When the dust settles those figures might well be different – but not because the UK did not join the euro. According to journalist Ambrose Evans-Pritchard, in 2009 the City still commanded 21 per cent of global hedge-fund business and 80 per cent of Europe's total, which is why Germany and France were behind the AIFM Directive to "get" the hedgies, despite the fact that the hedgies were almost last in line for blame for the recession but the first in line to spend for Britain. And they pay billions in taxes.

Our future lies outside the shackles of the EU, which includes not one of the world's 100 fastest-growing cities. Today, the EU has 7 per cent of the world's population, down from 12.5 per cent 50 years ago (when the organisation had far fewer members). Following current trends, it will account for 5 per cent by 2050. And since October 2007 it has been home to more elderly people (65+) than children (under 14). Europe has for some time had a problem with a shrinking population: Mussolini taxed bachelors more than married men during his "Battle For Births" and, from 1938, the Führer gave out "Mother's Crosses" to particularly fecund females (four children=bronze, six=silver, eight plus=gold) on his mother's birthday. The necessary replacement ratio is 2.1 children for every woman but it's well under two in Europe, with many Mediterranean countries coming in at just 1.3. As Carl Haub of the Population Reference Bureau in Washington DC put it, "If you compare the size of the 0-4 and 29-34 age groups in Spain and Italy right now, you see the younger is almost half the size of the older. You can't keep going with a completely upside-down age distribution, with the pyramid standing on its point. You can't have a country where everybody lives in a nursing home."[464] Surprisingly, the birth rate is much higher above "the olive line". In Scandinavia and the UK it's about 1.75. There are currently four times as many people aged under 65 in the EU27 as over but by 2050 it will be equal; this is the pensions timebomb.

Basil Fawlty said of the EEC and the British referendum of 1975: "I didn't vote for it myself quite honestly but now that we're in I'm determined to make it

---

[464] *No Babies?* by Russell Shorto, *New York Times Magazine*, 29 June 2008

work." [465] Well, it's now 35 years later, Basil, and the thing still doesn't work, and nor does it want to. Witness the hounding of every whistleblower – many British and almost always "good Europeans" (ie pro-EU) before their ordeal. They tried to help the EU clean up its act, to mop up its financial incontinence. All were telling the truth but the best any of them managed was an apology from Neil Kinnock. Anybody encouraged by the fact that the Commission's last anti-fraud man, Mr Kallas, was himself acquitted of fraud in his home country is setting their sights low. While he may have learnt something about chicanery from the arguments of his unsuccessful prosecutor – and only from him – his former domain continues to be a crook's paradise. It's built that way, and there is a distinct lack of appetite for reform of any kind. At the Conservative Party Conference in October 2006, David Heathcoat-Amory, who'd been on the European Convention which drafted the Constitution, said that the EU is "unreformable – I know because I tried". We married a drunk and we should have realised by now we can't change him, not least because he doesn't want to change. Anyone who thinks that an institution that won't take no for an answer in referendums is open to reform needs their head examined.

Nor is there any appetite for reform of the Common Agricultural Policy. The CAP is the lion's share of the budget and is guarded by the French, who do best from it. Tony Blair said he would not relinquish Britain's budget rebate without its reform. But at a European Council in London in December 2005 he did just that, having said to Jacques Chirac three years earlier, "How can you defend the CAP and then claim to be a supporter of aid to Africa? Failing to reform the CAP means being responsible for the starvation of the world's poor." Mr Chirac's successor has also made it plain that he will not budge. (And who can blame him? Apart from the rest of the world, obviously.) Mr Blair was the most overtly pro-EU prime minister for a generation and look what influence he had. If he and his silver tongue could not reform the inexcusable CAP, who in British politics can? No one on earth can, even if they wanted to. And if the CAP is immune from reform then that is another reason that we must leave or hasten the entire organisation's end.

The EU is vulnerable on many fronts but it really should have been a victim of its own failure by now. As it is, it's suffering from several slow punctures. What will do for it? A Boston Tea Party moment? A 21st century equivalent of the repeal of the Corn Laws? Perhaps it will be a fractured eurozone. The EU is unlikely to be a victim of enlargement, which deepens its remit while widening its reach – "dilution" is a myth.

---

[465] The quotation is from first-series episode *The Germans*, which was broadcast a couple of months after the 1975 referendum on continued British membership of the EEC

The EU is expensive, corrupt, propagandistic (and not above targeting children), anachronistic, secretive, counterproductive, anti-democratic, acquisitive and unfair to developing countries. It is a success only in terms of postponing the retirement of a few politicians, some of whom had spent their careers denouncing it. The sum of the EU is far smaller than its many magnificent parts. It is a doctrinaire catastrophe, harming almost everything it turns its self-promoting gaze to, be it the environment or transport. It's an article of faith, foisted on the peoples of Europe through bad faith, a Curia that refuses to accept that the rest of the world does not revolve around it. The attempted imposition of the Constitution after the French and Dutch no votes got what it deserved from the Irish. The second Irish vote was a cheat. The EU played the part of a boxer, floored by a right, a left and an uppercut, who got up and sucker-punched his vanquisher. It's not a wise long-term strategy. It may be that deeper political integration suits countries whose relationship with democracy is shorter and spottier than ours but it's not a good idea to try to impose it.

De Gaulle had the right idea: he wanted the EEC to be a "Europe des patries", a loosely bound intergovernmental organisation, one that would eschew coercion but still strive for mutual benefit through co-operation. Most reasonable people would agree that the EU needs to switch from dogmatism to pragmatism, from Procrustean thinking to flexibility. But no such magic switch exists.

Total integration is not inevitable but the EU pretends it is. Clive Crook in the *National Journal* wrote after the Irish 2008 vote: "Globalisation and distinctive national preferences can co-exist quite happily. The USA has comparatively low taxes and a small public sector; Sweden has high taxes and an elaborate welfare state. Both are open economies. Those differing national preferences can continue indefinitely – until governments, pursuing international political convergence as a goal in its own right, choose to lean against them. To be sure, there are areas where co-operation is valuable or even essential, such as measures to promote trade (mutual recognition of domestic regulation). Co-operation can be ad hoc, voluntary, limited to specific goals, and careful to leave discretion to members. Or it can express itself in supranational bodies with defined purposes, legal powers over the members, and a vision of a new political identity. The first is co-operation among unilateralists; the other the EU. What EU citizens have learned is that visionary forms of multilateralism widen the gap between political power and popular will, and are a far more potent threat to democracy than is globalisation. It is not the implacable logic of economic integration that sets the desires of the Irish, the French, the Dutch, and the rest at zero. It is EU governments, jointly pursuing an unwanted idea."[466]

---

[466] *Irish Lessons On Democracy* in *National Journal* (www.nationaljournal.com), 21 June 2008

None of us needs to marry our neighbour in order to sell him or her our car; the EU is unnecessary for trade. (But trade was never its point, which was and is to dissolve as many countries into one as possible, whatever the consequences.) We can survive outside the European Union just as surely as we have survived outside the euro. We in the UK were warned by the europhiles that we would perish without the single currency but we did not. Even Mandelson conceded in 2010 that "sterling's flexibility provided an additional support to demand" during the recession.

We will flourish outside the EU, too, and help many poorer nations to do so, many of them in the Commonwealth, whom we will again be able to trade with on our and their terms. The EU, as it well knows, is more often a trade block than a trade bloc. No other group of neighbouring countries is today coalescing by surrendering governance to the centre at the expense, literal and otherwise, of the people. Grown-up, developed nations do not feel the need to pass up their decision making to a supranational body. Does Australia ask Wellington to tell it and others what its import tariffs should be? In Nafta, does Ottawa boss Mexico and the USA over their employment and environmental laws? No, but the three enjoy free trade.

The European Economic Area was started in 1994 by Commission president Jacques Delors to try to ensnare non-participants in the EU project. Since then, three of its members, Sweden, Finland and Austria, have joined the EU, just as Delors wanted. Iceland, Norway and Liechtenstein remain in it but outside the EU.

We can leave the EU and stay in the EEA. But it might well be more attractive to rejoin the European Free Trade Association (Efta, which is the same three refuseniks plus Switzerland), which we set up in 1960. How about rejoining it in time for its 50th anniversary? Mimicking Berlin's "Europafest" of March 2007, we could have an "Eftafest" in London in 2010, with free alco-pops, Turkey Twizzlers and subsidised minibuses flitting between the capital's night spots, perhaps with a detour past The Ivy, to point out where Peter Mandelson's grandfather saved us all from the EEC's predecessor.

In a paper for the Bruges Group, Daniel Hannan wrote: "People in Efta are more than twice as rich as those in the EU. They also enjoy lower inflation, higher employment, healthier budget surpluses and lower real interest rates. Interestingly, they also export more per head than EU states, selling $16,498 per capita to overseas markets – the highest ratio in the world. Since British europhiles have always based their argument on economic necessity, Efta pretty well demolishes their case. Here, after all, is empirical evidence that countries that participate in the European market without subjecting themselves to the associated costs of membership are wealthier than full EU members... The Efta states participate fully in the four freedoms of the single market – free movement, that is, of goods, services, people and capital. But they are outside the Common Agricultural Policy. They control their own territorial resources, including fish stocks and energy reserves. They administer their own frontiers and admit whom they choose onto their territory... They are exempt from a good deal of EU social and employment law (all of it in the case of Switzerland). They are able to negotiate free-trade deals with third countries. They pay only a token contribution to the Brussels budget... And every member of Efta exports more per head to the EU than does Britain."[467]

That last point has also been made by Ruth Lea: "In 2003, 61.5 per cent of Swiss exports of goods and services went to EU25 countries and 83 per cent of Swiss imports were from EU25 countries. The equivalent data for Spain were 68 per cent and 64 per cent, and for Denmark they were 65 per cent and 70 per cent."[468]

The EU is not "going our way" and never has been. And it is not a buffet – we cannot pick and choose from it, which is what "renegotiation" suggests. One is either a member of an organisation committed to "ever closer union" and the relentless integrationist measures that go with that, or one is not. To "renegotiate" (if it were even possible) is merely to move seats in a train whose direction you cannot change. If a discretionary approach were possible, every country would be at it. The European Court Of Justice would be out of a job – nobody would bother with the EU laws they didn't fancy, so enforcement would not be an issue. Peter Hitchens has written that "You can't be in Europe and not run by Europe any more than you can be in Wormwood Scrubs and not run by Wormwood Scrubs". We are either in the EU and ruled by the EU – or outside it but trading with it.

To those who say that the latter course would mean being "ruled by fax machine" (see footnote for several dismissals of this argument[469]), well we are as it is drowning under the full weight of 170,000 pages of the acquis. Could we now have a go at associate (or "country") membership? It really couldn't be any worse. Besides, if Norway and Switzerland so much resent "rule by fax machine", why do they not become full members? In July 2006 a Swiss

---

[467] *Alternatives to the EU: The Case For Efta* by Daniel Hannan, available from www.brugesgroup.com
[468] *The Swiss model is a workable model for Britain* in *The European Journal*, January 2008
[469] This objection is demolished in *Alternatives to the EU: The Case For Efta* See also *Fax machine law?* (14 May 2008) and *The success of the EU* (24 March 2007) on eureferendum.blogspot.com

government survey predicted that joining the EU would cost the country €2.1billion a year. Switzerland believed that her bilateral agreement with the EU was far better value at €360million a year. Ian Milne, the editor of *eurofacts*, calculated in 2004 that between 1997 and 2003 Norway incorporated 2,129 of the 11,511 laws handed down by the EU (18.5 per cent). However, many of those 2,129 had come from the UN. Norway chose to receive them via the EU for the sake of convenience, in the same way that the UK and many others receive the non-EU Basel banking regulations via the EU.

After we left the EU, we would of course continue to respect EU standards when selling into the bloc – just as we have always borne in mind which side a country drives on when exporting cars – but designate our own standards, which might or might not be the same as now, for goods and services traded domestically, just as we put the steering wheel on the right when selling cars to ourselves. Some objectors seem to forget the principles of the EU when considering this: "Ah, but we'd have to negotiate 26 new arrangements with our former partners. What a palaver. How time-consuming and difficult." The whole point of the EU is that it is a single entity, with a single trade wall: we'd have to make only one arrangement.

So, how do we get to Efta from here? Withdrawal from the EU would be the easiest option: all roads lead away from the Treaty of Rome. As Robert The Bruce, no mean champion of independence, might have put it, "If at first you don't secede – try, try, try again." No one could today make the case for the UK joining the EU if we were not already in it, just as no one could now make the case for UK membership of the euro; you just wouldn't find enough buyers. However, now that we are in the EU, the reverse argument – the EU is appalling and we shouldn't have anything to do with it – doesn't have quite the same appeal. That unfair fact is the eurosceptics' problem.

What keeps us in the EU? Your MP, unless he or she is signed up to Better Off Out[470]. If the European Communities Act 1972 were repealed we would be out. It is this Act which absorbs each new EU treaty. No one forces us to be in the EU; we are sovereign. We are kept in the EU by the collective will of the 630 or so MPs who believe that people they have never met – and whom we cannot remove – do a better job of legislating for their own constituents than they (the non-Better Off Out MPs) themselves could. The man or woman who bothers you only every four years or so "for your support" is the problem. When he or she claims to want to represent your interests in Westminster, they're reciting an increasingly false prospectus. They know – or should know – that there's less and less they can do for you in a chamber that cannot change one iota of about three

---

[470] www.tfa.net/betteroffout

quarters of what it extrudes. And what is left to them is usually subject to indirect interference, such as rules on state aid – for example, railway fares, post offices and banks cannot be subsidised as much as some would like. Even the NHS is about to be taken out of MPs' hands. This is because, by giving away more and more of parliament's power, MPs have effectively locked themselves out of representing their constituents.

This is why the main parties have long looked as if they are converging; they have ceded most areas of legislation, and what little is left to them is often subject to EU rules. John Bright described England as the "mother of parliaments"[471]. It would be an appalling irony if she and the rest of the UK were now to surrender to a post-communist politburo.

Before the Lisbon Treaty passed through the UK parliament, Tony Benn said: "The EU is slowly turning Britain into a large local authority with a mayor in 10 Downing Street who has less power than the unelected commissioners who control Europe. The Lisbon Treaty is, as everyone admits, almost identical to the rejected constitution. Our political leaders promised us a referendum on that. Whatever view people take, it would be impossible to justify denying the people a vote. Electors are sovereign. They only lend their power for up to five years to MPs they elect. To transfer that power to those we don't elect is a theft of democratic rights. MPs of all parties should have a free Commons vote as to whether a referendum be held. By doing this MPs would be answerable to their constituents if they vote against and thus shut their own electors out of this major decision. We need an all-party referendum campaign in defence of our democratic rights. The decision would be democratic, not one which the European political establishment want to slip through."[472]

In 1996 the Referendum Party managed to persuade the governing party, the Tories, and then "New" Labour to pledge that they would not adopt the euro without a national vote; Sir James Goldsmith's millions had bounced John Major and Blair into making an unequivocal promise, which each published in his general election manifesto the following year. In 2005, both parties promised in their general election manifestos a referendum on the Constitution. Within weeks of the Labour victory, the Dutch and French electorates removed the need for a UK referendum.

The document then traded as the Lisbon Treaty (see the Appendix). The good news was that the Conservatives promised a referendum on it. The bad news

---

[471] Many people wrongly think that he said or meant that the Houses of Parliament were "the mother of parliaments"
[472] *The Sun*, 17 October 2007. The following March his son Hilary did not resign from the cabinet in order to vote for the referendum his father had urged

was that they, historically and recently, have told the truth about the EU much less often even than Labour. As a general rule, foreign politicians always tell the truth about the nature of the EU and what it has planned. The Tories have never publicly told the truth on the subject, from Harold Macmillan onwards. The Labour Party started fibbing from about 1988, when it abandoned opposition to the EU, having fallen for Jacques Delors' flannel about a "social Europe". (The trades unions would later twig that the EU meant lower wages when foreign workers undercut the natives.)

At the time of writing, David Cameron is PM in a coalition government. Of course, it matters less and less who is in Number 10 but what follows was his and the Tory party's position on the European Union up to that point.

On 26 September 2007, he wrote in the *Sun*: "Today, I will give this cast-iron guarantee: if I become PM a Conservative government will hold a referendum on any EU treaty that emerges from these negotiations [the intergovernmental conference that produced the Lisbon Treaty]. No treaty should be ratified without consulting the British people in a referendum." The Lisbon Treaty emerged from those talks. "Small wonder that so many people don't believe a word politicians ever say," added Cameron, "if they break their promises so casually." In 1997 Blair had said, "If a Labour government were to decide to enter a single currency – and that is a big if – I give my word that there would be a referendum before we committed ourselves to entering. This is our cast-iron pledge to the people." Tone was telling the truth, his heir not so much.

Six days later, on the Tuesday of the Tory party conference, Cameron was interviewed on the *Today* programme. He was trailing Brown in the polls. Just as when he had trailed David Davis and Liam Fox two years earlier in the leadership battle, he sought the same solution: to make a eurosceptic noise. He suggested that if a general election were not held that year and the Lisbon Treaty were in place when he came to power, the Conservatives would call a referendum.

Interviewer: If… there is a European treaty in place and you come into power, will you tear it up?

Cameron: We will hold a referendum on it and put it to the people. But it will be in…

Interviewer: If it's been ratified, if it's in place, what will you do?

Cameron: We will fight it through the House of Commons, we will put down amendments saying there should be a referendum. And as long as that treaty is being debated and discussed in the capitals of Europe…

Interviewer: What if it's there?

Cameron: If it's there, it won't have been accepted by every other European country [actually, it must have been to have been enacted] and we will hold a referendum. We think that this is just so wrong. Look, we put into our manifesto at the last election [which he mostly wrote] that we would hold a referendum [on the Constitution], the government put into their manifesto that they would have a referendum. They have broken trust with the British people. It's one of the most flagrant breaches of trust I can remember in British politics. And we promise a referendum. And that promise is good, *whenever Gordon Brown decides to hold this election* [emphasis added]."[473]

At the Tory conference that day, William Hague, the shadow foreign secretary, called Brown's reneging on a referendum "one of the most bare-faced and deliberate misrepresentations in the modern annals of political deceit".

Hague also called for a change to the 1972 European Communities Act, to allow for compulsory referendums on all future EU treaty changes: "If any future government agrees any treaty that transfers further competences from Britain to the EU, a national referendum before it could be ratified would be required by law."[474] Cynics even then said that it was all very well for him to say this because, as he knew or should have known, the Lisbon Treaty was largely self-amending and so any changes would not need the approval of member parliaments (who could later repeal such legislation anyway).

A few weeks later, Hague told BBC1's *Andrew Marr Show*: "We don't rule out a referendum in the future. Our discussions will take place against the background that this treaty, if passed without a referendum [in the UK], will lack democratic legitimacy and it will mean that the process of European political integration has gone too far. I think there are ways back."[475]

Two days later, his boss made an EU-turn. At his monthly press conference, on 23 October 2007, Cameron said that he refused to promise an unconditional, retrospective referendum if elected. Was this, in his words, "one of the most flagrant breaches of trust in British politics"? Or was it, in Hague's words, "one of the most bare-faced and deliberate misrepresentations in the modern annals of political deceit"? Why should Gordon Brown's reneging in 2007 on a 2005 manifesto pledge be a worse breach of trust than Cameron breaking two promises – neither of which was time-specific – only a month after making them in the nation's best-selling daily newspaper and on the nation's flagship radio show?

---

[473] *Today*, 2 October 2007
[474] In *The Sunday Times*, 7 October 2007, following the conference, Simon Jenkins wrote that, in his speech, "Hague derided the concept of an EU foreign policy shortly before demanding that 'the EU systematically turn the screw' on Zimbabwe, whatever that means. This is not policy but attitude"
[475] 21 October 2007

Six days earlier, 46 Tory MPs had signed a Commons Early Day Motion tabled by Bill Cash, the eurosceptic MP, that called for a referendum "before or after ratification" by parliament. Cameron had of course not signed it. The party leadership had by no means finished wriggling. If the treaty were implemented by the time the Tories were in office, Hague told the House on 12 November, "then we would be in a situation where we had a new treaty in force that lacked democratic legitimacy in this country and in our view gave the EU too much power over our national policies. This would not be acceptable to a Conservative government and we would not let matters rest there." Asked if that meant a post-ratification referendum, he replied: "It means what it says it means, exactly what I said earlier." "Not letting matters rest there" was the political equivalent of putting the alarm clock on "snooze": the problem would "go off" again.

In 2005, Cameron more or less sealed the party leadership by speaking to the party conference without notes. (This really shouldn't have impressed anyone who's ever watched a short play but it did. The heir to Blair, like his hero, is fluent, shallow and guided by focus groups rather than principle.) Aside from an absence of index cards, Cameron's other great crowd pleaser was a promise to withdraw Tory MEPs from the European Peoples' Party (EPP) grouping in the EU parliament. It was in response to a similar but weaker proposal from David Davis (who – let's not forget – had whipped the Maastricht vote for John Major).

Cameron's promise was arcane but symbolic, and welcome news to many of the party faithful. In order to qualify for funding, move amendments, propose debates and have a say in the parliament's admin and power structure, MEPs need to be in transnational groupings. The EPP grouping is strongly pro-EU. After he had won the leadership in December 2005, Cameron's promise looked shaky, and he had a problem: inaction spoke more loudly than words.

In February 2006 William Hague said of removing the Tory MEPs from the highly integrationist grouping, "We have said months, not weeks, but also we have said months not years." In June 2006, Hague said that plans to leave the EPP would be announced at the end of July. European politicians, including Merkel and Sarkozy, then French interior minister, had threatened to suspend dealings with the Tories if Cameron's MEPs left the grouping. Predictably, europhile Tory dinosaurs such as Patten also warned against such a move.

Tory party members were becoming restless about Cameron's unfulfilled promise but were not the only ones to be annoyed by it. So was he. A telling piece by Rachel Sylvester and Alice Thomson in the *Daily Telegraph* opened: "It is difficult to shake David Cameron's cool. His natural state is one of calm, collected Old Etonian charm. He is all open-necked shirts and smoothies. But I once saw him really lose it. When Alice Thomson and I last interviewed him...

we mentioned, in passing, his commitment to pull his MEPs out of the EPP. In return we got an absolute diatribe. 'Can we please not talk about the EPP?' he barked, with genuine anger in his voice. 'I'm sick to death of the EPP. It's so boring.' We persisted with our line of questioning for a bit, eliciting a variety of unrevealing non-responses, then gave up. But I came away with the impression that the Europe pledge, made when Mr Cameron desperately needed to win over Right-wingers during the Tory leadership campaign, had the potential to become his biggest headache – and that he knew it."[476] The EU, rather than the narrower matter of the EPP, would become Dave's biggest headache.

A month later, leaked emails from Cameron's "eyes and ears" in the Commons, Desmond Swayne, reported a worry among Tory MPs that the pledge to leave the EPP might be "blown off course" and that Hague's office was in any case "briefing against the move". A few weeks after that, Cameron announced that no new grouping could be formed until the Euro elections of June 2009. Later militating against the move would be a July 2008 rule change from the EP: new MEP groupings had, from 2009, to comprise at least 25 MEPs (up from 20), with members required to come from at least seven countries (up from six).

In a March 2006 speech at the Foreign Press Association, Cameron said that if elected he would try to restore the UK's opt-out from the Social Chapter (see below), but would not seek to take back control over trade policy: "Trade policy is decided in Europe and I don't propose to change that." (In 2009 he said: "I want us to be in the European Union. We are a trading nation." Tell that to the Commonwealth and developing world, Dave.)

He should have known that the EU is not a pick-and-mix organisation. He probably did. No country has *ever* managed to repatriate any powers, either individually or for all members. Implying that the EU was doomed – "there was life before the EU and there will be life after the EU" – he perhaps revealed his gameplan: to play along with the EU so as not to impede his ascent to Number 10, while making just enough eurosceptic feints.

Many people still considered Cameron to be eurosceptic. Perhaps they did not know that in the early 1990s he had worn cuff links decorated with the EU's ring of stars. Anyway, he had, by this point, abandoned plans for a Tory administration to derogate from the grotesque Common Fisheries Policy – which his three immediate predecessors had wanted to tear up. How "green" could he be to support that needless waste and avoidable pollution of the seabed? He had barred MPs who advocated EU withdrawal from his future front bench (but not those who favoured UK euro membership). And he had left unfulfilled a key

---

[476] *The Daily Telegraph*, 13 June 2006

pledge of his campaign to be elected party leader: to leave the EPP, which Michael Howard had forbidden during his time as Tory leader. Cameron, as Howard's protégé, could not have been unaware of how difficult it would be. (Meanwhile, the EPP high-ups were arguing for the return of the Constitution and were backing the parliament's leader as he announced the preservation of the Strasbourg seat.)

Cameron's chief of staff is Ed Llewellyn, an ardent europhile. Llewellyn used to work for Lord Patten, who made it clear in the summer of 2009 that he'd accept the EU foreign-affairs role if offered it (he had after all helped write the document that created the role). Cameron was weeks slower than Hague in criticising the candidacy of Blair for the Lisbon-sanctioned post of president of the European Council. Fittingly for an unelected role, Blair's candidacy was supported by another unelected politician, Lady (Glenys) Kinnock, of ACP-EU fame, when she was, for five minutes at least, Brown's EU minister in the Lords.

And, in 2009, Cameron's supposedly eurosceptic EU spokesman, Mark Francois, was suggesting that the party might cede even more of the UK's membership rebate if there were reform of the CAP. For a party that studies Blair so closely, this was a surprising thing to offer – had they not learnt that financial surrenders to the EU do not result in reform, especially not of the CAP?

Cameron then welcomed to his shadow cabinet the most ardently europhile Tory: Ken Clarke, a man who had campaigned on the same platform as Tony Blair to join the euro – against the most famous policy of then leader Hague (in the days when he had a backbone) – and who had similarly contradicted the party line and defied the whips by voting *against* a referendum on the Lisbon Treaty a few months earlier. However, Clarke was back on the front bench – but would not have been if he had advocated UK withdrawal from the EU.

At the 2009 Tory conference, Clarke suggested that he might campaign in favour of the Lisbon Treaty if there were a UK referendum, but later insisted he would not "contemplate campaigning against my colleagues". Elsewhere at the conference, he announced a "one in, one out" programme for business regulations: no new biz reg would reach the statute book before another had been repealed ("no new red tape will be introduced without a compensating cut in the costs and burden somewhere else"). Most business legislation emanates from Brussels and is therefore unstoppable or, if already law, unrepealable, so he was promising things that the Tories could not deliver: EU-derived law cannot be unilaterally repealed, not even to "make space" for another piece of EU-derived law. This rubbish found its way into the 2010 coalition agreement: "We will cut red tape by introducing a 'one-in, one-out' rule whereby no new regulation is brought in without other regulation being cut by a greater amount." Obviously not allowed, as the ConDems later conceded. Similarly, the coalition cannot say: "We will impose 'sunset clauses' on regulations and regulators to ensure that the need for each regulation is regularly reviewed." Ditto: "We will give the public the opportunity to challenge the worst regulations."

Before the 2010 general election Clarke travelled to Brussels to reassure Barroso that the EU had nothing to fear from a Tory victory. Why should it?

Like Michael Howard, Cameron found that the EU delighted in contradicting his promises. A pledge by the smoothie-drinking Old Etonian to guarantee small businesses a quarter of public-sector contracts was found to be in breach of single market anti-discrimination laws. (In the coalition agreement of 2010, this *still* appeared but had been deceitfully watered down: "We will promote small business procurement, in particular by introducing an *aspiration* that 25 per cent of government contracts should be awarded to small and medium-sized businesses" [emphasis added].) The Commission also said that it would not renegotiate WTO standards requiring companies to have three years' worth of accounts when bidding for contracts – another requirement Cameron had pledged to remove[477].

This was similar to his promise to repeal the Social Chapter, which had been incorporated into the Treaties years earlier. The Treaties, as we know from the impossibility of getting the parliament, like a hyperactive child, to sit in just one place, can be changed only unanimously, after an intergovernmental conference that drafts a new or amended text. On 26 February 2007, in a written answer to that parliament, Mr Barroso, the reliable reminder of a UK politician's limits, said that a country's withdrawal from the Social Chapter would be almost impossible: "These provisions are part of the whole treaty and cannot be isolated. All member states are bound by the Treaties they have signed and ratified and which have entered into force, including the social provisions they contain. Consequently, a withdrawal from these provisions by a member state would require an amendment of the EC Treaty in accordance with Article 48 of TEU." (This Article says that a member state can propose changes to the treaties but any change would have to be agreed by the European Council "after consulting the European parliament and, where appropriate, the Commission". The 27 countries would then each have to ratify the change domestically in their parliaments after an intergovernmental conference, the EU being the child of an international treaty.)

Despite Mr Barroso's helpful clarification, the Tories continued to pretend that the EU was an à la carte menu. In an interview with the *Financial Times* over a

---

[477] *The Financial Times*, 28 October 2006

year later, Hague said that a Tory government would seek to restore full British control over employment law and social policy. In addition, he said it was "important to point out that we [the Tories] are very positive about many aspects of the EU". He said that he favoured EU action in areas such as tackling climate change, fully opening the single market, and presenting a common front in foreign policy, for example in confronting Iran[478]. The EU's environmental efforts are a disaster. Hague may well wish to extend the single market but, as mentioned, our EU partners often guard their energy companies, among other sectors, rather jealously. And we can judge our partners' attitude to Iran from their reaction and inaction when that nation captured some of our sailors in 2007 (and two years later when Iran kidnapped staff of the British embassy in Teheran). Soon after becoming foreign secretary, Hague said, "Despite the present economic crisis, Europe has never been freer, more stable and more prosperous, and the European Union deserves considerable credit for that."

In December 2006, Cameron went to Brussels. In a speech, already quoted in the section on the CAP, he said, "Everyone keeps going on about a disconnection between the EU and its citizens. The way to end that disconnection is to deliver results on the environment, on competitiveness and getting the [WTO's Doha] trade round started and relieving poverty in the developing world. That is what people are marching on the streets for – trade justice and ending poverty and doing something about the environment." The EU is the enemy of the environment *and* a block on relieving poverty in the developing world – the CAP and CFP are designed that way. The EU's priorities are such that it was always going to cause Doha to fail, just as its priorities are not the environment or the world's poor. Cameron was appealing for results that the EU was not designed to deliver and he was perpetuating myths about what the EU could do.

He went on to say, "Commissioner Dimas was very optimistic that emissions trading can be made to work under the current set-up. Emissions trading is a great example of what I am talking about. The architecture is already there to make it work... we do not need institutional reform to do this." He managed also to peddle another myth, saying, "The Constitution is dead. As José Barroso said, there is a 0.000 per cent chance of getting it started again." Three months later, Mr Barroso, along with Ms Merkel and others, made the Berlin Declaration, which stated that a new form of the Constitution would be framed; it became, with the help of Chris Patten, the Lisbon Treaty.

Had Mr Cameron been gullible or complicit? Only a month earlier, the failures of the ETS had been all over the UK newspapers, with details of how NHS

---

478 *The Financial Times*, 23 July 2008

hospitals had been almost pauperised by paying oil companies for permission to function. Pointing out the failures of the ETS, Open Europe was surprised when a researcher from Conservative HQ told them that their research was unhelpful because "we want to be in favour of this". Which mattered more to the Tories – to do right or to *be seen* to do right?

It's often said – and it's true more often than not – that opposition leaders are eurosceptic until they assume office. Cameron wasn't even eurosceptic in opposition. When Brown announced the insane wind-farm-building programme, to comply with an EU directive, Cameron's response was that Brown should have started sooner. Cameron can promise to abolish any number of quangos but by far the costliest (and most divisive) are the regional development agencies. For as long as he supports UK membership of the EU, he is powerless to get rid of these. Membership is also entirely at odds with his supposed love of "localism" (which is also under threat from his habit of imposing his own shortlists on Tory constituency associations in lieu of their own, er, local nominees).

The inaugural meeting of the Movement for European Reform, which Cameron had set up in 2006, took place in Brussels in March 2007 (three weeks before the EU showed it was unreformable by dusting down the Constitution that Cameron said was dead). Cameron and the then Czech PM, Mirek Topolanek, leader of the country's ODS party, spoke – and wrote a joint article in that day's *Daily Telegraph*: "We want to work together with the peoples and parties of Europe who share our vision, to create a new union, a new union based not on uniformity and compulsion, but on diversity and voluntary co-operation of independent nation states[479]... It is only by responding to the challenges of global competition and by opening up our economies to free trade that we will fight poverty in Africa. Ultimately, it is enterprise, not aid, that will save the developing world... We are committed not only to establishing a new political grouping in the European parliament, but also to making the EU fit for the 21st century: one that is a force for good in the world; one that leads by example; and one that delivers. Join us in building an EU that we can all be proud of."[480]

And how did his desire to "open up our economies to free trade... to fight poverty in Africa" square with his statement a year earlier that "trade policy is decided in Europe and I don't propose to change that"? On the one hand he wants to help Africa through trade, on the other he is happy to participate in an

---

[479] This is an echo of Margaret Thatcher's famous speech at the College of Bruges, where many Eurocrats are trained, in 1988 (by which time the EEC scales had finally fallen from her eyes), in which she said, "... willing and active co-operation between independent sovereign states is the best way to build a successful European Community". She meant it. He did not
[480] *The Daily Telegraph*, 6 March 2007

inhumane customs union that specifically discriminates, through openly higher trade tariffs, against the poorest African nations. This is the same contradiction that Blair pointed out to Chirac: "How can you defend the CAP and then claim to be a supporter of aid to Africa? Failing to reform the CAP means being responsible for the starvation of the world's poor." Cameron should really study Blair even more closely.

In late 2008 Topolanek said, long after the Irish no vote, that he and his government were "dedicated to" Czech ratification of the Lisbon Treaty (his president, Václav Klaus, famously was not). If you were Cameron and you wanted to form a new, "eurorealist" MEP grouping, would you choose a supporter of the Lisbon Treaty to do it with? In 2009, after he'd lost office, Topolanek told the BBC that "This treaty is bad and we know it. We supported the treaty... because we were a party in government and because we signed it and because we agreed on a compromise at the level of the European Council... If we hadn't signed the Lisbon Treaty and had been pushed to the sidelines of the European Union, we would have had no chance of promoting our national interests. That's the main reason. It was the lesser of two evils." Mr Topolanek is now perhaps best known outside the Czech Republic for being photographed naked at one of Mr Berlusconi's lively parties.

A year before the 2009 EU elections, the Conservative Party entrenched its incumbent MEPs at the top of the party lists, a move that was clearly at odds with the membership, most of whom wanted to deselect the party's mostly pro-EU MEPs. And its MEPs were still in the EPP (although Daniel Hannan, to his and his supporters' delight as well as that of his opponents, had been expelled).

On 5 March 2008, MPs voted not to put the Lisbon Treaty to the British people. After that, most of them trotted off, their 2005 election promises to their constituents broken. A few of them, however, noticed that there was also to be a vote on a New Clause 9, proposed, like the October 2007 Early Day Motion, by Bill Cash. Cameron asked his MPs to abstain, and the Tory whips sent MPs texts seven minutes before the vote on Cash's proposal that said there were "no further official votes". This was true enough but slippery. Nevertheless, 40 of Cameron's 200-odd MPs ignored him and the whips to vote in favour.

In June 2008, a week before Ireland voted no to Lisbon, Cameron told an audience in Essex that if the Treaty had been implemented throughout the bloc by the time that he had assumed office, "We may have to say, well look, we're not happy with this situation, here are some of the powers we'd like to have back. But we can't give you that referendum on the Lisbon Treaty because it's already been put in place across the rest of Europe." Was that "one of the most flagrant breaches of trust in British politics"? When he said he'd like a few "powers" "back", had he not understood Barroso's reiteration that provisions of the treaties cannot be isolated? Apart from the euro, you're either wholly in or wholly out of the EU but, because not everyone understands that, Cameron pretended otherwise.

Back in 2003, Cameron had told *Guardian* readers that he wanted to maintain the UK's financial independence. Why not restore our trading independence, which he said he was happy to keep in Brussels? The artificially high prices created by CAP push people – here and elsewhere – into poverty. Is the affordability of food not part of his "quality of life" agenda? When the NHS is bankrupted by the HSD, what will the "quality of life" be like for those who cannot afford to channel hop for care? While EU directives on power generation drive energy bills ever higher, what will be the "quality of life" for those driven down into fuel poverty? That's why people, in Cameron's phrase, "bang on about Europe". It's hard not to conclude that, just as Gordon Brown dropped all mention of the EU in his last speech to the Labour Party Conference as chancellor, so Cameron was trying not to rock the boat as he, too, sensed the prospect of office. Blair taunted Cameron in the House of Commons on 25 June 2007 for "going through the motions a bit" when demanding a referendum. How right the old chancer was.

When the Brown government ratified the Lisbon Treaty, Hague said, in a press release of 17 July 2008, "… The government are joining in the ugly bullying of the Irish people, who have clearly rejected this treaty. Trying to push ahead with the treaty shows an utter lack of respect for the Irish voters' democratic decision. As long as the Irish decision is not reversed, the treaty will not be in force at the next general election. A new Conservative government would then take back the instruments of ratification [ie retrieve three pieces of goatskin parchment, signed by HM Queen, from a vault in Rome – the location being a legacy of the founding treaty] and put the Treaty to a referendum, recommending a no vote. That is the honourable and democratic thing to do."

"The honourable and democratic thing" for the Tories to do would have been to tell Ireland that she was not alone. A Tory government, Hague might have said, would also consult the people – irrespective of what the Irish did or didn't do, and so Ireland need not feel bullied about rejecting the Treaty because the UK might yet reject it as well. By *not* saying this, the Tories were implicitly "joining in the ugly bullying of the Irish people". Cameron could have killed the Lisbon Treaty quite easily by saying that he would hold a referendum regardless, and abrogate it if that is what the people of the UK wanted. Why could Cameron not have said to the Irish that they could, if they wished, wait until after the UK referendum that he was promising, and so perhaps not even have to bother voting again? In September 2008 Hague was still saying that the Tories might offer a referendum if the treaty were ratified when they won office. "We haven't made the decision," he said. "I certainly haven't ruled that out."[481]

Cameron believes in UK membership of the EU, whose central tenet has always been "ever closer union"; the Lisbon Treaty was a step towards "ever closer union"; therefore, you cannot be in favour of the EU and not Lisbon. (It's also illogical to be in favour of the EU – "ever closer union" – and to oppose membership of the euro, which is "economic and monetary union".)

Disingenuously, he announced to the 2008 Conservative Party conference that his MEPs would campaign on a Lisbon referendum ticket. As he well knew, those politicians were being elected to an entirely separate "legislature", which had no desire – or power – to order a referendum in the UK. But it was a call that *sounded* eurosceptic. How could Tory MEPs sitting in Strasbourg have forced a referendum in Brown's Britain? They couldn't. In any case, most Tory MEPs went native several hundred expenses claims ago, and so did not favour a UK referendum.

Six weeks before the 2009 Euro elections Dave returned to this cynical promise and launched a poster campaign that asked voters to return Tory MEPs in order to "Tell Labour you want the referendum they promised". Cameron also said, "Where you stand on the referendum says a lot about your politics. It says a lot about how much you value trust between the government and the governed. I believe that if you make a promise in your manifesto, and the country votes on that manifesto, then you are honour-bound to keep that promise."

A week before the 2009 Euro elections, with Labour nowhere (but Ukip presenting a more credible challenge), Cameron was at it again: "A progressive reform agenda demands that we redistribute power from the EU to Britain... We will therefore hold a referendum on the Lisbon Treaty, pass a law requiring a referendum to approve any further transfers of power to the EU, negotiate the return of powers, and require far more detailed scrutiny in parliament of EU legislation, regulation and spending." "A referendum on the Lisbon Treaty": it sounded unequivocal but was not. Speaking from a script, he had plenty of opportunity to say that the offer was conditional. He did not. As for the "return of powers", well, we've heard that joke before and it was never especially funny. And scrutiny of EU legislation is all very well but it has *never* led to an amendment. *Not one*. It can't.

There had been two notable interventions during the 2009 Euro campaign. Stuart Wheeler, the founder of spreadbetting firm IG Index who had given

---

[481] *The Sunday Times*, 28 September 2008

Hague's Conservatives £5million before the 2001 general election (the British record for a one-off donation), announced that he was – for the Euro election only – backing Ukip, putting £100,000 in their coffers. He wrote in the *Spectator*, on 20 May 2009, that "William Hague uses carefully chosen weasel words to give the impression that the Tories are getting tough about the EU. The exact reverse is the truth." The Tories expelled Wheeler. (After a visit to Britain almost a year later, Belgium's foreign minister said he could find no difference in attitude to the EU between the foreign secretary, David Miliband, and Hague, his shadow.) Ignoring Wheeler's fate, Lord Tebbit, the former Tory chairman, suggested that the electorate might like to withhold its vote from the three main parties (and the British National Party) in the Euro election[482]. Not known for embracing the Greens or Plaid Cymru, his Lordship must, therefore, have meant Ukip (or spoiling one's ballot or not voting – both unlikely). Cameron did not dare expel him. The party polled 28 per cent of the vote.

After the 2009 Euro election, the Tories left the EPP and formed the European Conservatives and Reformists (ECR) grouping in the European parliament. The ECR is headed by a Polish MEP, Michal Kaminski, a strong and unabashed supporter of the Lisbon Treaty, the CAP and of Mr Barroso's being given a second term as president of the Commission!

The ECR has 54 MEPs from eight countries, including the Polish Law and Justice Party, the Czech Civic Democratic Party, the Belgian Lijst Dedecker party, the Hungarian Democratic Forum, the Latvian National Independence Movement and the Dutch Christian Union. (There had also been a Finn but he scuttled back to the ALDE grouping of Liberals.) Although several of those parties were in government, the grouping was described as "extremist" by Labour and europhile Tories. The British Lib Dems sit in the ALDE with members of Latvia's First Party, which has campaigned against gay marches.

Meanwhile, the EPP accepted Italy's Alleanza Nazionale and was already home to a party that had run election posters showing a male gay couple with the slogan "Daddy and Papa? Say No!" (Forza Italia) and another that had campaigned against the immigration of some Indian computer programmers with the slogan "Children Before Indians" (Germany's CDU, Merkel's party).

Where the Tories sit in the Strasbourg and Brussels hemicycles is a sideshow. While the split with the EPP mollified some of his party – despite being 42 months late – it could not compensate for his many capitulations to the EU. Placing a supporter of the Lisbon Treaty at the head of the grouping was in any case a peculiar way for Cameron to show opposition to the Lisbon Treaty.

---

[482] Can Norman Tebbit and Tony Benn both be wrong about the EU?

After the Irish voted yes to Lisbon in October 2009, Cameron was pushed to explain what "not let matters rest there" meant. Hoping not to let Lisbon overshadow the Tory party conference, he said, "I don't want say anything or do anything that would undermine what is being decided and debated in other countries [the Czech Republic and Poland]." This was preposterous: there was no debate in those countries – both states' legislatures had ratified the treaty. Poland had been waiting to see what Ireland did before its president finally signed it off, while the Czech Republic's trip to Rome to drop off its instrument of ratification was delayed by a challenge by 17 senators in the country's constitutional court. The Czech judges were deciding on the treaty's compatibility with their constitution – nothing Cameron might have said could have altered the points of law that they were deliberating.

At the Tories' 2009 conference, Hague said: "We seek a European Union that acts by agreement among nations rather than by placing its own president or foreign minister above any nation [this option is not on offer, William]. Let us be clear on the reasons for our opposition to the Lisbon Treaty and our call for a referendum: the ever greater centralisation of power beyond the democratic control of the people is not in keeping with the needs of the 21st century; it is against the spirit of our age; it diminishes our ability to pursue our own global relationships, and in its lack of accountability and legitimacy it goes against our fundamental belief that people should only be led and governed with their consent."

Cameron's conference speech continued the deception:

"But if there is one political institution that needs decentralisation, transparency, and accountability, it is the EU. For the past few decades, something strange has been happening on the left of British politics. People who think of themselves as progressives have fallen in love with an institution that no one elects, no one can remove, and that hasn't signed off its accounts for over a decade. Indeed even to question these things is, apparently, completely beyond the pale [in your party especially, Dave – you told people not to "bang on" about it[483]]. Well, here is a progressive reform plan for Europe. Let's work together on the things where the EU can really help, like combating climate change [ahem], fighting global poverty and spreading free and fair trade [note to Dave: please re-read what Blair said about the CAP to Chirac]. But let's return to democratic and accountable politics the powers the EU shouldn't have. And if we win the election, we will have as the strongest voice for our country's interests, the man who is leading our campaign for a referendum, the man who will be our new British foreign secretary: William Hague."

---

[483] He had earlier said that UKIP are "fruitcakes, loonies and closet racists, mostly"

Dave didn't tell his audience whom William "We are very positive about many aspects of the EU" Hague would be fighting against for a referendum if the Tories were in office. The only impediment to a referendum would be the Conservatives themselves (coalitions aside). It's never been said that Hague could start a fight in an empty room but perhaps he can. Their desire for one was about as sincere as Blair's promise to *Sun* readers before the 1997 election that he would protect the pound (he was dying to get shot of it). Cameron never wanted to "waste" political capital on a referendum – or confront the issues it would raise.

The *Daily Telegraph*'s Benedict Brogan's wrote on his blog on 2 November 2009: "When I spoke to [Hague] before conference he said anyone who assumed the leadership will just roll over if Lisbon is ratified was making 'a serious mistake'. For good measure he added: 'We choose our words carefully. We mean what we say.' And: 'This is a democratic country whose people were promised a referendum. We will always make time for the people to have their say.'"

In the first 100 days of the coalition, the Tories agreed to the EU's plans to preview national budgets, opted in to the European Investigation Order, voted to approve Ashton's EU foreign office and tried to block the eurosceptic Bill Cash from chairing the EU scrutiny committee in the Commons.

On plans for an in-or-out referendum, Cameron has said, "If I thought that being a member of the EU was against the national interest, I would argue for us to come out, but I don't." If the Lisbon Treaty is bad for Britain, it certainly did not become less bad for Britain once it came into force. If Cameron believed Lisbon to be bad for Britain, then the logical thing to do would be to offer a no-strings referendum, retrospective if need be, just as Harold Wilson did in 1975. However, Cameron believes an "in/out" referendum would be won by the freedom fighters and has said he would not grant one.

As the journalist Andrew Alexander had earlier written, "[Cameron] says we should have a referendum on what he calls 'the European constitution'. Do not be deceived. He means on the *additional* powers which would be conferred by the Lisbon Treaty. If we were to have such a referendum and if we were to reject the Treaty, the powers of the EU would be what they are now – excessive, unpopular and very expensive. And Brussels would come up with another plan to extend its role. If he thought EU membership was damaging to British interests, he says, he would oppose our membership. But it does not do that. It is good for Britain, so he insists. There you have it. Here is a man who will never let it be thought that, however much the EU rejects his promise to return significant powers from Brussels, he won't ever use the crucial negotiating lever of threatening to leave. He is a dodger by nature, as he has always been one of politics' blatant opportunists. Sadly, he is not even a very good opportunist, since he could save money and cut household bills by leaving the EU."[484]

Before the 2010 general election the Tories had enjoyed 20-point poll leads against Gordon Brown, the most unpopular, spendthrift and incompetent PM for some time. Their lead dropped to about six or seven points at around the time that Cameron confirmed he would not hold a retrospective referendum on Lisbon, and it never recovered. Dave ended up 19 seats short of a majority. In 2005 it was thought that Ukip's 600,000 votes had cost the Tories about two dozen seats. In 2010, Ukip received about 920,000 votes, costing the Tories a similar number of seats (based on seats where the Ukip vote exceeded the Tory candidate's losing margin).

Three times in less than a year Dave had declined Ukip's offer not to stand in the general election, in return for a referendum on the UK's EU membership. There's no saying that all of those Ukip votes would have turned Tory even if Cameron had taken up Ukip's offer. And he may also have attracted a few votes by being EU compliant (and by abandoning Conservatism). But the balance of probability suggests that Ukip prevented him winning outright. The party under his leadership got 10.7million votes in the 2010 general election – 18 years earlier even John Major had got 3.3million more than that.

Cameron, a europhile, was himself already in a coalition with his mostly eurosceptic party – just as his hero Blair was a cuckoo in the Labour nest. Governing in tandem with the federast Lib Dems in order to save his skin was no hardship. The Lib Dem leader, Nick Clegg, is a former MEP and longtime admirer of the euro[485]. Before he was an MEP Clegg worked in Brussels for the European Commission's Tacis programme and for the rabidly europhile Tory EU commissar Leon Brittan (now Cameron's trade adviser). Clegg had met his wife, Miriam, when both were studying at the College of Bruges, the famous Eurocrat breeding ground. She would go on to work for Chris Patten, the Tory commissar who succeeded Brittan, and then Benita Ferrero-Rocher. She is also a former colleague of Cameron's EU-supporting chief of staff, Ed Llewellyn (and a former workmate of Peter Power, Mandelson's quondam press secretary). What a great fit the ConDem coalition is – at the top anyway. It's a heap of europhiles.

---

484 *The Daily Mail*, 3 June 2009
485 Eg "If we remain outside the euro, we will simply continue to subside into a position of relative poverty and inefficiency compared to our more prosperous European neighbours" in 2001, and "The euro may well come to be regarded in the coming years as part of the answer to saving the City from permanent decline. It was easy to dismiss the fledgling euro as a 'toilet currency' before we realised our own economic growth was built on sand" in 2009

Aside from its convenience, what makes politicians such invertebrates when faced with the European Union?

The columnist Charles Moore had a theory when Brown was pushing the Lisbon Treaty through the Commons: "The European process is, for its participants, almost compulsory. Europe is a bureaucracy. Just as a public company must always seek a better return for shareholders, so a bureaucracy must seek more power for its employees. When a politician takes over the leadership of his country, he is told that he must join the process... Any mere elected person who seriously tries to disturb it will have the whole official and diplomatic class against him, not only in his own country, but in 26 others. It requires someone of quite exceptional courage and tenacity to try to resist this – and even she failed. Mr Brown will not bother. But if I were a pro-European [ie pro-EU], I would be worried by the fact that the only people who any longer vociferously support ever-closer union are those whose living depends on it."[486]

Brown was no great fan of the EU, and was known for his boorishness at Ecofin meetings when chancellor. But he was not eurosceptic as some thought. The EU was useful to him and others for giving the illusion of action – particularly on environmental matters – even if the outfit's record in that area should disqualify it for life. Also, like many leaders, he found the EU useful for introducing and drafting unpopular or dreary legislation.

The EU is ideal for carrying the can for unpopular laws, such as the one enacted in the UK in April 2009 (Data Retention Directive 2006/24/EC), which mandated that internet service providers must store, for 12 months, the time and duration of customers' internet phone calls (but not their content), details of other internet use (including connection times but not sites visited), and details, but again not the content, of emails. It had been presented at EU level as a commercial law, which would need only QMV, rather than as a policing matter, which would need unanimity. (The measure, which Sweden refused to implement, followed a separate directive which required telecoms firms to hold on to telephone records for a year.) Directive 2006/24 had been lobbied for by Charles Clarke, then home secretary, after the July 2005 bombs in London. The beauty for governments is that such measures can be put on the statute book without parliamentary scrutiny. And the EU in return gets "more Europe" and is therefore a step closer to creating a single polity.

How can democracy be restored when it's not in politicians' interest? Labour changed its mind twice on the Constitution. Blair had always denied the people a referendum, pushing his Europe minister Peter Hain on to news programmes to

---

[486] *The Daily Telegraph*, 20 October 2007

say, "Put away your placards, there will be no referendum." Then in 2004 Blair granted one. The promise was used to try to take some of the sting out of the Euro elections, which were two months away and came a year after the unpopular invasion of Iraq, and the general election the following year. Then Brown reneged on the promise after the treaty was renamed. Cameron's position has been covered. His reneging was perhaps a disaster only for him: it probably prevented his winning outright in 2010 (but that is not to say he is uncomfortable sharing a bed with the Lib Dems). It wasn't necessarily a disaster for eurosceptics. As Andrew Alexander wrote, a repeal of the Lisbon Treaty would still leave us saddled with the previous five treaties, each corrosive and an enemy of freedom and prosperity in its own way. Also, there's no saying that the referendum would have been won.

Referendums tend to reinforce the status quo; people usually vote to carry on as they are. This cuts both ways for eurosceptics. The result of the British referendum of 1975 – let's leave aside the scaremongering and financial advantage of the yes side, which included even the *Daily Mail* and Thatcher's Tories – declared that we should, 29 months in, *remain* in the EEC (ie it was a passive vote; the country did not vote to *join* the EEC, which would have been an active vote)[487]. The Danish no to Maastricht (later overturned), the Irish no to Nice (ditto), the Danish and Swedish no to the euro, the French and Dutch no to the Constitution, and the Irish no in 2008 to Lisbon were all votes *against change*. There are exceptions, such as the yes to the Constitution in 2005 from Spain and Luxembourg but they are not significant – and the revised votes in Denmark (1993) and Ireland (2002 and 2009) were a result of hollow promises and bullying.

Electorates tend to be conservative in referendums. People may well say to a pollster that they wish to leave the EU. In a booth, however, there's a danger that the voter will stick with the devil that he or she knows and, in this case, vote to stay in the wretched con trick that is the European Union. This would be especially true if the government and opposition were throwing their weight behind the yes camp, which would be the case if they were some combination of the three main parties. The BBC, too, would support remaining inside the democracy-defying enterprise. And you have to be very suspicious of anything EU-related that the Lib Dems are or have been in favour of – they know the electorate could easily be spooked into voting to stay in, which is why they have recently been in favour of an in-out referendum (see Appendix). But the Tory party, as currently constituted, would not offer a referendum anyway.

---

[487] The 2004 local vote against the (EU-inspired) North East England assembly was also a vote against change

So, it is almost certainly not the right time to try to overturn 1975's travesty. It is MPs who must be targeted. Although Westminster's power has been sold down the River Thames to Belgium, it remains the case that only MPs can free us from bondage, by repealing the European Communities Act (1972). If an MP can resign in the face of public outrage over the cost of a duck house (cost to each of his constituents: about 2p), then they must surely be able to find it in their conscience to repeal an Act that impoverishes all of their constituents by thousands of pounds a year (as well as throttling those in developing countries and ruining the environment). It is *that* cost to the taxpayer – not the benefit, accrued also at the expense of the taxpayer, of switching second-home allowances – that should be a resigning matter.

Those who argue that the MP has not personally profited from voting for the Lisbon Treaty, or from not signing up to Better Off Out, are ignoring the fact that, by toeing the line, the MP deliberately does not rule himself or herself out of advancement or preferment. A minister's job is worth rather more over a year than a tin of pet food on expenses. Any MP who is now against at least pushing for an independent and scrupulous cost-benefit analysis of the UK's EU membership is cheating his or her constituent out of a lot more than the bill for removing wisteria from their home. Although some Labour MPs (and certainly some Tory MPs) voted out of principle not to give the people a referendum on being forced further into the EU sausage maker, most did so for their career. A cabinet minister earns more than twice a backbencher and gets red boxes and a chauffeur (with all the actual business of lawmaking done in Belgium). You need to claim for a lot of duck houses to match the higher salary. Obeying the whips to support EU membership is far more profitable than claiming for a duck house – but costs constituents and the wider world far more. This is an outrage on a far greater scale than any of the expenses claims.

Until MPs realise that the domestic and foreign injustices of the EU are their responsibility and that the people will soon be far angrier about those than the "John Lewis list" of allowances, there's no hope of freedom. But when enough constituents make it plain that they will not vote for someone who supports EU membership, this country won't need a referendum. And it won't matter who is nominally in "power" in Number 10. It is tempting, whether for tribalist reasons or because "the others haven't got a chance", to vote in general elections for the three longest-established parties but doing so means that the most important questions in politics – the economy, the health service, immigration etc – will be decided by people in Belgium one cannot remove. If people vote for the three longest-established parties, this will never change.

Britain has been responsible for much of the EU's intellectual construction. And, financially, we have always been a load-bearing wall. But it is not our duty to prop up an inhumane and anti-democratic anachronism. To atone for Salter, Cockfield, Kerr, Patten, Kinnock and the rest, Britain should now show the rest of the EU the way forward.

APPENDIX: THE LISBON TREATY
(to be confused with the Constitution)

The Lisbon Treaty was a product of the Laeken Declaration of December 2001, which established the "Convention on the Future of Europe". It was Belgium's EU presidency and in Laeken, a suburb of Brussels, the European Council pronounced that the Union was "at a crossroads". Moreover, the colleagues thought that the EU was "behaving too bureaucratically". They vowed that the EU would become "more democratic, more transparent and more efficient". They declared that the "institutions [should] be less unwieldy and rigid" and that the EU should be "brought closer to its citizens" (that's what Mr Tillack noticed).

As hollow jokes go, it wasn't a bad one. The *Economist* remarked, "According to the Laeken Declaration of 2001, [the Constitution] was supposed to simplify the EU's legal architecture, hand some powers back to member states and make the project intelligible to the voters. It has ended up doing the opposite – and its obfuscation will come back to hurt the EU in the long term, especially in Britain."[488]

The 2005 no votes in France and the Netherlands to the Constitution were followed by a yes vote in Luxembourg, and had been preceded by a convincing yes in Spain. Because of the need for unanimous backing of EU treaties, a "period of reflection" was declared. Despite that, the colleagues chose to reflect on only the first and last plebiscites. Very soon afterwards, the Austrian chancellor talked of plans to resurrect the document with "as little change in substance as possible". By 2006, the Finnish European affairs minister was telling the European parliament that her country's presidency (in the second half of the year) would hold secret talks on the Constitution's future. She said, "Our intention is to draft an intermediate report for the December 2006 European Council." The "consultations", she continued, had to be "in a very confidential spirit" so as to foster "honest and open discussion between member states".

Valéry Giscard d'Estaing, the French ex-president with the mien of a supercilious sommelier, had been chief drafter of the Constitution. When spirits flagged during the lengthy process, Giscard had tried to rouse colleagues by saying, "This is what you have to do if you want the people to build statues of you on horseback in the villages you come from." (He would later write a *roman à clef* that hinted he'd had an affair with Princess Diana.) In a lecture to the London School Of Economics on 28 February 2006, he said that "the rejection of the Constitution was a mistake which will have to be corrected... The Constitution will have to be given its second chance" and joked that "everyone

---

[488] *The Economist*, 26 October 2007

makes mistakes". He said people had voted no out of an "error of judgment" and "ignorance". He said, "In the end, the text will be adopted... It was a mistake to use the referendum process, but when you make a mistake you can correct it."

He told the *Financial Times* on 23 May that year much the same thing: "It is not France that has said no. It is 55 per cent of the French people – 45 per cent of the French people said yes... I wish that we will have a new chance, a second chance, for the constitutional project."

A month later, Chancellor Merkel and President Chirac held a Franco-German summit, after which she said, "We have agreed that the constitutional treaty will be reviewed during the German presidency [first half of 2007], after a period of reflection." Chirac said that France "trusts the German presidency to steer the ship in the right direction. We have certain problems but we will of course overcome them."

In spring 2007, the LSE was again hosting the diehard believers. In February, the Italian interior minister and ex-PM Giuliano Amato, spoke. He led Prodi's group of "Wise Men", the handsomely pensioned ex-Eurocrats, including Chris Patten and other has-beens, charged with reviving the Constitution. (Not to be confused with the "Wise Men" who filleted the Santer Commission in 1999.) Amato said in his lecture that he wished to "change the name, but not the substance" of the old text, adding that the "good thing about not calling it a Constitution is that no one can ask for a referendum on it".

By now, Germany had the EU presidency. The 50th birthday celebrations were over and the Berlin Declaration – a promise by the 27 leaders to revive the text – had been made. There was still a need for furtiveness, however. In April, Merkel wrote secretly – as she also had in January – to her 26 counterparts, saying that the successor text might use "different terminology without changing the legal substance" of the rejected Constitution. In June, Amato's group produced a "new" draft treaty. An accompanying report said that the text should "take over almost all the innovations contained in the constitutional treaty" and would "only leave aside the symbolic changes that were introduced by the constitutional treaty – such as the title of the treaty and the symbols of the Union". But it would include "the innovations of the 'substance' of the constitutional treaty".

This delighted Giscard. Later that month, in a frank article for *Le Monde*, he said, "This text is, in fact, a return of a great part of the substance of the Constitutional Treaty... the differences are few and far between and more cosmetic than real. The public is being led to adopt, without knowing it, the proposals that we dare not present to them directly [again]... All the earlier proposals will be in the new text but will be hidden or disguised in some way."

His next sentence was less widely quoted: "But [this method] will reinforce the idea among European citizens that European construction is a machinery organised behind their backs by jurists and diplomats." On 17 July, he told MEPs, "What was [already] difficult to understand will become utterly incomprehensible, but the substance has been retained... Why not have a single [consolidated] text [as before]? The only reason is that this would look too much like the constitutional treaty. Making cosmetic changes would make the text more easy to swallow... the substance remains the substance of the constitutional treaty."

At the European Council of June 2007, which concluded Merkel's EU presidency, she revealed her 16-page mandate for a new treaty. The mandate was a new development. It sought to tie the hands of the Intergovernmental Conference (IGC) in Lisbon in the second half of the year which would draft the treaty itself; this was the child (EU) dictating to the parents (27 separate states) and was highly irregular – a treaty-based organisation such as the EU cannot, under the Vienna Convention on Treaties, seek to amend itself, only the signatory states themselves can amend treaties. (Such behaviour was a foretaste of the Lisbon Treaty itself, which sought to amend itself without even the bother of any further treaties, giving itself the means to grab more power whenever it wished.) Christopher Booker described the agreement as a "legal coup d'état". He wrote that "for the first time, the European Council has given an 'exclusive mandate' to all the governments involved that they can be permitted to discuss only the treaty that the European Council wants. In other words, they are no longer allowed to act as sovereign governments, as the international rules on treaties require, but can act only under the orders given them by the European Council." [489]

When the draft text was revealed, there was no shortage of people to say how similar it was to the Constitution. Its near-identical nature – it even contained the word "Constitution" several times, making it plain that it was a cut-and-paste job – was telegraphed with glee by other leaders, many commissioners and also, of course, Giscard. It was the old text, rising like Lazarus (or perhaps Rasputin). Only Gordon Brown and his government thought otherwise.

So who disagreed with Brown? Angela Merkel said: "The substance of the constitution is preserved. That is a fact." Astrid Thors (Finland's minister of migration and European affairs) said: "There's nothing from the original institutional package [Constitution] that has been changed." Bertie Ahern (then Ireland's PM) said: "These changes haven't made any dramatic change to the substance of what was agreed back in 2004... 90 per cent of it is still there." Mr Ahern accused Brown of "running away" from a public vote, adding "if you believe in something, why not let your people have a say in it?" (It was when in

---

[489] *The Sunday Telegraph*, 24 June 2007

conversation with Ahern that Brown referred to the Lisbon Treaty as "the Constitution".) Luxembourg's PM Jean-Claude Juncker thought it "99 per cent the same". Spanish foreign minister Miguel Angel Moratinos said, "I believe that 98 per cent of the content, of what we consider the substance of the Constitutional Treaty, is to be found in the future EU Treaty. The wrapping has been changed, but not the content." His boss, José Zapatero, said, "We have not let a single substantial point of the Constitutional Treaty go… It is, without a doubt, much more than a treaty. This is a project of foundational character, a treaty for a new Europe." Even Ken Clarke, then on the back benches, said in the House of Commons to David Miliband, Brown's foreign secretary[490]: "Will you stop all this nonsense about it being different from the constitution because it is plainly the same in substance, and [instead] explain why it is better not to have a referendum but have it decided in parliament? You are getting into trouble because of the devious ridiculousness of the arguments you are using."

Of course, those who opposed Lisbon also thought it was the same as the Constitution, including a leading light from the 2005 no campaign in Holland, Harry Van Bommel, the Socialist Party leader, who said, "This is the Constitution in drag." President Klaus of the Czech Republic said, "Only cosmetic changes have been made and the basic document remains the same."

Just as the word "federal" was swapped for its synonym "communautaire" in an attempt to make the Constitution more palatable for Blair, the word "Constitution" had been done away with in the Lisbon Treaty (except where it was carelessly left in), also "to make a few people happy". After the October IGC, which finalised the document, Giscard said, "In the Lisbon Treaty, drawn up exclusively from the Constitutional Treaty, the tools are exactly the same. Only the order has been changed in the tool box." He described the few changes there were – the (eventual) disappearance of the word "Constitution", the flag and the anthem – as "ridiculous" and "thankfully destined to remain unapplied". He noted that the new treaty was "unreadable for citizens" and asked, "What is the point of this subtle manoeuvre? First and foremost to avoid the constraint of referendums." Echoing Giscard, Amato said that the Treaty should be unreadable so as to hoodwink electorates, principally Britain's, and so obviate referendums[491].

---

490 Why it should be the foreign secretary that deals with EU matters is a mystery when one thinks of the profound domestic implications of EU membership. But it has been ever thus

491 He wasn't the only one. The Belgian foreign minister, Karel De Gucht, now a commissar, said, "The aim of the Constitutional treaty was to be more readable; the aim of this treaty is to be unreadable… The Constitution aimed to be clear, whereas this treaty had to be unclear. It is a success"

The mostly Labour (nine of 16 members) House Of Commons European scrutiny committee[492] (ESC) pronounced it to be "substantially equivalent" to the Constitution. The committee's chairman, Labour MP Michael Connarty, said: "It's exactly the same apart from no songs and no symbols" and "Everything else that was in that treaty is in the reform treaty."

However, at the 11th hour, the 12 stars and friends were reinserted into the document. Giscard was right: such changes were "destined to remain unapplied", not that their absence from the document would have meant that they would ever have disappeared. Separately, the EU parliament had already voted to recognise officially the EU flag, motto and anthem: at the reopening of the Strasbourg parliament in July 2009, uniformed EU soldiers paraded to Beethoven's *Ninth Symphony* under the EU flag.

Just before the 27 leaders signed the Treaty, a new declaration (which, like European Council declarations, was non-binding) was added: "Belgium, Bulgaria, Germany, Greece, Spain, Italy, Cyprus, Lithuania, Luxemburg, Hungary, Malta, Austria, Portugal, Romania, Slovenia and the Slovak Republic declare that the flag with a circle of twelve golden stars on a blue background, the anthem based on the *Ode To Joy* from the *Ninth Symphony* by Ludwig Van Beethoven, the motto 'United In Diversity', the euro as the currency of the European Union and Europe Day on 9 May will for them continue as symbols to express the sense of community of the people in the European Union and their allegiance to it."

---

[492] "The scrutiny committee has just one power – the scrutiny reserve – which allows it to ask ministers not to sign up to important EU legislation until it has at least been discussed in the House. But the government has used its right to 'override' scrutiny about 400 times since 2001": Open Europe, comment on press summary, 7 June 2007

"The scrutiny override was used 350 times [in 2007], allowing ministers to take no notice of the committee's objections... Ms [Helen] Goodman told us that the committee had judged 500 documents worthy of comment, and of them, five had been debated on the floor of the House. One per cent... To bridge the democratic deficit [MPs] need to dispel the sense of futility in European scrutiny. For even if their objections lead to a debate on the floor of the House, the government overrides them. Structures or procedures won't really help. Effectiveness is not in the letter but in the spirit" Simon Carr, *The Independent*, 8 February 2008.

Since 2005 the scrutiny committee has chosen to deliberate in private, overturning a 2003 decision (though it still takes evidence in public). "The House of Lords EU select committee's 2008 annual report showed that between July 2007 and June 2008, the government gave agreement in Council to an EU proposal that was still under scrutiny in the House on 24 occasions. Matters on which the government used the override included an EU military operation in Chad and in the Central African Republic, restrictive measures against Iran, and a uniform format for residence permits for third-country nationals." From Open Europe press summary, 17 December 2008

The consensus that the Lisbon Treaty was the same as the Constitution was unhelpful to Gordon Brown because he and his predecessor had in 2004 promised a referendum on the Constitution. (Equally unhelpful was the 2007 TUC Conference, which on 12 September voted for a referendum[493].) Tony Blair said, in April 2004, over a year before the no votes: "What you cannot do is have a situation where you get a rejection of the [Constitution] and bring it back with a few amendments and say, 'Have another go.' You cannot do that." But that's exactly what happened – except we, the Dutch and the French did not get a "go" and nor did 23 other countries. A few weeks before the votes, he had written in the *Sun*, "Even if the French vote no, we would have a referendum. That is a government promise." A cast-iron one?

When reminded in June 2007 of Blair's 2004 remark, Peter Mandelson, then still an EU commissar, replied, "It depends what you're doing. If you're simply rearranging and altering the packaging, but retaining the original constitutional treaty as was, then I don't think you can or should get away with ratifying it without a referendum. But I don't believe that's what Chancellor Merkel is proposing." It was.

Brown and Miliband tried to prove that the Lisbon Treaty was not the Constitution by saying that "the constitutional concept has been abandoned", which was quite true – although it was a lawyerly misdirection. The ESC discussed claims that the new treaty no longer had the characteristics of a constitution: "We do not consider that references to abandoning a 'constitutional concept' or 'constitutional characteristics' are helpful and consider that they are even likely to be misleading in so far as they might suggest the Reform [ie Lisbon] Treaty is of lesser significance than the Constitutional Treaty."

The Constitution could be read, like America's, from start to finish; it was a document in itself that collated and added to its predecessors, underlining the power it already had and taking some more while it was about it. The Lisbon Treaty achieved the same effects – and many more – by merely listing amendments to its predecessors; it is not a standalone document – it cannot be

---

493 The unions, like the Labour Party, have had an on-off relationship with the EU – sometimes being pro and sometimes anti. (The Tory high command have mostly been in favour, despite the image given them by a few vocal MPs, since the days of Harold Macmillan and have signed most of the major treaties.)
At the TUC Conference in 1988, "the Brothers" approvingly sang "Frère Jacques" to guest speaker Jacques Delors, the highly integrationist president of the Commission, who had promised a "social Europe" and workers' rights. But by 2009 it was obvious to everyone that the EU might not after all be in British workers' interests, not least those who had hoped to work at the Lindsey oil refinery. In 2004, the TUC had decided not to issue a statement backing the government over the Constitution, worried that it would lose the debate. GMB, Unison, Transport & General Workers, and Amicus had been lukewarm at best

read in isolation and is not designed to be; those fluent in the language of software might think of the Lisbon Treaty as a "patch" or "update" for an existing program; useless by itself. If that analogy means nothing then imagine hearing only one side of a phone call.

What Brown and Miliband could not do was specify what was in only the Constitution that necessitated a referendum. What was the magical, referendum-triggering "Ingredient X" that had been omitted from the newer text? Of course, nothing was missing – but a lot had been added.

Tony Blair in 2004 – and in his general election manifesto the following year – promised a referendum because of a "partly successful campaign to persuade Britain that Europe is a conspiracy aimed at us" that he wanted to counter. In effect, he wanted the electorate, to borrow Major's phrase, "to put up or shut up" about the EU. "Let the issue be put and let the battle be joined!" said the great pretender. He did not offer the referendum on the Constitution because it was constitutional, but because he wanted, like Wilson in 1975, to shoot the fox of scepticism for another generation. Brown, however, rewrote recent history and said that the constitution's "constitutionality" had been the reason for granting a plebiscite. And people, not least the fourth estate, fell for it. The argument then pottered off down a philosophical cul-de-sac, exactly where Labour wanted it. To Brown and Miliband's delight, people discussed whether the feathered aquatic bird, which seemed to be quacking loudly, could really be called a "duck". It was a sideshow to distract from what was in the Lisbon Treaty.

There were five supposed opt-outs for the British from the Constitution but one of those concerned our rebate, which Blair surrendered at the European Council in London in December 2005. The four that "remained" for the Lisbon Treaty are:

a) An opt-out from the Charter of Fundamental Rights of the European Union (CFR)

Much of the Charter (see p347) and its vague language had been in the Treaties since Maastricht anyway, and the ECJ was already using it, relying on a December 2000 declaration by the European Council in Nice that approved the text (but which could not make it binding). Lisbon merely formalised that approval, giving the Charter equal legal billing with the Treaties. Swedish PM Frederick Reinfeldt pointed out to his parliament on 26 June 2007 that "it is important for this [the Swedish] government to keep the Charter legally binding, which now is the case... The UK accepted this... and it should be stressed that the UK was given a clarification, not an opt-out." An ESC report called into question the government's claim that the Charter would not affect UK law: "We express doubts on the effectiveness of the protocol on the [CFR] and do not consider that it guarantees that the Charter can have no effect on the law of the United Kingdom when it is combined with consideration of the implementation of Union law."

Jim Murphy, one of the many Labour Europe ministers, conceded that "the UK does not have an opt-out on the Charter of Fundamental Rights"[494]. Even if the UK did have an opt-out, consider the scenario: a prisoner in Stockholm successfully argues at the ECJ, using the CFR, that he be allowed a plasma TV in his cell. The judgment would then be part of EU case law – and the UK would then be open to the same challenge, via EU law, from which we certainly do not have a note from doctor. Like a disease jumping between species, provisions of the Charter (from which the UK is not shielded anyway) can jump into EU law (which applies everywhere).

b) An opt-out from justice and home affairs

c) Retaining the veto in foreign policy

d) An opt-out from social security and tax (tax was never under formal threat anyway)

Here's Mr Barroso, who's always so helpful when domestic politicians need to be told where their jurisdiction ends and his starts: he said that Brown's opt-outs or "red lines" were safe "only for the time being". The UK would face unlimited fines for non-compliance after this undefined period of grace. Michael Connarty and the ESC agreed: "We [the committee] believe that the red lines will not be sustainable. Looking at the legalities and use of the European Court of Justice, we believe these will be challenged bit by bit and eventually the UK will be in a position where all of the treaty will eventually apply to the UK."

He added, "If they can't get these things firmed up, we think they will basically leak like a sieve." He told the BBC, "They have given us five years to get in line... The redraft contains protocols that weren't there before which actually are much tougher for the UK and actually threaten those red lines very, very quickly. It's a bullying tactic and it's entirely unacceptable and the prime minister should say he won't accept it. Our red lines will basically be rubbed out five years after getting them"[495]. Ex-minister Gisela Stuart, who had helped to draft the Constitution, described the UK government's position as "patently dishonest" and said that Brown's "red lines" are "red herrings". She also said, "This document, irrespective of what you call it, substantively is still the same as the Constitution."

The ESC also criticised the lack of opportunity for proper parliamentary

---

[494] *A guide to the constitutional treaty,* Open Europe (second edition, February 2008)
[495] *The World This Weekend,* 14 October 2007

scrutiny and debate before the treaty would be signed: "The process could not have been better designed to marginalise the role of national parliaments and to curtail public debate, until it has become too late for such debate to have any effect on the agreements which have been reached."[496] On his blog (as at 27 November 2007), Giscard was delighted: "I have taken on the work of comparing the draft of the new Treaty of Lisbon with the Constitution on the 'nine essential points' published on this blog. To my surprise, and, to tell the truth, to my great satisfaction, these nine points reappear word for word in the new project. Not a comma has changed! The only thing is that you have to really look for them because they are dispersed in the texts the new Treaty refers to, namely the Treaties of Rome [TEC] and Maastricht [TEU]."

The absurdity and vanity of the entire project were demonstrated in November 2007 when disagreement arose over where the new text would be signed. After much debate, it was decided that the deed would be done in Lisbon (Portugal had the rotating presidency) by all 27 EU leaders and then, after a few hours in the Portuguese capital, the leaders would reboard their planes and follow one another to Brussels, where by evening they would be sitting together again around a different table. Just so that Belgium could share in the "glory". The *Times* "conservatively calculated" that 135 tonnes of CO_2 would be emitted as a result of the extra air travel[497].

On 13 December 2007 Gordon Brown signed the Lisbon Treaty at 3.15pm, about three hours after everyone else, including Miliband, had done so. He claimed that he had a diary clash, in order to avoid being seen signing the thing with the other leaders and foreign secretaries. Nevertheless, his signature was overseen by Miliband, José Socrates, the Portuguese PM, Mr Barroso for the Commission, and Hans-Gert Pöttering, the parliament's then president. As well as the world's press. His confected lateness satisfied neither pro-treaty nor anti-treaty camps.

Of course, the signing did not enact the treaty (see the Constitution's plaque below). Lisbon then had to navigate all 27 parliaments. Only Ireland was constitutionally bound to offer her people a vote. Remembering 2005, no other country risked it.

In January 2008, another UK parliamentary committee, the Commons foreign affairs select committee, reported: "We conclude that there is no material difference between the provisions on foreign affairs in the Constitutional Treaty which the government made subject to approval in a referendum and those in the Lisbon Treaty on which a referendum is being denied... We recommend

---

496 House of Commons European scrutiny committee: *European Union Intergovernmental Conference: Follow-up report, Third Report of Session 2007-08*, 14 November 2007, available via tinyurl.com/3c9xbz
497 *The Times*, 2 November 2007

that the government should publicly acknowledge the significance of the foreign policy aspects of the Lisbon Treaty."

On the same day, Michael Connarty told a newspaper that the Lisbon Treaty paved the way for "a massive and fundamental" shift of power to the EU: "The Reform Treaty and the red lines are just a postponement of what will be one system for all of Europe."[498] Also in that day's papers was Gisela Stuart, who told the *Guardian* that the Lisbon Treaty gave the EU a "toolbox" of powers that would allow it to "interfere in virtually every aspect of our lives". She also repeated that the treaty was virtually the same as the Constitution: "It's like a cookery recipe: all the same ingredients, but you've just rearranged them differently. Giscard d'Estaing came up with a wonderful phrase: he said, 'It's the same letter; just in a different envelope'."

Would you have bought a second-hand Constitution from Gordon Brown? He said, "We will ensure that there is sufficient time for debate on the floor of the House, so that the Bill can be examined in the fullest detail and all points of view heard." Twenty days were allotted but in the end the government granted only 12. A Lib Dem-supported Tory amendment for 18 days' debate was also defeated. Geoff Hoon, the chief whip, threatened all sorts against the Labour rebels, including Gisela Stuart and Frank Field, who said they would vote for a referendum. Field would say, "We are in the absurd position where we may actually be punished for trying to maintain a manifesto pledge."

During the dozen days' debate, the pro-EU Connarty said, "This treaty is the tipping point – it will take the centre of power away from this parliament to Brussels. There is no doubt about that." He also said that, post-ratification, "the role of national parliaments will be massively diminished."

On 5 March 2008, the House Of Commons voted 311-248 against an amendment that would have granted a referendum. In all, just 28 Labour MPs voted for what they had promised their constituents three years earlier. A handful of europhile Tories (Ken Clarke and John Gummer etc) went a small way to cancelling them out. An amendment, by Labour rebel Ian Davidson, for a two-question referendum (on membership itself, and on Lisbon) was defeated 311-247.

Previously, Nick Clegg had stormed out of the Commons when he was denied just such a membership-referendum amendment. The fact was that he thought that the British public might well vote to remain in the EU out of fear, but certainly would not endorse Lisbon. His bluff called, he looked ridiculous, and he had to whip his MPs to abstain from a vote he had called for not long before. But more than a quarter of his MPs voted aye, and three of the Lib Dem "front bench" had to resign.

---

498 *The Daily Telegraph*, 19 January 2008

Six days later, the Treaty was passed. Parliamentarians could not, even if they had voted to do so, have changed one comma[499].

During his state visit to Britain later that month, Sarkozy thanked Gordon Brown for his "courage and loyalty" in pushing through the Lisbon Treaty without a referendum. Tsarko said, "I am not the only one in Europe who appreciates what he has done. What he has done was necessary for Europe." Again, Britain helps the cause. (In June 2009, when Brown's position was very precarious after a string of resignations and very poor Euro election results, the same Treaty-supporting faces from around the EU urged him to remain in office so that there could be no general election – and promised Tory referendum – before Lisbon had been universally ratified.)

At the end of March 2008, at a Fabian Society meeting in the House Of Commons, Gisela Stuart said that she feared the EU would collapse if it did not find democratic legitimacy, warning "If the Treaty of Lisbon is ratified and implemented, and devolution to Wales, Scotland and Northern Ireland continues apace, in 15 to 20 years' time, this House of Commons will have only two functions – one will be to raise taxes, and the other will be to authorise war."

In May 2008, the Lords rejected an amendment on EU membership tabled by Lord Pearson. Lib Dem peers abstained on this in-out question, despite their leader huffing out of the Commons when just such an amendment of his was turned down by the Speaker. A spokesman said the party did not want to "give succour" to eurosceptics by voting with Ukip, stating that they wanted a referendum on whether Britain should remain in Europe from a "pro-European stance". The truth was that the arithmetic in the Upper House was such that the amendment might have been passed if the Lib Dems had been consistent.

In June, just before Ireland voted for the first time, the Upper House rejected the referendum amendment 280-218, the Lib Dem peers voting against. Had they not done so – ie if they had honoured the party's 2005 manifesto or had followed the lead of the MPs in abstaining – the amendment would have been passed. A fortnight after Ireland voted, Stuart Wheeler lost a High Court bid to prevent the UK ratification of the Lisbon Treaty without a referendum, as had been promised in all three parties' manifestos for its prototype, the Constitution.

Let's say the Treaty is the Constitution. What were the latter's aims? They were literally spelt out on a plaque: "On 29 October 2004 in this most sacred Capitoline Hill [Rome], which is the citadel of this bountiful city... the high contracting parties of the nations joined in the European Union signed a treaty about the form of constitution to be adopted, so that the races of Europe might coalesce into a body of one people with one mind, one will and one government." Those last two words were not included by mistake.

---

[499] Because of sections 2 and 3 of the original European Communities Act (1972)

The Constitution had been signed in the Campidoglio, the splendid Michelangelo hall where the Treaty of Rome had been signed. The Italian PM, Silvio Berlusconi, summoned lorryloads of flowers and commissioned the designer Valentino to tailor the staff uniforms, and the film director Franco Zeffirelli to direct the TV coverage.

Projects such as the EU embassies (nowadays the External Action Agencies) and Galileo, which were dependent on the Constitution, proved that much of the EU operated as if the Constitution had been ratified anyway; onwards hurtles the project. Amazingly – and comfortingly – there are some things that the EU cannot do without permission. Which is why it so badly needed the Lisbon Treaty. As mentioned, the EU did not need this treaty because there was an expansion-inspired logjam and lots of exciting new legislation was being held up; laws were passed *more quickly* after 2004. The EU wanted the Treaty because it wanted more powers.

Ruth Lea, the former head of the Institute of Directors and now director of Global Vision, summed up Lisbon: "It cannot be emphasised too strongly that, however significant the previous EU treaties were, the Lisbon Treaty is unique. Once enforced, there will quite simply be no more significant powers left solely with the governments of the member states, and outside the orbit of the EU's formal institutions."[500]

In February 2008, a diplomat in the British Embassy in Dublin was briefed by Ireland's director-general on the EU, Daniel Mulhall, on his country's preparation for the referendum. The Briton sent a secure (sic) email about the chat to the Foreign Office in London. In April, it was leaked. It revealed that Margot Wallström, the PR commissar, had told Dermot Ahern [the Irish foreign secretary, no relation to Bertie] that the Commission would "tone down or delay" any announcements before the vote "that might be unhelpful", such as the EU's proposed military capabilities and a standardised corporate tax base – though Sarkozy couldn't help letting slip that he planned those things for his EU presidency later in the year. Days before the vote, the French foreign minister, Bernard Kouchner, said, "It would be very, very, very troubling... that we could not count on the Irish, who themselves have counted a lot on Europe's money."

Later that month, the beleaguered PM Bertie Ahern stood down. His resignation was widely recognised as a way of preventing the Irish vote becoming about him and his troubles with undisclosed payments rather than about the Lisbon Treaty.

The new PM, Brian Cowen, said in May, "We are absolutely committed to the ratification of this treaty... And if there were to be anyone – and I don't know of anybody, but take it hypothetically – who had a conscientious problem, they would have to consider that outside the context of my parliamentary party." His

[500] Article for BBC news online, 24 July 2007. Her think tank is global-vision.net

finance chief said a no vote would be a "step into isolation for Ireland" and damage the Irish economy. Why had France and the Netherlands not suffered plagues of locusts when they voted no in 2005? It was never explained.

At the end of May 2008, Barroso again "warned" Ireland of the implications of voting no: "If there was a 'no' in Ireland or in another country, it would have a very negative effect for the EU. We will all pay a price for it, Ireland included, if this is not done in a proper way." Ireland's commissioner, Charlie McCreevy, admitted that he hadn't read the treaty – "no sane and sensible person" would do so, he said – and he said that "over 80 per cent of all legislation affecting the business community is adopted by majority voting at EU level".

Despite all this browbeating, the no camp, once trailing badly, was catching fast. It comprised, as the UK's no faction in 1975 had, some awkward bedfellows: Sinn Fein, anti-abortionists, Greens and others. The new boy was Declan Ganley and his Libertas movement. An Irish millionaire who'd been raised in Watford, he was pro-EU but anti-Lisbon. His fluent media performances – "We want a European Union that's credible, but we're sick of the failure of this Brussels elite to bring the people with them, it almost seems like some sect of secular cardinals who think they know better than us" – were in contrast to the vague but threatening establishment efforts (all major political parties and the print and broadcast media were urging a yes, also much like in the UK in 1975).

And then on 12 June 2008, the Irish voted no, by a margin of 53.4 per cent to 46.6 per cent.

The rules are that any treaty must be unanimously ratified by all member states, or it cannot come into force. Indeed, on the morning of the Irish count, French PM Francois Fillon said, "If the Irish decide to reject the Lisbon Treaty, obviously, there will be no Lisbon Treaty." The anti-Lisbon Czech President Václav Klaus declared that the Lisbon Treaty should be dead.

The other reactions were less than gracious.

"They [the Irish] are bloody fools. They have been stuffing their faces at Europe's expense for years and now they dump us in the shit." Nicolas Sarkozy, French president (the *Times*, 20 June)

"I don't think you can say the treaty of Lisbon is dead even if the ratification process will be delayed." Jean-Pierre Jouyet, French Europe minister (Reuters, 16 June)

"I am convinced that we need this Treaty. Therefore we are sticking with our goal for it to come into force. The ratification process must continue." Frank-Walter Steinmeier, German foreign minister (Reuters, 14 June)

"Of course we have to take the Irish referendum seriously. But a few million

Irish cannot decide on behalf of 495million Europeans." Wolfgang Schäuble, German interior minister (*Deutsche Welle*, 15 June)

"We think it is a real cheek that the country that has benefited most from the EU should do this. There is no other Europe than this treaty. With all respect for the Irish vote, we cannot allow the huge majority of Europe to be duped by a minority of a minority of a minority." Axel Schäfer, SPD leader, in the Bundestag (*Irish Times*, 14 June)

"The Treaty is not dead. The Treaty is alive, and we will try to work to find a solution." José Barroso

"The Treaty will be applied, albeit a few months late." Lopez Garrido, Spanish Europe Minister (*Forbes*, 15 June)

Giscard d'Estaing said, "The Lisbon Treaty is not dead. We are going to discuss it. The Lisbon Treaty can only be adopted when Ireland's position has been redefined." His interviewer said, "But the Irish position is defined – you're saying it needs to be redefined?" Giscard replied, "It is defined for the moment... But one can change one's opinion... It is imperative that they vote again."

The Commission tried to keep items such as re-evaluation of the British rebate and plans for harmonised corporate tax bases and farm reform off the agenda until all countries had ratified. This coincided with the boisterous Sarkozy's turn as president of the European Council, France having taken over on 1 July 2008.

At a European Council a week after the no vote, a statement was released: "The European Council noted the outcome of the referendum on Ireland on the Lisbon Treaty and took stock of the situation on the basis of an initial assessment provided by the Taoiseach Brian Cowen... The European Council agreed that more time was needed to analyse the situation. It noted that the Irish government will actively consult, both internally and with the other member states, in order to suggest a common way forward." Predictably, it was announced some months later that Ireland would have to vote again, as she had been made to do in 2002 – but France and the Netherlands had not.

In the summer of 2009, Gordon Brown was destabilised by several cabinet resignations. The ship of state was listing and a few rats thought it wise to seek alternative passage. Mandelson held the cabinet together with string and menaces – a general-election win might (it's a big "might") have made Cameron keep his promise of a referendum on Lisbon. For Mandy that would never do.

The Irish government sought legally binding "protocols" to the Treaty to hoodwink the electorate into thinking it was being asked to comment on a different proposition. The concessions given to Cowen were nothing of the kind. If they were legally watertight they would have triggered re-ratification in the other 26 provinces, which would have been the last thing the EU needed. As it was, the protocol, in the words of the European Council, "[clarified] but did not change either the content or the application of the Treaty of Lisbon."

The protocol was worse than worthless – it distracted from the harm of the treaty. And it gave no reason to vote yes if you had voted no in 2008. Our then Europe minister, Glenys Kinnock, confirmed that Ireland would vote on exactly the same text a second time around. She said in July 2009: "Those guarantees do not change the Lisbon Treaty; the European Council conclusions are very clear on them. The Lisbon Treaty, as debated and decided by our parliament, will not be changed and, on the basis of these guarantees, Ireland will proceed to have a second referendum." She added: "Nothing in the treaty will change and nothing in the guarantees will change the treaty."

The outgoing Irish commissar, Charlie McCreevy, said, "I think all of the politicians of Europe would have known quite well that if a similar question [referendum] had been put to their electorate in a referendum the answer in 95 per cent of countries would have been 'no' as well." He admitted that he still hadn't read the treaty but would do so over the summer.

Michael O'Leary, the Ryanair boss, said in a TV interview that one of the reasons he was campaigning for a yes vote in the second Irish referendum was that the government was "incompetent". "Yet," he said, "I needed to persuade them to sell me Aer Lingus." He was right on two levels: Brian Cowen and his cohorts were indeed "incompetent"[501], and they owned something that O'Leary wanted. However, O'Leary's true "government" – in Brussels – is also incompetent and it also needed persuading that any further sale of Aer Lingus to RyanAir (which already owned 30 per cent of its rival) was not anti-competitive. As O'Leary well knew, Neelie Kroes, then competition commissar, blocked the first of his two takeover bids. Commissar Tajani (then i/c transport) campaigned for a yes on a whistle-stop tour of Ireland with O'Leary on his airline. Shortly after Ireland voted yes in 2009, Aer Lingus announced that it was making over 15 per cent of its staff redundant.

Ireland had been a beneficiary of EU handouts since 1973 – well over 20 years before she started to get rich in the mid-1990s. And she got rich not because of Brussels cash given to arable farmers in Co Kerry but because her low-cut corporate taxes, together with a 1993 devaluation of the punt, attracted foreign tech firms. In 2009, assorted EU dependents, including commissars and the president of the EU parliament, tried – successfully – to scare the bejesus out of Ireland by saying that jobs depended on a yes vote. Intel gave hundreds of thousands towards a yes vote in the second Lisbon campaign, while it was appealing a €1billion fine from the ECJ. Literally the only jobs that depended on a yes were those of the new president of the Council and Foreign Affairs chief.

---

601 Cowen is nicknamed "Biffo" (big ignorant fecker from Offaly)

Brian M Carney wrote in the *Spectator* about how Barroso approached Ireland in 2009: "He used an interview in the *Irish Times* to make it clear that Brussels could hurt the Republic if it had to. When asked whether Ireland would be driven out of the EU over a second 'no' vote, he said that of course it would not. But then, in what was a master-class in the language of the veiled threat: 'There are some doubts now about the future situation of Ireland. Some people have asked me: is Ireland going to leave the EU? For investor confidence, it is important that there is certainty about the future of Ireland in the EU.' Not, of course, that Barroso was shameless enough to make baseless threats against Ireland in his own voice. So he attributed the quotes to anonymous others. He assured the Irish, in his best Don Corleone voice, that of course they will not be booted out of the EU if they don't do the bidding of Brussels. But still, better not to find out, non?"[502] France and the Netherlands hadn't been booted out in 2005, for the simple reason that there's nothing in the Treaties that allows the EU to do that.

A 16-page "information" supplement prepared by the Commission accompanied every Irish Sunday newspaper five days before the poll. Of course, it had been funded by those it sought to influence. It lied when it said that Lisbon ensured that every country retained a commissioner and it chose not to mention the defence consequences of Lisbon (see below). The Commission was also acting ultra vires: the EU under the Nice Treaty was a child of its signatory nations and it could not tell them or its peoples what to do regarding treaties. This was illegal pester power.

A challenge to the treaty in Karlsruhe, the German constitutional court, citing among other things the 2008 Irish no vote, hoped to repeat the success of three years earlier when a judge, respecting the French and Dutch results, instructed Germany's president not to sign the Constitution. After a two-day hearing, the constitutional court pointed out that Lisbon involved a clear extension of the EU's competences. A judge said, "One has to ask soberly: what competences are left with the Bundestag in the end?" He wondered if "it would not be more honest to just proclaim a European federal state" and if the transfer of powers to the EU really meant more freedom for EU citizens: "Is the idea of going ever more in this direction not a threat to freedom?"

The German constitution, the Karlsruhe judges noted, promotes peaceful co-operation within the EU and the UN, but this is not "tantamount to submission to alien powers". The German government, they said, must be denied the power "to abandon the right to self-determination of the German people", and EU integration "must, in principle, be revocable"[503]. The Bundestag and Bundesrat

502 *The godfather of Europe* in *The Spectator*, 24 October 2009
503 *Germans reel at prospect of 'submission to alien powers'* in *The Daily Telegraph*, 18 September 2009. This judgment was also quoted in the section on the European parliament

"have not been accorded sufficient rights of participation in European lawmaking procedures and treaty-amendment procedures". A press release accompanying the judgment said that "if one wanted to summarise, one could say: the [German] constitution says yes to the Lisbon Treaty but demands that parliament's right to participation be strengthened at the national level". Karlsruhe asked for a new law to safeguard the German parliament before the treaty could be ratified. It was rushed through.

The Czech Republic's president said that the 2008 Irish vote had been "a victory for democracy and reason". A year later the Czech constitutional court cleared Lisbon after the Irish changed their minds. President Klaus sought guarantees on the CFR, as the UK had done. Without legal bottom, his opt-outs looked as worthless as ours. He signed off the treaty, remarking with evident sadness that his country was giving up its sovereignty.

Poland was also cool on the treaty until it was hinted that "illegal" state aid of £2.1billion to the totemic Gdansk, Gdynia and Szczecin shipyards would be overlooked by the Commission. Nevertheless, despite the survival of the birthplace of Solidarity, President Kaczynski said, as Klaus did, that Poland would not sign the Lisbon Treaty until after the second Irish referendum – "to defend the Irish people's right to a sovereign decision" – and also after eventual German ratification. Poland signed a week after the Irish voted.

Four years earlier, ratification of the Constitution halted in the UK when France and Holland voted no. Why it did not halt in the UK and elsewhere for the Lisbon Treaty when Ireland voted no has not been satisfactorily explained. It's a decision that will always look condescending.

The lowlights of Lisbon

The Lisbon Treaty amended TEC (the Treaty of the European Community, which had started life in 1957 as the Treaty of Rome) and TEU (the Treaty of the European Union, which had started life in 1992 as the Treaty of Maastricht), occasionally shuffling articles between the two. Also, Lisbon renamed TEC as the Treaty on the Functioning of The Union (TFEU). The two treaties continue to be known as "the Treaties"; TFEU now has 358 articles, TEU 55.

Lisbon's two most visible contributions are the president of the European Council, the EU's semipermanent figurehead, and the high representative Of The Union For Foreign Affairs And Security Policy. These are Belgium's Mr Herman Van Rompuy (previously her caretaker prime minister) and the UK's Lady (Cathy) Ashton, both of whom we've met.

Because the Lisbon Treaty is an amending treaty (or software "patch") it's not quoted here: the quotations below are from the "consolidated versions" of the two treaties it amended. The treaties are big enough and ugly enough to speak for themselves, so they have here been allowed to do so. In the lingo, "the Union" means the EU. "The Council" means the Council Of Ministers, the collective of counterparts where nations' cabinet ministers go to get outvoted by people their electorate did not vote for, or else nod things through without much in the way of debate. The European Council is the 27 political leaders of the member states.

Unlike the anonymous-looking Van Rompuy and Ashton, the EU now has personality – "**legal personality**" in the vernacular (TEU 47). This makes the EU a state in itself, one that can sign treaties as a standalone entity. TFEU 217 makes a similar point: "The Union may conclude with one or more third countries or international organisations agreements establishing an association involving reciprocal rights and obligations, common action and special procedure."

Lisbon added many "**competences**" to the EU's bow. TFEU offers a round-up of these "competences", those areas that Westminster has outsourced to Brussels like an insurance company passing jobs to a call centre in India – but without the savings or efficiency.

TFEU 2(1): "When the Treaties confer on the Union exclusive competence in a specific area, only the Union may legislate and adopt legally binding acts, the member states being able to do so themselves only if so empowered by the Union or for the implementation of Union acts."

And those exclusive competences are: "the customs union; the establishing of the competition rules necessary for the functioning of the internal market; monetary policy for the member states whose currency is the euro; the conservation of marine biological resources under the common fisheries policy; and common commercial policy" (TFEU 3 (1)).

There are also "shared" competences. This might not be your definition of "sharing" but here is TFEU 2(2): "When the Treaties confer on the Union a competence shared with the member states in a specific area, the Union and the member states may legislate and adopt legally binding acts in that area. *The member states shall exercise their competence to the extent that the Union has not exercised its competence. The member states shall again exercise their competence to the extent that the Union has decided to cease exercising its competence*" [emphasis added]. However, because the EU never ceases to exercise its competence – legislation is what it does – the scope for national activity in the "shared" fields is extremely limited.

So what's "shared"? "The internal market; social policy, for the aspects defined in this Treaty; economic, social and territorial cohesion; agriculture and fisheries, excluding the conservation of marine biological resources; environment;

consumer protection; transport[504]; trans-European networks; energy; area of freedom, security and justice; common safety concerns in public health matters, for the aspects defined in this Treaty."

There's more: "The Union shall [also] have competence to carry out actions to support, co-ordinate or supplement the actions of the member states. The areas of such action shall, at European level, be: (a) protection and improvement of human health; (b) industry; (c) culture; (d) tourism; (e) education, vocational training, youth and sport" (TFEU 6). Whatever the EU does to "support" the "actions of the member states" will trump whatever the member states may themselves have decided to do.

* The European **Defence** Agency (which had anyway been operational since July 2004) was finally legitimised. It is not clear how the neutral countries of the EU, such as Austria, Finland, Ireland and Sweden, view TEU 42(1)'s calls to arms: "The common security and defence policy [CSDP] shall be an integral part of the common foreign and security policy. It shall provide the Union with an operational capacity drawing on civilian and military assets. The Union may use them on missions outside the Union for peacekeeping, conflict prevention and strengthening international security in accordance with the principles of the United Nations Charter. The performance of these tasks shall be undertaken using capabilities provided by the member states." In the same vein is 42(2): "The CSDP shall include the progressive framing of a common Union defence policy. This will lead to a common defence, when the European Council, acting unanimously, so decides."

Nato now has to do the EU's bidding, as TEU 42(3) makes clear: "Member states shall make civilian and military capabilities available to the Union for the implementation of the CSDP, to contribute to the objectives defined by the Council. Those member states which together establish multinational forces [eg Nato] may also make them available to the CSDP. Member states shall undertake progressively to improve their military capabilities. The European Defence Agency in the field of defence capabilities development, research, acquisition and armaments shall identify operational requirements, shall promote measures to satisfy those requirements, shall contribute to identifying and, where appropriate, implementing any measure needed to strengthen the industrial and technological base of the defence sector, shall participate in defining a European capabilities and armaments policy, and shall assist the

---

[504] An example of "shared" competence in transport was given in the Introduction – the UK could not legislate when it wanted to force foreign trucks to use mirrors better suited to driving on the left

Council in evaluating the improvement of military capabilities."[505]

Based on this remark from 2000, you could argue that an EU army is much older than Lisbon: "If you don't want to call it a European army, don't call it a European army. You can call it 'Margaret', you can call it 'Mary-Anne', you can find any name, but it is a joint effort for peacekeeping missions – the first time you have a joint, not bilateral, effort at European level." Then Commission president Romano Prodi on 4 February 2000 to the *Independent*.

The solidarity clause is TFEU 222: "The Union and its member states shall act jointly in a spirit of solidarity if a member state is the object of a terrorist attack or the victim of a natural or manmade disaster. The Union shall mobilise all the instruments at its disposal, including the military resources made available by the member states, to: prevent the terrorist threat in the territory of the member states; protect democratic institutions and the civilian population from any terrorist attack; assist a member state in its territory, at the request of its political authorities, in the event of a terrorist attack…"

How does the European Union *prevent* terrorist attacks? Compulsory ID cards? 92-day detention? RFID tags in everyone's shoes? It is vaguely worded and that is the point.

The language is even looser in TEU 42(7): "If a member state is the victim of armed aggression on its territory, the other member states shall have towards it an obligation of aid and assistance by all the means in their power, in accordance with Article 51 of the UN Charter."

Both articles have the same meaning as Nato's famous Article V (an attack on one member is an attack on all) – the UK had tried to kick out the equivalent clauses from the Constitution.

* As already mentioned, Lisbon made the **European Council** a formal EU institution, which means that its members have to hold – as the commissars, the ECB and the Luxembourg judges etc do – the "aims and objectives" of the EU above those of their own countries. TEU 13(1) says: "The Union shall have an institutional framework [including, for the first time, the European Council] which shall aim to promote its values, advance its objectives, serve its interests, those of its citizens and those of the member states, and ensure the consistency, effectiveness and continuity of its policies and actions."

The blog EU Referendum made the point just a few days after the 2007 Berlin

---

[505] Just to make sure, there's also TFEU 2(4): "The Union shall have competence, in accordance with the provisions of TEU, to define and implement a CSDP, including the progressive framing of a common defence policy"

Council's "mandate", highlighting how the Lisbon Treaty would be even more brazen than the rejected Constitution:

"Rather than representing their respective nations, they [the European Council's members, such as our PM and Angela Merkel] would act as a corporate body – an institution – the aims of which are, in respect of the Union, to: 'promote its values; advance its objectives; serve its interests, those of its citizens and those of member states; and ensure the consistency, effectiveness and continuity of its policies and actions'. Crucially, the requirement to serve the interest of the Union comes first, the 'citizens' come second and the member states come third. The order is neither accidental nor without significance. The European Council has to put the Union first. Serving the EU is, de facto, what the European Council already does, but this is now to become de jure. That such an important change is tucked into a paragraph of an obscure document that few will read – and fewer will understand – is another of those dangerous and deliberate obfuscations, designed to defeat easy analysis. It also represents a very significant transfer of power from member states, our leaders having been hijacked and impressed into the service of the Union – all the more dangerous because, as far as the media and the general public are concerned, they are part of an invisible institution, one that will, to them, remain a 'summit'."[506]

A similar trap was noticed by the ESC. On 23 July 2007, the *Daily Telegraph* reported: "The Commons' [ESC] has raised serious concerns over a section in the proposed wording of the treaty that states: 'National parliaments shall contribute actively to the good functioning of the Union' [now TEU 12]. MPs are concerned that the word 'shall' creates an obligation for parliament to put the 'good functioning' of the EU above its own interests and independence, and could allow European judges to block future opposition to Brussels from British MPs... Referring to the wording, Michael Connarty, the chairman of the committee, has warned Mr Murphy [then Europe minister] that 'no one should instruct parliament what to do' [bit late for that]. He added during a recent session of the committee: 'This is a takeover of the rights of this parliament.'" The word "shall" was dropped.

TEU 4(3) states that "The member states shall take any appropriate measure, general or particular, to ensure fulfilment of the obligations arising out of the Treaties or resulting from the acts of the institutions of the Union. The member states shall facilitate the achievement of the Union's tasks and refrain from any measure which could jeopardise the attainment of the Union's objectives."

* The treaty is **self-amending**: TEU 48 allows the European Council to

---

[506] *A dangerous and deliberate obfuscation*, eureferendum.blogspot.com, 26 June 2007

change the Treaties piecemeal, without the need for an entirely new one. Lisbon really was a constitutional blank cheque. Although any country's head of government could supposedly veto this, such nay-saying is legally impossible if one is, as a member of the European Council, contracted – as described above – to "advance the Union's objectives" (TEU 13(1)) and mandated to "refrain from any measure which could jeopardise the attainment of the Union's objectives" (TEU 4(3)).

A veto would certainly "jeopardise the attainment" of any EU objective so it's hard to see how a veto could ever be wielded. Besides, a yes can easily be bought in the European Council through horse-trading or by giving a browbeaten "colleague" a soundbite to take back to his or her people (eg John Major's "Game, set and match" from Maastricht).

The additional power of Article 48 – to move decision making in most areas from unanimity to QMV – is known as a "passerrelle" ("footbridge" in French) and is not new. The first passerelle (also the French for "gangplank", which is probably more apt) was in Maastricht, for certain police matters. Others appeared in the Amsterdam and Nice treaties. However, the passerrelle in Lisbon covered every area but defence, though aspects of the Common Foreign and Security Policy (ie defence) can be moved to QMV from unanimity by virtue of TEU 31(3).

Where such surrenders have to clear national parliaments, then statutory instruments can be used.

* From 2014, the **Commission** will be cut from the current 27 members to 18 (TEU 17(5)). Commissioners would be selected on a rotation system among the states. For long periods, therefore, the UK would be without representation in the only body that can initiate legislation.

* If you feel like going to a lot of trouble for nothing, you can **start a petition**, care of TEU 11(4): "Not less than one million citizens who are nationals of a significant number of member states may take the initiative of inviting the European Commission, within the framework of its powers, to submit any appropriate proposal on matters where citizens consider that a legal act of the Union is required for *the purpose of implementing the Treaties*" [emphasis added]. The important words are the last half dozen: you cannot propose scrapping the CAP, you can propose only to push the EU in the direction it wants to go – as laid out in the Treaties. Pre-Lisbon there was a million-plus petition to stop the shuttle of the European parliament, and it got nowhere. It would also get nowhere after Lisbon: the Treaties state that "the seat of the institutions of the Union shall be determined by common accord of the governments of the member states [eg France]" (TFEU 341). Each signatory would have to provide their postal

address, email address, date and place of birth, nationality and personal identification number (from a passport or ID or social-security card).

* TFEU 311 provides for guaranteed **revenue**: "The Union shall provide itself with the means necessary to attain its objectives and carry through its policies." Hence plans for carbon taxes and bank levies etc that do not rely on national treasuries.

* **Health** is explicitly in the EU's sights. As discussed, there are indirect pressures on healthcare: hospitals must conform with the 48-hour rule, they must buy "permits to pollute", and they must not bar from employment doctors whose English is fatally bad. The biggest direct pressure – and it hasn't nearly begun to exert itself – will come from the Health Services Directive, which merely "catches up" with ECJ rulings. Immigration from the EU and third countries (often via other EU countries) is another pressure on national healthcare provision.

But the other direct grab is TFEU 168(1), which says "Union action, which shall complement national policies, shall be directed towards improving public health, preventing physical and mental illness and diseases, and obviating sources of danger to physical and mental health." How wonderfully benevolent – but who defines the things that "improve public health"? How is illness prevented by the EU? With whose money? See also article 35 of the CFR below.

TFEU 168(2) is a variant of the Health Services Directive masquerading as "co-operation": "The Union shall encourage co-operation between the member states in the areas referred to in this Article and, if necessary, lend support to their action. It shall in particular encourage co-operation between the member states to improve the complementarity of their health services in cross-border areas."

The sixth clause of 168 says that "[the EU] may also adopt incentive measures designed to protect and improve human health and in particular to combat the major cross-border health scourges, measures concerning monitoring, early warning of and combating serious cross-border threats to health…" Who defines a "cross-border scourge"? What are they?

* **Law and order** sank far deeper into the EU quicksand with Lisbon. The very real possibility of a public prosecutor comes in TFEU 86(1): "In order to combat crimes affecting the financial interests of the Union [one of many catch-all phrases in Lisbon that does more than target currency speculators], the Council… may establish a European Public Prosecutor's Office from Eurojust". This is in addition to the existing European Arrest Warrant, which enables fast-

track extradition (and therefore imprisonment without trial in some countries) without prima facie evidence, for crimes not even on the UK statute book. It is from the same Eurojust whose chief stepped down in 2009 after being reprimanded for leaning on prosecutors back home in Portugal.

TFEU 82(1): "Judicial co-operation in criminal matters in the Union shall be based on the principle of mutual recognition of judgments and judicial decisions". This is an uncoded attempt to mould the member states into a single polity, so that plane-spotting is an offence not just in Greece but also in Helsinki, and trials in absentia, which are allowed in Britain only in extreme cases, would be part of our legal system because they are part of another country's concept of jurisprudence.

There is a similar judicial putsch, or attempt to season the disparate into the homogeneous, in TFEU 67(3): "The Union shall endeavour to ensure a high level of security through measures to prevent and combat crime, racism and xenophobia, and through measures for co-ordination and co-operation between police and judicial authorities and other competent authorities, as well as through the mutual recognition of judgments in criminal matters and, if necessary, through the approximation of criminal laws." Beneath the liberal veneer ("combat racism") is an authoritarian core ("approximation of criminal laws"). Holocaust denial is deeply unpleasant but it should not be a criminal act in the UK, thus making martyrs of its proponents (and nor should our courts ever hear cases involving any other crimes not on our statute book). However, holocaust denial is against the law in some EU countries. To adapt Niemöller: "First they came for the holocaust deniers."

In addition, TFEU 83(1) allows the EU to "establish minimum rules concerning the definition of criminal offences and sanctions in the areas of particularly serious crime with a cross-border dimension resulting from the nature or impact of such offences or from a special need to combat them on a common basis". These offences include "corruption, counterfeiting of means of payment, computer crime and organised crime". "Organised crime" is a catch-all and open to interpretation.

This is backed up by CFR Article 49(3): "The severity of penalties must not be disproportionate to the criminal offence." Now, the ECJ can decide what is or is not a "disproportionate" sentence.

Also, the role of Eurojust – whose chief, it bears repeating, stood down in 2009 for improper behaviour – would be expanded to include not just the co-ordination of investigations but also their "initiation". TFEU 85(1)(a) allows for "the initiation of criminal investigations, as well as proposing the initiation of prosecutions conducted by competent national authorities".

One of the ConDems' first acts was to opt in to the **European Investigation**

Order, which relied on Lisbon. It gives judicial authorities (acting on requests from local police forces) in any EU country the power to order British police forces to collect and surrender evidence (including but not limited to blood samples, fingerprints and DNA, bank account details and phone records), interrogate suspects or launch surveillance operations. (The Home Office can supposedly reject requests but only if they breach immunity rules, compromise national security, affect another investigation or breach human rights.) A 90-day deadline for requests to be met means that UK police will often have to prioritise foreign police work over their own. Foreign police can operate in the UK alongside British officers but would not (for the time being) have powers of arrest.

UK judges cannot block requests, even if they relate to offences that are trivial in the UK or not a crime here (such as Portugal's offence of criminal libel or other provinces' outlawing of holocaust denial). In this it's similar to its companion piece, the European Arrest Warrant.

As pointed out in the Lords, "there is no agreed basic standard across Europe for pre-trial evidence gathering and analysis, no implementation of basic minimum procedural defence safeguards and no coherent data-protection regime". The campaigning group Fair Trials International warned that, theoretically, Spanish police investigating a murder could demand the ID and DNA of every British citizen who visited the country in the month of the attack. They could also demand that UK police search the DNA database to see if any of the same people are on it and to provide their samples if so.

The powers are one-way, resting only with the state: the accused cannot demand evidence from foreign police forces and other agencies. The ConDem coalition agreement says, "We need to restore the rights of individuals in the face of encroaching state power" and to "protect Britain's civil liberties and preserve the integrity of our criminal justice system". More famously, it promised "no further transfer of sovereignty or powers" to the EU. This area of justice has been ceded irrevocably and now Her Majesty's constabulary cannot decline requests from overseas judges even if it hampers their own investigations. That's not a transfer of power? The Tories had made a manifesto pledge a few months earlier to repatriate powers over criminal justice.

TFEU 82(2)(a-d) governs admissibility of evidence in court, defendants' rights, victims' rights and – terrifyingly – "any other aspects of criminal procedure". If you want an amnesty for householders who prefer the American way when dealing with violent trespass, or if you'd like victims to enjoy more rights, you can no longer vote for those who make such decisions.

TFEU 89: "The Council, acting in accordance with a special legislative procedure, shall lay down the conditions and limitations under which the competent authorities of the member states referred to in Articles 82 [judges] and 87 [police officers] may operate in the territory of another member state in liaison and in agreement with the authorities of that State." This article – the "gendarmes in Piccadilly" provision – could easily go from veto to QMV. There is separate provision for a third of all police officers (ie 50,000 in the UK) to be given, before 2014, training in a "common culture" of policing.

The EU body Cepol (Collège européen de police) is part of the Police Staff College in Bramshill, Hampshire. Cepol's budget in 2008 was €8.7million. When asked to sign off its 2008 accounts, Cocubu said, "The audit shows there are irregularities, blatant ones, in terms of administration and finance, and that's why we would like to defer discharge."[507] Olaf was already investigating dodgy expense claims and worse for the years 2007 and 2008. No charges were brought but there were resignations.

* On **asylum and immigration**, TFEU 67(2) states "[The EU] shall ensure the absence of internal border controls for persons and shall frame a common policy on asylum, immigration and external border control, based on solidarity between member states, which is fair towards third-country nationals [ie anyone not from the EU]. For the purpose of this Title, stateless persons shall be treated as third-country nationals."

TFEU 78(1-2): "The Union shall develop a common policy on asylum, subsidiary protection and temporary protection with a view to offering appropriate status to any third-country national requiring international protection... The European parliament and the Council... shall adopt measures for a common European asylum system comprising: (a) a uniform status of asylum for nationals of third countries, valid throughout the Union; etc."

TFEU 77(1)(a) states that "the Union shall develop a policy with a view to ensuring the absence of any controls on persons, whatever their nationality, when crossing internal borders". As Booker noted: "In other words, once someone has entered any of the 27 countries making up the EU, it will become illegal to prevent them from entering any other EU country, regardless of their nationality. So if millions of Turks or Russians or Somalis somehow manage to enter any part of the EU, the British government will no longer have any right to stop them entering Britain and staying here."[508] This provision is echoed by CFR Article 45: "Every citizen of the Union has the right to move and reside freely within the territory of the member states. Freedom of movement and residence may be granted, in accordance with the Treaties, to nationals of third countries legally resident in the territory of a member state." Therefore, no

---

[507] *EU Observer*, 21 April 2010
[508] *The Sunday Telegraph*, 26 August 2007

British government – if it is Labour, Tory or Lib Dem – can "beef up Britain's borders". TFEU 77(1)(c) allows for "the gradual introduction of an integrated management system for external borders".

TFEU 77(2)(e) tells us how we must treat Commonwealth citizens by dictating "the conditions under which nationals of third countries shall have the freedom to travel within the Union for a short period". The abolition of the ancestry visa was probably an attempt to pre-empt this measure.

Put simply, TFEU 79(1) says "The Union shall develop a common immigration policy."

* **ID cards** are not decided on only in Westminster. TFEU 77(3) says, "If action by the Union should prove necessary to facilitate the exercise of the right referred to in Article 20(2)(a) ["to move and reside freely within the territory of the member states"], and if the Treaties have not provided the necessary powers, the Council, acting in accordance with a special legislative procedure, may adopt provisions concerning passports, identity cards, residence permits or any other such document." This was foreseen as long ago as 1980, in a *Yes Minister* episode: "Brussels is about to decree that there should be a new European identity card."[509] Since 2009, anyone in an EU country in the Schengen zone who applies for a passport, visa or residence permit needs to supply biometrics (fingerprints and digitised facial image). However, this is nothing compared to the provisions discussed under Articles 7 and 8 of the Charter of Fundamental Rights below.

* TFEU 122(1) gives the EU the power to ensure "in a spirit of solidarity" "the security of **energy supply**", with decisions taken by majority vote: "The Council, on a proposal from the Commission, may decide, in a spirit of solidarity between member states, upon the measures appropriate to the economic situation, in particular if severe difficulties arise in the supply of certain products, notably in the area of energy." This means that a country's right to allocate its own resources is taken away. There goes what's left of North Sea oil and gas. Remember what happened to our fish from the same area? Temporarily removed from the Constitution after the British made a fuss, the clause was inserted into Lisbon and approved by Gordon Brown.

* **Galileo** was legitimised several years late (but not as late as Galileo itself is), in TFEU 189: "To promote scientific and technical progress, industrial competitiveness and the implementation of its policies, the Union shall draw up a European space policy. To this end, it may promote joint initiatives, support

---

[509] *The writing on the wall*, series 1, episode 5 of *Yes Minister*, first broadcast 24 March 1980

346

research and technological development and co-ordinate the efforts needed for the exploration and exploitation of space."

* TEU 50 provides a lengthy and complicated procedure for "any member state [that] may decide to **withdraw** from the Union". It remains the case that repeal of the UK's European Communities Act (1972) requires only a one-line Bill in the House of Commons: a far simpler – and equally valid – exit strategy.

* On the **economic** front there's: "The member states shall co-ordinate their economic policies within the Union" (TFEU 5(1)). As well as the similar TFEU 121(1-2): "Member states shall regard their economic policies as a matter of common concern and shall co-ordinate them within the Council... The Council shall, on a recommendation from the Commission, formulate a draft for the broad guidelines of the economic policies of the member states and of the Union..." and, if still in doubt, there's also TFEU 2(3): "The member states shall coordinate their economic and employment policies within arrangements as determined by this Treaty, which the Union shall have competence to provide." And that's why the UK budget will have to be peer-(p)reviewed before being announced to the House.

* In short, countries lost over **60 vetoes**, in such areas as social policy, social security, employment and health policies.

* The **Charter of Fundamental Rights** (CFR) of the European Union is now part of EU law. The enactment of the Lisbon Treaty meant that the EU itself, not just its member states, acceded to the Convention for the Protection of Human Rights and Fundamental Freedoms, usually known as the European Convention on Human Rights. Even if Cameron had been sincere in wanting to repeal the Human Rights Act, most of its provisions are in the CFR anyway. It would have been an empty gesture (rather than a hollow promise).

The CFR includes:

Article 2(1): "Everyone has the right to life." Thanks.

Article 7: "Everyone has the right for his or her private and family life, home and communications."

Article 8(1): "Everyone has the right to the protection of personal data concerning him or her", which is identical to TFEU 16(1).

Article 8(2): "Such data must be processed fairly for specified purposes and on the basis of the consent of the person concerned or some other legitimate basis laid down by law. Everyone has the right of access to data which has been collected concerning him or her, and the right to have it rectified."

Article 8 has been relied on by the Human Rights Act (1998) in libel cases.

Do the following measures sound as if they abide by CFR articles 7 and 8?

On 30 May 2007 the European parliament voted in support of proposals to allow multiple agencies the right to monitor telephone, internet and email traffic (the Data Retention Directive, 2006/24). This directive forced internet service providers to store, for 12 months, the time and duration of customers' internet phone calls (but not their content), details of other internet use (including connection times but not sites visited), and details, but again not the content, of emails. It had been presented at EU level as a commercial law, which would need only QMV, rather than as a policing matter, which would have needed unanimity. (The measure followed a separate directive which required telecoms firms to hold on to telephone records for a year.) Directive 2006/24 EC had been lobbied for by Charles Clarke, then home secretary, after the July 2005 bombs in London although it was devised after the Madrid bombings a year earlier.

As the *Guardian* described it: "The measure will also cover VOIP – voice over internet protocol – calls such as Skype. The Home Office confirmed that access to personal internet and text data will also be available to all public bodies licensed under the 2000 Regulation of Investigatory Powers Act. This means that hundreds of public bodies, including local councils, health authorities, the Food Standards Agency, the Health and Safety Commission and even the education standards watchdog, Ofsted, will be able to require telecommunications companies to hand over the personal data."[510] At least 600 UK bodies have access to this data. In 2008 local councils, police and other UK bodies made more than 500,000 requests for confidential communications data. The various authorities requested and received info such as lists of phone numbers dialled and email addresses to which messages had been sent.

This new civil-liberties-violating law followed the preparation of a secret document by the EU's Hague-based police force, Europol. The Home Office has admitted that Europol, which is immune from prosecution, as are its officers, who cannot be compelled to give evidence in court, is also able to hold data including "information concerning a person's sexual orientation, religion, or politics". In 2001, its offices were raided by Dutch police in connection with a fraud investigation. Nine years later, its powers were extended so that it could monitor anyone thought to be involved in any "preparatory act" likely to lead to committing a crime, particularly if it were xenophobic or an offence against vehicles, the environment or computers. In the pursuit of "serious crimes" Europol was also granted the power to gather a person's "behavioural data", "lifestyle and routine; movements; places frequented", tax position, plus voice

---

[510] *'Snooper's charter' to check texts and emails* in *The Guardian*, 13 August 2008

and DNA profile. There was also scope to collect data about a person's "religious or philosophical beliefs or trade union membership and data concerning health or sex life". The full mandate was deliberately vague. The British rights group Liberty said: "We have huge concerns that Europol appears to have been given powers to hold very sensitive information and to investigate matters that aren't even crimes in this country. Any extension of police powers at any level needs to be properly debated and discussed."[511]

The EU's **Prum Treaty** (2005) came into force in 2007. It enables home secretaries from all EU countries to have automatic access to the DNA profiles, fingerprints and car registration details held in one another's police databases.

The **Inspire** ("infrastructure for spatial information") directive, as Open Europe reported, "includes common provisions for data on public health, including requirements for authorities to make information about citizens' personal health available to both authorities in other member states and the public"[512].

Indect is a computer program, nourished with €10.9million of EU funding, that scours the net (peer-to-peer networks, websites, social networks and forums) looking for trouble. In the Commission's words, it is "the elaboration of a concept, method and technology for intelligent monitoring of objects and urban areas for the purpose of automatic detection of threats related to crime, terrorism and violence acts". It will "monitor various people clusters and detect abnormal behaviour and situations of danger" through "intelligence gathering from the web and monitoring of suspicious activities in the internet".

Open Europe detailed other nasties: "Another project, Automatic Detection of Abnormal Behaviour and Threats in crowded Spaces (**ADABTS**), is seeking to develop models of 'suspicious behaviour' so these can be automatically detected using CCTV and other surveillance methods. The system would analyse the pitch of people's voices, the way their bodies move and track individuals within crowds. The project has received €3.2million of EU funding and has the co-operation of the UK Home Office. The system 'will communicate results to the various kinds of identified actors: security stakeholders such as European and national authorities, police organisations or event organisers; security system operators and security service companies; security system integrators; technology developers; the research communities for psychology, human factors, and signal processing communities.'"[513]

---

[511] *The Daily Express*, 26 March 2010
[512] *How the EU is watching you: the rise of Europe's surveillance state*, available from www.openeurope.org.uk
[513] *How the EU is watching you: the rise of Europe's surveillance state*, available from www.openeurope.org.uk

ADABTS is a project of BAE Systems, which had received £33million from the EU for it and **SCIIMS** ("strategic crime and immigration information management system"), which "will create 'a secure information infrastructure in accordance with EU crime and immigration agencies' information needs'. It will allow multiple systems to be scanned in order to 'predict, analyse and intervene' in crime before it happens."[514]

Similarly, the UK's love of CCTV means it must be salivating at the thought of "suspicious-and-abnormal-behaviour monitoring using a network of cameras and sensors for situation awareness enhancement" (**Samurai**), which aims to "develop an abnormal-behaviour detection system based on a heterogeneous sensor network consisting of both fix-positioned CCTV cameras and mobile wearable cameras with audio and positioning sensors." It has received €2.48million of EU funding.

Such projects are likely to report to the EU's secretive Joint Situation Centre, an embryonic CIA known as **SitCen**, staffed with member states' spooks. Cathy Ashton has plans to merge SitCen with its **Watch-keeping Capability** (which collates info from EU missions, such as EULex in Kosovo) as well as the EU's separate **Crisis Room** (media monitoring of the world's conflicts).

In turn, SitCen comes under a new agency, which sounds like an EU Home Office, that was created by the Lisbon treaty: the Standing Committee on Internal Security (**Cosi**, set up by TFEU 71). Cosi oversees Frontex (the borders agency), Europol and liaison between member states' "internal security authorities".

In the entry for the taxation commissar, we met **Eurofisc**, which is a proposal for all member states to pool their knowledge of your salary, level of savings and spending habits – in order to "combat VAT fraud".

Since at least 2006, the EU has been interested in the idea of tagging air passengers and has funded research into a programme called "**Optag**". Travellers would be tagged inside airports with wristbands or boarding passes embedded with computer chips in order to allow authorities to track passenger movement around terminal buildings. The information could then be twinned with CCTV footage[515]. Plans for scanning machines that virtually "strip" passengers are allowed subject to EU permission.

The Commission has put pressure on the UK to implement **eCall**, an in-car emergency system which, in the event of a crash, automatically alerts the

---

[514] *Brussels Sprouts* column, *Private Eye*, 19 March-1 April 2010
[515] *How tagging passengers could improve airport security* in *The Guardian*, 13 October 2006

emergency services. In order for it to take effect, all member states must sign up. The UK, Ireland, Denmark, France, Latvia and Malta have yet to do so.[516]

More sinister still is the **Co-operative Vehicle-Infrastructure Systems**, a £36million EU initiative backed by carmakers and the telecoms industry. As the *Guardian* reported, "Vehicles would emit a constant 'heartbeat' revealing their location, speed and direction of travel. EU officials believe it will reduce accidents, congestion and carbon emissions. A consortium of manufacturers has indicated that the device could be installed in all new cars as early as 2013."[517] For such a system to be of any use, uptake would need to be, as with vaccination, widespread. Because of civil-rights and privacy concerns, voluntary uptake would not be widespread. So, if the EU wishes not to waste its £36million, it will have to force it on us. It has also spent £2.4million on **Project Veronica** (Vehicle Event Recording based on Intelligent Crash Assessment), which investigated the viability of fitting all cars with £500 airplane-style black boxes.

All of these schemes mean that multiple agencies, from your local council's planning department all the way up to the Estonian chief of police, might one day very soon have access (if they don't already) to: your DNA, health records, tax return, bank account details, savings details, details of your internet usage, criminal record (or at least that of someone with a name similar to yours), details of your car journeys, phone calls and biometric data. The EU's Forward Group called this, approvingly, a "digital tsunami" which it suggested should be "meshed together". When you've been denied car, health or other insurance (sometimes because of a mix-up of your details with someone else's), or when you've been turned down for a job because of someone else's shoplifting conviction, you'll have some idea why.

Article 16 is "the freedom to conduct a business". As Open Europe has pointed out, "This is controversial with trade unions and the Left, who fear the ECJ may use this to apply internal-market rules to public services. The 'in principle' freedom to conduct a business could reverse the sorts of decision made by the ECJ – for example, in Sodemare v Regione Lombardia. In that case the ECJ ruled that Italy would still be allowed to specify that only non-profit organisations could get public contracts to run old people's homes."[518] Now the market can reach everywhere.

Article 20: "Everyone is equal before the law." Except the EU employees exempt from prosecution.

---

[516] Press Association, 10 September 2009

[517] *Big Brother is watching: surveillance box to track drivers is backed* in The *Guardian*, 31 March 2009

[518] *A guide to the constitutional treaty* (February 2008), available from www.openeurope.org.uk

Article 21 states "No discrimination on grounds of nationality." This is either badly drafted or it means that the UK is potentially liable for the welfare of seven billion people.

Just as Article 16 provokes the Left, Article 28 provokes the Right, by conferring the "right of collective bargaining and action [ie strikes]" in the workplace. Open Europe describe it as "a seemingly open-ended right to take industrial action."

Article 35 states "Everyone has the right of access to preventive medical care and the right to benefit from medical treatment under the conditions established by national laws and practices." The chronic drunk has as much right to a new liver as a young widowed mother. The NHS could be further hobbled – by claims from patients not availed of drugs that *might* have prevented their illness. This article is yet another provision that makes channel hopping for care possible, with or without the Health Services Directive.

Article 41(3) provides for recompense: "Every person has the right to have the Union make good any damage caused by its institutions or by its servants in the performance of their duties, in accordance with the general principles common to the laws of the member states." If this article were an insurance policy, would it cover the treatment meted out to Marta Andreasen or Hans-Martin Tillack? If not, what is the point of it?

Article 50 is the "Right not to be tried or punished in criminal proceedings for the same criminal offence". This is the return of our double jeopardy law. Repealing double jeopardy has advantages (the killers of Damilola Taylor were eventually convicted) and disadvantages (cases often come to trial opportunistically, without enough evidence, because the police think they might have another chance in the future) that are best weighed up in the UK parliament.

Article 52(1) states: "Any limitation on the exercise of the rights and freedoms recognised by this Charter must be provided for by law and respect the essence of those rights and freedoms. Subject to the principle of proportionality, limitations may be made only if they are necessary and genuinely meet objectives of general interest recognised by the Union or the need to protect the rights and freedoms of others." So, one's rights can be suspended if they are deemed to be against the "general interest" – however it is defined – of the EU. Article 2(1) is "Everyone has the right to life". Can that right be suspended in the "general interest"?

Index